Security, Conflict and Cooperation in the Contemporary World

Edited by **Effie G. H. Pedaliu**, LSE-Ideas and **John W. Young**, University of Nottingham

The Palgrave Macmillan series, Security, Conflict and Cooperation in the Contemporary World aims to make a significant contribution to academic and policy debates on cooperation, conflict and security since 1900. It evolved from the series Global Conflict and Security edited by Professor Saki Ruth Dockrill. The current series welcomes proposals that offer innovative historical perspectives, based on archival evidence and promoting an empirical understanding of economic and political cooperation, conflict and security, peace-making, diplomacy, humanitarian intervention, nation-building, intelligence, terrorism, the influence of ideology and religion on international relations, as well as the work of international organisations and non-governmental organisations.

Series Editors
Effie G. H. Pedaliu is Fellow at LSE IDEAS, UK. She is the author of *Britain, Italy and the Origins of the Cold War*, (Palgrave Macmillan, 2003) and many articles on the Cold War. She is a member of the peer review college of the Arts and Humanities Research Council.

John W. Young is Professor of International History at the University of Nottingham, UK, and Chair of the British International History Group. His recent publications include *Twentieth Century Diplomacy: A Case Study in British Practice, 1963-76* (2008) and, co-edited with Michael Hopkins and Saul Kelly of *The Washington Embassy: British Ambassadors to the United States, 1939-77* (Palgrave Macmillan, 2009).

Titles include:

Pablo Del Hierro Lecea
SPANISH-ITALIAN RELATIONS AND THE INFLUENCE OF THE MAJOR POWERS, 1943–1957

Aaron Donaghy
THE BRITISH GOVERNMENT AND THE FALKLAND ISLANDS 1974–79

Martín Abel González and Nigel J. Ashton
THE GENESIS OF THE FALKLANDS (MALVINAS) CONFLICT
Argentina, Britain and the Failed Negotiations of the 1960s

Christopher Baxter, Michael L. Dockrill and Keith Hamilton
BRITAIN IN GLOBAL POLITICS VOLUME 1
From Gladstone to Churchill

Rui Lopes
WEST GERMANY AND THE PORTUGUESE DICTATORSHIP
Between Cold War and Colonialism

Malcolm H. Murfett
SHAPING BRITISH FOREIGN AND DEFENCE POLICY IN THE TWENTIETH CENTURY
A Tough Ask in Turbulent Times

John W. Young, Effie G. H. Pedaliu and Michael D. Kandiah
BRITAIN IN GLOBAL POLITICS VOLUME 2
From Churchill to Blair

Security, Conflict and Cooperation in the Contemporary World
Series Standing Order ISBN 978–1–137–27284–3 (Hardback)
(*outside North America only*)

You can receive future titles in this series as they are published by placing a standing order. Please contact your bookseller or, in case of difficulty, write to us at the address below with your name and address, the title of the series and the ISBN quoted above.

Customer Services Department, Macmillan Distribution Ltd, Houndmills, Basingstoke, Hampshire RG21 6XS, England

---

Other books by Malcolm H. Murfett

NAVAL WARFARE 1919–1945: An Operational History of the Volatile War at Sea

IMPONDERABLE BUT NOT INEVITABLE: Warfare in the Twentieth Century

BETWEEN TWO OCEANS: A Military History of Singapore from 1275 to 1971

COLD WAR SOUTHEAST ASIA

HOSTAGE ON THE YANGTZE: Britain, China and the Amethyst Crisis of 1949

Shaping British Foreign and Defence Policy in the Twentieth Century

A Tough Ask in Turbulent Times

Edited by

Malcolm H. Murfett
Visiting Professor, King's College London, UK

palgrave
macmillan

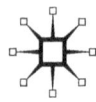

Editorial matter, selection and introduction © Malcolm H. Murfett 2014
Individual chapters © Respective authors 2014

All rights reserved. No reproduction, copy or transmission of this publication may be made without written permission.

No portion of this publication may be reproduced, copied or transmitted save with written permission or in accordance with the provisions of the Copyright, Designs and Patents Act 1988, or under the terms of any licence permitting limited copying issued by the Copyright Licensing Agency, Saffron House, 6–10 Kirby Street, London EC1N 8TS.

Any person who does any unauthorized act in relation to this publication may be liable to criminal prosecution and civil claims for damages.

The authors have asserted their rights to be identified as the authors of this work in accordance with the Copyright, Designs and Patents Act 1988.

First published 2014 by
PALGRAVE MACMILLAN

Palgrave Macmillan in the UK is an imprint of Macmillan Publishers Limited, registered in England, company number 785998, of Houndmills, Basingstoke, Hampshire RG21 6XS.

Palgrave Macmillan in the US is a division of St Martin's Press LLC, 175 Fifth Avenue, New York, NY 10010.

Palgrave Macmillan is the global academic imprint of the above companies and has companies and representatives throughout the world.

Palgrave® and Macmillan® are registered trademarks in the United States, the United Kingdom, Europe and other countries.

ISBN 978–1–137–43147–9

This book is printed on paper suitable for recycling and made from fully managed and sustained forest sources. Logging, pulping and manufacturing processes are expected to conform to the environmental regulations of the country of origin.

A catalogue record for this book is available from the British Library.

A catalog record for this book is available from the Library of Congress.

In Honour of Professor David Neville Dilks

A fine scholar, teacher, and administrator who has rarely taken the line of least resistance and has remained true to his principles throughout

Contents

Acknowledgements ix

Notes on Contributors x

Introduction 1
Malcolm H. Murfett

1 Professor David Neville Dilks, MA (Oxon), FRHistS, FRSL
 (1938–): An Appreciation from Afar 10
 Malcolm H. Murfett

2 The British Empire's Image of East Asia, 1900–41: Politics,
 Ideology and International Order 21
 Antony Best

3 The Struggle to Maintain Locarno Diplomacy: Britain and
 the Idea of a Political Truce in 1931 41
 Frank Magee

4 'Leaving Us in the Lurch': The British Government,
 the First DRC Enquiry and the United States,
 1933–34 64
 Peter Bell

5 Chamberlain, the British Army and the
 'Continental Commitment' 86
 G.C. Peden

6 Eden, the Foreign Office and the 'German Problem',
 1935–38 111
 G.T.P. Waddington

7 Harold Nicolson and Appeasement 136
 John W. Young

8 Another Jewel Forsaken: The Role of Singapore in British
 Foreign and Defence Policy, 1919–68 159
 Malcolm H. Murfett

9 Quadruple Failure? The British-American Split over
   Collective Security in Southeast Asia, 1963–66   193
   Brian P. Farrell

10 GCHQ and UK Computer Policy: Teddy Poulden,
   ICL and IBM   240
   Richard J. Aldrich

Select Bibliography   254

Index   273

Acknowledgements

I've always regarded it as a great privilege to acknowledge the individuals and organizations that have helped me in the publication of my research. In fact, it's the least I can do to thank them for being there for me. Editing a volume brings the same debts and I willingly place on record the assistance that has been given either to me personally or my contributors by The Arts & Humanities Research Council, Aamir Farooqi, Gill Bennett, the British Academy, Professor Xiaolan Curdt-Christiansen, Jill and David Dilks, Michael Emery, Kim Evans, Tiha Franulovic, Caroline Henry, Marianne McMahon, Clare Mence, Nicolas Murfett, Emily Russell, the late Professor Philip Taylor, Professor Odd Arne Westad, Stephanie Williams, and Allen and Cherry Yhearm. A final word of thanks must go to my wife Ulrike for being such a brilliant friend and partner of mine since our days at Oxford together.

As editor I'm ultimately responsible for what appears in this volume of essays. If there are any mistakes in this work, I should have spotted them and the fact that I haven't is down to me, alas.

Notes on Contributors

Richard J. Aldrich is Professor of International Security at the University of Warwick. He began his career in the Department of International History at the University of Leeds, where David Dilks was Head of Department. Among his many publications are *British Intelligence, Strategy and the Cold War, 1945–51* (1992); *The Key to the South. Britain, the United States and Thailand During the Approach of the Pacific War 1929–1942* (1993); *Espionage, Security and Intelligence in Britain 1945–70* (1998); *The Hidden Hand: Britain, America and Cold War Secret Intelligence* (2006); *Intelligence and the War Against Japan: Britain, America and the Politics of Secret Service* (2008); and *GCHQ: The Uncensored Story of Britain's Most Secret Intelligence Agency* (2010). Since 2008, he has been leading a team project funded by the AHRC entitled: 'Landscapes of Secrecy: The Central Intelligence Agency and the Contested Record of US Foreign Policy'. He currently serves on the Cabinet Office Consultative Group on Intelligence and Security Records, the UK Information Assurance Advisory Council and the UK Ministry of Defence Academic Advisory Forum.

Peter Bell taught History and American Studies at York St John University until 2011. He studied International History at the University of Leeds, specialising in British foreign policy between the world wars. Under David Dilks' tutelage, he conducted doctoral research into the widening debate, following the opening in 1969 of the 1930s archives, about Appeasement and the Origins of World War II. In 1996 Palgrave Macmillan published, as part of their Studies in Military and Strategic History series, his book *Chamberlain, Germany and Japan, 1931–34*. He also undertook research into newsreels, propaganda and diplomacy, and led, in conjunction with the late Professor Philip M. Taylor, the Inter-University History Film Consortium, which pioneered the application of news film to the study of history, bequeathing to the British Universities Film and Video Council a permanent on-line archive of the Consortium's entire catalogue of articles and film productions.

Antony Best is a Senior Lecturer in International History at the London School of Economics. He did his International History and Politics undergraduate degree at the University of Leeds between 1983 and 1986, where he studied under David Dilks. He is the author of *Britain, Japan and Pearl Harbor: Avoiding War in East Asia, 1936–1941* (1995), and *British Intelligence and the Japanese Challenge in Asia, 1914–1941* (2002) and co-author (with J. Hanhimaki, J. Maiolo and K.E. Schulze) of *International History of the Twentieth Century* (2008).

Brian P. Farrell is Professor and Head of the Department of History at the National University of Singapore, where he has been teaching since 1993. His main research interests include the military history of the British Empire, coalition warfare, and the Western military experience in Asia. David Dilks acted as external examiner for his PhD thesis, 'War by Consensus: Power, Perceptions and British Grand Strategy 1940–1943', completed at McGill University in 1992. This led to an active academic friendship that continues to this day, and this volume presents a welcome opportunity to present a chapter as grateful return for the staunch support of a most esteemed mentor, inspiration and role model, in person and in print. Publications include *The Basis and Making of British Grand Strategy 1940–1943: Was There a Plan?* (1998); *The Defence and Fall of Singapore 1940–1942* (2005); *Malaya 1942* (2010). He was also co-author of *Between Two Oceans: A Military History of Singapore from 1275 to 1971* (2011) and editor of *Churchill and the Lion City* (2011).

Frank Magee is Associate Head of the Department of International Studies and Social Science at Coventry University. He has written about aspects of British foreign policy in the inter-war period and become an authority on the Locarno period. He has also acted as a reviewer for the *Journal of Global History*, *The English Historical Review* and *Diplomacy and Statecraft*. In his final year as an undergraduate at Leeds, Frank was taught by David Dilks, who subsequently became his doctoral supervisor. His thesis was titled 'The British Government, the last Weimar Governments and the rise of Hitler, 1929–1933'.

Malcolm H. Murfett is Visiting Professor in the War Studies Department of King's College, London. He was in the first batch of International History and Politics students at Leeds under David Dilks' direction and did his doctorate on Anglo-American relations in the late 1930s at New College, Oxford where he worked for five years as the sole research assistant to the Earl of Birkenhead on the officially commissioned life of Sir Winston Churchill. He joined the Department of History at the National

University of Singapore in 1980 and was elected a Fellow of the Royal Historical Society in 1990. His publications include *Fool-Proof Relations: The Search for Anglo-American Naval Cooperation During the Chamberlain Years, 1937–40* (1984); *Hostage on the Yangtze: Britain, China and the Amethyst Crisis of 1949* (1991); *In Jeopardy: The Royal Navy and British Far Eastern Defence Policy 1945–1951* (1995); *Naval Warfare 1919–1945* (2013). He was also the lead author of *Between Two Oceans* (2011) and the editor of *Imponderable But Not Inevitable: Warfare in the 20th Century* (2010) and *Cold War Southeast Asia* (2012).

G.C. Peden is an Emeritus Professor at Stirling University. A graduate of Dundee and Oxford, he was a colleague of David Dilks while teaching international history at Leeds in 1976–77, before going on to teach economic history at Bristol. Publications include *British Rearmament and the Treasury, 1932–1939* (1979); *Keynes, the Treasury and British Economic Policy* (1988); *British Economic and Social Policy: Lloyd George to Margaret Thatcher* (1991); *The Treasury and British Public Policy, 1906–1959* (2000); *Arms, Economics and British Strategy: From Dreadnoughts to Hydrogen Bombs* (2007). He also edited *Keynes and his Critics: Treasury Responses to the Keynesian Revolution 1925–1946* (2004).

G.T.P. Waddington is Senior Lecturer in International History at the University of Leeds. He completed his PhD under the supervision of David Dilks in 1988. He is the author of numerous articles and chapters on aspects of Nazi diplomacy and translator of Reinhard Spitzy's celebrated memoirs *So Haben wir das Reich Verspielt*. He has recently completed a major study of Ribbentrop and the course of Nazi foreign policy between 1933 and 1945 and is currently working on a number of projects including a study of Franco-German relations in the 1930s, a survey of German foreign policy during the Nazi era and a commentary with documents on Hitler's interviews with statesmen, diplomats and private individuals between 1933 and 1941.

John W. Young has been Professor of International History at the University of Nottingham since 2000, having previously held chairs at the universities of Salford and Leicester. He was a colleague of David Dilks in the Department of History at Leeds University in the 1980s. Since 2003 he has also been Chair of the British International History Group. Among his many publications are *Winston's Churchill's Last Campaign: Britain and the Cold War 1951–5* (1996); *Cold War Europe, 1945–1991: A Political History* (1996); *Britain and the World in the Twentieth*

Century (1997); *The Longman Companion to America, Russia, and the Cold War, 1941–1998* (1999); *Britain and European unity, 1945–1999* (2000); *Twentieth Century Diplomacy: A Case Study in British Practice, 1963–76* (2008) and *David Bruce and Diplomatic Practice: an American ambassador in London, 1961–69* (2014).

Introduction

Malcolm H. Murfett

Devising any kind of operational strategy to cope with the turbulent years of the twentieth century was never going to be an easy undertaking and the British found this out to their cost both before and after World War II. It's easy enough to be an armchair critic – particularly after the fact – but policymakers are neither similarly placed nor blessed with the inestimable advantages of hindsight, so they must plot their future moves more in hope than certainty of success. This volume is devoted to reviewing the complexity of this decision-making process and showing why it's relatively easy for states to lose their way as they grope for a safe passage forward when confronted by mounting international crises and the antics of a few desperate men with considerable power at their disposal. We often talk of the 'fog of war' without acknowledging that there's a peace-time equivalent. It's a mistake to do so.

Professor David Dilks knows this only too well. His historical research has spanned the challenging inter-war era and beyond through the unremitting struggle of World War II to those dark and brooding years of the Cold War. He understands the complexity of geostrategic affairs and appreciates that these policy issues have often been rendered for press and public consumption alike into the lowest common denominator. Arguably, the most contentious example of this policy simplification was seen in the case of appeasement. This was never a simple matter of black and white, as it has often been portrayed. David Dilks saw it as being far more nuanced than that. He has made this point repeatedly over his entire career, but his message that Chamberlain was not a hopelessly naïve politician has been drowned out by the political and historical clamour that vilified the prime minister for trusting Hitler for so long when others, notably Churchill and Eden, were far swifter in rejecting all that the Austro-German dictator stood for.

This volume has been written as a tribute to Professor Dilks. By no means all the contributors (former students and colleagues of David's) are as sympathetic to Chamberlain as he is, but we all acknowledge that far too often historical issues are depicted as inevitable (when they are not) and obviously apparent from the outset to anyone with a degree of intelligence (ditto). It's our hope that this volume will capture the difficulties that British policymakers faced in trying to cope with some of the more intractable issues that arose both before and after World War II and which legitimately gave them such cause for concern.

Antony Best opens this volume with a fascinating essay on the British Empire's changing image of East Asia from the beginning of the twentieth century to the outbreak of the Pacific War in 1941. From a negative impression of a weak and feckless China in 1900, the British began to form a more nuanced and sympathetic opinion of the former 'Middle Kingdom' by the early 1930s, seeing it as a victim of bludgeoning imperialist forces. By the same token the British attitude to the Japanese went in the opposite direction. From hailing the latter as a dynamic state that had integrated modern Western ideas in an Oriental setting and welcoming it as an ally in 1902, the British Empire's relationship with Japan began to cool appreciably during World War I and in the years leading up to the Washington Conference of 1921–22. A sense of disillusionment grew once it became clear that the Japanese had every intention of becoming a bold player in the region with a blue-water navy that couldn't be relied upon to support British interests. This attitude hardened perceptibly as the 1920s wore on and increased in fervour once Taishō democracy was jettisoned in favour of a more militaristic approach illustrated by the Mukden incident and the founding of the puppet state of Manchukuo. Thereafter, the Japanese were seen as a powerful regional adversary and with good reason in London and the other Commonwealth capitals.

From the chaos and enmity of World War I and the baleful consequences of that tragic event culminating in the Ruhr invasion and the wretchedness of hyperinflation, came a kind of short term political salvation in the shape of the Locarno agreement. Fashioning a political understanding linking the British, French and Germans in 1925 was a work of diplomatic art since the prospects of gaining such an outcome were far from serene. No wonder it was dubbed a 'honeymoon' by some expansive commentators, while even dourer spirits were inclined to see it as a welcome return to normalcy. Unfortunately, an enduring European love affair it was not and once the rigours of the Great Depression descended upon the continent after the Wall Street Crash the once heady relationship fell apart as the German banking system hovered on the brink of bankruptcy and popular sympathy expressed at the ballot box lurched towards embracing Hitlerian extremism and a swift end to the Versailles Settlement. In such an intemperate atmosphere of simmering distrust, it was hardly any wonder that a proposed political truce between Berlin, London and Paris fell apart. Frank Magee's chapter on this ill-fated initiative vividly demonstrates just how far Locarno's diplomatic compact was fraying around the edges by 1931. Europe was in need of another Stresemann but what it got was Hitler. Locarno held no magic hold over this naturalized German from across the Austrian border. It wouldn't be restored. It was seen by him as part of the illegitimate Versailles system that ought to be swept away and with his march into the Rhineland on 7 March 1936 it was.

By the time Franklin Roosevelt reached the White House in March 1933 the problems facing the British government were already daunting. Stalwart allies were in remarkably short supply and potential enemies were jostling for an ever increasing piece of the action on the world's stage. FDR may have been a patrician but he wasn't one in thrall to the British. Anglophile though he may have been, these tendencies were kept in check by his recognition that the French weren't entirely far from the mark in describing the British as 'perfidious Albion'. It was a charge that Herbert Hoover's Secretary of State Henry Stimson would have echoed after his clashes with Sir John Simon, the British Foreign Secretary, in the aftermath of the Mukden incident. As a result, Anglo-American relations – often poor in the 1920s – had fallen upon hard times yet again. Unfortunately, by the time Hoover's presidential bid for a second term had collapsed in the face of the worsening economic slump, the Japanese had revealed what post-Taishō democracy was going to be like and Hitler was newly installed in the Reichskanzlei in Berlin and already using brutish methods to enforce his will over the state. Apart from recognizing the danger posed by a resurgent Germany, the National government in London was deeply divided on what to do for the best in dealing with the awkward and unreliable Americans and the strident and assertive Japanese. Peter Bell's essay 'Leaving us in the Lurch' captures this dilemma by illuminating the complex nature of policymaking in 1933–34 as well as the growing influence of Neville Chamberlain, the Chancellor of the Exchequer, upon those deliberations in Whitehall between the ministers of MacDonald's National government and their chief advisors.

In his chapter on Chamberlain and the Continental Commitment, George Peden underlines the important involvement of the much misunderstood and often reviled Chancellor and subsequent Prime Minister on defence matters throughout the 1930s. As the economic mouthpiece of the National government from 1931–37, Chamberlain naturally had firm ideas on what Britain could afford militarily, but his remit moved well beyond demanding ministerial economies of scale to envelop strategic matters in which he was unschooled. If this should have caused him pause for thought, it didn't seem to do so. In fact, he was quite strident in his beliefs. For instance, it became very evident from the outset of his time at the Treasury that Chamberlain was unconvinced that the army represented value for money and that Britain should not make any continental commitment to send an expeditionary force to the aid of France and Belgium in the event of war as it had done at the outset of World War I. What may have been appropriate in 1914 looked overblown to him by the early to mid-1930s. Chamberlain had become a Trenchard ally; he thought the former Chief of the Air Staff made a lot of sense when it came to discussing the strategic use of air power and the endearing idea for all accountants and economists that the RAF provided more 'bang for its buck' than the other two services did. Chamberlain was also influenced by Basil Liddell Hart's views on the value of the bomber in prosecuting British defence interests in Western Europe. While conceding that the Royal Navy had an appropriate role to play in shoring up imperial defence overseas, Chamberlain was more taciturn over the utility of the army and saw it as playing only a subordinate role in any continental war that might be fought in the short term. He maintained a reluctance to embrace the continental commitment until quite late in the proceedings, but once appeasement became a broken reed in March 1939 with the Nazi takeover of the rump of Czechoslovakia the architect of the failed policy shifted gears in the most remarkable fashion as Professor Peden masterfully illustrates.

Geoff Waddington's view of the interwar period is beautifully encapsulated in the opening sentence of his chapter: 'Of all the dilemmas that plagued the British Foreign Office during the interwar years none was more onerous or enduring than that which has passed into the history books as the "German problem".' His assertion matches that of Anthony Eden whose forlorn quest it was to maintain peace for the foreseeable future with European dictators who saw no reason for restraint and had little love of diplomacy when force could be applied to the problem at hand. Eden's dilemma was acute; coming into office after the shambles of the Hoare-Laval pact had been exposed and its authors vilified, he faced a German dictator whose confidence was rising perceptibly as events began flowing his way with a vengeance. After the Saar plebiscite had been overwhelmingly secured and the Anglo-German Naval Agreement had been freely negotiated, Hitler was even more obdurate than usual. Eden and the Foreign Office pinned their far from lofty hopes on eliminating the demilitarized zone in the Rhineland as a means of effecting an improvement in relations between London and Berlin. Unfortunately, the talks on arranging such a deal proceeded at a snail's pace until Germany rendered the scheme entirely redundant by marching into the Rhineland and reclaiming the entire territory for the Reich on 7 March 1936. It was a devastating blow for the British and French; it contravened both the Treaty of Versailles and that of Locarno, while reaffirming the notion that Europe was set upon a very dangerous course and one in which resort to yet another continental war could not be ruled out. Although Ribbentrop thereafter raised the spectre of an Anglo-German alliance, both Eden and the leading members of the Foreign Office were very wary of such a prospect and what it might entail. After the opening of the Spanish Civil War and the establishment of the Anti-Comintern Pact, however, this initiative looked increasingly woebegone. It didn't stop Chamberlain from trying to resurrect it once he came to power in May 1937, but Eden's sympathy for appeasing Hitler – never remotely strong – receded as the German Chancellor's price for such an accommodation grew ever more unsavoury.

John Young's chapter on Harold Nicolson is noteworthy because it reveals the dilemma and quandary of a talented and sensitive British politician, former diplomat and man of letters in confronting the robust challenge posed by the German and Italian dictators in the 1930s. That Nicolson, a National Labour MP, was trumped in the face of such a determined onslaught shouldn't surprise us. He was not alone in seeking an effective way forward. It proved to be a tortuous path. After all, appeasement wasn't resorted to for its equity, but because it appeared to offer the possibility of 'peace for our time' once the League of Nations had foundered after the Abyssinian invasion. Appeasement didn't prove to be the answer, of course, but Chamberlain naturally hoped that it would. Nicolson loathed all forms of dictatorship and didn't approve of appeasement because it provided a diplomatic gloss to violent conduct. He didn't trust Chamberlain and looked for leadership from Eden, but the former Foreign Secretary who promised much in early 1938 ultimately proved to be a disappointment. Churchill's circle didn't appeal either for whatever reason and so Nicolson was left to plough an inconsistent furrow – fearing war and yet hoping for allies should his fears of Hitler's megalomania prove justified.

As an example of just how difficult it was to form a coherent and effective British foreign and defence policy in the twentieth century, the case of Singapore is both instructive and revealing. It can also be read as an intermittent commentary on the much-hyped 'Special Relationship' that is supposed to exist between the UK and the US. In 'Another Jewel Forsaken' I demonstrate that bringing the Anglo-Japanese Alliance to an end in deference to American wishes after World War I didn't do the British any favours whatsoever. For that matter the quid pro quo given to the Japanese – a monopoly position in the Western Pacific – in order for them to sign the 5-Power Naval Limitation Treaty (February 1922) – wasn't exactly a bonus feature for His Majesty's Government (HMG) either. That, alas, wasn't the end of the chain of bad news. Worse was to follow. As a means of trying to combat the relatively unfavourable geo-strategic circumstances the British expected to find themselves in during the medium to long term, the Admiralty managed to indulge the Royal Navy in a comforting piece of wishful thinking when it came to defending HMG's interests east of Suez. In forging the 'Singapore Strategy', the Admiralty supported the construction of a first class naval base one degree north of the equator that would become home to the Main Fleet which would hypothetically be sent out east should the Japanese declare war on the British Empire. Unfortunately, the base was poorly sited, logistically and structurally deficient, and crucially indefensible against enemy forces both in the air and on the ground. Field Marshal Jan Smuts was never convinced by the 'Singapore Strategy' and his prescient warnings about the unlikelihood of the Main Fleet steaming out to Southeast Asia for weeks or months at a time ought to have been shared by successive Australasian governments, but somehow the penny didn't seem to drop in either Canberra or Wellington. It only seemed to do so in late 1941 when war was finally at hand. Although Churchill's National government did eventually send a 'flying squadron' to Singapore it proved, sadly, to be more a magnet rather than a deterrent to the Japanese. After the destruction of Force *Z* on 10 December 1941, the writing was clearly on the wall for British interests in Southeast Asia. When the Japanese duly completed their 70-day invasion of Malaya and Singapore on 15 February 1942, the colonial population as well as chastened British policymakers were shocked and the Commonwealth dominions were aghast. A sense of being palpably let down by the 'mother country' was acutely felt by all those who had to endure the painful 42-month Japanese occupation of Singapore before the Pacific War came to an abrupt end and the island was turned back over to the British in September 1945. Thereafter the problem of what to do about this equatorial island and the rest of the British territories in Southeast Asia became an unexpectedly expensive challenge for Attlee's government and its successors in Whitehall during the following two decades. From the Malayan Emergency (1948–60) to *Konfrontasi* (1963–66), the British and their Commonwealth partners found themselves pouring far more money into defending their hold over the region than the cost-benefit statistics suggested they should. Macmillan was alive to the situation from the time he succeeded Eden after the Suez debacle of late 1956. A 'wind of change' was already blowing strongly in Southeast Asia several years before it was associated with Africa. While recognizing the need to withdraw from the region was meritorious on Macmillan's behalf, designing an appropriate exit strategy in the Cold War era proved to be a far more arduous proposition than he had ever imagined. It was left to Wilson's administration to orchestrate this much criticized manoeuvre abandoning Singapore and flying in the face of US policy in Vietnam. Ratting on promises freely given in the past was not a noble way of treating friends or influencing people. Once again, therefore, another Singaporean episode had ended controversially with the UK accused of actively dissembling in order to secure its national objectives. It is hardly a new trick or one that's confined to HMG, but it looked disconcertingly self-serving which, of course, it was!

In picking up one of the threads of the strategic dilemma that the British faced in Southeast Asia when it came to maintaining the 'Special Relationship', Brian Farrell carefully traces the idea of collective security in the region from the days of the 'domino theory' in the 1950s to the explosive issue of Indonesian *Konfrontasi* from 1963 to 1966. It soon became obvious that London and Washington saw the momentous issues of dealing with the Cold War while trying to manage change in Southeast Asia in markedly different ways. Whereas the Americans believed that the existential threat posed by the communists had to be contained by surface engagement in Vietnam, the British were not at all convinced that committing ground forces against Ho Chi Minh's People's Army of Vietnam (PAVN) and Viet Cong was the most sensible way of diminishing the latent threat posed by Mao's PRC. These diametrically opposed views caused irritation on both sides of the Atlantic and fomented problems with both the Australians and New Zealanders for whom the Far East was the 'near north'. As Professor Farrell bluntly concedes: "The price for refusing to intervene in Vietnam was the Manila Pact...." This led to the birth of the Southeast Asia Treaty Organization (SEATO) which provided the only direct link between all the Western Powers with interests in the region. As SEATO planned for the direst of scenarios, the British were grappling the Malayan Emergency. Once the Malayan Communist Party's (MCP's) resistance had been finally broken, Macmillan's government – cognizant of the emerging force of nationalism – began applying a 'Grand Design' to its former empire subjects in Southeast Asia. This was much easier said than done. Not all the territories wished to be subsumed within a 'Greater Malaysia' and the Malay ruler Tunku Abdul Rahman was far from convinced that having Singapore in the mix would be beneficial to the new enlarged Malaysia. Unfortunately, matters didn't end there; the 'Grand Design' enraged the Indonesian President Sukarno who saw it as yet another piece of neo-colonialism which he was determined to sink without trace; and it frustrated the Philippine nationalists who still entertained visions of incorporating British North Borneo (Sabah) into their republic. When Sukarno proceeded beyond verbal criticism to the encouragement of violence against Malaysia, the tricky Anglo-American partnership in Southeast Asia was tested still further, not least because the US had been hoping to keep him from moving into a communist orbit. Crucially for the British, Sukarno overplayed his hand allowing a modus vivendi to be struck between Washington and London on tackling *Konfrontasi*. It was just as well since this gave the British a decent excuse for staying out of the Vietnam imbroglio. Harold Wilson's accession to power in mid-October 1964 and the PRC's detonation of its first thermo-nuclear device within a day of the changing of guard in Downing Street reinforced the impression that the 'Special Relationship' was now needed more than ever. Wilson's government beset with economic woes from the outset and determined not to give into devaluation, couldn't afford an open-ended commitment to defence spending. It would have to start cutting back and its role east of Suez looked particularly vulnerable if it could only bring *Konfrontasi* to an end. It was a strategic response that provided only short-term comfort to those of its allies with medium to long-term concerns in the region.

Bonus item

When this project was first mooted a few years back I had hoped that this volume would move into the post-war world of propaganda, communications and intelligence in addition to foreign and defence policy. Unfortunately Phil Taylor's sad and untimely death in December 2010 left a massive hole to fill. Out of respect for Phil I haven't endeavoured to try to replace him. He was a one-off and a Leeds man from first to last. Other less tragic events conspired to ensure that a planned contribution from Nick Cull fell by the wayside leaving Richard Aldrich alone to perform a cameo and admittedly tangential role in this festschrift. His paper on the role of Teddy Poulden and GCHQ's influence upon the rather woebegone British computer industry is offered as a bonus item to David Dilks and our readers with a warning that sometimes British is not always best!

1
Professor David Neville Dilks, MA (Oxon), FRHistS, FRSL (1938–)
An Appreciation from Afar
Malcolm H. Murfett

I need to state at the outset that I owe a huge debt of gratitude to David Dilks for the significant impact he had on my life at Leeds and Oxford in the 1970s and at Singapore ever since. Without David's influence and periodic intervention, my professional career would have almost certainly turned out quite differently.

Despite the fact that he has performed a number of cameo roles at various stages of my life, I have to confess I don't begin to know what really makes him tick. He is an elusive fellow who guards his privacy almost inordinately well. For someone who has been in the spotlight for much of his life, he was rather embarrassed at the thought that I was going to prepare an essay on him for this volume and hoped it would be a brief affair. I laughed as only a prolix fellow should and gave him no such guarantee.

I think it would be entirely appropriate to call David a 'high Tory' – someone who early on in his career found a congenial home in the corridors of the Conservative and Unionist Party working closely with a number of the leading luminaries of that institution – some of whom had reached the top of the greasy pole in British politics in the postwar world. It's clear that Anthony Eden, Harold Macmillan, Lord Home and RAB Butler trusted him and with good reason since he never let them down. Secrets that he became aware of were never divulged – at least not by him. David's moral integrity wasn't compromised. His sphinx-like persona gave nothing away. If Robert Blake was the older generation's official historian of the party, David was seen by many as his natural successor. His two volume study of another stalwart of the party – Lord Curzon – and his magisterial work on the much maligned figure of Neville Chamberlain, together with the scholarly grasp he acquired of Churchill's turbulent career, made him a natural choice for that role until university administration lured him away from the archives and began to take up an overwhelming amount of his time. Tertiary administration's gain was, alas, historical scholarship's loss.

A Baring Scholar at Hertford College, Oxford (1956–59), David's interests in International History were fostered by his two spells at the hothouse of St Antony's (1959–60, 1961–62) and by his early undergraduate teaching assignments at the LSE. These were busy and productive years as he spent the decade working as a research assistant on the memoirs of Eden (1960–62), Marshal of the RAF Lord Tedder (1963–65) and Macmillan (1964–70). There was much to do. Access to closed archival papers is usually fascinating and always a great privilege, but the staple of fact checking, draft writing, editing and endless amounts of reading that comes with it does so at a great cost to the individual's free time and often saps his energy. Working for prominent figures with a story to tell is rarely as easy as it sounds. Some can be considerable task masters and research assistants need as much enthusiasm and self-confidence as endurance and resilience to ride out the storms that occasionally erupt when material that they may have presented doesn't go down well with their host and paymaster! On balance, however, David gained vastly from the experience. He was seen as a safe pair of hands: bright, scholarly and agreeable, but far from being a cloying sycophant.

Working on several fronts appealed to David. As he devilled in the archives for biographical details, he was gathering a mass of material for his projected manuscript on the tenure of the rather superior Lord Curzon as the Governor-General and Viceroy of India, and editing the diaries of Sir Alexander Cadogan, the analytically shrewd and dependable former Permanent Under-Secretary of State at the Foreign Office. All of this hyperactivity was going on while he was moving through the lecturing ranks at the LSE. This fine institution proved to be an ideal launching pad for his assault in 1970 on the new position of Professor of International History and Politics (IHP) at the University of Leeds. Despite his unflagging energy and commitment to the cause, David at only 32 was hardly a cast iron certainty for a professorship at a well-established university in West Yorkshire that might have been expected to appoint a more seasoned academic with bags of administrative experience on his record. Although he had only eight years of university service to his name by this stage, David did have youth, flair and that key asset 'potential' on his side. When linked to an impressive maturity and a clear vision of where he wanted IHP to go, his inexperience no longer became an impediment to securing this post but actually a virtue. In 1970 professorships were not usually doled out to tall young willowy men of promise, but Leeds bucked the trend.

It helped that David was (and still is) very suave and engaging; with a compelling delivery and an ability to convince even the most sceptical that his views are worth listening to and deserving of attention. I rarely agreed with some of the positions he adopted and failed to see what there was to admire in Chamberlain's faulty grasp of foreign and defence issues, but David could fashion a heroic defence of the fallen 'anti-hero' of Munich like no other. His championing of Chamberlain was remarkable because it won him few favours among his peer group. Appeasement seemed as bankrupt in the 1970s as the Kreditanstalt had been in 1931. As for his students, we marvelled at how he seemed to turn black into white with the finesse of a master illusionist. In the face of overwhelming criticism of appeasement, David was stoically unmoved. He was convinced that history had given Chamberlain a raw deal and it was his task to enlighten the new wave of emerging historians that all was not what it may have seemed to have been back in the mid-to-late 1930s. His earnest conviction that Chamberlain had grasped the overall reality of the situation rather than merely a few straws of it certainly helped to underline the necessity for each of us to recognise that there is always another side to the argument no matter how stacked the odds are against it.

I invariably found him an amusing raconteur; an individual who could be relied upon to discover unfamiliar and yet captivating vignettes in the public records about the 'great and the good' which could then be used to enliven his lectures and improve their accessibility no matter whether his audience was student-orientated or non-university based. He had little difficulty in identifying the absurdities of life and the fecklessness of the human condition. As a tutor, I found him somewhat intimidating – a bit like an iceberg that you didn't mess with but steered around. Collisions were out of the question. I can only recall having him as my tutor in the first year of the IHP programme and it was soon entirely evident that he seemed to know so much more than I did about everything! It was extremely galling. I wasn't used to slipping under the radar screen, but tangling with David in his pomp when I hadn't read everything on the subject seemed like a very bad idea to me at the time and still does!

Whether in class or not, David could be always relied upon to inveigh against the smug, self-satisfied tyranny of the Oxbridge-London 'golden triangle' which he felt looked down on the other tertiary institutions in the UK. Despite the fact that he had passed through two of the three elite universities himself and had recently been a visiting fellow at All Souls, he genuinely thought that the 'golden triangle' – for all of its wonderful endowments – didn't have a monopoly on scholarly brilliance and its apparent disdain for the other academic outposts dotted about the country was both very demeaning and extremely unfair to them. In his view, Leeds and other universities like it weren't there just to make up the numbers even if they were woefully underestimated and critically under-funded by the British Establishment.

While the iniquities of the British university system with its uneven pattern of resources could immediately gain his undivided attention, another touchstone of David's passion lay in fostering links with the Commonwealth. While he was at LSE, he became a consultant to the Secretary-General of the Commonwealth (1968–75) and the founding member and first chairman of the Commonwealth Youth Exchange Council (1968–73), both roles he took to Leeds with him in 1970. During this time he also developed a close rapport with a number of leading figures within the Canadian higher education system and solidified these links by initially establishing the Canadian Studies Committee at Leeds and becoming its chairman for a decade as it proceeded from an informal grouping to a fully-fledged, University-funded body (1974–84). He also took on the additional role of advisor to all overseas students who joined the School of History at Leeds in the 16 years after 1975. In this role he lent an ear to the homesick and eased the financial burdens of others who found themselves struggling to keep afloat in an increasingly expensive UK on inadequate funding. While he was not one to crow about his achievements in these fields, he was quietly appreciated by those who came to see him with their problems and benefited from his kindness and consideration. These administrative roles were not undertaken by him to add an extra line or two to his burgeoning curriculum vitae. After all, in the days before annual league tables and the quinquennial Research Assessment Exercise became a way of life for British universities, tenured professors of his ilk weren't obliged to prove that they were instrumental in bringing extra value-added to their schools or departments. David helped because he wanted to. It was understated as usual with him. He wanted no publicity or fuss. He still doesn't.

At Leeds he was synonymous with the advancement of the IHP degree. He was its lightning rod and from the outset its admissions tutor. This enabled him to take a punt on the unorthodox – the 'second-chance', mature students – as well as the gifted younger candidates who had jumped through the examination hoops at school with great facility and on time. Not surprisingly, IHP had an edge to it and rapidly became a flagship programme within the School of History. In establishing the BA in International History and Politics he was aided by a set of excellent, if occasionally highly idiosyncratic, colleagues with eclectic tastes. They made for a vibrant community of scholars. Steering such an assorted group with considerable abilities and egos to match would have been challenging for anyone. Whether David was inclusive or exclusive in the running of the department and as chairman of the School (1974–79) is better answered by those who were there at the time.

Whatever went on in the professional domain, however, he always had the loyal and consistent support of his family and a close knit circle of friends to rely upon. In particular, his wife Jill knew the score and had seen it all before since her father, the celebrated academic and prolific historian W.N. Medlicott, had been the former Stevenson Professor of International History at the LSE. Jill could therefore provide both a reality check and a calming influence if and when things began to go awry as they occasionally must have done over the years. Anyone who has had to deal with us on a long-term basis knows that academics can be notoriously difficult characters at the best of times – our insecurities often reign supreme regardless of how high our personal IQs may be. In any case, university politics is often contentious and frustrating, so a retreat to a lovely home environment after tangling with the levers of bureaucracy all day long becomes crucial if sanity is to be preserved. Jill clearly provided that oasis for David and the strong bonds of their marriage (1963–) and the joy that came from witnessing the growing exploits of their only child Richard (born in 1979) illuminated their family life together and put everything else into a welcome sense of perspective.

Even at the best of times tertiary administration is an acquired taste; endless amounts of times stuck in committees arguing the toss about procedural items, government interference, policy matters, faculty budgets, and funding initiatives would test the patience of Job and drive most people to despair. Somehow David acquired the taste for navigating his way through the swirling shoals that lie in wait for even the most intrepid of administrative helmsmen. His motivation was laudable in that he sought to try to make the university he served more responsive to change and better able to cope with the compelling demands of the modern world. It wasn't a case of mere survival, by the 1970s that wasn't good enough any longer. David was hardly alone in recognizing that any institute of higher education needed to shake off the lethargy and complacency that may have arisen in the wake of the Robbins Report (1963) and the expansion of the tertiary sector to take account of the 'baby boomer' generation that would be beating a path to its door from then onwards. It was evident that all centres of higher learning needed to improve at all levels if they were to become more appreciated in a hyper-competitive world. David quite naturally wanted to attract the best students and staff to Leeds and subsequently to Hull and knew it wouldn't happen unless the university actively courted them and showed that it was a place worth coming to. He saw it as his task to try to lay the groundwork for that desired objective. It would require more than talk to bring this about but policy guidelines needed to be drawn up to facilitate progress in these fields and that was where David felt he could contribute in a meaningful capacity. While at Leeds he was Dean of the Faculty of Arts (1975–77); he had two spells on the Planning Committee of the Senate (1977–79 and 1981–84), the latter period coinciding with his chairmanship of its Research Policy Committee; and if that wasn't enough, he was also a member of the Council of the University (1977–79) and six other university committees ranging from industrial relations to military education.

Amazingly, that was not all. He also performed a number of non-university roles, in particular on the Advisory Council on Public Records (1977–85), the Central Council of the Royal Commonwealth Society (1982–85) and the Universities Funding Council in London (1988–91). In addition, he was a trustee of the memorial trusts established for two Privy Councillors and Companions of Honour he greatly admired: Baron Boyle of Handsworth (better known as Sir Edward Boyle) and Viscount Boyd of Merton (the former Alan Lennox-Boyd). Both had reached Cabinet rank – the former for education and the latter for the colonies – but had become disenchanted with the daily grind of knockabout politics and sought solace in organ music and scholarly pastimes (Boyle) and mapping out the fortunes of Arthur Guinness & Sons (Boyd). David's trustee work extended across a variety of other areas to embrace the Imperial War Museum, the Royal Commonwealth Society Library, the Heskel & Mary Nathaniel Trust, and the Young Historians Scheme. Worthy though these causes were, it remains a mystery to me how he found the time to conduct these extra-curricula activities and yet still keep his head above water. But there was more because he was also a Freeman and subsequently a Liveryman of the Goldsmiths' Company – one of the 12 great livery companies in the City of London. Need I go on?

When David arrived at Leeds in 1970, the Brotherton Library already had a very fine collection of printed works and published sources which it had built up assiduously over the years. Working closely with the librarian, however, he identified a whole range of additional public and private collections in the realm of international history that could be purchased in microform to complement the library's existing holdings. His efforts in this regard helped to ensure that an impressive array of primary research materials was made available for project work at all levels of the IHP scholarly community. David also played a vital role in raising £250,000 as a precursor to acquiring the vast Liddle Collection of materials on World War I – the largest of its kind in existence – for the Brotherton.

Supported by an increasingly strong research environment, he supervised a raft of MPhil and PhD theses on a diverse range of topics covering many aspects of modern foreign and Commonwealth affairs. It was not unusual for him to have eight or nine graduate students working on their dissertations at any one time. In the ultra-competitive era of the 1980s British universities were expected to vie for the best students not only domestically but internationally. David saw this as an ideal opportunity to draw on the strengths and attractions of Leeds to reach out to a much wider audience. Using his high profile position on the British National Committee on the History of the Second World War (1983–2005) and as a founder member of the Study Group on Intelligence (1982–91) to great effect, he began organizing a series of stellar conferences throughout the decade in which a cast of leading academics from Europe, the US, and the wider world beyond were persuaded to come to Leeds to thrash out a number of hugely contentious issues within the realm of modern international history. These proved to be intellectually engaging affairs and showed Leeds in a very positive light. Building on this momentum, he became instrumental in promoting the establishment of the MA in Modern International Studies. An advanced degree by course work and dissertation, the new Masters course proved to be a very attractive magnet drawing students from around the globe to Leeds in the post-1989 period. Already postgraduate admissions tutor since 1985, he was the natural candidate to become appointed director of the Institute for International Studies in 1989, a post he retained until Hull hove into view in 1991.

I never thought that David would end his career at Leeds even though he had done so much to raise its profile as a cool place to do history at university. I imagined that he would ultimately return to the 'golden triangle' as a master or warden of a college. I was wrong. A vacancy as vice-chancellor arose at the University of Hull and David, already something of an institution at Leeds, opted to apply for it. After two decades in West Yorkshire, he was ready to face another challenge. Going to Humberside would prove to be all of that and more. By the time of his appointment David could draw upon a vast well of university administration. Much of that, of course, had been devoted to preserving the interests of the historical discipline from administrative intervention and the impact of government policy. Now he was directly in the firing line on behalf of the entire university. He couldn't seek to protect one discipline or faculty over another. History would have to take a back seat for the duration.

Funding issues were, naturally, of paramount importance in higher education in the 1990s. A university could have a great strategic plan for the future but the ability to implement it was almost always driven by the financial health of the institution. New sources of revenue were therefore vital if a university was to move forward in this new and rather unsatisfactory 'bums on seats' era. Vice-Chancellors like David were forced to spend a good deal of their time on financial matters, making earnest appeals to alumni as well as potential donors to sponsor a multiplicity of academic initiatives and infrastructural needs. It was often a 'fire fighting' exercise in which some success on one front was mitigated by failure to arrest its depressing negative momentum on another. Even at the best of times administrators are rarely beloved by academics who accuse them of being divorced from the reality of the classroom, lecture theatre or laboratory and obsessed by the minutiae of box ticking, form filling and number crunching. Sitting on the top of this unforgiving pyramidal structure are the well-heeled Vice-Chancellors who chair high powered committees, meet visiting dignitaries and preside over matriculation and graduation ceremonies. In the past they were often seen as being largely inaccessible figures surrounded by an equally remote entourage who lived 'inside the academic tent' with them. In recent years they were encouraged to get out more and David didn't need any cue to follow suit. As a result, he travelled abroad extensively presiding at degree days and cultivating links with an extensive cast of government officials, business executives and potential or actual benefactors who could be used to Hull's advantage. In my experience, however, teaching staff don't have to be querulous and disputatious to consider all bureaucrats – elite or otherwise – as a frictional element in their lives. Rarely are they embraced for their foresight or initiative, let alone the formal work that they do. David's time at Hull, therefore, was hardly likely to be a bed of roses. I'm sure he realised that from the beginning as he began negotiating the congested M62 from Leeds out to the East Riding of Yorkshire.

Nonetheless, whatever difficulties the staff might have posed for him, the students at Hull during the 1990s were consistently known for having a great time, being very satisfied with their courses, and finding little difficulty in getting jobs once they graduated. Such very positive student feedback suggests that Hull had got its act together under David's resolute leadership. This was independently confirmed by *The Times Good University Guide* which saw Hull vaulting more than 20 places up its ranking list during the eight years that he remained at the helm in University House (1991–99). A marked improvement of this nature was no mean feat in a restless tertiary sector. Moreover, it wasn't a marketing ploy devised by the public relations unit on campus or some spurious claim on a website; the fact was that Hull's fortunes were distinctly and officially 'on the up'. While there are many causes for this startling progress, team work obviously played a vital part. Although I know David shrinks from gratuitous displays of self-promotion, as the team leader at Hull even he ought to derive a certain quiet satisfaction from this substantial achievement.

Despite the fact that much of his time at Hull was taken up on official duties, the historian in him refused to disappear entirely from the scene. Formal lectures and occasional publishing ventures offered him an abiding connection to the discipline and there was always his work as vice-president of the International Committee for the History of the Second World War (1990–92) and thereafter the presidency of that august body over the course of the next eight years (1992–2000) to ensure that university administration didn't claim all of his attention. His work in the field of international history was recognized by the award of the Médaille de Vermeil of the Académie Française in 1994 and by an Honorary Doctorate of History which was conferred on him by the Russian Academy of Sciences in Moscow in 1996.

If one imagined he would retreat to pottering about his garden in Adel or gliding around the Dales in his Bentley upon his retirement from Hull in 1999, David had other ideas. He had already worked on a series of critically well-acclaimed programmes for both the BBC and Granada Television before he left Leeds and his historical expertise was to be tapped once more in the post-Hull era. In the autumn of 2001 he was engaged as a consultant for the television play 'A Lonely War' which revolved around Churchill's life during the 1930s. David provided detailed guidance about the draft text of the play, as well as more general interpretations of Churchill's activities and relations with his friends and parliamentary colleagues. It was broadcast in 2002 with Albert Finney and Vanessa Redgrave in the leading roles. He performed a similar role in the 2009 documentary drama 'Into the Storm' which was concerned with Churchill's wartime premiership from 1940 to 1945.

Notwithstanding his other academic accomplishments, David has produced a corpus of historical studies worthy of close attention. It essentially falls into six main and often-overarching subject areas, namely, the making and impact of British foreign policy in the twentieth century; the life and times of Neville Chamberlain; the role of Churchill both in and out of power; Colonial and Commonwealth affairs and the so-called 'End of Empire'; the world of Intelligence and its application to policy making; and the road to World War II and its diplomatic and political aftermath.

Whatever the merits of his examination of the Raj in the 1920s, the meticulous editing of the Cadogan diaries, let alone his fascination with Anglo-Canadian affairs, David will be most frequently associated with being an apologist for appeasement and its architect Neville Chamberlain. This has been unfashionable from the winter of 1938–39, but David has consistently maintained that history has been profoundly unkind to the former Lord Mayor of Birmingham. Chamberlain's critics have always blamed him for being duped by Hitler and for being willing to accept peace at almost any price. David doesn't believe he was that naïve, misguided or cynically detached from the fate of those who would be enslaved by the forces of Nazism. Regardless of Chamberlain's understandable horror of war, anti-appeasement sentiment has endured in the UK with apologists for the concept of negotiating with dictators in very short supply. Given the number of historians who have plundered the field of appeasement studies, one wonders just what defence can be mounted by David in his second and concluding volume of the Chamberlain biography which British and European historians await with some avidity. We all know that Chamberlain's critics have never forgiven him for supposedly being out of his depth in foreign affairs and for living in a fantasy world in which ruthless dictators can be relied upon to keep their word to him. At its basic level, however, this is far too simplistic and sweeping an indictment, even if it has stubbornly persisted for more than seven decades. While David has presented certain aspects of the other side of this story in a number of persuasive articles and lectures, the collective wisdom needs to be drawn together before an informed, retrospective judgement can be satisfactorily passed on Chamberlain's embattled premiership. Let us hope David can summon up the requisite energy in his retirement to complete the poignant study of a much derided premier who is still so much associated with him.

David's impact can also be felt in his growing body of illuminating work on Churchill, the quality of which deservedly won him the Emery Reves Award in 2006 and which can be strikingly seen in both *'The Great Dominion': Winston Churchill in Canada 1900–1954* (2005) and his latest volume *Churchill and Company: Allies and Rivals in War and Peace* (2012); his pioneering studies in the world of intelligence, in collaboration with Christopher Andrew, which helped to bring attention to bear on a crucial determinant in the vital area of policy formulation; and in the rich contributions he has made to the diplomatic history of World War II and the re-orientation of British foreign policy towards Europe and the Commonwealth in the turbulent era of the Cold War.

Looking back on David's career, I am struck not only by the sheer magnitude of the administrative workload he absorbed, but also by the extensive teaching and academic roles he performed at the LSE and Leeds, as well as for the wider tertiary world. How this was all fitted in with his extensive research activities is anyone's guess. Clearly, he mastered the knack of academic juggling to an exemplary degree, but didn't the constraints of time apply to him as well as the rest of us? Perhaps the key to what he did and to who he is lies in Churchill's summing up of Russia in October 1939: 'It is a riddle, wrapped in a mystery, inside an enigma.' David may not agree, even ruefully, that this observation is appropriate to him personally; but in my privileged position of being the editor of his festschrift, I'm prepared to take that risk!

2
The British Empire's Image of East Asia, 1900–41
Politics, Ideology and International Order
Antony Best

In recent years historians have become increasingly interested in trying to understand the nature of the interaction between the West and East Asia during the imperialist age. In the light of the advances made over the past three decades by post-colonial history, much of this new work has dwelt on the impact that the arrival of Western ideas had on the countries of East Asia and the consequent cultural, economic and even linguistic challenges that the latter faced.[1] However, the danger with this focus on the 'victims' of imperialism is that the interests and ambitions of the imperial powers themselves tend to be forgotten or at best treated as if imperialist behaviour, wherever it took place in the world, was constant.[2] Another problem, which is linked to this, is the assumption that the imperial powers had fairly static and uniform views of those that they controlled and/or interacted with. That this mental straitjacket should exist is rather surprising, for it is surely self-evident that political events and the evolution of any observer's ideological and cultural beliefs have a transformative effect on the way in which s/he views the world.[3] In order to demonstrate how Western views of Eastern societies and polities could evolve, this chapter looks at the changing images that Britain had of East Asia in the period between 1900 and 1941 and relates how these were influenced both by events and ideological innovations, and how perception in turn had an effect on the political and diplomatic process.

During the first half of the twentieth century East Asia played a significant role in world affairs for a variety of reasons. In economic terms, in China it possessed a country whose potential to become a great market led to much international investment, while in Japan it had a state that was emerging as an important exporter of consumer goods, most notably cotton textiles. In regard to world politics and strategy, Japan's emergence as the first non-Western Great Power acted as both an inspiration and a threat, while China's resurgent nationalism and chronic political instability created interest in its development but also fear of its becoming a power vacuum. The realm of culture also played a part in the region's prominence, for its rich tradition in the arts provided both an inspiration to the avant-garde and a foil to those who sought to proclaim the moral and cultural superiority of the West. Another aspect that cannot be forgotten is that the very fact that the region was rapidly modernizing led to concern in the West that if Asia should ever politically unite it might present a challenge to the former's dominance of international politics. Even if that did not occur, its rapidly burgeoning population caused concern, for there seemed to be no simple solution to this Malthusian crisis, which could bring in its wake dire political and economic consequences. East Asia was then a volatile region, whose future evolution had ramifications not just for the countries that bordered on the Pacific but for the world as a whole.

Among the European Great Powers, Britain was the state with the greatest interest in East Asia. Aside from the factors outlined above, it had its own specific concerns in regard to East Asia, for it had a considerable economic stake in China itself and possessed a number of territories that bordered on the region. In China it attempted to uphold its commercial presence through supporting the fragile 'open door' and its attendant institutions, which were beset with potential enemies.[4] In regard to its colonies in South and Southeast Asia, Britain sought to defend them from any direct strategic threat that might emerge from East Asia. In addition, however, it was conscious of the indirect influence that events in the latter region might have on its possessions. For example, it was all too aware that the successful modernization of the countries in East Asia and their emergence as a force in world politics might undermine the prestige of European rule. Thus in the period under review much concern was caused by developments such as the mobilization of overseas Chinese opinion to support the Guomindang (GMD) and the steady growth of Japanese trade with India and Malaya.[5] In addition, East Asia demanded attention for, while it might have been the 'Far East' for Britain, it was the 'near north' for the White Dominions of Australia and New Zealand, who feared both the arrival of Asian immigrants and the threat of Japanese military expansion.

Armed with these myriad concerns, British observers, both official and private, made a close study of East Asia in this period looking for signs of stability and disorder in a bid to read the future. To a degree it may be said that the foundations of the British perception of the region lay in certain set stereotypes. It is important to note though that the clichés adopted by the British tended to concentrate on specific countries and nationalities rather than treating all 'Orientals' as essentially similar. This reflected the nature of the British interaction with the region, for it was clear to most observers that the states and peoples that made up the region were reacting in different ways to the arrival of Western imperialism and thus posed different problems and opportunities. As Rotem Kowner has observed in regard to the development of racial science, this tendency to treat the Chinese and Japanese as races in their own right went back to the mid-nineteenth century, when already their different approaches to the West began to be apparent.[6]

The place to begin in any survey of the images that the British had of the individual East Asian countries is with China, for, as noted above, trade with this country was Britain's primary motivation for taking an interest in the region. As Nicholas Clifford has outlined in his excellent study of British and American travel writing, most observers tended to treat China as an entity whose once great civilization had lost its way and sunk into decadence. Visitors to China were thus more often than not struck by the decay of its cities, palaces and temples, a facet which was reinforced by the constant references to the ubiquitous dirt of the country.[7] Thus, for example, in 1927 the journalist and former foreign editor of *The Times*, Sir Valentine Chirol, recalled in his memoirs his first visit to Peking in 1895:

> all my senses seemed to be assailed at the same time – my nose by the most pungent and unsavoury smells, my ears by the discordant din of a strange and uncouth tongue, my eyes by weird and often revolting sights.[8]

Six years later in 1933, the poetically inclined and rather precious Canadian diplomat, Kenneth Kirkwood, noted, during his tour of China: 'To me sadness was the dominant note in Peking. The sadness of faded glory, forgotten splendour, wasting, rotting, decaying beauty.'[9] As Robert Bickers has observed, so prevalent were those images of China and so similar the vocabulary used that it is hard not to believe that most visitors to the country had already, through familiarity with the discourse on all things Chinese, decided what they were going to experience before they had even arrived![10]

Reinforcing this image of decline were certain patterns of behaviour that were commonly associated with the Chinese. One of these was the belief that while the Chinese people shared a culture they did not possess any real sense of patriotism and thus were constitutionally ill-prepared to introduce a far-going policy of reform in order to deliver their country from the West. Exacerbating this apparent lack of public spirit was the perception in British circles that the Chinese displayed a marked indifference to Western knowledge, which not surprisingly in its turn fostered an image of both their misplaced arrogance and profound ignorance. Another problem that further emphasized the essential passivity of the Chinese population was, of course, its association with the smoking of opium. The high levels of opium use and addiction in China could do little but reinforce the perception that the country had succumbed to narcotics and was content to sleep and dream while modernity left it far behind. Redeeming features undoubtedly existed in the population's capacity for hard work and shrewdness in business, but no observer was left oblivious to the massive changes that China needed to throw off the weight of its history. At the same time, however, this impression of China as a country stuck in the past placed it in a position where some were inspired to take a keen paternal interest in shaping its future. Its weakness thus both repelled and attracted.[11]

The way in which visitors reacted to Japan tended to be quite different. Japan was clearly not in a state of terminal decay. Indeed, most of the visitors who came to Japan saw it as possessing an advanced civilization and a vigorous society that was inquisitive about learning from the best of Western practice. Indeed, as Akira Iriye has noted, it was praised at a relatively early stage for its having so rapidly leapt from a state approximating the European Middle Ages to something approaching modernity.[12] Underlining this positive impression was the relative order, good manners and cleanliness that greeted visitors in Japan. This was seen as standing in marked contrast to Chinese customs. Thus the Australian scientist and internationalist, Ian Clunies Ross noted on his arrival in Peking in 1930 after having spent the past few months in Japan:

> As we never thought possible one plunges back into the dirt, the squalor, the picturesqueness and the incompetence of the Middle Ages. We have never realised how unfair it is to lump the Orient and its peoples in one. Japan is as different from that China we have

glimpsed as England is from India & the Japanese we feel are as something known & kindly with whom we are as much at home as here we are alien and apart.[13]

To some what was particularly beguiling was the mixture of modernity and tradition that existed in Japan. One aspect of the country that particularly entranced new arrivals was the discovery that Japanese women still wore kimono out-of-doors. As both Sir Ian Hamilton, one of the British military observers of the Russo-Japanese War, and the Canadian politician, Sir Vincent Massey, observed, in 1904 and 1931 respectively, the effect was to make one feel that one had walked into a Japanese painting.[14] However, the very fact that Japan had proved to be such an apt pupil of Western ways meant that its ambitions for the future were sometimes treated with suspicion. For example, Japanese migrants in South-East Asia and the Dominions were wont to be seen as spies and as an underground vanguard preparing the way for invasion.[15] Thus, while China was viewed as mired in the past, Japan was treated with some circumspection for possibly having learnt too well.

It is, however, important to see that, although these stereotypes were powerful, they were not uniformly accepted among all British observers. After all, the image adopted by any one observer depended to a considerable degree on his or her relative experience and outlook: the intrepid explorer, the devoted missionary, the dilettante traveller, the aesthete, the journalist, and the long-term resident merchant or banker would all have their own version of the truth to relate. Nor were the images of China and Japan necessarily static. Indeed, considering that these were years of marked political and economic turbulence including events such as the Boxer rebellion, the Russo-Japanese War, the collapse of Imperial China and the crises of the 1930s, it is no surprise to find that, although certain stereotypes lingered, perceptions were subject to considerable change. Moreover, as attitudes towards race, modernity and internationalism rapidly evolved in the West, so opinions on the 'East' came increasingly to be defined by the observer's ideological standpoint.

The stereotypical images of the countries of East Asia had their roots in the nineteenth century, but only really came into their own in the 1890s after Japan defeated China in the war of 1894–95. That conflict naturally cast doubt on China's viability as a state and thus brought to an end the period in which Britain had, as James Hevia has noted in his recent book, focused its efforts on the pedagogical exercise of trying to bring the Chinese government to accept modernity.[16] From 1895 it was clear that Japan was the coming power in the East, although opinions differed in British circles about whether this constituted a threat or an opportunity. Resentful of Japanese high-handedness in Korea, a minority already talked of a 'yellow peril' and warned of the threat posed by 'a people... energetic, crafty, unscrupulous, hating of the white race, and imbued with a sense of their coming greatness as a nation'.[17] Most observers though were more positive, largely because they saw Japan, which had proved its worth in war, as a possible balance to Russian ambitions in the region and as a state that would help to preserve the 'open door' in China. Thus it was the 1890s that sealed the stereotype that Japan represented progress, while China became a symbol of 'Oriental' backwardness.

Eventually the sense that the national interests of Britain and Japan complemented each other led to the countries signing an alliance in January 1902. Over the next few years Britain's faith in Japan was amply rewarded by the strategic benefits that the former accrued when its ally defeated Russia in 1905. As Colin Holmes and Hamish Ion have observed, Japan's victory over Russia and its general impression of vitality and discipline had a dramatic effect on British thinking.[18] Wracked with insecurity after the hard-won campaign against the Boers, British politicians and publicists were deeply impressed by Japan's resilience and martial spirit, feeling that these were qualities that Britain somehow had lost. No less a figure than Lord Curzon, the viceroy to India, observed in 1905 that:

> we could not have done what the Japanese have done: for as a nation we are growing stale, flaccid, and nerveless. In point of national ardour and power of self-sacrifice the Japs [sic] stand about where we did at Agincourt.[19]

Japan was thus not just a state that should be admired because of the progress it had made since 1868, but one that could in itself act as an example to Britain. This belief that Japan had become a beacon of modernization in Asia was reflected in the following years in the writings of a number of visitors and observers. Most famously this complimentary view was adopted by Sidney and Beatrice Webb, whose visit to East Asia in 1911 led them to contrast Japan's modernity with what they saw as the hopeless feudal backwardness of Korea and China.[20] Reinforcing this trait was the tendency, as seen in Curzon's comment, to draw parallels between the histories of the two countries and to emphasize their similarity of outlook by referring to the alliance as an association between 'two island empires'.

This admiration for Japan's achievements led, moreover, to a marked change in how it was treated at the diplomatic level. In October 1905 Britain announced its decision to raise the status of its diplomatic representation in Japan from a legation to an embassy. In doing so, it indicated that it now perceived Japan to be one of the highest-ranking countries on a par with the Great Powers in Europe and the United States. This privileged treatment of Japan was also reflected in the development of the relationship between the British and Japanese royal courts. In 1906 a British mission to Japan led by Prince Arthur of Connaught bestowed the Order of the Garter on Emperor Meiji and the same honour was granted to his successor in 1912.[21] The sense of trust that developed in the diplomatic sphere is neatly reflected in the recollections of one British diplomat, Thomas Hohler, who served in the Tokyo legation at the time of the Russo-Japanese War. In his memoirs Hohler observed: 'People talk of the gulf which separates the European from the Japanese, but I found them to be a good deal more like us than many other foreigners.'[22]

However, as noted above, Japan's remarkable progress in the 1900s came at a price, for some in Britain saw the former's advancement as an unwelcome factor in international politics. Once again a minority reacted by indulging in 'yellow peril' rhetoric, which warned of Japan's pretensions to lead Asia and the possibility of racial war in the future. As Akira Iikura has noted, these sentiments, although they held appeal in continental Europe, were not particularly widespread in Britain.[23] They did though find a home in the British Dominions bordering the Pacific where fears of Japanese immigration became more concrete than they had been in the 1890s. A more important strain of thinking in Britain was that Japan, having emerged as the major regional power in East Asia, might now pose a threat to British interests. In other words, the awareness existed that with Russia's defeat the balance of power in the region had changed and that Japan was now capable of challenging any of the Western Powers.

Allied to this recognition of Japan's improved standing was the sense that the Japanese had by no means satiated their ambitions and that they aimed at the steady accumulation of influence over China. These fears were particularly prevalent among the British trading community in China, which began to see Japan as a rival that was undercutting the interests of its own ally.[24] Some in Britain, including the pushy young seventh Earl Stanhope who was looking for a cause to champion, and, perhaps more surprisingly, the erstwhile Japanophile Ian Hamilton sympathized with their concerns. The latter, indeed, went as far as to declare, with his usual tendency towards hyperbole, that, 'we have no more deadly enemies in the world than our Japanese allies.'[25] In addition, concern about Japanese ambitions was expressed within the wider British Empire. In Australia the government of Alfred Deakin perceived Japan as a potential menace to its security, which in turn led to a debate over whether the newly formed federation ought to have its own navy.[26] Similar concerns were expressed in Canada, where Lord Grey, the Governor-General, noted to the Prime Minister Sir Wilfrid Laurier he feared that the Japanese might be able to strike against the undefended coast of British Columbia.[27] However, others were dismissive of the Japanese threat by contending that Japan's talent was overwhelmingly focused on merely copying the West and that it had no initiative of its own. Thus, for example, in 1912 when the young Philip Kerr (later as Lord Lothian to be British ambassador in Washington in 1939–40) visited Japan, he observed: 'In truth most people at home are quite unnecessarily afraid of the Japs [sic]. Their reputation I fancy will rapidly decline. They are quite competent imitators of the West, but no more.'[28]

Thus even in the years preceding World War I, when the alliance was supposed to be at its height, an ambivalent image of Japan existed within British circles. The Japanese victory in the conflict against Russia in 1905 had confirmed that Britain had chosen correctly three years earlier when it had sought an ally in order to deal with the Russian menace, but this did not mean that Britain had unshakeable faith in Japan. Ironically, British doubts were entertained about its ally precisely because Japan had been so successful. Modernization thus may have made Japan an equal to the West, but in this process it had merely replaced its former image of weakness for a new one of lingering distrust.

Japan's rise to international prominence not surprisingly led to questions about whether China would follow in its wake. Some in the late 1900s claimed to witness shoots of recovery, most notably the Australian journalist G.E. Morrison who worked as Peking correspondent of *The Times*. In 1910 Morrison gave a talk to the Author's Club in London on the subject of 'The Awakening of China' in which he drew a favourable picture of the recent reforms made in the areas of education and communications. His assertions attracted some interest, but this was in the main limited to those, such as Stanhope, who had already begun to evince suspicion of Japan's ambitions.[29] Moreover, any immediate hope in China's resuscitation was rendered premature when in 1911–12 a revolution swept the Manchu monarchy from power replacing it with a weak and divided republic. As the new state struggled, and failed, to achieve national unity over the following years, the stereotype of China as a country that was lost in slumber as the world progressed around it was reinforced. Apparently not even the adoption of republicanism could stir China into real reform and modernization.

The next event that precipitated change in the way in which East Asia was perceived was World War I. In regard to British perceptions of Japan, that conflict led to both a deepening of the doubts about its ambitions and a broadening of the constituency that accepted the need for suspicion. This sense of unease arose largely out of the belief that Japan was cynically using the power vacuum in East Asia created by the war to pursue its own national interests; a tendency that was symbolized above all else by the 'twenty-one demands' that it attempted to impose on China in 1915. As one observer commented, in exerting such pressure on the Chinese: 'The Japs [sic] do not seem to be playing the game.'[30] Another disturbing development was the rise of vocal pan-Asianism in Japan, in which radical right-wing pressure groups called on the government to do much more to liberate their Asian brothers from the European colonial yoke. Japan's wartime behaviour confirmed the British trading community in China in its distrust, but also, unlike in the pre-war period, this suspicion also spread to the British diplomatic corps. Indeed, by the end of World War I it was difficult to find many diplomats with East Asian experience who believed that the alliance should be maintained.[31] In public, British statesmen continued to express faith in their Japanese ally, but, as one Australian observer discovered to his satisfaction, this represented expediency rather than 'any particular affection for our Eastern neighbours'.[32]

Reinforcing this heightened suspicion of Japan was the fact that the nature of international politics was changing. With the American entry into World War I, the conflict against Germany shifted from being one of clashing national interests to one designed to extinguish German militarism and build a world based on democracy and internationalist principles. This shift towards a more overtly moralistic diplomacy had global implications. In East Asia it quickly began to merge with the consistently held Anglo-American belief that the 'open door' constituted the best way to manage international rivalries and encourage Chinese reform.[33] The obvious consequence of such thinking was that as Japan stood as the greatest danger to the future of the 'open door', it came to be viewed as a potentially hostile state. Moreover, it did not help matters that the Imperial Japanese Army (IJA) showed a marked propensity to involve itself in high politics and to attempt to inculcate society with its values. This led its critics to say that Japan was imbued with distinctively German traits and to christen it the 'Prussia of the East'.

This criticism, which, in particular, stressed the IJA's past training at the hands of German advisers, was heard in both British and American circles, and led to speculation that in the future Japan might be drawn towards an alliance with Germany.[34]

The problem, however, was that although critics of Japan existed in both conservative and liberal circles within the British Empire, the increasing ideological divide between these two groups meant that they did not necessarily worry about the same things or seek similar solutions. On the conservative side of the spectrum, Australia played a complicating role in deciding the empire's attitude towards Japan. Concerned about preserving the 'White Australia' policy, the Australian Prime Minister William Morris Hughes, took the leading part at the Paris Peace Conference of 1919 in wrecking Japan's attempt to have a racial equality clause drawn into the League of Nations Covenant. However, just two years later in 1921, at an Imperial Conference in London, Hughes emerged, perhaps surprisingly, as the chief proponent of maintaining the Anglo-Japanese Alliance. He did not, of course, do this out of any newfound love for Japan; it was rather the case that he saw the alliance as the best practical means of containing its ambitions and thus preserving 'White Australia'. The Japan that he feared can thus be categorized as one that posed both a racial and strategic threat to his country and which had to be kept in its proper place as Britain's junior partner in Asia.[35]

In both of these years, 1919 and 1921, Hughes took the opposite path to that espoused by the liberal internationalists who were also attempting to influence British foreign policy in this period. Their critical image of Japan rested on its perceived tendency towards imperialism and militarism, which was seen as dangerously anachronistic. As such, these figures, argued that the Japanese alliance should be terminated and that Britain should instead align its foreign policy in the Pacific with that of the United States. Thus, for example, Austin Harrison, the liberal editor of the *English Review*, argued in the run-up to the Washington Conference of 1921, at which the future of the alliance was bound to be discussed, that:

> The conference will give us the opportunity to declare our policy, above all to prove whether we have learnt any lesson from the war, whether we are to remain the 'flaming second' of Japan, or to move constrictively and culturally at the side of America as the example of world-peace.[36]

A corollary to this position was that if in future Japan was denied the strategic protection that was explicit in the alliance it might possibly be persuaded that it had more to gain from internationalist cooperation with the West than from continuing to pursue a policy of imperialist expansion. A crucial element in this argument, and one that was particularly evident among the intellectuals and publicists who contributed to *The Round Table* journal, was that Britain needed to avoid any complete severance of its ties with Japan lest this merely exacerbate racial tensions between Asia and the West, which clearly could only have the most unfortunate consequences for the British Empire. The alliance, it was argued, had acted as a useful bridge between the races and this advantage should not be cast aside, thus any future arrangement had to reassure Japan and Asia in general that it was not being slighted on racial grounds.[37] Thus the optimum solution was for the United States to be persuaded to adhere to a drastically watered-down version of the alliance that would bring internationalist principles into East Asia without at the same time offending Japan.

The irony of the situation was that both the conservative and liberal critics of Japan achieved only half of their goals. Hughes defeated racial equality but could not preserve the alliance: the liberals were able to bring about a multilateral order based on internationalist principles at the Washington Conference of 1921–22, but this contained nothing that explicitly bridged the racial divide. Moreover, only two years after the end of the conference the United States in its Immigration Act of 1924 aggravated the racial problem by introducing the total exclusion of Japanese immigrants.[38] In retrospect, one might say that this represented the worst of all possible worlds, for Japan had been deprived of its security alliance but at the same time still nursed the grievance that it was being treated as an inferior for racial reasons. Moreover, as many recognised at the time, the danger was that the latter of these issues could become a serious problem as Japan was entering into a particularly difficult period where its population growth threatened to out-run its economy and resources.[39] Thus, while the Japanese threat subsided in the 1920s, it was not felt that it had disappeared entirely and a number of observers continued to write about the possibility that at some future date a 'real Armageddon will be fought between the white and yellow peoples'.[40]

Just as World War I and the internationalist moment led to a change in the way in which Japan was perceived, so it had a similar effect on how some in the West treated China. Despite the fact that the latter country descended from 1916 to 1928 into the chaos of the warlord years, there was increasing hope among liberals that it might finally be on the verge of moving along the road towards modernization. An important stimulus to this sense of optimism was the appearance of a new, young, Western-educated intelligentsia in China who spoke the language of reform and internationalism. British commentators felt that this group had to be encouraged, for they were in a sense the West's own creation.[41] Even the arrival of radical anti-imperialist nationalism in the Chinese treaty ports around the mid-1920s did not entirely dent this faith in 'Young China', for liberal observers of the scene had little sympathy with those who wished to preserve Western privileges and, in particular, looked down on the anachronistic views of the British trading community. One such figure was Basil Riley, a young Australian, who was sent out to Shanghai by *The Times* in 1927. In a letter to Harold Williams, the director of the Foreign Department at *The Times*, Riley observed:

> a really big upheaval is needed here in Shanghai. The rigidity of mind is trying & the amount of utter bunk dealt out to newcomers by alleged leaders of the British community is just appalling. One might be in the nineteenth century.[42]

Influenced by such views, the former prime minister David Lloyd George wrote in the foreword to a book of essays on China by the *Manchester Guardian* journalist, Arthur Ransome, that was published in 1927, the year of greatest tension between Britain and China, that, 'Chinese nationalism is essentially a just cause' and that 'we must at all costs avoid the impression that the Nationalists are our enemies.'[43]

Accordingly, as Nicholas Clifford has noted, these years also marked the arrival in China of a new kind of visitor, one who sought to find evidence of the country's progress and to speculate about its future. Included among their number were Ransome, Peter Fleming and Gerald Yorke and their conclusions, which were relatively positive, seem to have reached a sizeable audience in Britain.[44] However, China's image was not just changed by those who visited its shores, but also by the increasing willingness of Chinese intellectuals to engage with their Western counterparts. For example, in 1926 the prominent Chinese philosopher, Hu Shih, engaged in a successful and high-profile visit to London in which he presented a paper to the British Institute of International Affairs on the theme of reform and education in China.[45] In addition, it is noteworthy that the private papers of British internationalists for the interwar years often reveal them to have been in regular contact with one or more Chinese intellectual. In part this seems to have arisen from the genuine Chinese enthusiasm for the League of Nations, but, in addition, it is worth noting the significance of the establishment in 1925 of the Institute of Pacific Relations (IPR) by American Christians and philanthropists. The IPR provided with its biannual (later triennial) conferences a new forum for discussion of regional events, which allowed Chinese intellectuals to make personal contact with their British and American counterparts. For example, it is notable that the private papers of Sir Charles Webster, who attended the IPR conferences in 1927 and 1929, and Sir Arnold Toynbee, who attended in 1931, both contain letters from Chinese correspondents in the mid-to-late-1930s asking them to use their influence to help China in its struggle with Japan.[46] Strangely, there is little evidence that Japanese intellectuals attempted to use correspondence in this manner.

This interest in China also had its cultural side. Some intellectuals, such as Bertrand Russell and Harold Acton, were now drawn to visit China because, in the wake of World War I, they were wracked with doubt about the future of Western civilization. They thus sought to find a balm in Chinese culture before it too was snuffed out by the unforgiving weight of 'progress'.[47] Others, however, looked to the process of modernization as hopefully finally bringing about the rejuvenation of China as a civilization and thus putting it back on a par with the West. It is perhaps in this sense that we can understand the immense success of the exhibition of Chinese art that took place at the Royal Academy in London in the autumn and winter of 1935–36, for this seemed to confirm China's re-emergence from its own 'dark ages'.[48]

It would, however, be a mistake to see the interwar period as an age in which the previous British sympathy for Japan was simply replaced by affection for China. As I have noted elsewhere, there were sharp divisions among British opinion-makers during these years, which to a large degree reflected the increasingly serious ideological dispute between liberals and conservatives over how to approach international politics.[49] Conservatives in this period were deeply sceptical about the ideas associated with internationalism, such as the emphasis put on collective security rather than national interest and the preference for conciliation rather than the demonstration of force. They, therefore, tended to view events in East Asia from a very different perspective. In regard to China, they had little faith in its rejuvenation for, relying on the traditional stereotypes of the country, they entertained profound doubts about whether the GMD could ever bring about unity or introduce adequate governance. As one conservative journal, the *English Review*, observed in 1927 Chinese nationalism was no more than its traditional xenophobia and that:

> Of 'patriotic ideals', consciously and unselfishly pursued towards definite ends of national security and progress, of any genuine determination to help China win her rightful place in the comity of nations, as Japan has done, by discipline, efficiency and honest administrative reforms, there has never been, and there is not, any sign.[50]

Accordingly, they saw no reason to revise British treaty rights and saw the Chinese threats of unilateral abrogation that were made between 1925 and 1931 as lacking any legal or practical basis. Indeed, their desired response to Chinese infringements of treaty rights was to revert to 'gunboat diplomacy'.

Moreover, as indicated in the quotation above, the right within British politics continued to be considerably impressed by Japan. In part, this can be seen as a reflection of an assumed similarity between Britain and Japan both in terms of institutions and outlook. Japan, after all, still possessed a monarchy, which China did not. Japan was a state that put a high premium on patriotism, discipline and service, which were all traits that were highly attractive to British conservatives. Beyond that, however, was another important factor, and one which went to the heart of the ideological dispute in Britain. This was the idea on the right that the alliance with Japan, which had secured British interests in the Pacific for two decades, had been needlessly sacrificed at the Washington Conference in the name of internationalism and Anglo-American solidarity. It had been replaced by reliance on the League of Nations and the United States which, it was contended, would surely be of little assistance at Britain's moment of crisis. The support for Japan has, therefore, to be understood as one front in a much broader war that was taking place between the opponents and advocates of 'new diplomacy'.[51]

The fact that these competing images of Japan and China existed is important for they help to make sense of the vagaries of British foreign policy towards East Asia in the 1930s. In that decade the British government reacted to the growing confrontation between Japan and China by trying to keep a middle distance between the two protagonists and avoiding controversy. It did so in part for strategic reasons, but, in addition, its lack of any definite initiative needs to be seen in the light of the fact that there was no domestic consensus on how to deal with this situation. The right presented Japanese grievances against China as being similar to Britain's, castigated the League for its unwise intervention into the Manchurian crisis and even called for a new alliance with Japan. Meanwhile the left watched for any signs of heresy against internationalism and talked of 'democratic' China struggling to resist 'fascist' Japan. Thus, for example, in May 1937, when rumours about the possibility of Anglo-Japanese talks surfaced at Westminster the Labour politician, Philip Noel-Baker, noted to an academic friend, 'The Government are now trying to patch up an Imperialist deal with the fascist dictatorship in Japan for sharing the swag in China on precisely the lines your note predicted...'[52] Faced with such a febrile environment the government was placed in an exceedingly difficult position which only heightened its natural reticence.

What is also interesting about the 1930s is that some of the more extreme and abstract arguments of the previous decades that were connected to racially derived images seem to have been forgotten. Clearly now Japanese expansion posed a direct threat to British interests, but, surprisingly, there was little talk within Britain of any future conflict constituting a race war. Why this was so is not entirely clear, especially as Japanese trade competition did lead to a short-lived recrudescence of 'yellow peril' rhetoric.[53] One explanation might be that while some Japanese commentators espoused pan-Asian ideas their credentials were hardly burnished by Japan's domineering attitude towards the Chinese, which reached its peak with the outbreak of the Sino-Japanese War in July 1937 and the appalling massacres that followed in December that year in Nanjing.[54] In addition, one needs to recollect that Japan's rhetoric about its being unjustly discriminated against by the status quo powers was the same as that emanating from two European powers, Germany and Italy. This then was an alliance of the 'have-not' late industrializing states rather than a racial combination.

This chapter has presented a rough sketch of the evolution of British images of East Asia in the first four decades of the twentieth century and much more might be said. However, what is apparent from this still incomplete picture is that the stereotypes that existed in British minds were to an extent malleable and that opinion was far from uniform. In particular, this was the case in the interwar period. During these latter years conservatives continued to base their images of East Asia very largely on the shop-worn clichés of the previous generation, in which Japan was largely eulogized and China damned with criticism. This was, though, as much due to political expediency, in the sense of having a stick to beat the left with, as it was to any sense of conviction. However, the shift on the left after 1918 towards a more internationalist perspective on foreign affairs and the adoption of an increasingly critical attitude towards imperialism led to a marked change in attitudes, whereby China rather than Japan became the preferred symbol of modernity. This in part reflected some of the real changes that were taking place in the region, but must also be understood as a more abstract intellectual choice that expressed the left's aspirations for the region and for world politics more broadly. After all, to claim in the 1930s that Japan was fascist, but not to see that Jiang Jieshi's GMD regime flirted with fascism in the form of the Blue Shirts and the espousal of the New Life movement was nothing more than an exercise in wilful myopia.[55] However, Japan had aligned itself with the Axis powers and in that sense it logically followed that one could draw direct parallels between the suffering of the Chinese people as victims of Japanese aggression and those of Republican Spain at the hands of Franco and his allies.

What the above hopefully does is to underline the degree to which historians must be careful in studying images as part of international and imperial history. It is clearly vital to understand how one country viewed another if one is to make any sense of the policy-making process. At the same time, however, one has to acknowledge that, while particular tropes often maintain their resonance over time, they can also be subject to revision. Clearly events can change how one country perceives another; for many in Britain the alliance with Japan was never the same after World War I due to their knowledge that the Japanese had not been the most loyal of allies. In addition, however, ideas and ideologies evolve and this too affects perception. In the period after the Paris Peace Conference and the establishment of the League of Nations it was inevitable that some Britons would now judge other states on how loyally they committed themselves to the tenets of internationalism. In 1931 Japan failed that test, while China passed and was seen by the League enthusiasts as the victim of Japanese aggression. It is also, however, important to remember in a discipline that seems increasingly obsessed with Orientalism and ideas of 'the Other', that images of foreign peoples are not simply tools used by the observers to define national identity, they are also used as weapons within national discourse where they become exemplars of policies or attitudes that particular parties or factions support or deprecate. The example of how the British viewed Japan and China is a case in point, for in reality the arguments used tell one not so much about British identity as about the ideological divisions that were, almost fatally, paralysing the political process while the country was faced with the challenge from what became the Tripartite Powers.

Acknowledgements

I wish to thank the British Academy for its help in financing some of the research used in this chapter.

This chapter does not directly address issues raised in the writings of David Dilks, but, as with all of my work, the approach is shaped by my experience as one of his final-year undergraduates and the thorough and questioning methodology that he drilled into us when it came to understanding the motives and actions of British policy-makers during the interwar period.

Notes

1. See, for example, Lydia H. Liu, *The Clash of Empires: The Invention of China in Modern World Making* (Cambridge, MA: Harvard University Press, 2004) and Shogo Suzuki, *Civilization and Empire: China and Japan's Encounter with European International Society* (London: Routledge, 2009).
2. This is a point that is made in James L. Hevia, *English Lessons: The Pedagogy of Imperialism in Nineteenth Century China* (Durham, NC: Duke University Press, 2003) ch.1.
3. See, for example, Akira Iriye's masterful treatment of changing perceptions in his *Across the Pacific: An Inner History of American-East Asian Relations* (New York: Harcourt, Brace and World, 1967).
4. For an excellent overview of British interests in China, see Jürgen Osterhammel, 'China', in Judith M. Brown and Wm Roger Louis (eds), *The Oxford History of the British Empire, vol. 4: The Twentieth Century*, (Oxford: Oxford University Press, 1999) pp. 643–66.
5. See, for example, C.F. Yong and R.B. McKenna, *The Kuomintang Movement in British Malaya, 1912–1949* (Singapore: Singapore University Press, 1990) and D.S.J. Koh and K. Tanaka, 'Japanese Competition in the Trade of Malaya in the 1930s', *Southeast Asian Studies*, 21 (1984), pp. 374–99.
6. Rotem Kowner, '"Lighter Than Yellow", But Not Enough: Western Discourse on the Japanese "Race", 1854–1904', *Historical Journal*, 43 (2000), pp. 103–31.
7. Nicholas Clifford, *'A Truthful Impression of the Country': British and American Travel Writing in China, 1880–1949* (Ann Arbor: University of Michigan Press, 2001). See also Michael Adas, *Machines as the Measure of Man: Science, Technology, and Ideologies of Western Dominance* (Ithaca: Cornell University Press, 1989) pp. 133–270.
8. Sir Valentine Chirol, *Fifty Years in a Changing World* (London: Jonathan Cape, 1927) p. 177.
9. Kirkwood papers, Library and Archives Canada (LAC), MG27 III E3, vol.2, 'Journal of a Tour of China September 1933', pp. 62–3. (I am grateful to the Library and Archives Canada for permission to quote from the Kirkwood papers.)
10. Robert Bickers, *Britain in China: Community, Culture and Colonialism, 1900–1949* (Manchester: Manchester University Press, 1999) pp. 58–9.

11. See Clifford, 'A Truthful Impression', passim and Bickers, *Britain in China*, ch. 1. On the use of opium and its effect on Western perception of China, Yangwen Zheng, *The Social Life of Opium in China* (Cambridge, Cambridge University Press, 2005).
12. Iriye, *Across the Pacific*, pp. 23–8. See, for example, Lord Redesdale, 'Old and New Japan', lecture to the Japan Society of London, 14 November 1906, in H. Cortazzi (ed.), *The Memoirs and Recollections, 1866–1906, of Algernon Bertram Mitford, the First Lord Redesdale* (London: Athlone Press, 1985) pp. 1–14.
13. Clunies Ross papers, National Library of Australia (NLA), Canberra, MS7485 Clunies Ross to 'Ranee' 6 March 1930 (By permission of the National Library of Australia). See also Joseph M. Henning, *Outposts of Civilization: Race, Religion and the Formative Years of American-Japanese Relations* (New York: New York University Press, 2000) p. 66.
14. Hamilton papers, Liddell Hart Centre for Military Archives, (LHCMA) King's College London, 3/2/3 Hamilton (Tokyo) to Lady Hamilton 15 March 1904. (I am grateful to the Trustees of the Liddell Hart Centre for Military Archives for permission to quote from the Hamilton papers.) Massey papers, University of Toronto Archives, B87-0082, Box 308, no. 33, diary entry 26 September 1931.
15. Antony Best, *British Intelligence and the Japanese Challenge in Asia, 1914–41* (Basingstoke: Palgrave, 2002) p. 17, and David Walker, *Anxious Nation: Australia and the Rise of Asia 1850–1939* (Brisbane: University of Queensland Press, 1999) pp. 173–5.
16. Hevia, *English Lessons*, ch.1.
17. Curzon papers, Asian, African and Pacific room, British Library, London, Mss.Eur.F111/74B Hunt (Pusan) to Curzon 10 April 1895.
18. Colin Holmes and A. Hamish Ion, 'Bushidō and the Samurai: Images in British Public Opinion, 1894–1914', *Modern Asian Studies*, 14 (1980), pp. 309–29.
19. Curzon papers, Mss.Eur.F111/168 Curzon (Calcutta) to Godley (IO) 23 March 1905.
20. Colin Holmes, 'Sidney Webb and Beatrice Webb and Japan', in Hugh Cortazzi and Gordon Daniels (eds), *Britain and Japan 1859–1991: Themes and Personalities* (London: Routledge, 1991) pp. 166–76.
21. Michio Yoshimura, 'Nichi-Ei kyūtei kōryu shi no ichimen: sono seijiteki seikaku to hiseijiteki seikaku', in Yoichi Kibata, Ian Nish, Chihiro Hosoya and Takahiko Tanaka (eds), *Nichi-Ei kōryu shi, vol.1, Seiji-Gaikō* (Tokyo: Tokyo Daigaku Shuppankai, 2000) pp. 315–19, and Antony Best, 'Race, Monarchy and the Anglo-Japanese Alliance, 1902–1922', *Social Science Japan Journal*, 9, 2 (2006), pp. 171–86.
22. Thomas Hohler, *Diplomatic Petrel* (London: John Murray, 1942) p. 91.
23. Akira Iikura, 'The Anglo-Japanese Alliance and the Question of Race', in Phillips O'Brien (ed.), *The Anglo-Japanese Alliance* (London: Routledge, 2004) pp. 222–35.
24. E.W. Edwards, *British Diplomacy and Finance in China 1895–1914* (Oxford: Clarendon Press, 1987), pp. 144–6.
25. Hamilton papers, LHCMA, 4/1/8, Hamilton to Amery 7 August 1909.

26. Neville Meaney, *The Search for Security in the Pacific 1901–14* (Sydney: University of Sydney Press, 1976) pp. 120–58.
27. Laurier papers, LAC, MG26-G, vol. 732, fos. 204821-8 Grey to Laurier 20 December 1907.
28. Lothian papers, National Archives of Scotland, Edinburgh, GD40/17/462 Kerr (Yokohama) to 'Mother' 16 June 1912 f.22. (I am grateful to the National Archives of Scotland and Rt Hon. Michael Ancram MP for permission to quote from the Lothian papers.)
29. Cyril Pearl, *Morrison of Peking* (Sydney: Angus & Robertson, 1967) pp. 211–13.
30. James Stewart Lockhart papers, National Library of Scotland, Edinburgh, Acc.4138, file 11(h) Clementi-Smith to Lockhart 7 January 1915.
31. For British suspicions of Japan, see Peter Lowe, *Britain and Japan, 1911–15: A Study of British Far Eastern Policy* (London: Macmillan, 1969); Ian Nish, *Alliance in Decline: A Study in Anglo-Japanese Relations, 1908–23*, (London: Athlone Press, 1972) pp. 115–262, and Best, *British Intelligence*, ch.3.
32. Piesse papers, NLA, MS882/3/8, Latham (Paris) to Piesse 21 February 1919 (by permission of the National Library of Australia).
33. For the relationship between the Anglo-Japanese Alliance and the 'open door', see Antony Best, 'The Anglo-Japanese Alliance and International Politics in Asia, 1902–23', in Antony Best (ed.), *The International History of East Asia, 1900–1968: Trade, Ideology and the Quest for Order* (Routledge, London, 2010) pp. 21–34.
34. Best, *British Intelligence*, pp. 45–6, and Iriye, *Across the Pacific*, pp. 139–40.
35. For Hughes and Australian foreign policy see Peter G. Edwards, *Prime Ministers and Diplomats: The Making of Australian Foreign Policy 1901–1949* (Melbourne: Oxford University Press, 1983) pp. 29–65.
36. Austin Harrison, 'Great Prospects', *English Review*, August 1921, p. 159.
37. 'The Imperial Conference', *The Round Table*, September 1921, pp. 735–58. The same kind of argument can also be found in a memorandum by the Round Table affiliate Edward Grigg, who was acting by mid-1921 as Lloyd George's private secretary, see Lloyd George papers, Parliamentary Archives, London, LG/F/86/1 'The Anglo-Japanese Alliance' Grigg memorandum 25 May 1921. See also Peter Lowe, 'The Round Table, the Dominions and the Anglo-Japanese Alliance 1911–1922' in Andrea Bosco and Alex May (eds), *The Round Table: The Empire/Commonwealth and British Foreign Policy* (London: Lothian Foundation Press, 1997) pp. 423–36.
38. For a recent analysis of the 1924 Act and its consequences for American-Japanese relations, see Jon Thares Davidann, *Cultural Diplomacy in U.S.-Japanese Relations, 1919–1941* (Basingstoke: Palgrave/Macmillan, 2007) pp. 81–102.
39. See, for example, 'The Problem of Japan', *The Round Table*, June 1930, pp. 524–35.
40. Sir Frederick Maurice, 'The Chances of War in the Pacific', *Empire Review*, January 1926, p. 12.
41. 'News of the Week', *The Spectator*, 29 August 1925, and Arthur Ransome, *The Chinese Puzzle* (London: George Allen & Unwin, 1927) p. 63.
42. Times Newspaper Limited Archive, News International Limited, London, Harold Williams papers, Riley (Shanghai) to Williams, 11 June 1927. (I am

grateful to News International Limited for permission to quote from the Williams papers.)
43. Lloyd George's foreword to Ransome, *The Chinese Puzzle*, p. 10.
44. Clifford, 'A Truthful Impression', pp. 220–38.
45. Hu Shih, 'The Renaissance in China', *Journal of the British Institute of International Affairs*, November 1926, pp. 265–77.
46. See, for example, Toynbee papers, Bodleian Library, Oxford, file 116, Chien (Kunming) to Toynbee 23 January 1939, and Webster papers, British Library of Economics and Political Science, LSE London, file 1/14, Tsiang (Peiping) to Webster 7 December 1935.
47. Clifford, 'A Truthful Impression', pp. 101–5, 115–16.
48. According to *The Times* of 3 March 1936, the exhibition attracted 400,000 visitors.
49. Antony Best, 'British Intellectuals and East Asia in the Interwar Years', in Wm Roger Louis (ed.), *Yet More Adventures with Britannia* (Austin: IB Taurus/University of Texas Press, 2005) pp. 307–20, and Antony Best, 'The "Ghost" of the Anglo-Japanese Alliance: An Examination into Historical Mythmaking', *Historical Journal*, 49, 3 (2006), pp. 811–31.
50. 'Current Comments', *English Review*, February 1927, p. 132.
51. Best, 'The "Ghost" of the Anglo-Japanese Alliance', passim.
52. Noel-Baker papers, Churchill College Archives Centre, Cambridge, NBKR 4/64 Noel-Baker to Wright 7 May 1937. (I am grateful to Churchill College Archives and the Noel-Baker family for permission to quote from the Noel-Baker papers.)
53. Antony Best, 'Economic Appeasement or Economic Nationalism?: A Political Perspective on the British Empire, Japan and the Rise of Intra-Asian Trade, 1933–37', *Journal of Imperial and Commonwealth Studies*, 30, 2 (2002), p. 81.
54. See Hans van de Ven, 'Bombing, Japanese Pan-Asianism and Chinese Nationalism' in Antony Best (ed.), The International History of East Asia, 1900–1968 (London: Routledge, 2010) pp. 99–117.
55. For useful essays on fascism in Japan and China, see Gregory C. Kasza, 'Fascism from Above? Japan's Kakushin Right in Comparative Perspective', and William C. Kirby, 'Images and Realities of Chinese Fascism', in Stein Ugelvik Larsen (ed.), *Fascism Outside Europe: The European Impulse against Domestic Conditions in the Diffusion of Global Fascism* (New York: Columbia University Press, 2001) pp. 183–232 and 233–68 respectively.

3
The Struggle to Maintain Locarno Diplomacy
Britain and the Idea of a Political Truce in 1931

Frank Magee

As far as British policy makers were concerned the central issue in European diplomacy since the end of World War I was how to deal with the German problem and the associated question of French security. It was hoped in London that Britain's adherence to the Treaty of Locarno in 1925 had gone a long way to satisfy French anxieties; anxieties that had to be addressed if the preferred option in London – some revision of the Treaty of Versailles in Germany's favour – could be tackled. The early 1920s had demonstrated how difficult it was for Britain to persuade France to accept British policy in Europe without some kind of security commitment over and above the somewhat nebulous obligations outlined in the Covenant of the League of Nations. The Anglo-American guarantee offered to France during the Paris Peace Conference had lapsed when the United States Senate refused to ratify the Peace treaty with Germany. Further attempts to provide for French security through a bilateral Anglo-French alliance failed due to Lloyd George's refusal to undertake commitments in Eastern Europe to underpin the Cordon Sanitaire of states around Germany which France had constructed as a makeweight against German revival. Conscious of its global commitments, Britain after 1918 was more anxious to limit its commitments than extend them, especially into areas such as Eastern Europe which were not perceived to be areas of vital British interest. Security initiatives through the agency of the League of Nations, such as the Draft Treaty of Mutual Guarantee and the Geneva Protocol, were similarly dashed upon the rocks of Britain's unwillingness to undertake further, and apparently unlimited responsibility for international security.[1]

The continuing refusal, however, to make a further contribution to the security of France, while it obviously limited Britain's commitments, also had the effect of straining Anglo-French relations almost to breaking point on a number of occasions – most notably at the time of the Ruhr Crisis in 1923 – and completely handicapped British policy makers when trying to persuade the French to adopt a line more acceptable to Whitehall. The conclusion of the Treaty of Locarno, which, in theory at least, provided a British guarantee to France and an obligation to act if the demilitarised Rhineland were 'flagrantly' violated, went some way to satisfy French fears of a revived Germany. The Treaty of Locarno also had the effect, which was seen as a distinct advantage in London, of making France wary of weakening the new found commitment from Britain. Thus, Locarno gave the British government a much greater influence over French policy than had formerly been the case. From 1925 to 1930, therefore, and especially during Sir Austen Chamberlain's period as Foreign Secretary, Anglo-French relations developed a closeness which had all too evidently been lacking in the immediate post-war period. With renewed confidence in Britain's attachment to France, and with gentle coaxing from London, after Locarno French leaders found it possible to agree to ameliorate some of the provisions of Versailles. In 1927 the Inter-Allied Military Control Commission was wound up and in 1929 at The Hague Conference, Briand, the French Foreign Minister, agreed to abandon the military occupation of the two remaining Rhineland zones in return for Germany's acceptance of the Young Plan.[2] Moreover, Britain had gained distinct advantages as a result of the Rhineland Pact which it wished to retain. Not only did Britain have a much greater influence over France than in the immediate post-war period, but political stability also brought with it the hope of improved trade. Locarno also added to Britain's own security by obliging the German Army to remain to the east of the Rhine and by encouraging continuing Franco-German reconciliation.

The deepening economic crisis that gathered momentum after 1929, however, served to derail further efforts at Franco-German detente. The collapse of the Grand Coalition in Germany and its replacement by a Cabinet led by Dr. Brüning and reliant upon Article 48 of the Constitution to govern, created unease. The amazing emergence of the Nazis from a tiny splinter party on the radical Right into the second largest party in the Reichstag in September 1930 turned that unease into anxiety. The trend in German political rhetoric to vehement denunciations of Versailles made French governments less willing to concede to the German point of view. Naturally, the movement of opinion in France and the growing right-wing radicalism in Germany, threatened British hopes of continuing Franco-German detente and therefore the political stability of Europe. At the end of June 1930 the German government had issued a manifesto promising with reference to the Saarland, 'to do all that lies in us to assure that their desire for reunion may soon be realised'.[3] The election campaign for the new Reichstag due to meet in September 1930, gave further evidence of the further nationalistic shift in German opinion. The Minister for the Occupied Territories, Treviranus, had declared, 'Now the East demands the unification of all German people.'[4] The question of the revision of the recently agreed Young Plan was also much to the fore in the election campaign and remained a feature of international relations during the rest of 1930 and into1931. If these developments were not sufficient to create Franco-German tension, then the attempt by Germany and Austria to conclude a Customs Union, announced to an unprepared world in March 1931, confirmed the worst fears of French leaders. Despite the repeated assertions of German and Austrian ministers that the proposal was merely an attempt to alleviate the impact of the depression, French ministers took it to be the first step towards the Anschluss. As a consequence of this latest German move, Franco-German relations descended to a new low.[5]

It was against this background that the idea of a political moratorium, or political truce as it was called in the Foreign Office, first appeared in early June 1931. The idea emerged from a letter which Sir Eric Drummond, the Secretary-General of the League of Nations, sent to Philip Noel-Baker, the Parliamentary Under-Secretary to the Foreign Secretary, recording a conversation with Comert, the Press Director of the League Secretariat.

Following visits to Vienna, Budapest and Berlin, Comert had become convinced that the severity of the economic crisis facing European countries was of such magnitude that the question of treaty revision, which had dominated European diplomacy since the end of the Great War, was being pushed by responsible people firmly into the background. Firmly in the foreground, on the other hand, Comert argued, was the fear of social unrest caused by the economic depression. He suggested that one way of lowering unemployment in Central and Eastern Europe, and thus lessening the potential for revolutionary outbreaks, would be for the French to inject a large amount of capital into the German economy. He fully realised the reluctance of France to do this for fear of a revived Germany pressing its demands for treaty revision with renewed vigour. To allay French anxieties on this point, Comert suggested that Germany, as a quid pro quo for the help she would receive, should agree to a political truce for ten years. Comert believed that this would be a very reasonable request since, in his view, the principal question of the next ten years in Europe would be the maintenance of social and economic stability.[6]

The initial response in the Foreign Office to Comert's idea of a political truce between Britain, France, Germany and Italy was to doubt its feasibility. With Britain wishing to see peace and tranquillity on the continent, and France wishing to maintain her position of superiority over Germany, no difficulty was envisaged in the acceptance by these two countries of a political truce. Indeed, even Italy, with her 'somewhat indeterminate' aims, aspiring perhaps to expansion in the Mediterranean and influence in the Danube Basin, was thought to represent no obstacle to such a truce since Italy, the Permanent Under-Secretary Sir Robert Vansittart asserted, 'requires ten years to grow'.[7] The central problem was, of course, the probable attitude of Germany. Both Nichols, a member of the Foreign Office's Central Department, and his departmental head, Orme Sargent, doubted whether any German statesman would make a bargain on the basis of economic help for the abandonment of ten years of such issues as the Polish Corridor, the customs union with Austria, or disarmament. Vansittart, on the other hand, was not inclined to agree with his colleagues. He replied to their views on 16 June:

> It is not at all impossible for the idea to be linked up with any thoroughgoing reparations concession to Germany. She should be made, if possible, to pay a fair price for that. Nothing short of that will serve, and even so it may be difficult: but it must be borne in mind, for if ever the French and the Americans were to play up this might well be one of the conditions they would be disposed to lay down.[8]

Vansittart's assessment of future developments was to be fully borne out by events. On 20 June 1931 President Hoover, worried about American financial exposure in Germany and the possibility that independent action by the latter might raise the issue of war debt payments to the United States, announced his proposal to place a moratorium on international debts for one year in an effort to relieve the financial crisis threatening to engulf the world.[9] The French, however, refused to accept the Hoover Moratorium without modification and pressure was applied in Berlin by London and Washington to persuade the Germans to make some contribution for the debt relief they would be receiving. In Paris during his conversation on 15 July 1931 Arthur Henderson, the Foreign Secretary, was told by Laval, the French Prime Minister, that no substantial French help would be rendered to Germany without political conditions. Henderson, who had gone to Paris with a copy of a memorandum by Noel-Baker dealing with the question of a political truce, suggested the idea of a truce to Laval and almost certainly intended to press the idea on the Germans during his planned visit to Berlin later the same summer.

In his memorandum, Noel-Baker painted a highly pessimistic picture of the position in the 'storm centre' of Europe: Germany. If Germany collapsed it would bring the countries of Central Europe down with it, and 'London, as the financial centre with the greatest commitments in Germany, would be seriously affected'.[10] Even if the Reich surmounted its present financial crisis, Noel-Baker argued that without a revival in trade, German unemployment, currently at more than four million, would rise to seven or eight million in the approaching winter; but 'long before that happens the country must have fallen under a Hitler or Communist dictatorship'. The economic and political results of such a development would be disastrous and

> almost certainly involve the withdrawal of Germany from the League [of Nations], the failure of the Disarmament Conference, and a complete set-back to the whole cause of European co-operation.[11]

Faced with this stark scenario, Noel-Baker stressed Europe's need for a German economic revival to forestall the forces of revolution inside Germany and throughout Central and Eastern Europe. No country could view the possibility of a continuation of the economic crisis without alarm; therefore governments 'must desire to take every measure possible to bring about the stimulation of investment and the revival of trade'.[12] For this to take place the major countries of Europe, together with the Central Banks, had to adopt a policy of 'concerted economic co-operation', and secondly, confidence had to be restored. For that to happen, 'the fear of political and social unrest, and above all the fear of war' had to be removed. In short, the essential prerequisite was for 'friendly relations and understanding between Germany and France' to be re-established which lay at the heart of Britain's Locarno diplomacy.[13]

French good faith in German intentions had been shaken by the customs union crisis, the growth of the Nazi Party and continuing propaganda regarding the Polish Corridor. 'In order to re-establish

French confidence and French support for M. Briand's policy', Noel-Baker wrote,

> it is plain that Germany must give some kind of reassurance to France that she does not intend to break up the peace treaty system by faits accomplis or by violence, but only to secure modifications in her favour as and when they can be attained by mutual consent.[14]

Such a declaration, Noel-Baker realised, could not be imposed upon Germany; it would have to take the form of a general declaration undertaken by all the major European countries. If the Brüning government issued such a declaration unilaterally, such was the internal political situation inside Germany, it 'would be swept from power, leaving the road open to Hitler and the Communist parties'.[15]

Noel-Baker argued that for Brüning to accept the declaration of a political truce, even in a multilateral form, public opinion in Germany would have to be brought round by certain concessions. He highlighted a number of areas where such concessions might be made. In regard to disarmament, Noel-Baker suggested that the European powers should declare their intention of making the Disarmament Conference, due to meet in February 1932, succeed, with the aim of producing real reductions and applying the same system of regulation and measures of disarmament to all countries. Such a policy would, Noel-Baker hoped, lessen the 'inferiority complex' the Germans were taken to feel.[16] He further suggested that a financial bargain might bring about the reunion of the Saarland with Germany before the plebiscite due in January 1935. Here, Noel-Baker felt, the French had much to gain in terms of German good will at minimum cost to themselves. After all, it was highly likely that the plebiscite would produce a result favouring a return to the Reich.[17] Noel-Baker's other ideas on concessions to German public opinion dealt with a possible private assurance that reparations would be scaled down in proportion to the fall in prices; the possibility of a further declaration from European countries affirming their determination to see the rights of minorities effectively protected; and, finally, the transformation of the Austro-German customs union proposal 'into something which would be free from political objection and which would be of economic value to Europe as a whole'.[18] Should this policy of economic co-operation and political truce fail, Noel-Baker believed Germany could look forward to economic collapse, 'with communism probably added to the miseries'; while France would face 'a Germany inspired by undying hatred and determined sooner or later to seek revenge'.[19]

These ideas were given added impetus by the negotiations that were proceeding in Paris between the French and the Americans regarding the implementation of the Hoover moratorium. These negotiations were particularly galling to the British for a number of reasons. First, it appeared that while Laval fiddled Europe's financial structure was crashing down: Germany was struck by a banking crisis in early July, a crisis whose shock waves would eventually undermine London as the next weak link in the chain. Second, it was undoubtedly exasperating for the British to be forced to play a passive role in negotiations the outcome of which was of the utmost interest to them. Third, France was comparatively immune from the ravages of the slump at this stage. Unemployment was low, the franc stable and the Bank of France held gold reserves second only to the Federal Reserve in New York.[20] In Britain unemployment was rising and a run on the gold reserves of the Bank of England in July and August was about to produce a collapse. Despite this weak hand, the British nevertheless applied pressure in Washington, Paris and Berlin in order to try to secure their interests. The British, and in particular the Prime Minister and the Chancellor of the Exchequer, were worried that the Americans would concede too much to the French; that the French would demand too much and thus wreck the effectiveness of Hoover's proposal, and that the Germans, by refusing to offer anything as a quid pro quo for the benefits of the moratorium, would encourage the French to stand firm.

Britain was the first of the world's major nations to accept Hoover's proposal wholeheartedly. It was hoped that an immediate statement in the House of Commons announcing Britain's adherence to the Hoover scheme would add to the beneficial psychological impact of the move, and by outlining British losses of between £11 and £12.6 million per annum, the French would be encouraged to accept their proposed losses. It was further thought that such an announcement would anticipate 'any possible announcement by a foreign Government which might jeopardize the scheme'.[21] Although it was considered possible that the French might raise difficulties it was not certain at this stage. However, should that prove to be the case the Cabinet agreed that the Americans were better placed than the British to persuade Paris.[22]

The French were not slow in bringing forward their objections. As early as 22 June Berthelot, the head of the Quai d'Orsay, had warned Sir Walter Layton, the owner of *The Economist*, and J.R. Cahill, the Commercial Counsellor at the British Embassy in Paris, 'that France would undoubtedly accept [the Hoover Moratorium] in principle, though the scheme would require adaption'.[23] Berthelot pointed out that the loss of the unconditional annuities when the budget was already heading for a deficit would prove 'a serious matter for France'. His principal objection, however, centred on the fear that 'Germany would never resume payment once [it had been] definitely suspended.'[24] Nevertheless, he was confident of ways being found to render Germany help while securing the principle of continuing reparations payments.[25] In short, this was the line to which France held in the summer of 1931.

The Foreign Office was sympathetic to French difficulties, particularly in relation to public opinion and the hostility in the Chamber to unilateral concessions in Germany's favour. However, if the French held out against the American initiative then public opinion across the Atlantic might become increasingly critical of the President's move and force him to withdraw the offer. Naturally, the position of Europe 'would be immeasurably worse' should events take this turn.[26] Accordingly Sargent suggested that Germany, the only country from whom no sacrifice was called, should make a contribution to the success of the negotiations in Paris. Sargent thought Germany might be asked to abandon the customs union with Austria and promise 'not to revive it'. Germany might agree to an investigation of its economic position and thus satisfy the French of the desperate nature of Germany's condition. Further, Germany could suspend expenditure on the pocket battleship *Deutschland*, and she might also promise not to relax the provisions of the June emergency decrees following the moratorium. These suggestions were adopted and sent to Lindsay in Washington with the purpose of providing the American administration with 'some ideas which would promote the U[nited] S[tates'] chances of obtaining French assent and also of obtaining some very legitimate return from Germany for all the help and consideration – not wholly deserved – which she is getting."[27] The Foreign Office deprecated the attachment by France of political conditions to the acceptance of the Hoover Moratorium, but suggested that the voluntary abandonment of the customs union and some reduction in Germany's military budget would facilitate the common goal.[28] The French viewed concessions by Germany as integral to their acceptance of the Hoover Moratorium. In essence the French agreed to suspend the conditional and unconditional annuities of the Young Plan provided that the French share of the unconditional annuity was deposited by the Germans at the Bank for International Settlements, with the money being used to render financial assistance to Germany and other countries in Central and Eastern Europe. France also sought an undertaking from Berlin to uphold and observe international treaties.[29] Although the German government had, without the prompting of any other power, declared its intention not to alter the 'total financial results of the emergency decree', this was not sufficient for the French, or indeed the British, though it was seen as helpful in London, as indeed was Brüning's suggestion of a meeting of French and German ministers.[30]

The French insistence that Germany should still pay a proportion of the unconditional annuity in the moratorium year was utterly rejected by the Treasury in London. Germany was not in a position to pay. The Treasury also found statements of French losses which had appeared in the French press to be exaggerated.

> The choice for France is not between getting full payment and no payment, but between suspension of all payments and continuing to meet her debt liabilities while not receiving payments from Germany.[31]

While Mellon, the Amercian Treasury Secretary, and Walter Edge, the American Ambassador in Paris, were negotiating with the French, the Foreign Office, which was not in total agreement with the Treasury's case, concentrated its efforts on persuading the Germans to make their contribution in order to facilitate agreement in Paris.[32]

In the knowledge that the Hoover Administration shared the British government's view that Germany should make a contribution to the settlement of the dispute in Paris, Henderson wasted no time in telegraphing to Newton in Berlin suggesting 'that they [the German government] could make no better contribution to the restoration of international confidence' than by allowing the Austro-German customs union to drop.[33] On discovering that Sackett, the American Ambassador in Berlin, had received instructions to support Britain's view of the customs union, and to point out to German ministers the 'inadvisability of proceeding with the construction of the battleships"' Newton was told to support Sackett's representations on this latter point, while Henderson himself tackled the German Ambassador in London von Neurath.[34]

These representations in Berlin had assumed a more particular urgency following the breakdown of the Franco-American talks on 28 June. At the Cabinet meeting on 1 July Henderson gave his colleagues a summary of the continuing difficulties being experienced in Paris. The Foreign Secretary could think of only one way of putting pressure on the French to come to terms over the moratorium. Washington had requested London to make forceful representations in Paris supporting the stand taken by the administration. The Cabinet decided this was impossible and would be ineffective; however, it agreed with Henderson that an international conference might be an effective way of 'putting pressure on France'.[35] Accordingly both Washington and Paris were sounded on the feasibility of calling a conference in London which both accepted in principle, though Briand, the French Foreign Minister, pleaded for it to be held in Paris.[36] Clearly, if the conference moved to France part of the object of calling it would be defeated. In the following few weeks the French continually resisted calls for a conference in London and indeed attempted to turn an informal gathering of French, German, American and British ministers into an alternative conference in mid-July. The resumption of Franco-American talks in Paris put all talk of a conference in London temporarily into abeyance.

Anglo-American representations in Berlin about the customs union and the battleships proved forlorn. Curtius, the German Foreign Minister, told Sackett on 30 June that the replacement of ships was unavoidable. Moreover, if the German government acceded to the request, Hindenburg would resign. This argument was regarded as 'poor sob stuff' in London.[37] The Americans and the British returned to the charge but it proved impossible to move the Germans. The most that could be wrung from Berlin was a statement that the financial relief gained by Germany from the moratorium would not be used to increase armaments expenditure.[38]

On the night of the 6–7 July agreement was at last reached in Paris. Almost all of France's desiderata had been met, perhaps not surprisingly since it was deemed essential that France join in the moratorium and there appeared to be few means available to pressurize her. All inter-governmental debts were postponed except for the unconditional annuities. These were to be paid by the Germans to the Bank of International Settlements (BIS) in the form of German railway bonds. The suspended payments were to be repaid in ten instalments beginning on 1 July 1932. Of course, although this was only a Franco-American agreement, it could affect the rights of other Powers signatory to the Young Plan and this necessitated a meeting of those Powers which was eventually held in London. But the fact that France had now reached an understanding with the Americans made it very difficult for others, especially the British, to stand out against it as Vansittart noted.[39] This settlement did not alleviate Germany's plight. In early July a banking crisis almost toppled the German economy over the precipice.

The run on German credit had been magnified by the government's emergency decree of 6 June. Investors, German and foreign, anticipated a major upheaval affecting German finance. Indeed, had it not been for President Hoover's intervention, Brüning had already decided to call for a moratorium under the Young Plan. Hoover's announcement did much initially to steady the jittery Berlin markets.[40] However, the attitude of France and the prolonged negotiations in Paris had dissipated the good effect of the announcement. Moreover, the news on 3 July that the Norddeutsch Wollkämmerei was unable to meet its creditors, principally the Danat Bank saw the resumption of withdrawals from Germany and the movement of German funds abroad.

On 9 and 10 July the President of the Reichsbank, Hans Luther, made 'secret' flights to London, Paris and Basle, in an effort to gain further credits, but to no avail. London was unable to extend any further help, being already over committed in Central Europe, while the Bank of France was willing to extend further credits but only if Germany accepted political conditions such as the abandonment of the customs union, and the cancellation of any further work on the battleships. The Brüning government could not have met these conditions even if it wished to, which it did not. Luther, therefore, was forced to return home empty-handed to deal with the ramifications of the collapse of the Danat Bank on 12 July, to be followed by government imposed bank holidays on 14 and 15 July.[41]

Against this background of mounting financial panic, with the possibility of a German collapse which 'would carry with it most of the countries in Central Europe and involve obvious risks of social and political disorders', the discussions between London and Paris for the convening of the London Conference took place.[42] Throughout these discussions, as through the Conference itself, the strength of the French position was clear. This fact alone, of course, was sufficient to produce tension in London, exacerbated by disagreements between the Foreign Office and the Treasury, and between MacDonald, the Prime Minister, and Henderson. It was probably unfortunate that the Foreign Secretary should have been in Paris fulfilling a long standing engagement to visit the Colonial Exhibition, and in his capacity as President of the forthcoming World Disarmament Conference, when the discussions over the London Conference were at their height. Undoubtedly the distance between Henderson and MacDonald added to the difficulties, but not as much as the fact that they were pursuing policies independently of one another. The impending visit of MacDonald and Henderson to Berlin, announced on 19 June and due to take place between 17–19 July, injected a further element of confusion into the proceedings taking place in Paris.

As soon as he arrived in the French capital on the evening of 14 July, Henderson received word that the Americans were pressing for an immediate convening of the London Conference.[43] The next morning MacDonald telephoned Henderson and suggested that the ministerial visit to Berlin be postponed and replaced by a conference in London.[44] The French were not impressed by the idea of an immediate meeting in London. 'A Conference', Briand told Henderson, 'without a programme, without a definite object, is to court failure'.[45] With Stimson, the American Secretary of State, Henderson and the French ministers already in Paris, Briand thought 'certain common decisions' could be reached in 'a kind of conference'. However, before any such conference could take place, Laval insisted upon 'substantial guarantees' from Germany, specially the abandonment of the customs union with Austria, and the postponement of the second battleship.[46]

Henderson agreed with Laval over these issues and had already raised them with Neurath in London and through Newton with Curtius in Berlin. Indeed he had gone further. On 9 July Henderson contacted A.L. Kennedy at *The Times* and requested a leader pressing Germany to postpone the customs union and the battleship during the Hoover year.[47] The Foreign Secretary was prepared to go further. He now wanted Germany to accept 'a political moratorium of five and even ten years. We must put an end to all these discussions.'[48] Laval, unsurprisingly, leapt at this suggestion:

> Certainly, we might arrange for a political moratorium which would last as long as we are helping Germany – that is, for the period of the loan.[49]

Henderson was completely satisfied, 'I agree with you', he told Laval. 'There is nothing between us.'[50]

In pursuance of this new course Henderson proposed that he and MacDonald should stick to their timetable and visit Berlin. Following the visit Henderson would return to Paris to report to the French government on the situation in Berlin and the attitude of Brüning. While in Berlin he would also attempt to persuade the German ministers to go to Paris. Laval insisted throughout his talks with Henderson that France would help Germany – principally by offering a long-term loan – only if German ministers travelled to Paris and agreed to political concessions. In short, Laval would not go to London unless Brüning visited Paris first. Henderson, who was under pressure from MacDonald to get the French to attend the London Conference immediately, conceived of the Berlin visit as a useful means of persuading the Germans to go to Paris and thereby facilitate the convening of the London Conference. He also had another motive. In his talks with Laval he had suggested the idea of a political moratorium. It is highly likely that he intended to press the idea on the Germans in Berlin.[51]

The idea of a political moratorium now became central to Henderson's policy. Finding the French Prime Minister strongly in favour of the proposal, the Foreign Secretary, contrary to the British Prime Minister's own intentions, decided to visit Berlin himself alone, first to induce the German Chancellor and Foreign Minister to go to Paris before the London Conference – an essential prerequisite the French demanded to ensure their own attendance at the London Conference – and second, to suggest the idea of a political truce to Brüning. In this way Henderson no doubt hoped to produce a measure of Franco-German reconciliation so essential for the further appeasement of Europe, especially with the Disarmament Conference due to open in February 1932. His plans, however, were thwarted by Downing Street which feared that the Foreign Secretary was exceeding his remit and prejudicing MacDonald's own policy.

The financial position in London was becoming more acute as the days passed. On 15 July London had lost £3 million sterling, and on 16 July a further £4.5 million was lost. In these circumstances MacDonald telegraphed to Henderson demanding 'immediate action' in order to convene the London Conference.[52] Despite Henderson's request, Laval would not accept an invitation to the London Conference unless the German ministers first visited Paris. Henderson decided to travel to Berlin the following day to hurry the departure of Brüning and Curtius.[53] His decision, however, was pre-empted by the news that in the early hours of 16 July London had issued the invitations for the Conference to open on Monday, 20 July at 6.00 pm. The telegram containing the news continued:

> [The] Prime Minister and Mr. Henderson will go to Berlin as arranged on Friday, returning in time for [the] Conference of Ministers on Monday, when it is hoped Dr. Brüning will accompany them.[54]

MacDonald was most anxious to prevent two possibilities. First, he wanted to prevent the German ministers from travelling to Paris and being bullied by the French. Second, he wished to prevent the Paris conversations turning into an alternative London Conference. To these ends the Prime Minister had hurriedly issued the invitations to the

London Conference. He had also telephoned to the British Ambassador in Berlin, Sir Horace Rumbold, at about 9.30 pm on Thursday 16 July to request him to tell Chancellor Brüning that, in the Prime Minister's opinion, 'the Germans would be unable to accomplish anything useful if they went to Paris first before seeing our Ministers.'[55] MacDonald also refused Henderson's request to send Leith-Ross, the Treasury's Controller of Finance, to Paris for the preliminary conversations.[56]

When he received the Prime Minister's message, Rumbold hastened to Brüning who was with Curtius, and the State Secretary to the Foreign Ministry, von Bülow. A rather embarrassing conversation followed. The Germans had learnt from their Ambassador in Paris, Leopold von Hoesch, who had been summoned to the British Embassy in Paris in the early hours of the morning by Henderson, that the Foreign Secretary was urging the German ministers to travel to Paris at once to have preliminary talks before the London Conference met, with the French, himself and the American Secretary of State, Stimson. Rumbold returned to the Embassy and telephoned MacDonald 'and explained the difficulty in which the Germans were'.[57] In the meantime MacDonald had received news from the *Berliner Tageblatt*, announcing the cancellation of the British ministerial visit to Berlin. In these circumstances the Prime Minister instructed Rumbold to return to the Chancellor and inform him officially that the visit had been postponed.[58] MacDonald was beside himself as he confided to his diary on 16 July:

> A day of confusion. Henderson's vanity has overcome him. He is working to keep everyone 'off his grass' except himself. Telephones to Paris and Berlin reveal that he has cancelled the Berlin visit without consulting me or the Germans. He has assured me that the Germans have agreed whilst our Ambassador at Berlin tells direct from Brüning that they have not and [the] German Ambassador has called to tell me that Brüning is in consternation and that the cancellation will do harm. Henderson says proposal to cancel was made by German Ambassador in Paris. Brüning says it was made to the Ambassador by Henderson. The Government has been doing everything it could to prevent [the] Germans from going to Paris and having an ultimatum presented by the French. Henderson has thwarted us. F[oreign] O[ffice] here is furious.[59]

Although he was at odds with his Prime Minister, Henderson had clearly been in an awkward position. MacDonald was pressing for the London Conference to begin at once, yet Henderson realised that the French would not attend without a preliminary meeting with the Germans. Had the Berlin visit gone ahead there would not have been enough time for Franco-German discussions before 20 July. In terms of having the London Conference meet on that date Henderson's was probably the more realistic approach. However, by being 'economical with the truth', he had certainly deceived the Prime Minister and the Foreign Office which undoubtedly helped to strain further the relations between MacDonald and Henderson. Apart from their difficult personal relationship, MacDonald and Henderson also differed on their attitudes towards France. Henderson had been converted to the necessity of good relations with Paris, and the need for Franco-British co-operation in order to achieve the continuing pacification of Europe. MacDonald, however, entertained the most serious reservations concerning French motives. He once wrote,

> I do my best to have confidence in [the] French, but I am always defeated. They seem to be incapable of disinterested diplomacy... The diplomacy of France is an ever active force for evil in Europe.[60]

Despite his refusal to allow Leith-Ross to join Henderson in Paris, and his warning to the Foreign Secretary that the discussions in Paris must not degenerate into a full scale conference, MacDonald remained worried that Henderson would fall in with French plans to hold the conference in Paris. Accordingly, and almost certainly springing from the concerns of Downing Street and the Treasury, Rex Leeper of the Foreign Office News Department, telephoned *The Times'* leader writer, A.L. Kennedy, at about 6.00 pm on 17 July. Leeper asked Kennedy to announce in his columns that there would be a meeting of the Cabinet on 20 July. This announcement was designed to forestall any French designs to hold an alternative conference in Paris, and also to prise the Foreign Secretary out of the hands of the French. 'The whole point is that Henderson', Kennedy wrote in his journal,

> has gone to Paris, and in the opinion of the F[oreign] O[ffice] and of MacDonald, apparently, he has been nobbled by Briand, and there is a danger of the Conference being held in Paris instead of London.[61]

Under intense pressure from London, Henderson, along with Stimson, made it clear to the French that the meetings in Paris could not be regarded as a substitute for the meeting in London, and no discussions could be entered into in Paris with the aim of anticipating the decisions to be reached in London.[62] Laval was prepared to accept these conditions but insisted that if agreement in principle was not reached with the Germans when they arrived in Paris on 18 July, the French would not proceed thereafter to London.

The French hope that the Germans would accept a moratorium on political action in return for a large French loan were dashed at the first Franco-German meeting on 18 July. However, once Laval was satisfied that the London Conference would discuss only the issue of financial aid to the Reich, he was prepared to acquiesce in a French presence.[63]

The French had been suspicious of German and British motives throughout the period following the announcement of the Hoover Moratorium. While the French were working to secure the unconditional annuities under the Young Plan during the Franco-American negotiations, Berthelot, the Secretary General of the Quai d'Orsay, had learnt that the 'British Treasury acted constantly in Washington... and preached an uncompromising attitude and worked against the unconditional and [sic] reparations'.[64] The French also feared that the British would attempt to use the London Conference to force the abandonment of the Franco-American agreement and demand the application of the Hoover Moratorium in its entirety.[65] The Laval government entertained similar fears regarding the German attitude. However, once it became clear that the London Conference would not discuss the whole question of debts and reparations, the French were prepared to accept the invitation to attend. Unfortunately, the Franco-German discussions in Paris on 18 July had precluded any large settlement of Germany's financial difficulties. The Germans would not accede to French political demands and without this the French would not offer financial assistance to the Reich.

The negotiations in Paris and the Proceedings of the London Conference itself were to demonstrate the differences between the Treasury and the Foreign Office. These differences had arisen due to a change of attitude on behalf of the Treasury. In November 1930 both departments had been united in their approach to the question of German reparations. In the crisis of June–July 1931 the Treasury reversed its stand of the previous November and attempted to secure an end of reparations and war debts, or at least a drastic downward revision of both. While Henderson pressed for a political moratorium tied to a further large international loan to Germany, the Treasury under Philip Snowden, and following the advice of the Governor of the Bank of England, Montagu Norman, deprecated the idea of a further loan to Germany and sought to pressurise the French directly, and indirectly through Washington, into abandoning the Franco-American agreement worked out in Paris. Henderson, on the other hand, concentrated his efforts on getting the Germans to make some contribution to a settlement. It was small wonder then that when Henderson returned from Paris on 19 July and met MacDonald and Snowden, the conversation was described as 'a bit spiky'.[66]

In spite of the tremendous efforts which had gone into the convening of the London Conference, it produced little tangible result, at least in its immediate aftermath. The Conference's major achievements were its recommendation that the financial institutions should agree to maintain their credits in Germany, and the decision to empower the BIS to establish a committee to investigate Germany's credit needs.[67] This committee, the Wiggin-Layton or Basle Committee, as it came to be known, was to have an important impact on the future development of the reparations issue and the lead up to the Lausanne Conference on reparations in June and July 1932.

The London Conference also witnessed the defeat of the policies which the Treasury and Foreign Office had been pursuing. Snowden, the Chancellor of the Exchequer, received a public rebuff at the Conference from his own Prime Minister when, at the third meeting of the conference on 22 July, he attempted to introduce the question of reparations. He accused the Conference of failing to tackle 'the fundamental causes of the trouble from which Germany is suffering at the present time'. In his view 'it was quite impossible for Germany to maintain her internal economy and at the same time have to meet the huge drain of political reparations.' MacDonald's reaction to this outburst was to pass a note to Stimson saying, 'I know nothing of this.'[68] Certainly Snowden's intervention flew in the face of French and American views expressed during the Paris conversations the week before. Both had insisted that the London Conference should confine itself to the issue of returning Germany to financial stability. Stimson attempted to undermine Snowden's argument by pointing out that the Chancellor had already agreed that Germany's financial stability had to be established first before any other measures could be contemplated. No further reference was made to reparations and the conference moved to discuss the standstill agreement.[69]

Henderson was altogether more circumspect in the advancement of his policy. On 21 July Curtius and von Bülow called at the Foreign Office to discuss the postponed visit of British ministers to Berlin with the Foreign Secretary. The German Foreign Minister hoped that MacDonald and Henderson would be able to go to Berlin at the end of that week, or during the following one. He regarded the visit 'as most important', there being questions which he wanted to discuss, such as disarmament.[70] For his part Henderson was anxious to know what had passed between the French and German ministers when they met in Paris. When it became clear that Brüning and Curtius had not been able to accommodate French wishes, Henderson expressed his hope that he might be able to take action if he was informed of the differences between the two countries rather in the fashion of Sir Austen Chamberlain after the signing of Locarno. 'In his opinion', Henderson told Curtius, 'it was necessary to issue some declaration which would have the effect of restoring confidence throughout Europe'.[71] Foiled in his attempt to press the idea of a political truce on the Germans during his planned trip to Berlin the week before, Henderson now pushed the idea on the Germans in London and was firmly rebuffed.'"The idea of a declaration involving a political moratorium', Curtius told Henderson, 'was impossible in the present state of German opinion'. Henderson attempted to persuade Curtius by pointing out that Germany would not be asked to abandon any of its rights under the peace treaty, merely to place them in abeyance for a period. At this Bülow asserted that 'abeyance would amount to the same thing' as abandonment, which German opinion would never accept. This flat rejection of his proposal provoked Henderson's temper. He accused the Germans of adopting 'an impossible position' which 'amounted to nothing else than fiddling while Rome was burning'. Later the same day Henderson had a further meeting with Curtius covering much the same ground, and again Curtius insisted Germany could not 'make any concession towards the elaboration of a formula which would give satisfaction to the French.' With that exchange the idea of a political truce died.[72]

In September when referring to the idea, Vansittart highlighted the fundamental difficulty that had prevented its realisation:

> What the French want, as Sir H. Rumbold has recently pointed out, is that Germany should accept the Treaty of Versailles as it stands, in other words capitulate: in fact that Germany should alter her entire mentality.

Despite this Vansittart remained hopeful that 'something on the lines of the political truce may become possible'.[73]

Sir Austen Chamberlain once told the Imperial Conference that he 'regarded the spirit of Locarno as more important than the treaties themselves'. Locarno, he argued, had restored the 'peace mentality' to

Europe and this, rather than the theoretical obligations Britain had undertaken to defend the inviolability of the demilitarized Rhineland zone and the frontiers of Germany, France and Belgium, remained at the core of Britain's Locarno diplomacy.[74] Put simply, if the 'peace mentality' Chamberlain spoke of disappeared then the resolution of the differences between Germany and the Allies which had characterized the period 1925 to 1930 would be replaced by increasing tension between France and Germany. No one could be quite sure how that tension would manifest itself, but a return to the instability of the immediate post-war period was conceivable. Should this happen then the British guarantee enshrined in Locarno might be called upon. This of course would represent the negation of Britain's Locarno diplomacy because the European Great Powers would have divided and potentially cause Britain to choose sides. Many people believed that such divisions in Europe had helped to bring on war in 1914. From this perceptive the maintenance of Locarno diplomacy offered real advantages to Britain. Instability in Europe directly affected Britain's ability to act as a global power and if the European powers were at each other's throats Britain's own security could be called in to question. Indeed, Locarno appeared to underpin Britain's security because it obliged the German army to remain east of the Rhine and thereby protected the English Channel.[75]

Given the distinct advantages Locarno offered to Britain it was not surprising that British diplomats pursued the idea of a political truce in 1931. Under the impact of the Great Depression with the financial and economic turmoil that event brought forth, relations between the leading European powers came under great strain. The rise of intense nationalism, most evident with the emergence of the Nazi Party in Germany as the second largest party in the Reichstag following the September 1930 elections, drew countries back from international co-operation upon which Locarno diplomacy was predicated. For France in particular, the Nazis' anti-Versailles, anti-French propaganda, was alarming and undermined confidence in Germany. Indeed, the decision of German politicians to attempt to push revision unilaterally with, for example, the Austro-German customs union project sprung on the world in March 1931, persuaded France that Germany had turned against Stresemann's policy. Simultaneous German initiatives on the issues of reparations and disarmament heightened French fears of German intentions. With France and Germany dividing over a range of political issues the core of Locarno diplomacy was undermined. The idea of a political truce was designed to prevent the further drift to greater Franco-German tension. Perhaps the idea was unrealistic from the start but the effort to achieve a truce reflected Britain's fears for the gains it had received from Locarno and it also reflected Britain's weakness in the crisis of 1931. London came under increasing financial pressure in that year and eventually it brought down the second Labour government and led to the establishment of a National government coalition. National financial weakness and a rising tide of nationalism in Europe limited British influence and made the successful pursuit of a political truce highly unlikely. It may have been impossible to achieve a political truce, but the attempt did demonstrate the commitment of Britain to Locarno diplomacy.

Notes

1. Anne Orde, *Great Britain and International Security, 1920–1926* (London: Royal Historical Society, 1978).
2. On Chamberlain's period at the Foreign Office see R.S. Grayson, *Austen Chamberlain and the Commitment to Europe* (London: Frank Cass, 1997). Specifically on Britain and the Treaty of Locarno see Frank Magee, 'Limited Liability? Britain and the Treaty of Locarno', *Twentieth Century British History*, 6 (1995), pp. 1–22. For Curzon's period at the Foreign Office see, G.H. Bennett, *British Foreign Policy During the Curzon Period* (Basingstoke: Macmillan, 1995). For a very detailed account of the Ruhr crisis, see E. O'Riordan, *Britain and the Ruhr Crisis* (Basingstoke: Palgrave Macmillan, 2001).
3. Sir Horace Rumbold (Berlin) to Arthur Henderson, 3 July, 1930, FO (Foreign Office) 371/14355, C 5481/16/18. All FO references are to found in the National Archives, Kew, London unless otherwise stated.
4. Rumbold to Henderson, 3 July 1930, FO 371/14370, C 5484/680/18.
5. On the Austro-German Customs Union Crisis see F.G. Stambrook, 'The German-Austrian Customs Union Project of 1931: A Study of German Methods and Motives', *Journal of Central European Affairs*, 21 (1961–62), pp. 15–44; A. Orde, 'The Origins of the German-Austrian Customs Union Affair of 1931', *Central European History*, 13 (1980), pp. 34–59; F. Magee, 'Conducting Locarno Diplomacy; Britain and the Austro-German Customs Union Crisis, 1931', *Twentieth Century British History*, 11 (2000), pp. 105–34.
6. Drummond to Noel Baker, 5 June 1931, FO 371/15218, C 3892/49/18.
7. Undated marginalia by Vansittart, possibly 16 June 1931 on Drummond to Noel Baker, 5 June 1931, FO 371/151218, C 3892/49/18.
8. Minute by Vansittart, 16 June 1931 on Drummond to Noel Baker, 5 June 1931, FO 371/15218, C3892/49/18.
9. Bruce Kent, *The Spoils of War: The Politics, Economics, and Diplomacy of Reparations, 1918–32* (Oxford: Clarendon Press, 1989), pp. 343–6.
10. Memorandum by Noel Baker, 13 July 1931, FO371/15187, C5233/172/62.
11. Ibid.
12. Ibid.
13. Ibid.

14. Ibid.
15. Ibid.
16. Ibid.
17. Ibid
18. Ibid
19. Ibid. A copy of this memorandum was sent to the Prime Minister.
20. H. Blumenthal, *Illusion and Reality in Franco-American Diplomacy, 1914–45* (Baton Rouge, Louisiana State University Press, 1986), pp. 139–144.
21. Cabinet minutes. Meeting of 24 June 1931. CAB23/67, 35(31).
22. Ibid. The statement by the Chancellor to the House of Commons on 24 June 1931 may be found in E. L. Woodward, M. E. Lambert, W. N. Medlicott et al (eds), *Documents on British Foreign Policy* (DBFP), Ser. 2, vol. 2, no. 80.
23. Tyrrell to Henderson, 22 June 1931. FO 371/15182, C4340/172/62.
24. Ibid.
25. Ibid.
26. Minute by Sargent, 24 June 1931 on Henderson to Lindsay (Washington), 26 June 1931. FO 371/15182, C4386/172/62.
27. Minute by Vansittart, 24 June 1931 on Henderson to Lindsay, 26 June 1931. FO 371/15182, C4386/172/62.
28. Henderson to Lindsay, 26 June 1931. Ser. 2, vol. 2, no. 87.
29. Tyrrell to Henderson, 24 June 1931. DBFP, Ser. 2, vol. 2, no. 81.
30. Newton (Berlin) to Henderson, 24 June 1931. FO 371/15209, C4459/9/18.
31. Henderson to Lindsay, 27 June 1931. FO 371/15183, C4516/172/62.
32. The Treasury argued that Germany could not pay the unconditional annuities; the French believed she could. 'It is', wrote Nichols, 'surely up to the Treasury to produce convincing reasons and arguments in the support of their attitude – which they have certainly not done hitherto.' Sargent too had a good deal of sympathy for the French point of view: 'The French argument that what Germany is suffering from is a credit crisis and not a budgetary crisis would appear – to the layman – to have a good deal of weight. It would account for the phenomenon of the Reichsbank on the verge of default – and only maintained by international support – side by side with a balanced budget.' Minutes by Nichols and Sargent, 29 June 1931 on Tyrrell to Henderson, 28 June 1931. FO 371/15183, C4549/172/62.
33. Lindsay to Henderson, 27 June 1931. DBFP, Ser. 2, vol. 2, no. 89; Henderson to Newton, 29 June 1931. DBFP, Ser. 2,vol. 2, no. 93.
34. Lindsay to Henderson, 30 June 1931. DBFP, Ser. 2, vol. 2, no. 97; Henderson to Newton, 1 July 1931. DBFP, Ser. 2, vol. 2, no. 104.
35. Cabinet Minutes. Meeting of 1 July 1931. CAB23/67, 67(31).
36. Lindsay to Henderson, 1 July 1931. DBFP, Ser. 2, vol. 2, no. 110; Henderson to Lindsay, 2 July 1931. DBFP, Ser. 2, vol. 2, no. 112.
37. H. Dalton, *Call Back Yesterday* (London: Muller, 1953) p. 254.
38. Newton to Henderson, 6 July 1931. DBFP, Ser. 2, vol. 2, no. 142.
39. Minute by Vansittart, 8 July 1931 on Lindsay to Henderson, 6 July 1931. FO 371/15185, C4862/172/62.
40. H. James, 'The Causes of the German Banking Crisis of 1931', *Economic History Review*, 2, 37 (1984), pp. 68–87.
41. B. Kent, *The Spoils of War*, p. 350; Henderson to Tyrrell, Lindsay and Rumbold, 10 July 1931. DBFP, Ser. 2, vol. 2, no. 177; Newton to Henderson

10 July 1931. DBFP, Ser. 2, vol. 2, no. 178; Newton to Henderson, 8 July 1931. DBFP, Ser. 2, vol. 2, no. 180; Newton to Henderson, 13 July 1931. DBFP, Ser. 2, vol. 2, no. 188.
42. Minute by Vansittart, 17 June 1931 on Lindsay to Henderson, 16 June 1931. FO 371/15226, C4196/2018/18.
43. Lindsay to Henderson, 14 July 1931. DBFP, Ser. 2, vol. 2, no. 191.
44. Tyrrell to Vansittart, 16 July 1931. FO 371/15187, C5295/172/62.
45. Ibid.
46. Ibid.
47. Journal of A.L. Kennedy, entry for 9 July 1931. Kennedy Papers, LKEN11. Churchill College, Cambridge.
48. Tyrrell to Vansittart, 16 July 1931. FO 371/15187, C5295/172/62.
49. Ibid.
50. Ibid.
51. D. Carlton, *MacDonald versus Henderson* (London: Macmillan, 1970), p. 204.
52. Tyrrell to Vansittart, 16 July 1931. DBFP, Ser. 2, vol. 2, no. 207; D. Carlton, *MacDonald versus Henderson*, pp. 202–3.
53. Memorandum by Henderson on discussions in Paris, 15–19 July 1931. DBFP, Ser. 2, vol. 2, no. 193.
54. Vansittart to Washington, Paris, Berlin, Tokyo, Brussels and Rome, 16 July 1931. DBFP, Ser. 2, vol. 2, no. 198.
55. Rumbold to Sir Clive Wigram, 22 July 1931. Rumbold Papers, Bodleian Library, Oxford. MS Rumbold, dep.38.
56. Memorandum by Henderson on discussions in Paris, 15–19 July 1931. DBFP, Ser. 2, vol. 2, no. 193.
57. Rumbold to Sir Clive Wigram, 22 July 1931. Rumbold Papers, Bodleian Library, Oxford. MS Rumbold, dep.38.
58. Ibid.
59. MacDonald Diary, entry for 16 July 1931. MacDonald Papers, PRO 30/69/1753.
60. Ibid, entry for 7 April 1932.
61. Kennedy Journals, entry for 17 July 1931. Kennedy Papers, LKEN11.
62. Memorandum by Henderson on discussions in Paris, 15–19 July 1931, DBFP, Ser. 2, vol. 2, no. 193.
63. Notes of a conversation between representatives of France, Britain, Germany, Italy, Belgium and Japan held in Paris, 19 July 1931, DBFP, Ser. 2, vol. 2, no. 219.
64. Ibid.
65. Tyrrell to Henderson, 9 July 1931, FO 371/15185, C4971/172/62.
66. H. Dalton, *Call Back Yesterday*, p. 256.
67. Proceedings of the London Conference, DBFP, Ser. 2, vol. 2, app. 1.
68. Ibid.; E.W. Bennett, *Germany and the Diplomacy of the Financial Crisis, 1931*, (Cambridge, MA: Harvard University Press, 1962), pp. 176–7.
69. Stenographic notes of the London Conference, DBFP, Ser. 2, vol. 2, app. 1.
70. Notes of a conversation between Henderson and Curtius, 21 July 1931, DBFP, Ser. 2, vol. 2, no. 221.
71. Ibid.
72. Ibid.

73. Postscript by Vansittart, 21 September 1931 on a Memorandum by Vansittart, 21 September 1931, FO 371/15707, W12764/47/98.
74. Statement by Sir Austen Chamberlain at the Imperial Conference, 20 October 1926, DBFP, Ser. 1A, ii, app.
75. K. Neilson and T.G. Otte, *The Permanent Under-Secretary for Foreign Affairs, 1854–1946* (Abingdon: Routledge, 2009), p. 196.

4
'Leaving Us in the Lurch'
The British Government, the First DRC Enquiry and the United States, 1933–34

Peter Bell

The failure of the United States to play a more active role during the 1930s in the containment of international aggression remains an important issue for historians interested in whether World War II could have been prevented; and is intimately connected with the debate concerning Britain's ill-fated policy of appeasement – whether misguided capitulation to German, Italian and Japanese expansion, or pragmatic response to insuperable burdens contingent upon British decline. Could more have been done by the British government to establish a closer association with America, and thereby deter war? Did London miss the chance to follow leads from Washington, confounding Franklin D. Roosevelt's attempts to wean Congress away from isolationism? Or was Britain's desperate, febrile policy towards potential enemies – consequence of ineluctable constraints – further weakened by America's persistently ambiguous posture: one that, if aligned with, risked antagonising hostile powers without providing the practical support necessary to justify such risk? Did British policy, thus, merely help entrench isolationism, or was the latter itself one of the determinants of appeasement?

Central to this debate is the reputation of Neville Chamberlain – still contentious, despite four decades of frequently favourable reappraisal.[1] As an unusually influential Chancellor of the Exchequer, and as Prime Minister, his presence dominates the 1930s.[2] Churchill's charge in his notoriously unreliable memoirs that Chamberlain 'waved away the proffered hand stretched across the Atlantic', casting aside 'the last frail chance to save the world from tyranny otherwise than by war', met with ready approval after 1945, in an era wise with hindsight, keen to distance itself from past mistakes.[3] It was not seriously challenged by historians until the revisionist debate that emerged in the 1970s, with the opening up of the British archives under the 30-year rule – though Keith Feiling's sympathetic 1946 biography, based on Chamberlain's private papers, had already offered generous assessment, not least regarding his attitude towards the United States.[4] Churchill's view, however, dies hard, especially among politicians and the public; and indeed, in recent years, has undergone something of a resurrection among historians, a major contention of counter-revisionists being the alleged mishandling of America. According to this thinking, better strategies, were, if admittedly imperfect, nevertheless available, but subverted by Chamberlain's blinkered leadership. However, counter-revisionists have yet to prove that viable alternatives existed sufficient either to counter isolationism or to create an Anglo-American front capable of deterring Germany, Italy and Japan; they have done little more than reaffirm the Churchillian myth, even the 'Guilty Men' thesis of Cato.[5]

Britain's cautious handling of America, moreover, cannot be attributed to the supposed prejudice of one man; for scepticism regarding the Unites States' reliability had a long and well-justified history in London. Ever since the United States' refusal in 1919 to join the League of Nations and underwrite the Treaty of Versailles, isolationism remained an awkward political reality that no British government could ignore; a difficulty intensified after 1929 by global economic crisis and the breakdown of stability in Europe and the Far East – crowned by the alarmingly restrictive neutrality laws enacted by Congress during 1934–37. Even if it be accepted that the isolation of the United States is a misconception understating the nation's and Roosevelt's true international posture; and that by insisting on 'specific, presumably military, commitments', Chamberlain applied a 'self-defeating test',[6] the fact remains that no policy was proposed by Washington, throughout the 1930s, sufficient to reassure any responsible British leader. That Britain could not risk a multi-theatre war without American assistance was an axiom shared by almost everyone within the government, whatever varied nuances emerged as to its likelihood; on the other hand, pending any credible commitment, Britain had perforce to conduct policy unilaterally, prioritising her own security against burgeoning threats, however unpalatable to Washington.

The period of this study is that of the Defence Requirements Committee (DRC) of 1933–34: the official interdepartmental investigation, representing The Foreign Office, the Treasury and the Military Departments; the ministerial discussions and decisions within Cabinet and its Disarmament Committee; and the wider platforms of debate impinging on the enquiry, notably those pertaining to the forthcoming 1935 Naval Conference. The DRC enquiry – the first major review of Britain's global strategy since World War I – was established in response to the emergence of a double danger from Japan and Germany. It was the most significant threshold in interwar planning, not only in addressing Britain's gravely depleted defences – consequence of financial constraints, domestic and international pacifism and the absence of serious enemy danger until 1931 – but in defining a strategy appropriate to a rapidly worsening global scene, where an obsolete British Imperial hegemony was under challenge from hostile, militarised 'have-not' powers, and when no strong, reliable ally was assured.

The basic facts are well known: the designation of Germany as ultimate potential enemy; the placation of Japan by diplomacy while 'showing a tooth' by completing Singapore; Russia as a third potential enemy in India; the rearrangement of defence priorities, favouring the RAF, defender of the homeland, over the Army and a continental commitment and over the Navy and Imperial Defence. Less well recognised is that the enquiry led to a changed emphasis in policy towards the United States. Hitherto resigned to working around ambiguous and frustrating American forays on the world stage, London resolved for the foreseeable future not to allow the objective of preserving good relations with America to override more immediate security needs against a menace from two – and after 1935, with the alienation of Italy, three – aggressive, well-armed opponents. Far from the image of laxity portrayed by critics of the National Government, a working strategy evolved towards isolationist America, which enjoyed the support of almost all senior officials and the Cabinet. The aim was to mend relations if possible with Japan, so as to prioritise preparations against the longer-term German threat; and to try to achieve this without wholly alienating the United States, whose assistance would be critical in the event of another global conflict. A diplomatic tightrope, indeed it was, one of several the British had to walk in the 1930s, as they struggled to pitch inadequate resources against overwhelming odds – not least the imponderable policy of Washington.

In this context, comment must be passed on the role of the allegedly anti-American Chancellor of the Exchequer, Neville Chamberlain, who was instrumental in instigating the DRC, influencing its terms of debate and arbitrating on its final recommendations. Chamberlain's pervasive influence over all aspects of defence and foreign policy – stemming from the weakness of senior colleagues, his own determination and the inherent power of the Chancellor in a government mandated to prioritise economic and financial recovery – should not obscure the fact that, regarding the United States (as indeed on the whole matter of appeasement) he commanded a broad consensus. The following discussion exemplifies the range of dissatisfaction, suspicion, frustration, wariness and under-confidence *vis à vis* America permeating the official mind in London, which cannot be attributed to the supposed prejudice of one man. Indeed, as part of this consensus, Chamberlain displayed not prejudice but pragmatism: in recognising that, however vital for ultimate security, a firm Anglo-American front was, as things stood, no more than a chimera, the pursuit of which was liable to worsen rather than improve Britain's strategic predicament.

The DRC deliberated against the backdrop of a rapidly deteriorating international scene, notably the collapsing disarmament and security talks on Europe and the departure of Japan and Germany from the League of Nations. It also met in the shadow of two notorious disagreements between Britain and the United States: first, the controversies associated with war debts, reparations, trade and the World Economic Conference, setting Chamberlain and the newly elect President Roosevelt at odds; second, the quarrel between the US Secretary of State, Henry Stimson, and the British Foreign Secretary, Sir John Simon, over the handling of Japan in the Far Eastern Crisis. Both events cast a long shadow over Anglo-American relations throughout the remainder of the decade and have been seen as factors entrenching a predisposition to negative thinking in London, in particular, in Chamberlain's mind – which effectively thwarted any chance of an alliance being constructed or seriously considered with Roosevelt's America.[7] What must also be stressed is that the reason for the long currency of such bad feeling was due not to prejudices formed at that time, from which the protagonists were unable or unwilling to revise, but to the continued validation of suspicion by the constant uncertainty of America's foreign policy.

While economics and finance soured relations, it was the Far Eastern Crisis that focused London's attention on the dilemma of balancing between immediate, unilateral steps to avoid war and pleasing a half-heartedly committed Washington. With Britain's skeleton forces incapable of resisting Japan, and the League of Nations a toothless hound without America, Britain had to ask which came first: protecting interests by compromise with Japan or preserving long-term security by aligning with Stimson's provocative proposal for a naval display and verbal condemnation. Simon defined the quandary, warning the Prime Minister, Ramsay MacDonald, a staunch pro-American, that Britain risked 'falling between two stools, offending Japan without completely satisfying America'.[8] Sir John Pratt, the Far Eastern Department's expert on China, stressed the need to avoid 'rebuffing America' and simultaneously 'incurring the hostility of Japan'.[9] Deputy Undersecretary, Sir Victor Wellesley, in a memorandum sufficiently prescient to be tabled at Cabinet, warned against 'a definite Anglo-American anti-Japanese attitude', which Tokyo would regard as 'abandonment by her old ally'.[10]

The Foreign Office's impatience was aggravated by parallel frustration with America's unhelpful stand at the Geneva Disarmament Conference, which had opened against the adverse background of Japanese bombardment of Shanghai. The Permanent Undersecretary, Sir Robert Vansittart, complained that despite careful cultivation of cordiality, Britain had been let down: 'when it came to deeds rather than words' collaboration with Washington had proved 'little easier than with the *Quai d'Orsay*';[11] a view shared by Chamberlain, who, as well as criticising the French for being 'as difficult as can be', professed himself infuriated with the 'idiotic Yankees' cynically advising 'what we should and should not do with sole regard to their own party politics'.[12] Chamberlain, likewise, worried about the Far East, confessing himself 'nervous' at the Prime Minister's belief that he had 'special influence' with the Americans.[13] Though exasperation with Washington was also enhanced by war debts, the Lausanne Conference on reparations, and the World Economic Conference in London, it is misleading to speak of a specific 'Treasury view', anti-American and pro-Japanese, for subsequent debates reveal a more complex alignment of opinions.

Though nominally reviewing service deficiencies, the DRC could not divorce them from the foreign political conditions underlying defence strategy. Chaired by the Cabinet Secretary, Sir Maurice Hankey, with representatives of the Services, it specifically included the Foreign Office and the Treasury; it was destined from its inception to become a broad strategic, diplomatic and political review. Proposing what would become the DRC at the Cabinet's Committee of Imperial Defence in November 1933, Chamberlain stressed the grave world situation, emphasising the Nazi menace and consequent need to insure against the hostility of Japan,[14] a view that would be later endorsed and developed throughout the enquiry. The perilous situation inevitably raised questions about the reliability of America; indeed, it became, after the assessment of Germany and Japan, the most dominant political question. The matter was first raised by Sir Warren Fisher, Permanent Undersecretary to the Treasury, who insisted that fruitless pandering to America over the past decade represented one of Britain's 'worst deficiencies'.[15] So large did the issue loom, and so obsessively was it canvassed by Fisher, that Hankey eventually ruled it beyond the terms of reference.[16] This was, however, not simply an attempt to muzzle the obdurate Fisher; it made sense to refer such a dominating issue to wider ministerial review, especially as the ensuing Naval Conference would soon present a stark choice between conciliating Japan and backing the United States. That the DRC Report did include as a 'governing consideration' a paragraph on Anglo-American relations testifies to that factor's gravity in its deliberations. It stated: 'There is much to be said for the view that our subservience to the United States of America in past years has been one of the principal factors in the deterioration of our former good relations with Japan, and that, before the Naval Disarmament Conference, 1935, we ought thoroughly to reconsider our general attitude.'[17] This was advice of crucial significance to future British policy; for the Cabinet was effectively being invited to reconsider relations with Washington in the context of Britain's worsening strategic predicament.

Fisher's tirade against America, developed in three substantial memoranda, arose from a conviction that the emergent Nazi menace dictated agreement with Japan, a priority eclipsing conciliation of, as he saw it, the treacherous Americans: driven by 'profiteering instincts plus some "Rule Columbia" thrown in', it suited their commercial ambitions in East Asia for Britain to become embroiled with Japan. It was vital, therefore, to remove the impression that the British were 'morally spineless sycophants of the USA', and to escape a 'policy of subservience'; the worst of our deficiencies was 'entanglement with the USA with all its dangerous consequences'.[18] Fisher's vexation with America, like that of the Chancellor, was certainly conditioned by the recent financial differences; but it would be an injustice to ignore the wider geopolitical anxieties conditioning his view. In common with Vansittart, he recognised the menacing potential of the new Germany and the consequent need for cautious handling of Japan. It was the latter priority as much as financial pique that fuelled his ire at America. Like Chamberlain he deplored how surrender to the American agenda in East Asia since 1919, notably the termination of the Anglo-Japanese Alliance, had alienated Japan, transmuting her into a potential enemy, with no compensating security from Washington. The USA, he declared, had 'bamboozled' us into renouncing the 'invaluable asset' of the old Alliance; satisfactory terms with Japan could never be achieved unless we were 'emancipated' from America. In like vein, he condemned the Naval Treaties of 1922 and 1930, with Japan's inferior ratio, as instruments of American dominance that drove a wedge between Tokyo and London.[19]

A more sober and constructive, yet critical, view of America was presented by Vansittart. Despite the two officials' common geopolitical outlook and their shared anxiety about Britain's strategic problems, there was significant difference of emphasis regarding the United States. Vansittart agreed with much of Fisher's critique of America, but was sceptical at his simplistic solution; and he displayed a more astute suspicion of Japan, reflecting his absorption of the many qualms held at departmental level within the Foreign Office. Resurrection of the Anglo-Japanese Alliance, or anything resembling it, which Fisher seemed to be implying, Vansittart considered 'quite outside the range of practical politics'.[20] There was, he believed, a fundamental disharmony between British and Japanese ambitions in China; and although he shared great frustration toward America, felt that to fall out with her would ultimately harm British security, not least because of this country's dependence, in the event of a long war, on a well-disposed America. Already he had advised the Committee that while Anglo-American relations were disappointing, it would be unwise to discard any benefits of recent progress, however limited, by chasing Japan.[21] There was much sense in his argument. At Geneva, where Britain was mediating between a revisionist Germany and an intransigent France, tolerable relations with the USA prevailed despite their continuing failure to underwrite a security guarantee, and notwithstanding the irritating Norman Davis; and in the Far East, despite the Stimson-Simon row, a dialogue still existed, crucially important for the forthcoming Naval Conference.

Fisher, by contrast, was unprepared to acknowledge either value or progress in Anglo-American relations, refusing even to accept that in a war America's support, or even benevolent neutrality, would be likely. The Americans, he urged, would never help us in another conflict; far from trusting to her benevolence, he suggested they might well, as had occurred before 1917, impair a British blockade.[22] According to this logic, there could be no advantage in placating the USA if it were at the price of mending fences with the Japanese – and the consequent improved insurance against Germany. Complete severance with America, however, was a position no other official or minister was willing to countenance, including Chamberlain; and it singles out Fisher as the only truly anti-American voice. Nevertheless, it is testimony to the Committee's sympathy with his basic premise, that relations with America had caused serious problems and conferred few advantages, that the Report's conclusion should have so closely followed his choice of words.

Fisher's extremism, though there was sympathy with his grievances, was countered by Hankey, Vansittart and the Chief of Naval Staff, Sir Ernle Chatfield – though the Army and Air Force Chiefs, Sir Archibald Montgomery-Massingberd and Sir Edward Ellington, as on most issues, remained silent. Hankey was worried about undermining traditional policy, stressing the Prime Minister's 'very warm spot for the Americans generally, and President Roosevelt in particular'.[23] Chatfield, like Hankey, was anxious not to alienate the United States, Britain's only feasible naval ally in a war against Japan; though he did endorse much of Fisher's case.[24] In contrast to the Euro-centric focus of Vansittart and Fisher, Chatfield and Hankey prioritised imperial defence, considering Germany a lesser urgency than Japan. On Chatfield's mind was the gloomy prospect for the Naval Conference, where Britain would have to balance between probably incompatible Japanese and American positions, with the likely worst contingency of falling out simultaneously with a rearming Japan and a disgruntled United States. For the Admiralty, improved relations with Japan could only be a good thing – if practicable (and which would subsequently be endorsed by the First Lord of the Admiralty, Sir Bolton Eyres-Monsell, until he recognised the corollary of reduced naval expenditure).[25] On the other hand, Japan's vast potential for immediate devastation of the British position in the Far East reinforced the case for continuing to court America, a view shared by Sir Robert Craigie, Foreign Office expert on naval matters and Head of the American Department, a leading advocate of a firm Anglo-American front at the Conference.[26]

Vansittart's carefully qualified position on the United States, expressed not only in the Committee but in numerous Foreign Office memoranda, reflected the wide spectrum of departmental indecision, itself a symptom of the conundrum presented by Washington. Internal opinion was pessimistic about both Japan and America, the latter frequently the object of trenchant criticism, notably from Far Eastern Department officials, still smarting at Mr Stimson. Pratt deplored America's 'deep seated hostility' to Japan and tactless 'criticism and condemnation'. She often suggested 'as a common policy' actions capable of 'no ameliorative effect' yet likely to cause 'dangerous tension'. Having induced others to participate, she was liable to 'drop out and leave her associates to pursue it alone'. As he succinctly noted: 'We may sail the same general course but we should at all times retain full control of our own vessel.'[27] Sir Francis Lindley, Ambassador to Tokyo, shared the frustration, tersely defining the problem: there was much to be said for an Anglo-American front if 'cemented by a hard and fast military alliance', otherwise it was 'a particularly foolish policy'.[28] Conviction of the inevitability of war with Japan, on the other hand, made Charles Orde, Far Eastern Department Head, anxious lest an overfriendly approach to her cause a 'virtual breach' with the United States.[29] The most optimistic gloss on America was offered by Craigie, who suggested her currently unhelpful attitude might not last indefinitely. He warned that to draw closer to Japan risked provoking an adverse reaction across the Atlantic.[30] Deputy Undersecretary Wellesley gloomily summarised the predominant view, that the United States was 'an entirely uncertain factor'.[31]

Even as the Committee deliberated, American representatives continued to behave in a typically obtuse manner, in relation both to the Far East and Europe. Sir Eric Phipps, British Ambassador to Berlin, reported disquieting conversations with American diplomats, William E. Dodd and William C. Bullitt. Seeking American support for the faltering Geneva Conference, Phipps was told by Dodd that Roosevelt was inclined to make closer collaboration with Britain in Europe 'contingent upon greater cooperation with the USA in the Far East'. Bullitt said the President wanted Britain to use all her influence with Japan to prevent further encroachments in China.[32] As Orde acidly minuted, this was 'rather nonsensical for we haven't the faintest idea what the United States Government wants us to do'.[33] The matter was further complicated by the frequently prevailing uncertainty as to whether such observations represented official policy or stemmed from the undisciplined ideas of the American diplomats; a problem that equally irritated Chamberlain.[34] The events typified the perplexity of trying to do business with the Americans at a time when the storm clouds of danger were gathering over Britain and the Empire. Phipps' report goaded Vansittart into sharp criticism of America, prefiguring his comments to the DRC; his somewhat convoluted assessment accurately reflected the situation's complexity and the dilemma regularly posed by Washington.

Vansittart urged great care, even obstinacy, regarding American requests for cooperative action in the Far East; they wanted us rather than them to get in wrong with Japan and would 'let us down at every turn'. 'We cannot afford such a luxury (given the state of our defences)', he argued, 'as American "cooperation"', in which role they had proven 'mostly futile or disloyal'. Cooperation might come but the United States made it presently impossible. No-one desired good Anglo-Americans more than he and no-one had worked harder for them, but a point had been reached where, if they wanted more, they must make the running. Failing that, the aim should be 'good relations, of course, but not undue sacrifice to the present myth of cooperation'. On the other hand, he did not wish 'to sacrifice any of the ground gained with the USA during the last decade – ground for good relations though not for effective cooperation – by any tardy recourting of Japan'. He therefore urged a balanced policy, with immediate emphasis on exploiting Tokyo's currently friendly overtures. Over the next five years – when it was essential to prepare against Germany – we should be 'more preoccupied in keeping Japan as friendly, i.e. as non-dangerous as possible, than in endeavouring to better our existing relations with the USA, which are as good as that unreliable will or can allow them to be.'[35] This was indeed a delicately poised policy; much would depend on the outcome of the Naval Conference, let alone the course of Japanese ambitions in China. But at least it was grasping at a policy suited to Britain's predicament. This he developed in the DRC, and further refined in the context of the Ministerial Committee on the Naval Conference.

That Committee, created to prepare for the Conference, furnished a further platform for continuing debate about America throughout 1934–35, among ministers and advisers, with Hankey, Chatfield, Fisher and Vansittart in high profile. America figured prominently also in the Cabinet and its Disarmament Committee, theoretically addressing European disarmament but ironically increasingly concerned with rearmament and war; it served as the principal forum for discussion of the DRC Report. Hankey regarded prospects for the Conference as 'extremely gloomy'.[36] Although the Admiralty shared Washington's wish to maintain existing naval ratios against Japan's demand for parity, it disagreed over tactics: the British wishing to deal cautiously behind the scenes with Tokyo, the United States favouring a joint rebuttal of Japan – raising echoes of the Stimson-Simon storm. Lord Stanhope, Parliamentary Undersecretary at the Foreign Office, thought a slim chance of agreement possible if we approached Japan independently, but 'not a hope' hand in hand with America.[37] Chatfield warned the Committee to not give 'the impression that an Anglo-American agreement had been arrived at in advance of consultation with Japan'.[38] When Simon told the Committee of Washington's preferred approach Chamberlain hoped the government 'would do nothing of the kind'.[39]

Washington's insensitivity to Britain's predicament was further shown in conversations during March and April between Simon and the US Ambassador to London, Robert Bingham, as well as with Davis. Bingham urged joint resistance to Japan's 'inadmissible and unreasonable' agenda. According to him, Simon reported, 'the present situation was one in which a policy of cooperation between the United States and ourselves for promoting the peace of the world, or at any rate for limiting the area for conflict if conflict broke out, was worthy of special consideration.'[40] Davis, true to form, proved equally capricious: asked by Simon if America might be willing, as he had implied the previous May, to support a European security scheme, he vaguely replied it was 'not impossible'; then immediately changed the subject, stressing the importance of close cooperation against Japan: if she refused to agree terms at the Conference, then Britain and America should maintain their own parity and adjust their forces 'in unison' as the situation demanded.[41] It was the usual combination of hot air and finger wagging, both diplomats confirming the worst fears about doing business with the Americans. The 'real trouble with the Yanks', as Chamberlain acidly remarked later in the year, was that they could 'never deliver the goods'.[42]

Comparably pessimistic information reached the Foreign Office from East Asia. Admiral Sir Frederick Dreyer, Commander of the China Station, reported a worrying conversation with Admiral F.B. Upham, US Commander of the Asiatic Fleet. Upham talked of America's probable withdrawal from the Philippines; he doubted she needed a fleet in the China Seas; it was awkward having the Japanese-controlled League mandates on the flank of her advance from Honolulu; and Manila was so vulnerable to air attack it would be better for the Americans to get out 'before they were kicked out'. He even insinuated – with striking ignorance of conditions at Singapore – that Britain could more easily police the region in view of the base's 'magnificent strategic position' compared to Manila; and when Dreyer mentioned the threat to the Dutch East Indies, Upham's complacent response was: 'Oh, the British will look after them.' Even if these were the Admiral's personal views, Dreyer warned, he must be to some extent informed about future US policy in the Pacific; it was 'not a pleasant prospect if they intend to do what he said, i.e. leave us in the lurch'. Dreyer concluded on an all too familiar note: 'I am very much afraid that we shall never be able to *rely* on American support in emergency, or at any rate not until sufficient time has elapsed after a crisis has developed, for the American people to be educated in the Pacific situation.'[43] This was prophetic, given the events leading up to Pearl Harbor.

Further corroboration of a possible withdrawal from the Far East was furnished by Sir Ronald Lindsay, the British Ambassador to Washington, covering a report on US press opinion by the British Naval Attaché, Captain A.R. Dewar: the Roosevelt administration was under pressure to make drastic concessions, such as relaxing immigration controls, waiving extra-territorial rights in China, conceding Japan's position in East Asia and abandoning Philippine naval bases. Though even Congress would reject such extremes, he thought Americans were 'at the moment in a mood to shed their direct political commitments overseas as fast as they can'.[44] Nevertheless – and despite Bingham's airy reassurance to Simon as to Roosevelt's 'extraordinarily strong position in Congress', the most 'solid backing' in US history – such a mood was worrying, and would soon not seem so far-fetched with the enactment of the neutrality laws.[45] It could not but fuel fears that Britain would indeed be 'left in the lurch' if trouble ensued with Japan.

The Naval Conference Committee allowed Fisher to reinforce his critique of America, which he feared was being sidestepped. Chamberlain, having digested the DRC's advice, had reasserted his conviction on the need to conciliate Japan, whatever the attitude in Washington. Though the Chancellor had not endorsed Fisher's outright anti-Americanism, the Treasury Chief drew succour from a seeming identity of view. He was vehemently opposed by Chatfield and Vansittart. Fisher traversed familiar ground: as Britain could neither fight a two-front war nor afford a two-power naval standard, imperial security depended on protection of the homeland first, with the corollary of negotiating friendly terms with Japan. There was everything to gain and nothing to lose by seeking an agreement 'in substance though not in form' like the former alliance; but it would be essential to dispel Japan's impression of the British as 'servile adherents' of Washington. Japanese friendship would be less urgent if American support were not 'the very last thing in the world' to be counted on; it was 'singularly ill-advised' to jeopardise her goodwill 'by paying any regard to the United States'. Japan would respect independent British overtures, convinced 'we proposed to order our own doings instead of having them ordered from Washington'.[46]

Fisher's case, which offered the seductive lure of the easy solution, had grave flaws, identified by the Admiralty, the Dominions Office, the Foreign Office and various members of the Cabinet, as well as its Secretary. Although the Admiralty had long been irritated by what it regarded as the United States' selfish naval agenda, and the negative impact on Anglo-Japanese relations, it remained its objective to handle the 1935 Conference in a manner that maintained cordiality with both nations. Indeed, it shared the US determination to preserve the existing ratios – the sole brake on Japanese aggression, given their immense strategic privileges, and pending completion of Singapore. Where it differed from the Americans was over tactics: while the latter wished to tell Tokyo at the outset that equal ratios were not on the table, the British preferred a diplomatic approach, in which the final goal would hopefully emerge from preparatory discussions, which might render possible the placation of Japan by other concessions. This, for Fisher, was not enough: the Admiralty's resistance to Japanese parity still smacked too much of appeasing the Americans; and, in fairness, the Admiralty's hopes looked – and proved to be – wishful thinking. In contrast, Chatfield contended that whatever naval deal Britain might reach with Japan would not moderate demands determined by her rivalry with America.[47] In the absence of any certainty that Japan could be conciliated, in relation to naval matters or China, by diplomacy, the Admiralty believed that Britain could not risk antagonising the United States, without whom any prospect of defeating Japan would be questionable. Fisher saw this position as inconsistent with the logic of designating Germany as the principal enemy – which the Chancellor was busy translating into practice in the Disarmament Committee by prioritising resources towards metropolitan air defence – but Chatfield was backed by Hankey, Eyres-Monsell, Sir Edward Harding, Permanent Undersecretary at the Dominions Office, and to an extent by Vansittart. None wished to snub a potential ally in a Far Eastern conflict or to countenance uncontrolled naval building. On the other hand, was their really any prospect of American help in the Far East? As Harding put it, while unlikely Britain would stand alone in a European war, she 'might or might not' be allied to the USA in conflict with Japan.[48] The naval lobby was trapped in its own dilemma: the possibility of war with Japan necessitated US support, and although evidence denied its certainty, it was dangerous to slam the door in Washington's face by conciliation of Japan, especially as there was only frail hope it would moderate her ambitions or forestall a collision with Britain. The dilemma matched Vansittart's parallel concern lest American benevolence be sacrificed with regard to a potential European war. This underlined a fundamental truth, apparent since the US intervention in World War I, reinforced by the subsequent alienation of Britain's former Far Eastern ally, Japan: that without something resembling an alliance with America, there would be little hope of successfully conducting simultaneous war in Europe and East Asia.

Fisher's intervention was considered by Craigie to be so 'based on a misconception of the facts' that he persuaded Vansittart to make clear the views of the Foreign Office.[49] In a letter to Fisher, also proposed as a brief for the Foreign Secretary at the Conference Committee, Vansittart set down his ideas – in what amounted to a brief for the conduct of relations with Washington for the rest of the decade. He emphasised 'fundamental reasons' why no British government, despite frustrations, could 'treat Anglo-American relations with anything but considerable respect when it comes to a showdown'. He supported Chatfield, affirming his contention that Japan's Conference agenda was decided by comparison with the US Navy, rather than Britain. He accused Fisher of oversimplifying the 'formidable' obstacles to rapprochement with Japan, notably the necessary respect for America. While deploring 'an ostentatious parade of Anglo-American cooperation in the Far East, with a free use of the "big stick"', he cautioned against forfeiting the 'useful and marked advance' achieved with difficulty over the past decade; Britain had paid for what she had got and should not waste what she had already bought. On balance, Japan would be less likely to risk war if existing Anglo-American relations prevailed than if they deteriorated. Britain should not make sacrifices merely to retain America's friendship; but, although 'little reliance' could currently be placed on her, antagonising her would harm British interests. He gave four reasons. First, public and press opinion in Britain and the Dominions would oppose any breach with America. Second, it would weaken Britain's dwindling capacity to satisfy French security demands at Geneva, which were 'dependent on some degree of American cooperation – or at least benevolent neutrality'; British influence in Europe depended ultimately on good relations with Washington. Third, he stressed the commonality of interests and objectives shared by Britain and America – greater than between any other powers. Finally, and most important, he warned that if Britain were ever engaged in another major conflict it would again be vital to obtain from across the Atlantic 'the sinews of war'. Commercial greed alone would ensure this, 'notwithstanding Senator Johnson and all his works', but only if the two countries remained friends.[50]

Throughout the middle of 1934 intensive ministerial discussions took place on the related topics of the DRC Report, the Naval Conference and the Disarmament Conference, in Cabinet and in the Ministerial Committees on Disarmament and on the Naval Conference. The dilemmas defined by their official advisers were echoed, and assumed more pointed form as ministers tried to translate the advice into coherent policy. Largely driven by Chamberlain, the Cabinet endorsed the order of priority that placed Germany first; indeed, within a less costly programme than that recommended by the Committee, conditioned by continuing caution about economic recovery, the Chancellor tilted the bias still further towards the Nazi menace by extra air force spending, in which he took the cue from Vansittart.[51] Chamberlain willingly accepted the logic which, placing Germany first, carried the corollary of defusing the Japanese threat by diplomacy; though not a return to the old alliance, it corresponded to a degree with Fisher's view. It differed from that of Vansittart only in holding more sanguine hopes. As regards America, Chamberlain's position corresponded more closely to that of Vansittart than that of Fisher. If anything, there was a Chamberlain-Foreign Office axis, rather than a distinct Treasury position.

The United States loomed large in the discussions. The strongest pro-American voice was MacDonald – though frequent illness-related absences had all but eliminated his influence. The Prime Minister worried lest agreement with Japan compromise Anglo-American relations, lest it be perceived in the United States as an alliance.[52] Even he, however, shared the general frustration, complaining about her obsession with a navy second to none, dismissed as 'really a toy and not essential'.[53] Stanley Baldwin, Deputy Prime Minister, also much out of touch, cautioned against jilting the Americans, towards whom he maintained residual confidence: 'Whilst he blamed America for many things which had happened since 1918, nevertheless he thought it possible that American feeling might be tempted to undertake a naval war against Japan. Although they would not do it for love of us, yet he thought it hard to believe that America would leave us alone to bear the full weight of Japanese attack.'[54] Canada's sensibilities and her alignment with the United States placed Dominions Secretary, J.H. Thomas, in the same camp.[55] Eyres-Monsell, the First Lord, was tempted by the possibility of an Anglo-Japanese political agreement easing naval negotiations, and perhaps impressing Washington with our influence in Tokyo; on the other hand, with a view to the long term, he feared snubbing the Americans at the Conference.[56]

The Foreign Secretary could offer little escape from the dilemma. Indeed, Simon's indecision was a matter of irritation to Chamberlain, who thought him 'temperamentally unable to make up his mind to action when a difficult situation arises'.[57] Adept, like the excellent lawyer he was, at balancing the different sides of an argument, he tended to pour cold water on all options. Bruised by his encounter with Stimson, he was ever on guard against 'putting her [the Unites States'] nose out of joint'.[58] He prevaricated on the proposed strategy towards Japan, simultaneously endorsing its desirability and disputing its practicality; it was into this breach that Chamberlain stepped. The Foreign Secretary recognised the need to balance between America and Japan, but made no definite counsel. In fairness to Simon, it may well be that his was the most accurate analysis: for the government was addressing a problem that was well-nigh insoluble – indication of the terrible predicament that Britain was facing by 1934; but something had to be done, and this was left to Vansittart and Chamberlain. It is notable that Anthony Eden, then Junior Minister at the Foreign Office – soon to become chief critic of Chamberlain's American policy – shared at this stage in the general scepticism, warning that America would expect 'sacrifices' for closer relations; it was difficult, he said, 'to place implicit confidence in her'.[59]

Chamberlain, certainly, emerged from his early financial dealings with the United States and from the Far Eastern Crisis, deeply mistrustful of America. He had little patience in 'flirting' with US diplomats, especially 'that detestable Norman Davis', or 'those unofficial Americans who always seem to hang around their official representatives'.[60] A practical politician, anxious for solutions, he disliked their inconsistency, their habit of exceeding their brief, airing policies later disowned by Washington. As the Ministerial Committee concluded its discussion of the DRC report in July, he privately noted – with prescient accuracy in view of Pearl Harbor: 'we ought to know by this time that USA will give us no undertaking to resist by force any action by Japan, short of an attack on Hawaii or Honolulu. She will give us plenty of assurances of goodwill especially if we will promise to do all the fighting but the moment she is asked to contribute something she invariably takes refuge behind Congress.'[61] Regarding Europe, he expressed equal distrust. The Far Eastern Crisis had demonstrated the League's impotence without American participation in sanctions; thus when Simon optimistically suggested, à propos the security plans under debate at Geneva in March 1934, that the United States 'would probably give it her blessing', Chamberlain stressed the futility of sanctions without definite US involvement.[62] Already, in October 1933, he had complained that the Americans were 'chiefly anxious to convince their people that they are not going to be drawn into doing anything helpful to the rest of the world'.[63] Roosevelt he found 'a dangerous and unreliable horse in any team'.[64]

Chamberlain's advocacy of agreement with Japan, even at the risk of upsetting America, stemmed from recognition that, without any definite policy from Washington, and given Britain's rapidly worsening predicament, it was vital to formulate an independent strategy. Indeed, he saw agreement with Japan and British policy at Geneva as complementary aspects of a 'general pacification'.[65] Introducing the idea of agreement with Japan in late 1933, he deplored the lack of compensation for having acquiesced in America's wish to end the Anglo-Japanese Alliance.[66] Favouring an agreement with Japan in which naval difficulties would be subsumed, he deprecated aligning with the United States at the

Conference, where it should be clarified we 'could not pull the chestnuts out of the fire for them'.[67] Most of the Cabinet actively agreed. Viscount Sankey, Lord Chancellor, voiced the common view: he 'wondered what we had to lose'. Only the Prime Minister – whom Chamberlain thought 'timid' about America – demurred, fearing its perception in Washington as an alliance.[68] Although subsequent discussions raised qualms about a pact's practicability, it related more to China than America. Indeed, one minister, Walter Elliot, anxious at rumours of possible withdrawal from the Philippines and the improbability of US assistance in the event of trouble with Japan, even suggested consideration of an alliance with Russia – though eliciting no support.[69]

The DRC enquiry of 1933–34 established in a variety of respects a blueprint for Britain's international policy up to the outbreak of World War II. Germany had been accurately identified as the principal enemy, liable to present immediate danger by 1939; as had the risk that Japan, or other hostile powers, would be disposed to exploit that threat in pursuit of policies also inimical to Britain; while they in turn tempted Germany. The enquiry underlined a truth that had remained disguised during the peaceful 1920s: that the British Empire, seriously ill-defended, beset by multiple enemy threats, lacking a powerful and reliable ally, in an era of unprecedented financial constraint, was in the words of the First Sea Lord, 'highly vulnerable' and arguably not 'in reality strategically defensible'.[70] In these circumstances the government, as Vansittart put it, could no longer afford the 'luxury' of 'cooperation' with the United States – unless this translated into a meaningful commitment, whether to deter Japan or underwrite a security guarantee in Europe. At the very least she would have to acknowledge Britain's right to make unilateral arrangements for her own security, however unpalatable. As Chamberlain put it, 'we must not sacrifice our own vital interests to the hope, probably very meagre, of conciliating American opinion'.[71] This led, however, neither to indecision, nor to a rejection of Washington; Fisher's anti-Americanism advice was overruled. The policy pursued henceforth towards the United States – prioritising unilateral security, while continuing to work where opportunity arose for good relations with Washington – was defined by Vansittart, endorsed by Chamberlain and enjoyed, amidst officials and ministers alike, a wide consensus.[72]

Ironically, in view of their later, more notorious disagreement over appeasing Germany, Chamberlain and Vansittart shared a common view concerning Britain's strategic predicament – that would soon be reinforced *vis à vis* Italy – belying the conventional idea of a

Treasury policy imposed against the wisdom of the Foreign Office. Certainly, there were different emphases, notably regarding the probability of achieving agreement with Tokyo. It is wrong, however, to see Chamberlain's subsequent dogged pursuit of such a goal as indicative of Treasury myopia, defying the clear-sighted objections of the Foreign Office.[73] Chamberlain, note, never entertained as a price the total rejection of America, or concessions at the expense of China.[74] That the idea of rapprochement with Japan should at least be explored, even if unappealing to Washington, was generally supported, not least by the Foreign Office.

American policy into the later 1930s continued to vindicate the anxieties voiced earlier in the decade. When the Naval Conference met, London's worst fears were confirmed: proceeding, in Chamberlain's words, 'on the assumption that we two honest-to-God Anglo-Saxons would deal kindly but firmly with the little yellow men'.[75] Advocating a placatory approach to Japan, Vansittart noted: 'We have Germany to consider as well. The Americans haven't.'[76] The laws enacted by Congress from 1934 to 1937, designed to forestall the scenario that precipitated the United States' intervention in 1917, made it look ever less likely, even as dangers multiplied, that Britain could expect direct assistance or benevolent neutrality in another conflict. Despite the efforts of the pro-American Foreign Secretary, Anthony Eden, no common action proved negotiable even when ships of both nations were attacked in the 'Panay' incident; indeed US press opinion called for withdrawal from the Far East. At the Brussels Conference the Americans opposed firm action, yet chose to denounce Japan in a declaration with 'five or six pages of indictment', recalling their provocative yet ineffective policy in the first Far Eastern Crisis.[77] Regarding Italian and German aggression, Washington persistently enunciated high-sounding condemnation, more likely to provoke than deter, with little sensitivity to the grave predicament facing Britain and the paramount necessity to reduce, as the Service Chiefs constantly urged, the number of potential enemies. Roosevelt's ostensible efforts to push America into a more proactive international role, particularly the so-called 'initiative' of early 1938 – which Chamberlain was unwilling to embrace but did not reject outright – must be seen in the preceding context.

Hindsight creates mythologies of lost opportunity. Churchill's memoirs spawned the myth of an Anglo-American alliance in waiting, thwarted by Chamberlain's misguided pursuit of appeasement and anti-American prejudice. Recent accounts have shown that during the 1930s far more constructive dialogues were emerging at departmental level than supposed, which later proved essential foundations of Anglo-American cooperation in World War II and the 'Special Relationship'; it is implied, however, that Chamberlain's purblind anti-American prejudice blocked trends that could have established a more robust Anglo-American partnership.[78] Yet there is no evidence to suggest that, at the highest level in Washington, any alternative scenario to that prevailing could have emerged, whatever valuable contacts were being developed at lower levels, or whoever was Prime Minister in London. Roosevelt's wish to reform the neutrality laws was perpetually stymied until Britain lay naked before the might of a German-occupied Europe, and arguably not until Japan's attack on Pearl Harbor and Hitler's gratuitous declaration of war on the United States. Roosevelt's agreement in 1938 to the Ingersoll mission to London, to discuss contingency planning for Anglo-American naval cooperation in event of a Far Eastern war, is instructive: as it had to be conducted in secrecy to avoid antagonising Congress.[79] Likewise, the visit of the British King and Queen to Washington in June 1939, while contributing greatly to public sympathy for the British, did not achieve Ambassador Sir Ronald Lindsay's objective of assisting Roosevelt's struggle with Congress over neutrality legislation.[80]

Throughout the 1930s the United States chose to speak loudly but not to carry a big stick: the British would have preferred fewer words and greater force. In the circumstances they were driven down a unilateralist road that would terminate in appeasement, an attempt by a weakened empire to fend off multiple threats by whatever resources of diplomacy and deterrence were available. Chamberlain believed that an Anglo-American alliance would be the greatest benefit to world peace; but the pragmatist in him recognised there was little imminent prospect.[81] The frustrations of dealing with Washington were neatly captured by Craigie, a convinced pro-American; who complained to Davis that while the Americans wished to register 'moral indignation' the British preferred to 'get on with the business of finding some practical means of preventing things from going from bad to worse'.[82]

Notes

1. David N. Dilks, 'Appeasement Revisited', *The University of Leeds Review* (1972); David N. Dilks, ' "We must hope for the best and prepare for the worst": The Prime Minister, the Cabinet and Hitler's Germany, 1937–1939', *Proceedings of the British Academy*, 73 (1987), pp. 309–352; John Charmley, *Chamberlain and the Lost Peace* (London: Hodder and Stoughton, 1989); Peter Bell, *Chamberlain, Germany and Japan, 1933–34* (New York: St Martin's Press,

1996); David Dutton, *Neville Chamberlain* (London: Edward Arnold, 2001); Robert Self, *Neville Chamberlain: a Biography* (Farnham: Ashgate, 2006).
2. Bell, *Chamberlain, Germany and Japan*; for a more critical appraisal see Keith Neilson, 'The Defence Requirements Sub-Committee, British Strategic Foreign Policy, Neville Chamberlain and the Path to Appeasement', *English Historical Review*, cxviii, 477 (2003), pp. 652–84; for an extremely negative appraisal see John Ruggiero *Neville Chamberlain and British Rearmament: Pride, Prejudice and Politics* (Westport, CT: Greenwood Press, 1999).
3. Winston S. Churchill, *The Second World War, Vol. 1, The Gathering Storm* (New York: Houghton Mifflin, 1948), pp. 197–9; see also Earl of Avon, *Facing the Dictators* (London: Cassell, 1962) ch. XII; and David Reynolds, *In Command of History* (New York: Basic Books, 2007) for a critical appraisal of Churchill's memoirs and influence upon historical perspectives.
4. Keith Feiling, *The Life of Neville Chamberlain* (London: Macmillan, 1946).
5. 'Cato', *Guilty Men* (London: Victor Gollancz, 1940); Sidney Aster, ' "Guilty Men": The Case of Neville Chamberlain', in Robert Boyce and Esmonde Robertson (eds), *Paths to War: New Essays on the Origins of the Second World War* (London Macmillan, 1989); R.A.C. Parker, *Chamberlain and Appeasement: British Policy and the Coming of the Second World War* (London: Macmillan, 1993); B.J.C. McKercher, *Transition of Power: Britain's Loss of Global Preeminence to the United States, 1930–1945* (Cambridge: Cambridge University Press, 1999); Ruggiero, *Neville Chamberlain and British Rearmament*; Neilson, The Defence Requirements Sub-Committee; Greg Kennedy, 'Neville Chamberlain and Strategic Relations with the US during his Chancellorship', *Diplomacy & Statecraft*, 13, 1 (2002), pp. 95–120; Greg Kennedy, ' "Rat in Power": Neville Chamberlain and the Creation of British Foreign Policy, 1931–39', in T.G. Otte (ed.), *The Makers of British Foreign Policy from Pitt to Thatcher* (Basingstoke: PalgraveMacmillan, 2002), pp. 173–95; Greg Kennedy, *Anglo-American Strategic Relations and the Far East, 1933–1939* (London: Frank Cass, 2002).
6. Warren F. Kimball *Forged in War: Churchill, Roosevelt and the Second World War* (New York: William Morrow, 1997) pp. 25–6.
7. Robert Self, 'Perception and Posture in Anglo-American Relations: The War Debt Controversy in the "Official Mind", 1919–1940', *International History Review*, 29, 2 (2007), pp. 282–313; Keith Neilson, 'Perception and Posture in Anglo-American Relations: The Legacy of the Simon-Stimson Affair, 1932–41', *International History Review*, 29, 2 (2007), pp. 313–37.
8. Letter, Simon to MacDonald, 29/1/32, in E.L. Woodward, M.E. Lambert, W.N. Medlicott et al (eds), *Documents on British Foreign Policy 1919-1939* (DBFP) (London: HMSO, 1947–84), Ser. 2, vol. IX, pp. 215–17.
9. Memorandum, Pratt, 26/1/32, DBFP, Ser. 2, vol. 1X, pp 183–5.
10. Memorandum, 'Anglo-Japanese Relations and the Present Crisis in China', Wellesley, 1/2/32, DBFP, Ser. 2, vol. IX, pp. 283–91, CAB 14 (32), 17/2/32, CAB 23/70.
11. Memorandum, 'The British Position in Relation to European Policy', Vansittart, 1/1/32, CP 4 (32), CAB 24/227.
12. Chamberlain Papers, letter, 5/6/32.
13. Chamberlain Papers, letter, 11/6/32.
14. CID 261st, 9/11/33, CAB 2/6.

15. Letter, Fisher to Hankey, 17/2/34, CAB 21/434.
16. Letter, Hankey to Fisher, 17/2/34, CAB 21/434.
17. DRC Report, 28/2/34, Paragraph 9, DRC 14, CAB 16/109.
18. Note by Fisher, 29/1/34, DRC 19, CAB 16/109; letter, Fisher to Hankey, 17/2/34, CAB 21/434.
19. Note by Fisher, 17/2/34, DRC 19, CAB 16/109; DRC 10th Meeting, 16/2/34, CAB 16/109.
20. DRC 10th Meeting, 16/2/34, CAB 16/109.
21. DRC 3rd Meeting, 4/12/34, CAB 16/109.
22. Note by Fisher, 29/1/34, DRC 19, CAB 16/109.
23. Letter, Hankey to Fisher, 17/2/34, CAB 21/434.
24. DRC 11th Meeting, 19/2/34, CAB 16/109.
25. Bell, *Chamberlain, Germany and Japan*, pp. 70, 136; Eyres-Monsell switched from warmly supporting a pact with Japan as a concession at the Naval Conference to denouncing the Chancellor's naval proposals as a policy 'not advocated even by the Communists in this country'.
26. Minute by Craigie, 2/11/33, W11987/11987/50, FO 371/17338.
27. Minute by Pratt, 1/12/33, DRC 20, CAB 16/109.
28. Lindley to Simon, 27/12/33, FO 677/591/23, FO 371/18184.
29. Minute by Orde, 14/12/33, DRC 20, CAB 16/109.
30. Minute by Craigie, 2/11/33, W11987/11987/50, FO 371/17338.
31. Memorandum by Wellesley, 18/1/34, F295/295/61, FO 371/18160.
32. Phipps to Simon, 10/12/33, W14129/40/98, FO 371/17375.
33. Minutes by Orde, 13/12/33, W14129/40/98, FO 371/17375.
34. Chamberlain Papers, letter, 28/7/34.
35. Minute by Vansittart, 14/12/33, W14129/40/98, FO371/17375; 15/12/33, A9235/252/45, FO371/16612.
36. Letter, Hankey to Craigie, 31/1/34, CAB 21/404.
37. Minute by Stanhope, 1/2/34, A1977/1938/45. FO371/17596.
38. Minute by Stanhope, A2176/1938/45, FO371/17596.
39. NCM(35) 1st Meeting, 16/4/34, CAB 29/147.
40. Simon to Lindley, 5/3/34, BD, 2, VI, 604–607.
41. Record of conversation with Davis at Foreign Office, 6/4/34, ibid.
42. Chamberlain Papers, letter, 27/10/34.
43. Record of conversation at Manila, 23/3/34, F3397/107/10, FO371/18098.
44. Lindsay to FO, 31/5/34, A4595/1938/45, FO 371/17697.
45. Simon to Lindsay, 5/3/34, BD, 2, VI, 519–520.
46. Memorandum by Fisher, 19/4/34, NCM(35)3, CAB 29/148.
47. Memorandum by Chatfield, 18/5/34, NCM(35)10, CAB 29/148.
48. Note by Harding, 21/6/34, CAB 21/388.
49. Letter, Craigie to Vansittart, 18/5/34, A4114/1938/45, FO371/17597.
50. Letter, Vansittart to Fisher, undated, c.18/5/34, A4114/1938/45, FO371/17597.
51. Bell, *Chamberlain, Germany and Japan*, ch. 6.
52. CAB 9(34), 14/3/34, CAB 23/78.
53. NCM(35) 7th Meeting, 29/10/34, CAB 29/147.
54. DCM(32), 55th Meeting, 24/7/34, CAB 16/110.
55. NCM(35) 1st Meeting, 16/4/34, CAB 29/147.
56. NCM(35) 3rd Meeting, 19/4/34, CAB 29/147.

57. Chamberlain Papers, Diary, January 1934, cited in Feiling, *The Life of Neville Chamberlain*, p 249.
58. DCM(32) 41st Meeting, 3/5/34, CAB 16/110.
59. DCM(32) 55th Meeting, 24/7/34, CAB 16/110.
60. Chamberlain Papers, letter, 28/7/34.
61. Ibid, letter, 28/7/34.
62. Ibid, diary, 25/3/34.
63. Ibid, letter, 21/10/33.
64. Ibid, letter, 28/10/33.
65. Ibid, diary, 25/3/34.
66. CID 261st Meeting, 9/11/33, CAB 2/6.
67. CAB(34)9, 14/3/34, CAB 23/78.
68. CAB9(34), 14/3/34, CAB 23/78.
69. DCM(32) 51st Meeting, 26/6/34, CAB 16/110.
70. Memorandum, August 1936, Chatfield Papers, in L. Pratt *East of Malta, West of Suez: Britain's Mediterranean Crisis, 1936–39* (Cambridge: Cambridge University Press, 1975), p. 3.
71. Chamberlain Papers, diary, 9/10/34.
72. Bell, *Chamberlain, Germany and Japan*, especially ch. 6.
73. A. Trotter *Britain and East Asia 1933–1937* (London: Cambridge University Press, 1975); A. Trotter, 'Tentative Steps for an Anglo-Japanese Rapprochement in 1934', *Modern Asian Studies*, 8, 1 (1974), pp. 59–83; Neilson, 'Perception and Posture'.
74. Bell, *Chamberlain, Germany and Japan*; Trotter, 'Tentative Steps'; Trotter, *Britain and East Asia*.
75. Diary, 30/10/34, Chamberlain Papers.
76. Minute by Vansittart, 13/9/34, F7186/1938/10, FO 371/17599.
77. CAB 43 (37), 24/9/34, CAB 23/89.
78. Kennedy, *Anglo-American Strategic Relations*.
79. L. Pratt, 'The Anglo-American Naval Conversations on the Far East of January 1938', in *International Affairs*, XLVII (1971), pp. 745–63; I. Hamill, *The Strategic Illusion: The Singapore Strategy and the Defence of Australia and New Zealand, 1919–42* (Singapore: Singapore University Press, 1981) pp. 303–4; Earl of Avon *Facing the Dictators*, pp. 544–6; M.H. Murfett, *Fool-Proof Relations: The Search for Anglo-American Naval Cooperation During the Chamberlain Years, 1937–40* (Singapore: Singapore University Press, 1984).
80. P. Bell, 'The Foreign Office and the 1939 Royal Visit to America: Courting the United States in an Era of Isolationism', *Journal of Contemporary History*, 37, 4 (2002), pp. 599–616.
81. Diary, 19/2/38; Letter, 16/1/38; cited in Feiling, *The Life of Neville Chamberlain*, pp. 322–4.
82. Record of a conversation between Craigie and Davis, 26/11/34, DBFP, Ser. 2, vol. VI, p. 136.

5
Chamberlain, the British Army and the 'Continental Commitment'

G.C. Peden

Field-Marshal Montgomery had no doubt that the British army was totally unfit to fight a first-class war on the continent of Europe in September 1939, and that successive governments in the inter-war period were to blame. He pointed to their belief in the 1930s that Britain's contribution to a future war with Germany should be made mainly through air and sea power, and remarked: 'how any politician could imagine that, in a world war, Britain could avoid sending her army to fight alongside the French passes all understanding.'[1] No politician did more to delay the commitment to send a British expeditionary force to the continent than Neville Chamberlain, who was Chancellor of the Exchequer from 1931 to 1937 and Prime Minister from 1937 to 1940.[2] There was no Ministry of Defence in the 1930s, and policy was laid down by the Cabinet after discussions by ministers in Cabinet committees or in the Committee of Imperial Defence (CID), which brought together ministers and the professional heads of the armed forces (the Chiefs of Staff) and senior civil servants. It was Chamberlain who persuaded the Cabinet in 1934 to give a lower priority to the army than to the Royal Air Force (RAF). It was he who initiated a review of the defence departments' programmes that resulted in a Cabinet decision at the end of 1937 that the army's first priority should be the air defence of Great Britain, and that the expeditionary force, or field force, as it was then known, should be equipped on a scale sufficient only for operations in defence of British territories and interests outside Europe. It was not until February 1939 that he reluctantly agreed that the army must be prepared to fight alongside the French. Sir Michael Howard, in his seminal book, *The Continental Commitment*, describes Chamberlain as 'implacably hostile', prior to that date, to any idea of involvement in Europe.[3] On the other hand, Chamberlain's most recent biographer,

Robert Self, believes that Chamberlain consistently regarded the army as 'an insurance' if the primary deterrent provided by the RAF bombers should fail.[4] This chapter looks first at the evidence for Chamberlain having ever imagined that it would be possible to avoid fighting on land alongside the French in a world war, and then considers briefly the extent of his responsibility for the shortcomings of the British army in France and Belgium in 1939–40.

Both as Chancellor and Prime Minister, Chamberlain thought about the army within the contexts of foreign policy, the economy and public opinion. As David Dilks points out, Chamberlain believed in preparing for the worst while hoping for the best.[5] Defence policy was intended to deter aggression while diplomacy removed potential causes of war; consequently the scale of the armed forces created by rearmament had to be no larger than what the economy could sustain over however long a period might be required to appease Europe. The National Government had been formed to deal with a financial crisis and mass unemployment in 1931, and until early 1939 the Cabinet accepted Treasury arguments about the need to maintain long-term economic stability and therefore the need to make choices regarding priorities in defence expenditure. Prior to 1939 even the Chiefs of Staff advised against military conversations that would lead the French to assume that the British were morally committed to them (as was believed to have been the case in 1914) and which would, therefore, limit Britain's freedom of action to decide what form of intervention she should take if and when war broke out.[6] The issue between Chamberlain and the Chiefs of Staff down to February 1939 was whether and when Britain should have the capability to despatch an expeditionary force.

As regards public opinion, the army had less support in Parliament or the press than the RAF and the navy. For example, in 1934 Stanley Baldwin, the leader of the Conservative party, told ministers considering defence programmes for future years that there were 'semi-panic' conditions regarding the danger of air attack, and they ought also to bear in mind possible activities of the Navy League.[7] No such support was forthcoming for the army. Even Winston Churchill, the leading advocate in Parliament of greater rearmament, was chiefly concerned with the government's failure to fulfil its pledge, first made in 1934, that parity would be maintained with Germany in the air. In July 1936 he advised Baldwin, who was by then Prime Minister, against a repetition of pre-1914 plans to commit the British army to a European campaign, and said that it should be made clear to France and Belgium that they would have to make their own arrangements to defend their frontiers, with any British contribution being additional and dependent upon what Britain was able to do. In March 1938, five days before the German occupation of Austria, Churchill told the House of Commons that 'the army is not at the present time a prime factor in our safety.'[8] It is not surprising that Chamberlain found it easier to persuade his Cabinet colleagues to agree to economies in the army's programmes than in those of the other two services.

The deficiency programme, 1934

Debate on defence priorities began in November 1933 when the Defence Requirements Sub-Committee (DRC) of the CID, comprising the Chiefs of Staff, the Permanent Secretary of the Treasury, the Permanent Under-Secretary of the Foreign Office and the Cabinet Secretary, was asked to prepare a programme for dealing with the worst deficiencies in the armed forces. The DRC reported at the end of February 1934 that immediate steps should be taken to improve Britain's position versus Japan, but that the ultimate potential enemy against whom long-range defence policy must be planned was Germany. In relation to the German menace, the most important deficiency in the army was stated to be the expeditionary force. The DRC identified the independence of Belgium and Holland as a vital interest, especially as regards the air defence of Great Britain. The situation in 1934 was that only single divisions could be despatched in each of the first two months of a war, followed by a third in the fourth month and the remaining two divisions at the end of the sixth month, and the DRC recommended that the regular army should be capable of fielding four infantry divisions, a horsed cavalry division and a tank brigade within one month. The report added that the army's fifth infantry division should not be included in the expeditionary force but should instead be used to provide reserves and help to train the Territorial Army (TA). The TA lacked modern weapons and training was normally limited to 30 evening drills and two weeks' camp each year. During the DRC's discussions, the Chief of the Imperial General Staff (CIGS), Sir Archibald Montgomery-Massingberd, had said that four TA divisions would be needed to support the regular expeditionary force four months after the outbreak of war, but he had not given an estimate of their cost, remarking that 'the full bill for TA requirements would be enormous'.[9]

The CIGS had good reason for being coy. The DRC report gave the cost of making good the army's deficiencies as £36.23 million spread over five years (in addition to the 1933/4 level of expenditure). Of this figure,

£25.68 million was for the capital cost of the expeditionary force and only £1.25 million was for the TA.[10] Major Henry Pownall of the CID secretariat thought that to produce an expeditionary force and prepare the TA properly would require £145 million over five years, a figure that he described as 'impossible... and dangerous too', for if ministers were presented with it they might decide that the army was too expensive and that the RAF would give better value for money.[11] Even after the omission of almost all of the potential cost of the TA, the army's share of the deficiency programme drawn up by the DRC was 40 per cent, compared with 13.5 per cent for the RAF.

Chamberlain's principal adviser at the Treasury was Sir Warren Fisher, the Permanent Secretary. Participation in the DRC's discussions had made Fisher aware that the deficiencies programme did not include the full cost of the TA, and that the reason why the army's programme for anti-aircraft guns and searchlights was spread over eight years, instead of the five-year period of the rest of the deficiency programme, was the CIGS's fear that the additional money required to complete air defence programme in five years would be found at the expense of the expeditionary force.[12] Fisher consulted Lord Trenchard, the former Chief of Air Staff (CAS), to whom he sent a copy of the DRC report. Trenchard's advice was that the items in the first order of priority included anti-aircraft guns and searchlights for England south of the Wash; an increase in the RAF based in Britain to 100 squadrons (compared with the 52 recommended by the DRC); and what Trenchard called 'the "spearhead" expeditionary force for securing continental air bases', but of these three items the first two were the most urgent.[13] Trenchard believed that two-thirds of the RAF's squadrons should be bombers, but the bombers in service in 1934 lacked the range to attack Germany effectively from British bases. What he was advocating was that the army should act as an auxiliary to the RAF, and presumably this advice reached Chamberlain via Fisher.

Nevertheless, when the army's programme was first discussed in the Cabinet's Disarmament Committee on 3 May, Chamberlain made no mention of this auxiliary role for the army. Instead he challenged the need for another British expeditionary force along the lines of 1914, when four regular divisions of infantry and one of cavalry had been sent to France within 12 days, followed by a further two regular infantry divisions about a month later. He argued that the strength of the French frontier defences and the nature of trench warfare would make it impossible for the German army to make progress, whereas the German air force could fly over the French defences. In these circumstances, he claimed, the best contributions that Britain could make to the defence of the west would be air power and sea power. When the Secretary of State for War, Viscount Hailsham, responded that a British expeditionary force was required to deny the Germans air and submarine bases in Belgium and Holland, Chamberlain asked whether a British force could reach these countries in time to prevent them being over-run. Rather than send troops, could Britain not instead finance the frontier defences that Belgium had planned but not yet built? Would the French be content with an air contribution from Britain?[14] Robert Self is unwilling to accept my suggestion that on this occasion Chamberlain was probably acting as the devil's advocate rather than expressing his own fixed opinions.[15] However, a literal reading of Chamberlain's arguments and questions about the need for *any* expeditionary force would seem to support Howard's belief that he was implacably hostile to a continental commitment, rather than Self's belief that he saw the army as an insurance should deterrence fail. In fact Chamberlain's role as Chancellor was to challenge proponents of a large-scale and, in the case of the TA, indefinite expenditure to prove their case.

When ministers resumed their discussion on 10 May Chamberlain admitted that he had previously misunderstood the proposal regarding the expeditionary force. He now realised that it was not proposed to create an expeditionary force out of something that did not exist, but rather to prepare the army's existing field force to act as an expeditionary force. He was still not convinced that Germany would be prepared to go to war in 1939, or that it would be necessary to have an expeditionary force ready by that date to go to Belgium and Holland within a month. Ministers agreed with Chamberlain that the Chiefs of Staff should be asked to consider whether the Germans could be prevented from making air attacks on Britain from continental air bases if the RAF was superior to the German air force. In reply the Chiefs of Staff advised that the successful defence of Belgium and Holland was the best means of mitigating air attacks on London, but on 15 May Chamberlain said he remained unconvinced that it would be possible to transport land forces from Britain in time to prevent the Germans overrunning Belgium. He was prepared to accept in principle the DRC's recommendation on modernising the army, but he had reservations on how much of it should ready to go overseas at any given moment, and how quickly it should be re-equipped.[16]

On 20 June Chamberlain produced what he described as his personal conclusions based on the discussions in the Disarmament Committee, financial limitations, and the probable reactions of public opinion. Since he did not believe that the public would agree to pay for the whole of the deficiencies programme, he urged that priority should be given to preparations against Germany rather than those against Japan. He therefore proposed to cut the navy's programme, much of which was intended for the defence of Britain's territories and interests in the Far East. As regards the German threat, the committee's discussions had, he said, brought out 'two salient facts': first, the danger of air attack; second, the exclusion of Germany from Belgium and Holland was essential to Britain's security. The best defence policy would be to create a deterrent, which he defined as an air force based in Britain 'of a size and efficiency calculated to inspire respect'. Should that deterrent fail, Britain's defences would take the form partly of the enlarged RAF, partly in the completion of anti-aircraft defences, and 'finally' in the 'conversion of the army into an effectively equipped force capable of operating with allies in holding the Low Countries'. These second thoughts, in contrast to the views expressed in May, do support Self's belief that Chamberlain saw the army as an insurance policy. In order to build up a deterrent, the Chancellor proposed that the RAF should have more money than had been allotted to it by the DRC, but that the army's deficiencies programme should be spread over a longer period than five years.[17]

Ministers were too concerned about the threat from Japan to accept Chamberlain's cut in navy's programme, but after some debate they increased funding for the RAF by more than he had proposed. As regards the army, Hailsham pointed out that Chamberlain had reached a figure of £19.1 million for the five financial years 1934/5 to 1938/9 by including in his calculation the DRC's proposals for anti-aircraft defence and coastal defences for the naval base at Singapore, but only a small residuum for the expeditionary force. Chamberlain argued that some kind of arbitrary cut was necessary on financial grounds, and that only the time scale of the army's deficiencies programme was being altered, with most of the expenditure being delayed until after 1938/9.[18] Hailsham gained little support from his colleagues, who agreed with Chamberlain that the public would not favour expenditure on the army, and on 31 July the committee merely rounded up the army's allocation for the five years to 1938/9 from £19.1 million to £20 million.[19] The Chancellor was doubtless content as regards the RAF and army since, as he had told his sister Hilda on 1 July, he had pitched his proposals 'on purpose a little high'.[20]

The debate on the deficiencies programme well illustrates Chamberlain's style within government. He pushed the Chiefs of Staff hard to ensure that they had really thought out strategic issues rather than merely come to a harmonious agreement on the basis of existing allocations of funds between them. He did not simply take the advice he received from Trenchard via Fisher, but ultimately, in the light of discussion in the Disarmament Committee, accepted that an expeditionary force would be necessary if war came. As he told his sister, 'we shall be more likely to deter Germany from mad dogging if we have an air force which in case of need could bomb the Ruhr from Belgium.'[21] The delay imposed on the army's programme also reflected Chamberlain's belief in 1934 that Germany would not be ready to attack in the west within five years.

The rearmament programme, 1936

There was growing evidence in late 1934 of German rearmament. Following intelligence reports early in 1935 on the scale of German borrowing, and on Fisher's suggestion, the Treasury agreed in principle to a defence loan to supplement revenue from taxation. Thereafter the ability of industry to fulfil defence contracts, and the effects of rearmament on the economy, rather than the Chancellor's annual budget, determined the pace of the departments' programmes. The Cabinet agreed that rearmament should not interfere with normal trade, and it was only after the German occupation of Austria in March 1938 that this condition was relaxed to any great extent. Detailed Treasury control of expenditure continued to be used to enforce priorities as between departments: in particular, the RAF had first call on new industrial capacity; and the army's expeditionary force had the lowest priority until 1939.[22]

In July 1935 the DRC was authorised by ministers to work out a rearmament programme on the assumption that by April 1939 each armed service should be as ready as possible 'in relation to the needs of national defence and within the limits of practicality'. Despite warnings from the Permanent Under-Secretary of the Foreign Office, Sir Robert Vansittart, the Chiefs of Staff were not disposed to think that war was likely in 1939. Montgomery-Massingberd estimated that the Germans would still be inferior in numbers on land to the combined French and Belgian armies in 1939, and he thought that if the Germans decided to go to war before 1942 they would be taking a bigger risk than they had done in 1914. The main differences between the army's proposals in 1935 compared with 1934 were the inclusion of the TA's 12 infantry divisions to reinforce the regular expeditionary force, and the mechanization of the cavalry division, which was to be combined with the tank brigade in a new mobile division (renamed 1st Armoured Division in April 1939). In a discussion on air defence on 3 October Montgomery-Massingberd admitted that the TA units that would operate the anti-aircraft guns and search lights were 'in a bad way', but the army's contribution to the air defence of Great Britain was only 'to be in sight of completion' in five years. According to the Master-General of the Ordnance – the officer in charge of the army's equipment – the army's deficiency programme as a whole was too big to be completed in three years with existing industrial capacity.[23]

In the DRC's proposed programme submitted to the Cabinet on 21 November more money was allocated to the army than to the RAF (see Table 5.1). However, ministers, led by Chamberlain, were much more concerned about air defence, and army expenditure rose more slowly than the RAF's (see Table 5.2). As in 1934, Chamberlain was a

Table 5.1 Army's and RAF's shares of DRC programme of 21 November 1935

Financial year	Army		RAF	
	£000s	%	£000s	%
1936/7	54,000	31.1	45,000	25.9
1937/8	62,000	29.4	60,000	28.4
1938/9	72,000	31.8	64,000	28.2
1939/40	72,000	33.9	50,000	23.5
1940/1	82,000	39.2	44,000	21.0

Source: DRC 37, CAB 16/112.

Table 5.2 Army's and RAF's shares of actual defence expenditure

Financial year	Army		RAF	
	£000s	%	£000s	%
1935/6	44,647	32.6	27,496	20.1
1936/7	54,846	29.5	50,134	26.9
1937/8	77,877	29.7	82,290	31.4
1938/9	121,361	31.7	133,800	35.0
1939/40	242,438	33.7	294,834	41.0

Sources: Cmd 6232, Parl. Papers 1939–40, x, 367, and (for 1939/40 only) Robert P. Shay, *British Rearmament in the Thirties* (Princeton, NJ: Princeton University Press, 1977), p. 297.

member of the Cabinet committee – the Defence Policy and Requirements Committee (DPRC) – which considered the DRC report. He had a powerful ally in his friend Lord Weir, the businessman and former Secretary of State for Air, who was advising the government on how best to secure industrial capacity for rearmament, and who was a full member of the DPRC. Weir warned at the committee's first meeting on 13 January 1936 that the programme recommended by the DRC could not be carried out on schedule without imposing on industry controls of a nature that he (and ministers) believed would be unacceptable except in wartime. However, he did not limit himself to his industrial brief. He argued that the army was the most expensive and least effective way of helping allies, and that it would take longer for an expeditionary force than the RAF to reach the scene of action.[24] Weir was evidently influenced by Basil Liddell Hart's articles in *The Times*, which had suggested that the offensive role of an expeditionary force should be entrusted to the RAF.[25]

Chamberlain's arguments and the responses to them in the DPRC in January 1936 followed similar lines to the discussions in the Disarmament Committee in 1934. He now believed that the Germans had already established a lead in rearmament and that it would take a long time for the British to catch up. He thought it was vitally important to find a deterrent, and that the threat of an air offensive would perhaps be a more effective deterrent to German aggression than defensive action on the part of land forces. He was prepared to accept that the army could not be left in its present condition, and that the TA must be revived, but the army's programme made the heaviest demands on industry. If it were decided to concentrate on the RAF's bomber force, it might be possible to reduce these demands. The Secretary of State for War, now Duff Cooper, circulated a memorandum by Montgomery-Massingberd which argued that Germany's superior industrial organisation meant that Britain was bound to lose an air armaments race, and that the vulnerability of London to air attack placed Britain at a disadvantage in air warfare. European nations, the CIGS believed, were primarily interested in land warfare, and a failure to send an expeditionary force would be interpreted by France and Belgium as tantamount to abandoning them to their fate. Most ministers, however, were primarily interested in reports that German aircraft output was greater than British output, and were disposed therefore to give the RAF priority. Duff Cooper successfully resisted a suggestion (whether by Chamberlain or Weir is not clear) that the size of the expeditionary force should be reduced. Instead, on 16 January, he accepted a compromise put forward by Baldwin whereby the War Office would be authorised to bring the regular units of the expeditionary force to as high a level of efficiency as possible within five years, and to provide the TA with modern equipment, but no war reserves, pending a review three years hence or whenever the industrial position had changed. Duff Cooper tried, but failed, to persuade the committee to take a decision in principle on the continental role of the TA infantry divisions; that question was reserved for later decision.[26]

Chamberlain was not prepared to wait. On 19 October 1936 he told Sir Thomas Inskip, who had been appointed Minister for Co-ordination of Defence in March, that there must be an early decision on the future of the army, and what he (Chamberlain) thought the decision should be. At this stage Chamberlain still believed that the RAF's bomber force could provide the 'most formidable deterrent to war', but he also spoke in public of having an army which, although 'trifling in numbers beside the vast conscript armies' of Europe, would be 'equipped with the most modern weapons and mechanical devices that science can give us'.[27] This force would comprise four infantry divisions and one mobile division of the regular army, with the necessary drafts to maintain its strength. Chamberlain believed that this was all that Britain could provide for a European war if it came, since there would not be enough manpower to produce all the munitions required for a million-man army. He was aware that Britain and her allies had come to rely upon imports of munitions from the United States in 1914–18 and that American isolationism made such imports doubtful in future. In these circumstances, the role of the TA, he thought, should be confined to anti-aircraft and home defence.[28]

These ideas were very much Chamberlain's own. Indeed, after hearing them, Fisher produced a memorandum on 23 October which was both a defence of the DRC's recommendation that the 12 TA infantry divisions should be properly equipped and a claim that 17 divisions (the regulars plus the TA), or about 600,000 men, should be Britain's maximum commitment for war on the European continent. Fisher believed that the British people would never again consent to be conscripted by the million for service in the trenches, and that, even if they were, air power would be a better use of resources. He tried to win the support of the Cabinet Secretary, Sir Maurice Hankey, for these views, but Hankey replied that, if at a future date the German army had six million men and the French only two million, the British would have to mobilise their millions, for the Germans would never allow Britain to achieve decisive air superiority.[29] Hankey's views were important because Inskip lacked a department of his own and relied on Hankey for advice.

Inskip took up Chamberlain's idea that the expeditionary force should be limited to five divisions with the CIGS, now Sir Cyril Deverell, and Vansittart. Vansittart believed that diplomacy could secure some easement of American neutrality legislation, so that the difficulty of maintaining in the field an army of half a million to one million was not as great as Chamberlain believed. Deverell said that Britain could not enter a European war with any limitation of liability. Inskip took the view that he was not in a position to controvert these expert opinions and told Chamberlain on 5 November that the size of the army in war could not be determined in advance.[30]

Inskip was also coming under pressure from Duff Cooper for a decision on the role of the army, since the Treasury used the fact that the Cabinet had not approved the DRC's recommendations for the TA's infantry divisions as a reason for holding up any plans for industrial capacity beyond what was required for the regular army. Inskip agreed that an early decision was necessary for the efficient planning and execution of the rearmament programme and he encouraged Duff Cooper to make his case in Cabinet.[31] While the Secretary of State for War was still preparing his Cabinet paper on the role of the army, Chamberlain consulted Fisher on what seemed to the Chancellor to be two separate questions. First, should the War Office proceed with the DRC plan to prepare to send 17 divisions to Europe on or within a limited time after the outbreak of war? – to which Fisher replied: 'As an *ultimate* policy I think yes.' Second, should resources be used to equip the TA rather than in strengthening the RAF? – to which Fisher replied: 'No. Air strength should be an *absolute priority*, accompanied by naval development.'[32] On this view, what could be done about the army would depend upon Britain's progress compared with Germany's in air rearmament.

Duff Cooper's paper on 3 December argued that war could not be fought on the principle of limited liability, and that the maximum effort should be made with the minimum delay. It followed, he claimed, that the TA should be available to support the expeditionary force as soon as possible after the outbreak of war, and that a start should be made in placing orders and expanding industrial capacity to enable at least part of the TA to be ready within two years.[33] In Cabinet discussion on 9 December Inskip gave Duff Cooper support from the point of view of the need to let the army's contractors know the scale of orders they should prepare for, but Chamberlain told Inskip that as Minister for Co-ordination of Defence he had a responsibility for strategy as well as supply, and that he (Chamberlain) doubted the wisdom of equipping the TA for the trenches.[34] In a Cabinet paper of 11 December, replying to Duff Cooper, Chamberlain denied that he was suggesting that war could be made on the principle of limited liability; but he also pointed out that resources were not unlimited and that choices would have to be made as to the best use of air, sea and land power at the outbreak of war. What readjustment of the national effort would be required during a war would depend upon circumstances that could not be foreseen. Although the Cabinet, in approving the rearmament programme, had agreed that there should be no interference with normal trade, there were already signs that industry was being diverted from exports to rearmament, and overseas markets once lost would not easily be recovered. Any substantial addition to the programme approved by the Cabinet in February would, he believed, lead to a breakdown of the whole scheme. He submitted that, before a decision was taken on TA contingents for the expeditionary force, the alternative use of resources by the RAF, the navy and the TA units responsible for air defence should be surveyed by 'the competent authorities'.[35] The Cabinet decided on 16 December that Inskip should conduct an inquiry into the role of the army after consultation with the three Chiefs of Staff, but Chamberlain told Inskip that he doubted if the Chiefs of Staff alone were sufficient for the task, and asked him to consider including in the inquiry someone who could put the point of view which he had urged. Hankey's tart comment was that if someone was to put Chamberlain's point of view it would have to be the Chancellor himself for he (Hankey) knew of no one else who shared it with sufficient conviction to put it forward.[36]

In fact Chamberlain was not alone in his views. The head of the Treasury's division dealing with defence expenditure, Edward Bridges, sent the Chancellor a note before the Cabinet meeting of 16 December saying that he personally could conceive of the Treasury agreeing to a small but highly effective and modern expeditionary force limited to the five regular divisions, but not a larger force including several TA divisions equipped to the same standard as the regulars. Bridges, who had served as an infantry officer on the Western Front from 1915 to 1917, pointed out that the War Office had not explained how the part-time soldiers in TA divisions could be trained in peace-time up to the necessary level of efficiency so as to be available for service in Europe on, or soon after, the outbreak of war. He himself doubted if that were possible, given the greater complexity of military equipment compared with 1914.[37]

The Chiefs of Staff's report on 28 January 1937 on the role of the army said that it would take four months' intensive training after the outbreak of war before the TA would be fit for service overseas. The only land forces available immediately would be the five regular divisions, all of which could be landed on the Continent within 15 days. While they might not arrive in time to take part in the initial fighting, their moral and material effect might prove to be of great importance for potential allies. Experience in 1914 had shown the need for reinforcements, which could only come from the 12 TA infantry divisions, some of which might also be required for imperial defence against first-rate military powers (Japan, Russia and Italy were mentioned). The Chiefs of Staff therefore recommended that the ultimate aim should be to equip the TA on a scale that would enable it to be ready to proceed overseas four months after the outbreak of war, and that industrial capacity available to the War Office should be increased.[38] Hankey drafted a letter for Inskip to send on 1 February to Chamberlain in which it was pointed out that the Chiefs of Staff recognised that the development of the RAF, the mechanisation of the army, and the uncertainty of the availability of supplies from the United States ruled out an army on the same size as in the last war, some 70 divisions. On the other hand, the letter noted, European countries attached great importance to armies, and the Chiefs of Staff believed that Britain must be able to send an expeditionary force to support France and Belgium in a war with Germany as soon as circumstances permitted. While Trenchard had said that a stronger air force would make it possible to limit the expeditionary force to the regular divisions, Hankey thought it was impossible for ministers to prefer the former CAS's views to those of their official advisers. He added that the evidence of recent warfare in China, Abyssinia and Spain did not suggest that air power alone could be decisive against infantry in defensive positions. Through Inskip, he warned: 'It would be a terrible responsibility, after the experience of the late war, if we had to send an ill equipped army or were unable to sustain it with war material, or to reinforce it within a reasonable time.'[39]

On 3 February the Cabinet adopted Inskip's suggestion that the regular army and the TA's two anti-aircraft divisions should be provided with the most modern and complete equipment, and the rest of the TA should receive enough equipment for training purposes, which would be the equivalent of equipment for two divisions. Chamberlain, however, insisted on knowing the cost, which the War Office was not able to provide until April. When the Cabinet met on 28 April Chamberlain pointed to the rising cost of rearmament as all three services added to their original programmes. In the army's case, the figure in the DRC Report of February 1934 had been £146 million, which the Cabinet had cut down to £100 million; by December 1936 it was £177 million, and now it was over £204 million (excluding the 12

TA divisions). The War Office was now asking for £9 million for training equipment for the TA and a further £33 million for equipment and war reserves for four TA infantry divisions. It was this last item which the Cabinet cut at a further meeting on 5 May. Chamberlain said he was challenging the advice of the military advisers because the matter was not purely military: the country was being asked to increase the size of the navy and RAF, as well as an army for use on the Continent. He believed that if Britain had to fight it would be with allies who had in any case to maintain large armies, and the British contribution on land should be on a limited scale. At his suggestion, the Cabinet remitted the question of the role of the army to one of its committees, the Defence Plans (Policy) Committee, which was already considering proposals for a new standard of naval strength.[40]

The Inskip Report, 1937

Chamberlain became prime minister on 28 May 1937, greatly strengthening his influence over defence policy. In the concluding weeks of his chancellorship Treasury officials had already begun a study of how to re-impose financial control over defence expenditure. On 30 June the Cabinet agreed to a proposal put forward by the new Chancellor, Sir John Simon, that the defence departments should work out how long it would take to complete their approved programmes; what their annual expenditure would be over that period, taking account of the rising trend of prices; and what their normal expenditure would be once rearmament was complete. In the light of the figures produced, ministers would fix maximum limits to each department's expenditure. Meanwhile decisions on major additions to the approved programmes were to be postponed.[41] Consequently, when Leslie Hore-Belisha, whom Chamberlain had appointed as Secretary of State for War in place of the intransigent Duff Cooper, submitted a plan to the Defence Plans (Policy) Committee on 13 July for new equipment for four TA infantry divisions, Simon was able to point out that a proposal which would increase expenditure on the army from £204 million to £250 million was not consistent with the Cabinet's decision a fortnight earlier. At Chamberlain's suggestion the committee deferred a decision until the review of all the defence programmes was complete, but agreed that the four TA divisions should be included in plans for the allocation of industrial capacity.[42]

Hore-Belisha looked to Liddell Hart for alternative advice to what he was receiving from the CIGS (Deverell) and other members of the Army

Council. Liddell Hart believed that modern weapon developments had increased the superiority of defence over attack in land warfare, and that an expeditionary force made up mainly of infantry divisions would be drawn into offensive operations, in which they would have little effect. What were required, he said, were one or two mechanised (armoured) divisions.[43] It would seem to have been preconceptions arising from this advice that led Hore-Belisha, following a visit to the French manoeuvres in September 1937, to tell the Cabinet that in the event of war the French wanted the British to send two mechanised divisions rather than a large number of infantry divisions. Hore-Belisha's understanding was that France's frontier defences (the Maginot Line) could be held by a garrison of 100,000 men, releasing the bulk of the French army for mobile operations. Chamberlain thanked Hore-Belisha for this statement, but the latter had almost certainly misunderstood what he had heard in France, his French not being good enough for military conversations.[44] According to Inskip, no one in the Cabinet believed Hore-Belisha's report to be well founded.[45]

Chamberlain too was impressed by Liddell Hart's ideas. On 29 October he told Hore-Belisha that he had been reading Liddell Hart's book, *Europe in Arms*, and recommended the chapter on the role of the British army. Hore-Belisha replied two days later that he had immediately read the chapter and was impressed by Liddell Hart's theories.[46] In *Europe in Arms* Liddell Hart argued that Britain should give up the idea of sending an expeditionary force to France or Belgium and should develop an air force that could intervene from British bases at the outbreak of war. 'The promise of such help', he wrote, 'would be more comfort to a threatened neighbour, and more deterrent to a would-be aggressor, than any force of the 1914 pattern – a mere drop in the bucket of a Continental struggle between mass armies'.[47] Inskip thought that Chamberlain had been 'bitten' by Liddell Hart and described the Prime Minister as 'a bitter opponent' of a continental role for the army.[48] That may be so, but Chamberlain did not dictate what the role of the army should be; he left the task of making recommendations on defence policy to the responsible minister, Inskip.

By 27 October the Cabinet had the revised figures for the cost of rearmament. On the basis of approved programmes, estimated defence expenditure over the five financial years 1937/8 to 1941/2 would be £1,470 million, but if additions which the Admiralty and Air Ministry wanted were included, the total would be £1,717 million.[49] The Treasury had calculated that the money available over the period, on the existing basis of taxation and within the level of borrowing authorised by the Defence Loans Act of 1937, would be £1,500 million. The Cabinet decided to refer the problem of reconciling these figures to Inskip, who was advised by senior officials, including Hankey and Bridges. Inskip and Hankey accepted the Treasury's argument that maintenance of the country's economic stability was a 'fourth arm' of defence, which would confront an aggressor with the prospect of a long war in which, as the Chiefs of Staff had advised earlier in the year, Britain and France, with their naval power, were likely to have the advantage.[50] On 23 November Hankey suggested to Inskip that the order of priorities for defence policy should be: (1) security of the United Kingdom; (2) safeguarding of sea communications; (3) defence of British territory overseas; (4) co-operation in defence of any allies Britain might have in war. The expeditionary force required such large resources of ammunition and stores for its continental role that he would in any case have been compelled, if reluctantly, to recommend that the Cabinet should place it low in the order of priority. Hankey then claimed that events had occurred that justified a change in policy. First, (echoing Hore-Belisha) he said that France no longer looked to Britain to provide an expeditionary force on the scale hitherto proposed. Second, the German government had guaranteed the neutrality of Belgium, and the vulnerability of the Ruhr to attack across Belgian territory suggested that the Germans had sound motives for not violating the guarantee. Third, the increasing cost of aircraft made it more difficult to provide a large army as well. Fourth, the Empire might absorb the whole of Britain's military forces in a major war.[51] (In 1914 there had been no Italian danger to Egypt; Japan had been an ally; and there had been no commitment comparable to Palestine, where at the end of 1937 three brigades were deployed to maintain British authority.)

Hankey's suggestions formed the basis of Inskip's interim report on defence expenditure in future years which was presented to the Cabinet on 22 December. Inskip recommended that provision for co-operation in defence of the territories of allies should only be made once the first three priorities of protecting the United Kingdom and its trade routes, and British overseas territories had been met. The primary roles of the regular army were now to be the air defence of Great Britain and the defence of the Empire. The latter role would still require modern armaments, but not the scale of reserves of munitions or the industrial capacity necessary for taking part in European warfare from the outbreak of war. Inskip made clear that he made this recommendation with reluctance and asked his Cabinet colleagues to share responsibility for it with their eyes open:

> If France were again to be in danger of being overrun by land armies, a situation might arise when, as in the last war, we had to improvise an army to assist her. Should this happen, the Government of the day would most certainly be criticised for having neglected to provide against so obvious a contingency.[52]

The Cabinet nevertheless accepted his proposals.

Inskip produced a second report in February 1938, making financial allocations between the departments and spelling out the implications for their programmes. Previously it had been planned that the regular army would be able to disembark on the Continent four infantry divisions and one mobile division within 15 days of mobilisation. Now it was proposed to have two infantry divisions and one mobile division with full reserves of munitions, ready to complete disembarkation within 21 days, and two infantry divisions with war equipment but only half scales of reserves of munitions, ready to begin embarkation in 40 days. The army also wanted to have a pool of equipment to enable either two TA divisions or two further regular divisions to take the field after four months. It was assumed that this force would be called upon to operate in an 'Eastern' theatre, with the defence of Egypt the most likely commitment, and substantial reductions were made in planned provision of tanks and reserves of ammunition compared with a European campaign.[53] In a separate paper on the army Hore-Belisha remarked that the expeditionary force should be despatched to Europe only if the situation in the rest of the world permitted.[54] Howard comments that 'what was generally termed a policy of "limited liability" in continental warfare had now shrunk to one of no liability at all.'[55]

The Inskip report did not in fact preclude a continental commitment at some future date. When briefing the Chancellor for a discussion in the CID of Hore-Belisha's proposals, Bridges commented: 'it now appears... that the reserves of ammunition for [the first three] divisions would, as it so happens, be to all intents on a Continental scale! This is what we always suspected and feared, namely that the War Office... are still, in effect, clinging to an Army capable of fighting in the Continental role.'[56] At the CID meeting on 17 March Hore-Belisha urged that, notwithstanding the priority for air defence, the War Office should be allowed to place orders for field guns and howitzers as well as anti-aircraft guns. Chamberlain asked for information and the CIGS, now Lord Gort, explained that the field guns were of a 1905 pattern and the howitzers were also outranged by foreign artillery. The CID therefore agreed that the War Office could allocate new capacity for gun production to the requirements of the expeditionary force. It was also agreed that the War Office could accumulate reserves and allocate industrial capacity in peace time to enable the seven divisions to be sent abroad at the dates specified in Hore-Belisha's paper, the reserves being adequate for defensive warfare in Europe.[57]

In terms of Self's analogy of Chamberlain seeing the army as an insurance if deterrence should fail, it could be said that the premium was reduced in 1937 so that it was uncertain if and when the expeditionary force would be available for continental service. Moreover, the nature of Britain's deterrent had changed. British aircraft production was lagging behind that of Germany and the Inskip Report marked the beginning of a greater emphasis on fighter aircraft rather than a bomber deterrent. Deterrence now meant facing Germany with the prospect of a long war in which British economic stability and naval blockade would be decisive. To make such a deterrent credible, the United Kingdom had to be proof against a 'knock-out' blow from the *Luftwaffe*. Only once Britain's air defences, including the army's anti-aircraft guns and search lights, were in better shape than they were in 1937, or indeed throughout 1938, was priority likely to be given to preparing the expeditionary force to fight alongside the French.

Continental commitment, 1939

The French had good reason to be disappointed by the news in February 1938 that the largest force that the British could send to their aid would be two incomplete infantry divisions (the mobile division was still being formed). The French Chief of the General Staff General Maurice Gamelin reported in April that he had only 80 of the 88 divisions required simply to defend France's frontiers against the 92 that Germany could rapidly deploy against her, and account had also to be taken of the Italian army.[58] With the loss of the Czech army after Munich the balance of power swung further in favour of the Axis powers and French pressure for a greater effort on land by Britain became insistent. The Chiefs of Staff warned in December 1938 that Britain's very existence would be threatened if the Germans established air and naval bases in Holland, Belgium and Northern France, which they were in a position to do. Intelligence reports at the beginning of 1939 that Germany might occupy

Holland alarmed British ministers. Pownall, now Director of Military Operations and Intelligence at the War Office, noted in his diary on 23 January: 'The French know we regard the Low Countries as vital to our security and they are using that as a lever to put a bit of ginger into us. More power to them!'[59]

Inskip's second report in February 1938 had said that there should be a further enquiry in 1939 as to whether, in the light of the international situation, higher defence expenditure should be authorised. By January 1939 it was clear that Munich had not brought about the improvement in Anglo-German relations for which Chamberlain had hoped. On 25 January 1939 the Foreign Secretary, Lord Halifax, told the Cabinet that Germany's economic problems arising from rearmament were such that it seemed likely that within the next 12 months Hitler would have to go to war to secure the vast supplies of raw materials that Germany could no longer pay for by exports.[60] In these circumstances Chamberlain and Simon were the only ministers who attached much importance to maintaining long-term economic stability as a fourth arm of defence. When Hore-Belisha presented the case in Cabinet on 2 February 1939 for equipping the army for service in Europe, Chamberlain still hoped that the French could be persuaded that it would be in the common interest that Britain should not attempt to expand her land forces in addition to the 'gigantic effort' she was making in the air and at sea. He insisted that Inskip's successor as Minister for the Co-ordination of Defence, Lord Chatfield, should have time to consider Hore-Belisha's proposal for the expeditionary force alongside War Office plans for increased expenditure on air defence. However, by 22 February the Prime Minister had been persuaded, reluctantly, that most of Hore-Belisha's proposals, which were supported by the Chiefs of Staff, should be accepted. Thus the mobile division was to be organised into two smaller divisions; the equipment and reserves of four regular infantry divisions were to be brought up to the scale required for continental warfare, with the first two being ready to embark in 21 days after mobilisation and the second two after 60 days; and four TA divisions were similarly to be made ready to embark six months after the outbreak of war, with the remaining eight or nine TA infantry divisions receiving training equipment. Although these measures would add £67 million to the cost of the army, Chamberlain accepted that there was no alternative, given the feeling in France that Britain must make some contribution on land.[61] Nevertheless, apart from the reorganisation of the mobile division, the size of that contribution would be no greater than what the DRC had proposed in 1935.

Then on 28 March, 13 days after the German seizure of the rump of Czechoslovakia, and the day before Anglo-French staff talks were due to begin, Chamberlain suddenly altered the whole scale of British military planning. He was due to address the 1922 Committee that evening and he wished to say something about how the recent increase in the number of men wishing to join the TA was to be utilised. There had been reports that volunteers were being turned away because the units in which they wished to enlist were up to establishment. Sir Horace Wilson, Chamberlain's confidential adviser, wrote to Hore-Belisha asking if men could be enrolled and given some training, even if, for the time being, equipment was not available for them. Hore-Belisha saw the Prime Minister in the afternoon and, when told that some action was required to show that Britain was determined to resist aggression, suggested doubling the TA. Chamberlain was anxious to have an announcement made in the next 24 hours, and Hore-Belisha called a meeting of the Army Council so that a plan could be presented to the Cabinet the next day. Within hours Treasury officials were astonished to learn that it was proposed to increase the existing establishment of the TA of 130,000 to its war strength of 170,000, and then to double it to 340,000 by duplicating every unit. Sir Alan Barlow remarked that since the immediate military value of such a force would be nil, the effect of the proposed announcement would be likely to make Hitler think he would be better to strike at once. Sir Richard Hopkins remarked that the proposal was unrelated to any strategic plan.[62] Even so, at the Cabinet meeting the next day the Chancellor of the Exchequer, Simon, agreed with Halifax that the need to impress public opinion at home and abroad was more important than the financial aspects (capital cost £80 million to £100 million).[63] The only echo of limited liability was that Chamberlain told Chatfield that Britain's freedom to decide the destination of the 26-division TA should be emphasised in staff talks with the French in April.[64]

The creation of a Ministry of Supply to deal with the greatly enlarged requirements on the army followed on 20 April. The introduction of conscription was delayed until 26 April only because Chamberlain feared to alienate the trade union movement at a time when it was being co-operative over changes in industrial practices required to expedite rearmament. Chamberlain explained this breach of earlier pledges not to introduce conscription in peacetime by saying that, although Britain was not in a state of war, international conditions could not be described as peacetime in any normal sense of the word.[65] However, Chamberlain still hoped to avoid war and his purpose in increasing the size of the army was to deter Germany, not to prepare for war in September 1939.

Conclusion and consequences

Was Chamberlain a politician who, in Montgomery's words, imagined that Britain could avoid sending her army to fight alongside the French in a world war? Was he implacably hostile to the idea, as Howard believes, or did he consistently regard the expeditionary force as insurance should deterrence fail, as Self claims? In answering these questions it is important to distinguish between the role of the army at the outbreak of war and what might happen later. Chamberlain focused on what could be done to deter Germany, and to prevent defeat in the early stages of a war if deterrence failed, rather than on what might happen in a prolonged war. Thus in 1934 Chamberlain wanted priority to be given to the RAF's bombers, but he accepted that a small, well-equipped army had a role to play in securing continental air bases. With Inskip's report of December 1937 deterrence changed to take the form of ability to outlast Germany in a long war. The prospect of the army being able to fight alongside the French at the outbreak of war was delayed sine die until Britain's air defences, trade routes and overseas possessions were secure. Even in 1938, however, Chamberlain agreed that the expeditionary force must be able to fight the army of a first-class power, and the difference between a force equipped for continental warfare and one equipped for imperial defence lay mainly in the reserves of munitions required for what was assumed to be more intensive fighting in Western Europe than in Egypt or elsewhere. The decisions in early 1939 first to prepare the regular army to fight in Western Europe at the outbreak of war, and then to double the size of the TA, threatened the stability of the economy and represented a new kind of deterrence designed for a period of about 12 months. In short, Montgomery's and Howard's criticisms contain an element of truth, but seem to exaggerate the consistency of Chamberlain's opposition to a continental commitment. Self likewise exaggerates Chamberlain's consistency in regarding the army as insurance at the outbreak of war; Chamberlain was flexible in his views as he responded to changes in the international situation, the economy and public opinion.

It is hard not to sympathise with Montgomery, who, as a divisional commander in the British Expeditionary Force in 1939–40, saw its deficiencies at first hand, and who heard from Chamberlain's own lips the latter's belief as late as December 1939 that the Germans had no intention of attacking.[66] The army paid a high price for political decisions to hold back its rearmament until air defence and sea routes had been made secure, and then to increase its size as a vain attempt at deterrence. Lack of up-to-date equipment made realistic training difficult even for the regular army. The enlarged TA of 1939 was short of equipment and instructors for its raw recruits and there was little time in which units could learn to work together. Even so, hasty and incomplete rearmament was not peculiar to the British army. In April 1939 the German army faced similar problems: 34 of its divisions were only half equipped; reserve units had only 10 per cent of their rifles and machine guns; and the total amount of ammunition was estimated to be sufficient for only 15 days' fighting.[67] What the German army had and the British army lacked was effective armoured divisions. It is not clear that financial restraint was wholly responsible for this deficiency. It was not until early in 1939 that the British army settled on tank designs for mass production and on the organisation of armoured divisions.[68] Bond points out that, had it not been for the Cardwell system, whereby roughly equal numbers of cavalry and infantry battalions were stationed at home and overseas, the regular army could have devoted more resources to armoured forces and could also have had more than five divisions available for the expeditionary force.[69] David French argues convincingly that the British army was outthought and outmanoeuvred by the Germans in 1940 on account of an inflexible command, control and communications system, defective tactical doctrine and inadequate air support, none of which was an inevitable result of financial restraint.[70] It would be quite wrong, therefore, to assume that the British army's deficiencies were wholly the result of Chamberlain's influence. That said, Chamberlain was too easily impressed by the claims made by Trenchard and the Air Staff in favour of the bomber, and by Liddell Hart's belief that air power could be a substitute for an expeditionary force. In the event, the RAF was largely ineffective against the German army in France and Belgium in 1940, and even in strategic bombing until 1942.[71]

Acknowledgement

I am grateful to Gill Bennett for comments on an earlier draft. Responsibility for errors remains with the author.

Notes

1. Viscount Montgomery, *The Memoirs of Field-Marshal the Viscount Montgomery of Alamein* (London: Collins, 1958), pp. 49–50.
2. B.J.C. McKercher, 'Deterrence and the European Balance of Power: The Field Force and British Grand Strategy, 1934–1938', *English Historical Review*, 123

(2008), pp. 98–131. McKercher is primarily concerned to challenge the arguments of Greg Kennedy and Keith Neilson that historians have focused too much on the threat to British power from Germany rather than Japan – see G.C. Kennedy, *Anglo-American Strategic Relations and the Far East, 1933–1939* (London: Frank Cass, 2002) and K. Neilson, 'The Defence Requirements Sub-Committee, British Strategic Foreign Policy, Neville Chamberlain and the Path to Appeasement', *English Historical Review*, 118 (2003), 651–84. Lack of space precludes me from engaging in that debate.

3. Michael Howard, *The Continental Commitment* (London: Temple Smith, 1972), p. 114.
4. Robert Self, *Neville Chamberlain, a Biography* (Farnham: Ashgate, 2006), pp. 238–9.
5. David Dilks, 'We Must Hope for the Best and Prepare for the Worst: The Prime Minister, the Cabinet and Hitler's Germany, 1937–1939', *Proceedings of the British Academy*, 73 (1987), pp. 309–52.
6. N.H. Gibbs, *Grand Strategy* (London: HMSO, 1976), pp. 610–13, 620–2, 625, 653–7.
7. Disarmament Committee (Ministerial) – hereafter DC(M) – conclusions, 2 July 1934, Cabinet Office papers, series 27, vol. 507 (CAB 27/507), part 3, the National Archives of the United Kingdom: Public Record Office, London (TNA).
8. Minutes of meeting between Prime Minister and Parliamentary Delegation on Defence, 29 July 1936, Prime Minister's Office papers, series 1, file 193 (PREM 1/193), TNA; *Parliamentary Debates (Commons)*, vol. 332, 7 March 1938, col. 1600.
9. DRC minutes, 23 Jan. 1934, and Report, DRC 14, 28 Feb. 1934, pp. 9 and 21, CAB 16/109.
10. DRC 14, tables A1 and A2, CAB 16/109.
11. Brian Bond (ed.), *Chief of Staff: The Diaries of Lieutenant-General Sir Henry Pownall*, vol. I (London: Leo Cooper, 1972), 18 December 1933, p. 29.
12. DRC minutes, 23 and 25 Jan., and 26 Feb. 1934, CAB 16/109.
13. Andrew Boyle, *Trenchard, Man of Vision* (London: Collins, 1962), p. 681.
14. DC(M) conclusions, 3 May 1934, CAB 27/507.
15. Self, *Neville Chamberlain*, p. 238, cf. G.C. Peden, *British Rearmament and the Treasury, 1932–1939* (Edinburgh: Scottish Academic Press, 1979), p. 123.
16. DC(M) conclusions, 10 and 15 May 1934, CAB 27/507.
17. DCM(32) 120, CAB 27/511.
18. DC(M) conclusions, 26 June 1934, CAB 27/507.
19. CP 205(34), CAB 24/250.
20. Robert Self (ed.), *The Neville Chamberlain Diary Letters*, vol. 4 (Aldershot: Ashgate, 2005), p. 77.
21. Ibid.
22. See Peden, *British Rearmament*, esp. pp. 73–4, 83, 151–2, 169–77.
23. DRC minutes, 11 July, 19 July and 3 Oct. 1935; DRC 29, 2 Oct., and DRC 37, 21 Nov., 1935, CAB 16/112.
24. DPR(DR) 4, 9 Jan. 1936, and DPR(DR) conclusions, 13 Jan. 1936, CAB 16/123.
25. Cuttings from *The Times*, 1935, Weir papers 17/10, Churchill College, Cambridge.

26. DPR(DR) conclusions, 13, 14 and 16 Jan. 1936; DPR(DR) 6, 15 Jan. 1936, CAB 16/123.
27. *The Times*, 3 Oct. 1936, p. 7.
28. Chamberlain's diary 25 Oct. 1936, NC 2/23A, Birmingham University Library.
29. Memorandum by Fisher, with Hankey's marginal comments, 23 Oct. 1936, CAB 64/35.
30. Inskip to Chamberlain, 5 November 1936, CAB 64/35.
31. Inskip to Duff Cooper, 27 Nov. 1936, CAB 64/35.
32. Chamberlain to Fisher, 30 Nov. 1936, Treasury papers, series 161, box 1071, file S.42580/1 (T 161/1071/S.42580/1), TNA.
33. CP 326 (36), 3 Dec. 1936, CAB 24/265.
34. Cabinet conclusions, 9 Dec. 1936, CAB 23/86.
35. CP 334 (36), 11 Dec. 1936, CAB 24/265.
36. Chamberlain to Inskip, 16 Dec. 1936, and Hankey to Inskip, 17 Dec. 1936, CAB 64/35.
37. Bridges to J.H.E. Woods (Chamberlain's principal private secretary), 15 Dec. 1936, T 161/1071/S.42580/1.
38. CP 41 (37), 28 Jan. 1937, CAB 24/267.
39. To Chancellor of the Exchequer, 1 Feb. 1937, CAB 64/35.
40. Cabinet conclusions, 3 Feb. 1937, CAB 23/87; CP 115 (37), 23 April 1937, Cab 24/269; and Cabinet conclusions, 28 April and 5 May 1937, CAB 23/88.
41. CP 165, 25 June 1937, CAB 24/270, and Cabinet conclusions, 30 June 1937, CAB 23/88.
42. DP(P) 6, 1 July 1937, CAB 16/182; DP(P) conclusions, 13 July 1937, CAB 16/181.
43. Brian Bond, *British Military Policy between the Two World Wars* (Oxford: Clarendon Press, 1980), p. 246; Brian Bond, *Liddell Hart: A Study of His Military Thought* (London: Cassell, 1977), pp. 91–4.
44. Cabinet conclusions, 29 September 1937, CAB 23/89; Sir John Kennedy, *The Business of War* (London: Hutchinson, 1957), p. 43.
45. Inskip diary, 11 Jan. 1939, INKP 2, Churchill, College, Cambridge.
46. R.J. Minney, *The Private Papers of Hore-Belisha* (London: Collins, 1960), p. 54.
47. Basil Liddell Hart, *Europe in Arms* (London: Faber and Faber, 1937), pp. 78–9.
48. Inskip diary 16 Dec. 1939, INKP 2.
49. CP 257 (37), Oct. 1937, CAB 24/272.
50. Gibbs, *Grand Strategy*, pp. 283–4.
51. Memoranda by Inskip and Hankey, 23 Nov. 1937, T 161/855/S.48431. For rising cost of aircraft see G.C. Peden, *Arms, Economics and British Strategy* (Cambridge University Press, 2007), p. 117.
52. CP 316 (37), 15 Dec. 1937, esp. para.75, CAB 24/273.
53. CP 24(38), 8 Feb. 1938, CAB 24/274.
54. CP 26(38), 10 Feb. 1938, CAB 24/274.
55. Howard, *Continental Commitment*, p. 117.
56. Note by Bridges, 10 Mar. 1938, T 161/1071/S.42580/3.
57. CID minutes, 17 Mar. 1938, CAB 2/7.

58. Jean Delmas, 'La perception de la puissance militaire française', in René Girault and Robert Frank (eds.), *La Puissance en Europe 1938–1940* (Paris: Publications de la Sorbonne, 1984), pp. 129, 133.
59. Bond (ed.), *Chief of Staff*, vol. I, p. 183.
60. Cabinet conclusions, 25 Jan. 1939, CAB 23/97.
61. Cabinet conclusions, 22 Feb. 1939, CAB 23/97.
62. Minney, *Hore-Belisha*, pp. 186–7; Hopkins' comment on memorandum by J.A.N. Barlow, 28 Mar. 1939, T 175/104 (part 2).
63. Cabinet conclusions, 29 March 1939, CAB 23/98.
64. Osmund Cleverly (Chamberlain's principal private secretary) to H.H. Sellar, 24 Apr. 1939, PREM 1/308.
65. Peter Dennis, *Decision by Default: Peacetime Conscription and British Defence 1919–39* (London: Routledge and Kegan Paul, 1972), pp. 206–7, 212–21.
66. Montgomery, *Memoirs*, pp. 50, 58.
67. Manfred Messerschmidt, 'German Military Effectiveness between 1919 and 1939', in Allan R. Millett and Williamson Murray (eds), *Military Effectiveness*, vol. II (Boston: Unwin Hyman, 1988), p. 227.
68. J. P. Harris, *Men, Ideas and Tanks* (Manchester: Manchester University Press, 1995), pp. 260–5, 274–9, 282–90, 297–307.
69. Bond, *British Military Policy*, pp. 73–4, 99–126, 188.
70. David French, *Raising Churchill's Army* (Oxford: Oxford University Press, 2000), esp. pp. 156–66, 174–8.
71. Richard Overy, *Air Power, Armies and the War in the West, 1940* (Colorado: US Air Force Academy, 1989); Sir Charles Webster and Noble Frankland, *The Strategic Air Offensive against Germany*, vol. I (London: HMSO, 1961), pp. 125, 129, 178–9, 309–11.

6
Eden, the Foreign Office and the 'German Problem', 1935–38

G.T.P. Waddington

Of all the dilemmas that plagued the British Foreign Office during the interwar years none was more onerous or enduring than that which has passed into the history books as the 'German problem'. The term itself was an unfortunate echo of failure, a nagging reminder that the primary objective that the British had pursued at such appalling sacrifice during the war of 1914–18 had not been realised. To be sure, the defeat of the *Kaiserreich* had eliminated a dangerous naval competitor and commercial rival, but the peace treaties had signally failed to deliver that continental equilibrium which was considered vital to the safety of the homeland and the promotion of British interests across the globe. Indeed, the manifest shortcomings of the peace settlement, the continental dominance of France, the disputes which continued to rage between the newly emerged states of Eastern and Central Europe and, most importantly, the severe weakening of Germany had created a situation which was in some senses even more challenging than that which had confronted the British before 1914. Well might they have wished to 'heal the wounds of war, to oppose far-reaching alterations in the law of Europe, to return to normal',[1] not least in view of their pressing domestic concerns and new imperial burdens, but the authorities in London were quick to appreciate that a German revival, a contingency not entirely undesirable in itself, if only from an economic point of view, was merely a question of time. Thus, unlike their French counterparts, who unrealistically aspired to keep the Reich in a state of permanent disrepair, the British adopted a proactive policy towards Germany during the early 1920s which was ultimately designed to facilitate the controlled reintegration of the fledgling republic into an international environment in which all could recover and prosper.

Following a series of disputes with the French, culminating in a rancorous disagreement over the occupation of the Ruhr, this approach appeared to be bearing fruit, reaching a high point with the Locarno treaties of 1925 and Germany's subsequent entry into the League of Nations. Locarno, however, would prove to be something of an illusion, for not only did it fail to usher in a lasting Franco-German rapprochement, the crucial lynchpin of future continental stability, but it served more to stimulate than to satisfy German ambitions. By the time Stresemann departed the scene in 1929 even the much vaunted 'spirit of Locarno' was visibly crumbling as Paris and Berlin once more locked horns over reparations and troop evacuations while Germany's brief flirtation with democracy began to fall victim to the world economic crisis and the heightened appeal of radical doctrines. Nevertheless, the emergence of Hitler in January 1933 and the reappearance of an overtly aggressive German nationalism brought no fundamental departure in Britain's approach to continental affairs. Indeed, the dangers posed by National Socialism, which were fully appreciated in the higher echelons of the British diplomatic service,[2] served only to provide an additional stimulus in the search for a lasting accommodation with Germany. On the other hand, coming in the wake of the Great Depression and the Manchurian crisis, and in the midst of the 'long-drawn agony' of the Geneva Disarmament Conference,[3] the very nature of National Socialism meant that the 'German problem' of the 1930s was of a fundamentally different order to that which had faced the British during the previous decade. Moreover, once the Defence Requirements Committee (DRC) had established that Germany was the 'ultimate potential enemy' against which Britain's long-term defence planning would have to be based, the policy agenda for Anglo-German relations had effectively been settled: reconcile and contain Hitler or prepare for the consequences of alienation and, ultimately, the possibility of war.[4]

By the time of Anthony Eden's appointment as British Foreign Secretary in December 1935 it was already apparent to the German experts in the Foreign Office that a satisfactory settlement with Hitler was unlikely to be achieved.[5] An initial attempt to open general discussions with the Nazi regime on the basis of the legalisation of limited German rearmament had already been thwarted by the first of the Führer's unilateral treaty violations. Moreover, despite the soothing words that continued to issue forth from Berlin,[6] Hitler had steadfastly refused to engage in any meaningful discussion on issues of arms limitation, multilateral security or a possible return to Geneva, each an essential element of the so-called 'general settlement' that the Foreign Office had long since prioritised as the foremost objective of its European policy. Ironically, the only advance of any significance that was made during 1935 was the Anglo-German Naval Agreement which was not only concluded on terms to which the British were initially wholly opposed, but which, by its very nature, and much to Hitler's satisfaction, exercised a deeply divisive influence on the powers that had only recently sought to advertise their solidarity against him at Stresa. Now, six months on from the naval agreement, and with relations between the Western Powers and Italy severely strained as a result of the Abyssinian crisis, the new Foreign Secretary was under no illusions as to the magnitude of the task that lay before him in framing a constructive policy towards the Third Reich.

Although Eden had formed a relatively favourable impression of Hitler during their first meeting in February 1934, describing him to Jan Masaryk as a 'sincere fanatic' who was not seeking war,[7] the subsequent course of German policy, most notably in Austria, coupled with the alarming pace of German rearmament, clearly boded ill for the future. When in March 1935 he had accompanied Sir John Simon to Berlin in the wake of the conscription decree, the change in the tone and demeanour of the German dictator was palpable. Confident of his growing strength, recently affirmed by his success in the Saar plebiscite and the feeble reaction of the other powers to his treaty violations, Hitler was markedly self-assured and firmly uncooperative on every issue of substance. Eden came away from the conversations deeply disappointed and sceptical about the prospects of any eventual settlement.[8] As he subsequently informed Stalin and Litvinov, the Germans had been asked whether they were prepared to contribute to 'a collective and co-operative effort to organise European peace and security, and... the answer was no'.[9] The experience clearly made a significant impression on the then Lord Privy Seal who told Aubrey Kennedy of *The Times* on the eve of Stresa that the only way to deal with Germany was to 'browbeat' her in the hope and expectation that a firm hand now would produce a workable settlement at some point in the future.[10]

As the third British Foreign Secretary to face Hitler within the space of a year, Eden came to preside over a crucial period in the international relations of the 1930s from the reoccupation of the Rhineland, which saw the strategic initiative pass decisively to Germany to the eve of the Anschluss, the first major act of the crisis years of 1938–39. Although his appointment was greeted with widespread approval in Britain, *The New Statesman* going so far as to call it Baldwin's 'Christmas present to the nation',[11] it is impossible to dispute Eden's own contention that he had succeeded to a 'wretchedly disordered heritage'.[12] As a result of the Abyssinian imbroglio, Italy, formerly an integral factor in British schemes for the containment of Germany, had become hopelessly alienated from the Western Powers and had already begun its fatal drift into the German orbit; Anglo-French relations were in a worse state than at any time since the Ruhr crisis; collective security had been exposed as an unworkable sham and British diplomacy revealed as hypocritical, self-seeking and duplicitous. As Neville Chamberlain wrote to his sister on 15 December, 'nothing could be worse than our position. Our whole prestige in foreign affairs at home and abroad has tumbled to pieces like a house of cards.'[13] While the Hoare-Laval plan had placed even greater strains on Anglo-Italian and Anglo-French relations, the position *vis-à-vis* Germany was also a source of mounting concern. On 13 December the British Ambassador in Berlin, Sir Eric Phipps, had had an interview with Hitler, their first encounter since the conclusion of the naval agreement, the outcome of which had been, in the words of the Ambassador, 'most unsatisfactory'. The German Chancellor had shown no interest in any of the issues that were of concern to the British, such as the proposed air pact and the limitation of armaments, preferring instead to indulge in a violent denunciation of the Soviets and to voice his criticisms of Britain's recent policy towards Italy.[14] As far as the Foreign Office was concerned, however, the interview had been useful in terms of providing confirmation of two important considerations which had underpinned British policy since at least the appearance of the DRC report. If a settlement with Germany were to be negotiated, noted Sir Orme Sargent, '(a) we must be materially stronger than we are at present; and (b) we must not be isolated politically from the other great European Powers.'[15] This latter point was not lost on the Permanent Under-Secretary of State, Sir Robert Vansittart, who, mourning the loss of Italy, was already toying with the idea of an improvement in Anglo-Soviet relations as a means of redressing the balance.[16] Vansittart was under no illusions about the tribulations which lay ahead. 'What is going on now', he wrote to Phipps on 20 December:

> is a very indifferent dress rehearsal of the drama that awaits us. At present collective security is a word and nothing more. Nobody so far has contributed but ourselves, and nobody really wants to contribute even though we have been reduced to going round knocking loudly on many doors. So far the result has been some tardy and reluctant paper alone. This country is therefore embarked on a foreign policy which outruns its material means. This seems to me a

grave danger unless it is remedied, and I had hoped that this crisis might remedy it, but the speaking has, I fear, not been plain <u>enough</u>. Next time the aggressor will be Germany, and that next time <u>will not</u> now be very far off. Then will be the moment, on present form, when all the surrounding States of Germany will have to be asked how much they intend to contribute, and, on present form, the answer will be 'Nothing'.[17]

If the British reaction to Eden's appointment had been largely positive, it was an altogether different story in Germany. Indeed, it was deeply lamented in Berlin not only because of Eden's strong identification with the League and the support he had shown for those very mutual assistance schemes and arms limitation proposals that the Nazis were determined to sabotage, but also because Hitler and his acolytes had regarded him as ideologically suspect since his visit to Moscow in the spring of 1935. This perceived act of heresy, coupled with the deep-seated conviction that the British Foreign Office was in any case an endemically 'anti-German' institution, made the appointment a very unattractive proposition for the Nazis.[18] It was a 'bad swop', noted Goebbels,[19] while in an interview with Leni Riefenstahl in February 1936 Hitler vilified Eden as a 'small, vain individual', a 'madman' whose leanings towards the USSR would lead Britain to catastrophe.[20] Coupled with the truculent attitude adopted by Hitler during his recent interview with Phipps, the prospects of any early breakthrough with Germany seemed slim indeed.

Understandably enough, Eden spent his first weeks in office picking through the debris of the Hoare-Laval fiasco and seeking to restore both domestic and international confidence in British statesmanship. Inevitably, however, German issues were not far from his mind; nor could they fail to be in view of the widespread rumours about an imminent move in the Rhineland.[21] In mid-January 1936 he submitted a paper reminding his Cabinet colleagues of the nature and magnitude of the threat that now faced Britain across the North Sea. Aptly entitled 'The German Danger', Eden's succinct memorandum covered some 30 despatches from Phipps and his predecessor in Berlin, the equally prescient Sir Horace Rumbold, which demonstrated unequivocally that Hitler was aiming at the 'destruction of the peace settlement and [the] re-establishment of Germany as the dominant Power in Europe'. The Foreign Secretary drew two conclusions from the evidence: first, that it was vital for the British to accelerate and complete their rearmament, and second that it would be well to consider if a *modus vivendi*, 'to put it no higher', could be reached with Hitler.[22] A few weeks later he returned to this latter point. Although the policy was certainly not without its risks, he declared himself, on balance:

> in favour of making some attempt to come to terms with Germany, but upon one indispensable condition: that we offer no sops to Germany. There must be no concession merely to keep Germany quiet, for that process only stimulates the appetite it is intended to satisfy. We should be prepared to make concessions to Germany, and they will have to be concessions of value to her if they are to achieve their object, but these concessions must only be offered as part of a final settlement which includes some further arms limitation and Germany's return to the League.[23]

This was a timely initiative which may have been prompted by the advice Eden had been receiving from the German experts in the Foreign Office. From the autumn of 1935 senior figures in the Central Department had been engaged in a comprehensive review of policy towards Germany which had principally been triggered by considerations relating to the likely repercussions of the Abyssinian crisis.[24] Consultations about a short-term policy towards Germany had revolved initially around three alternatives: an air settlement, the future of the demilitarised zone and a League inquiry into the colonial and raw materials situation. Although Hitler was clearly reluctant to contemplate the opening of negotiations for an air pact – on the interchangeable pretexts that the Franco-Soviet Pact and the on-going conflict in East Africa made such a course impossible – it was calculated that the prospect might be made more appealing to him by linking it to the possible restoration of full German sovereignty in the demilitarised Rhineland zone.[25] As far as the zone itself was concerned there had for some time been growing anxiety in London and Paris about the German propaganda campaign against the Franco-Soviet Pact which, so the Nazi pundits claimed, was incompatible with Locarno. In early January Ralph Wigram, head of the Central Department, had articulated his thoughts on the matter:

> The situation as regards the demilitarised zone does arouse disquiet. Can we expect that it will last indefinitely? Is not its insecurity really the strongest argument for getting on more intimate terms with the Germans with the least possible delay? Of course, theoretically, it would be better to wait until our rearmament has proceeded further. But can we do that? It seems to go so slowly. What is important in

the west is to keep the frontiers out of the discussion. The zone itself may have to go. The thing is to see that it goes peacefully and by agreement.[26]

Eden found himself in full agreement with this analysis and in the weeks that followed he and his colleagues elaborated a scheme which envisaged the negotiated disappearance of the demilitarised status of the Rhineland which, it was hoped, would be bait enough to draw Hitler into serious discussion of other and, for the British, more pressing matters.[27] These calculations were thrown into utter disarray, however, when on 7 March 1936 German troops marched into the Rhineland in contravention of the treaties of Versailles and Locarno.

Irrespective of its devastating strategic consequences for France and her Eastern allies, the remilitarisation of the Rhineland was a colossal diplomatic setback for the British, undoing in a matter of hours over five months of painstaking deliberation. As Eden famously recorded shortly after the coup, Hitler's action had not only provided further evidence of the 'scant respect paid by German Governments to the sanctity of treaties', it had also 'deprived us of the possibility of making to him a concession which might otherwise have been a useful bargaining counter in our hands in the general negotiations with Germany which we had it in contemplation to initiate'.[28] History had effectively repeated itself; for it was now twice within the space of a year that a unilateral German treaty violation had wrecked a British project to initiate wide-ranging negotiations towards the elusive 'general settlement'. With their diplomatic strategy in tatters, Eden and his advisers were subsequently compelled to engage in a delicate process of crisis management, vainly searching for a German contribution towards the pacification of the situation while simultaneously seeking to exercise a steadying influence in Paris.[29] Their task was made all the more difficult not only by Hitler's persistent refusal to accept any limitations on German sovereignty in the Rhineland, which he immediately proceeded to fortify, but also because Ribbentrop's purpose in the ensuing negotiations was first and foremost to persuade the British of the benefits of an Anglo-German alliance which, so he was heard to announce, would be for Germany 'the beginning of the golden age'.[30] It was thus no surprise that Eden's celebrated questionnaire, a somewhat ill-judged device designed to probe the offers which had accompanied the coup, was left subsequently to gather dust in a dark corner of the *Wilhelmstrasse*. Hitler was operating on an altogether different agenda. As Phipps observed, the Führer had 'no intention of binding himself in any way in [the] present fluid state of Europe';[31] on the contrary, his sights remained firmly fixed upon the long-coveted goal of an 'Anglo-German understanding, to the exclusion of third or fourth parties'.[32] Indeed, in the late spring of 1936, having long wearied of the regular diplomatic exchanges, the Führer sought to arrange a clandestine meeting with Baldwin with the very purpose of furthering that objective.[33] Naturally enough, Eden protested strongly and the initiative was quickly stifled, much to German chagrin.[34]

The combination of Hoare-Laval, the loss of the Rhineland and Mussolini's triumph over Abyssinia, finally confirmed by the fall of Addis Ababa on 5 May, impacted disastrously on Eden's hopes of basing Britain's foreign policy on collective security and thus, in turn, of utilising the League to contain the German threat.[35] In the wake of these developments the momentum now clearly lay with Hitler and Mussolini which made the prospect of a satisfactory settlement with either more remote than ever. At the Cabinet meeting on 6 July Eden painted a depressing picture of current conditions, citing inter alia the present weakness of France and the League, the tardy progress of British rearmament, Germany's growing strength and the unscrupulous nature of the Nazi leaders as elements of an international situation that had now become 'so serious that from day to day there was the risk of some dangerous incident arising'; indeed, 'even an outbreak of war could not be excluded'. In these circumstances the Foreign Secretary was unable to give any guarantee that peace could be maintained 'even during the present year'.[36] The recent setbacks had clearly taken their toll on Eden whose pessimism was echoed in the higher echelons of the Foreign Office where the development of German policy in particular had had a deeply stultifying effect. 'Hitler has never meant business in our sense of the word,' noted Vansittart angrily on 1 June. 'The sooner the Cabinet realise that, the better for this long misguided country.' It would nonetheless be necessary to ' "play" Hitler for some time', not least because 'we need time more than anyone, on account of the deficiencies in our equipment'. In the interim it was of the utmost importance for Britain and France to remain focused and united and to undertake no separate initiative that might be open to exploitation by the Germans.[37]

Within weeks the prospects for European stability were dealt a further and severely damaging blow with the outbreak of the Spanish Civil War, a development that would plague the remainder of Eden's first tenure as Foreign Secretary. The Spanish conflict was replete with danger not only in view of the potential repercussions it might have for Britain's strategic position in the Mediterranean but also because of the possibility that it might escalate and spread as a result of the barely concealed intervention of foreign powers. It was, moreover, certain to drive Mussolini and Hitler closer together, harden the ideological fronts, particularly between Germany and the Soviet Union, and thus intensify those very antagonisms which the British were seeking to relax. As Eden and the new French Premier, Leon Blum, hastened to arrange a non-intervention agreement, this new dimension to the problems currently confronting London was highlighted by Sir Orme Sargent. The development of rival blocs based on ideological antagonisms, he noted on 12 August, 'would be a very different and far more horrible development than the creation of national and imperialistic blocs of satisfied versus dissatisfied powers which we have hitherto foreseen and feared, for the creation of ideological blocs would not merely divide Governments far more deeply than any political dispute, but would also cut across the domestic politics of each country'. Such a division, he continued, would probably wreck any prospect of a new Western European security arrangement to replace Locarno and also render 'our own task of working for a general settlement along present lines far more difficult and invidious'.[38]

As Sargent had foreseen, the problems inherent in constructing any new security system were already becoming apparent. Although the Germans had agreed to participate in the attempt to find a substitute for Locarno following initial consultations between Eden and representatives of France and Belgium in London on 23 July, it soon became clear that they would only do so at a price that the Western Powers could not possibly afford to contemplate, if only in the interests of their own safety. Determined to preserve absolute freedom of action to prosecute their ambitions in the East, the Germans were markedly unenthusiastic about the British proposal to link any new treaty to Geneva and adamantly opposed to any mechanism being built into the new arrangements that might accommodate the operation of the Franco-Soviet Pact. This refusal to admit the incorporation of any special provisions designed to cover the French alliances in Eastern Europe was designed to render explicit what the original Treaty of Locarno had always implied: that while Germany might be prepared to assume obligations in the West she would accept no limitations of her freedom of manoeuvre elsewhere. What the Germans wanted, noted Lord Allen of Hurtwood, recently returned from the 1936 Nuremberg rally, 'is safety in the West and a free hand in the East' where, he continued, faithfully echoing his German mentors, it was imperative to maintain absolute vigilance against the 'danger of Communist agitation emanating from Moscow'.[39] Any such limitations on the new security arrangements were clearly intolerable to the British who, although they were adamantly opposed to undertaking any further commitments, continued to insist on the principle that peace was indivisible. By late October Wigram confessed to the fear that the putative pact would be nothing more than a 'complete phantom' and that the approaching negotiations would serve no purpose other than to give 'the corpse a highly respectable and protracted burial'.[40] And so it would prove. Diplomatic exchanges on the proposed Western Pact would continue well into 1937 only eventually to run into the sand as a result of the irreconcilable positions adopted by the Western Powers, on the one hand, and the emerging Rome-Berlin 'Axis', on the other.

In the meantime Ribbentrop's nomination as the new German Ambassador in London briefly raised hopes in some quarters of positive developments in Anglo-German relations.[41] In the Foreign Office, however, the German envoy's slogans about the dangers emanating from the Soviet Union and the need for an Anglo-German front to stem the tide of Bolshevism fell completely on deaf ears. Moreover, the conclusion on 25 November of the German-Japanese Anti-Comintern Pact, a barely disguised anti-Soviet agreement to which Hitler hoped the British would accede, was deeply lamented in Whitehall where there was no inclination to encourage that division of Europe on ideological lines which now seemed to be one of the chief priorities of the Nazi leadership. German sensitivity on this issue was amply demonstrated by an angry press reaction to the speech made by Duff Cooper at Birkenhead in which the Secretary of State for War had announced that Britain regarded both Fascism and Bolshevism with equal distaste.[42] While the Germans continued to couple the anti-communist message with an increasingly aggressive attitude on the emerging colonial question, Eden himself ventured into the public arena in order firmly to establish in the minds of the British people, and indeed others, the principles upon which the foreign policy of His Majesty's Government was based. Speaking to his constituents in Leamington on 20 November the Foreign Secretary affirmed Britain's attachment to the principles of the League, explained the rationale for British rearmament, confirmed Britain's determination to fight for France and Belgium, if the occasion arose, and declared that British armaments '*may* be used in bringing help to a victim of aggression in any case where, in our judgement, it would be proper under the provisions of the Covenant to do so'.[43] Three weeks later, speaking at Bradford, he effectively dashed whatever lingering hopes the Germans might have been entertaining of basing Anglo-German friendship on common ideological antipathies.

Britain, he asserted, would have no truck with 'dangerous doctrines which would have us divide the world into dictatorships of the right and left'; nor would it seek to 'align its foreign policy with any group of States because they support the one or the other'.[44]

With these sentiments ringing in his ears it was hardly surprising that Ribbentrop was said to have returned to Berlin for the Christmas holidays in a 'very depressed and chastened frame of mind'.[45] As Sargent noted, the year appeared to be drawing to a close with a series of 'spectacular failures' for German foreign policy, for not only had Hitler failed in his endeavour to pose as Europe's saviour from Bolshevism, but he had also achieved no early breakthrough in Spain or in the colonial question.[46] This analysis appeared to be substantiated by other sources. According to a Secretary of the German Embassy in Moscow, for example, the *Wilhelmstrasse* was said to be 'thoroughly depressed' at the current state of affairs, particularly with regard to Anglo-German relations.[47] In the bigger picture, however, there was little comfort to be drawn from supposed German misfortunes for those relations were now markedly worse than had been the case twelve months earlier. That much was brought home vividly in the memorandum that Vansittart submitted on the final day of the year. Recently returned from a visit to Germany where he had had conversations with Hitler and other senior Nazis, the Permanent Under-Secretary of State not only re-emphasised the difficulties of coming to terms with Germany but also pointed to the 'systematic belittlement' of the United Kingdom that was increasingly coming to feature in German propaganda. Moreover, Germany, the 'recognised storm-centre of the earth' had not only drawn closer to Britain's other potential enemies but was rearming 'on a scale spiritually more ferocious and materially more formidable than anything ever seen before in this world'. If Anglo-German friendship failed to develop on the lines desired by the leaders of the Nazi party, many of whom now viewed Britain as the 'greatest obstacle to German expansion and to the "heroic conception" of life and German destiny', the situation could well turn ugly. In these circumstances the Foreign Office would have to continue to play for the 'vital' commodity of time. '*Our aim must be to stabilise the position till 1939*', concluded Vansittart. 'On present form we cannot at all be sure of doing so.'[48] In the light of these considerations, there was obviously much force in Harold Nicolson's observation that 1936 was drawing to a close 'clouded by menace upon the Continent'.[49]

Addressing the Cabinet at its first meeting of the New Year, Eden declared that the next twelve months were likely to be 'critical' in terms of foreign affairs. The Foreign Office, he explained, was receiving many reports to the effect that Germany's economic situation would probably be unable to sustain another winter, and, that being the case, it looked 'as though this year would determine Germany in following a policy alternatively of co-operation or foreign adventure'. In these circumstances it was more important than ever to seek to restrain the advocates of forward action in the Reich, an aim which, he thought, could best be achieved by continuing 'our present policy of being firm but always ready to talk'. The Foreign Office, he added, would be assisted in its endeavours by any measure that was designed 'to show both our determination to press forward with our armament policy and that the programmes were proceeding satisfactorily'.[50] These statements, while confirming the essential continuity of British policy towards Germany in the mid-1930s, would prove more significant than Eden could have imagined. Although in comparison to the years which immediately preceded and followed it, 1937 was relatively calm, particularly in so far as European affairs were concerned, it was a crucial year in the evolution of Anglo-German relations. During 1937 the conviction began to crystallise in influential quarters on both sides of the North Sea that a mutually satisfactory arrangement was not simply unlikely but impossible, a process that led to exasperation in the British Foreign Office and, more ominously, to growing hostility and a complete reorientation of policy towards Britain in the minds of the German leaders.[51]

For the moment, with the enduring stalemate in the Western Pact negotiations and Ribbentrop's failure to elicit the slightest British interest in the Anti-Comintern Pact, it was widely anticipated that the New Year might bring fresh developments in the colonial question.[52] During the early stages of his chancellorship Hitler had not permitted the issue of the former German colonies unduly to encumber Anglo-German relations for fear that it would upset his plans to forge a partnership with Britain. By late 1935, however, the political failure of the Anglo-German naval agreement had persuaded the Führer to exploit the colonial issue primarily in an attempt to pressurise the British into compliance with his European goals.[53] In the Foreign Office the idea of using the prospect of colonial concessions as a basis for discussions with Germany already had its advocates, including Vansittart who for a time speculated that it might just be possible thereby to divert Nazi expansionist ambitions away from the trouble spots of Central and South-Eastern Europe.[54] Moreover, following the loss of the Rhineland, the former German colonies were effectively the only asset deriving from the 1919 peace settlement with which the Western Powers could now legitimately bargain. Eden, however, was not especially taken with the idea. As David

Carlton notes, he 'long temporized both within the Foreign Office and at Cabinet' on the subject of a colonial bargain and preferred, if possible, to seek to deal with Germany's legitimate European grievances on the basis of controlled and measured concessions.[55] Eden did not believe that colonial revision would either satisfy or limit German ambitions, and from the autumn of 1936 onwards he gradually inclined to the policy, already favoured by some of his chief advisors and clearly implicit in his Leamington speech, of keeping Germany guessing about British intentions in Europe until Britain was able to negotiate from a position of strength.

As anticipated, the colonial claim came to feature highly on the German agenda in early 1937. On 11 February, during a lengthy discussion with Halifax, the Lord Privy Seal, then deputising for Eden at the Foreign Office, Ribbentrop advanced arguments which had long been familiar to the British authorities relating to the economic and psychological bases of Germany's claim. Of far greater significance from the British point of view, however, was his insistence that the colonial question could never be the object of a bargain. When Halifax suggested that a satisfactory solution of the problem partly depended upon the linking of a colonial settlement to the 'general stabilisation of peace', Ribbentrop insisted that this was wholly unacceptable to Germany for not only was this a question of German 'honour', but 'the experience of the last few years had shown that, if the solution of one question was always linked to the solution of another, no question at all was ever solved'. It was time, he believed, for Britain to make a 'voluntary and generous gesture'.[56] This would remain the German position on the colonial question up to and beyond Halifax's visit to Germany nine months later when he would hear much the same thing from Hitler himself. The message was as clear as it was unhelpful; it served to corroborate unsettling reports from the British Consul General in Munich to the effect that the current opinion at the Brown House was that Germany should seek to make as much capital as possible out of Britain's alleged colonial 'guilt' without necessarily offering anything in return. As St Clair Gainer reported shortly before Ribbentrop broached the question in London:

> So far indeed from offering a quid pro quo the feeling here is that Germany can and should first make her demand without compensatory offers and base her future policy upon the answer she receives. This policy might be one of 'blackmail'... a threat to keep Europe in a state of suspense by [a] refusal to discuss any question affecting the

peace either of Western or Eastern Europe unless the demands are granted – with, indeed, no specific assurance that if she gets what she wants she will be satisfied or more prepared to co-operate with other European nations.[57]

Germany's refusal to accept the linkage of the colonial question with the solution of other outstanding issues had brought the Foreign Office up against another dead end, the third in less than two years following previous attempts to strike a deal with Hitler over armaments and the Rhineland. Although Eden and his colleagues on the Foreign Policy Committee continued to examine the colonial issue in detail and while it remained a frequent topic of conversation with Ribbentrop and other German dignitaries, by the spring of 1937 it was becoming increasingly difficult to see where any progress might be made in Anglo-German relations. Hjalmar Schacht's involvement in the colonial sphere, which had included conversations with the French government in 1936 and with Sir Frederick Leith-Ross in early 1937 had proved inconclusive, raising more questions than it had answered.[58] During the coronation celebrations the principal German guest, Hitler's War Minister, General Werner von Blomberg, had been affability itself, but his discussions with Baldwin, Chamberlain and Eden had never progressed beyond superficialities.[59] Although both powers were pledged to non-intervention in Spain, they inevitably took up opposing positions during the deliberations of the London-based Non-Intervention Committee; over the proposed Western Pact Britain's insistence on the pacification of the continent could hardly be reconciled with Hitler's determination to keep his hands free for future adventures in Eastern Europe; and the British aim to subsume the colonial question in a 'general settlement' stood at complete variance with Berlin's insistence that the former German colonies were stolen loot that should be returned as a matter of course.

British diplomats with long experience of the Nazis had already begun to draw the inescapable conclusions. Shortly after his transfer from Berlin to Paris, Phipps told his American colleague that there was not the 'faintest possibility' of coming to an agreement with Hitler who was 'a fanatic who would be satisfied with nothing less than [the] domination of Europe'.[60] When Bullitt suggested a further round of 'talks with Hitler' in an effort to persuade him to put his cards on the table, Phipps retorted that the only card he had caught sight of during nearly four years in Berlin had been 'carte blanche'.[61] For his part, Vansittart held that Germany was bent upon expansion 'at the expense of her neighbours, by force if necessary'. This was a 'policy of violence and robbery'; Britain and Germany were separated by 'a fundamental difference of conception, of morality'.[62] Even Eden, who generally took a less pessimistic view of German issues than Vansittart, was forced to admit to his Austrian counterpart that the road to Berlin was 'strewn with obstacles'.[63] Commenting on Eden's suggestion of a possible visit to London by the German Foreign Minister, William Strang, head of the Central Department since Wigram's untimely death in December 1936, confessed that he regarded the prospect with considerable misgivings, not least because it was difficult to see where the two parties might find common ground on any of the burning international questions of the day. To that extent, the proposed visit, by highlighting gulfs and resulting in little more than an anodyne communiqué, might well do more harm than good. Echoing Vansittart, Strang pointed out that the two powers were separated by a 'fundamental divergence... in their outlook on foreign affairs', the crux of which was that whereas Germany was clearly being geared up for 'drastic change' to the European status quo, if necessary through war, the British ultimately were seeking to 'preserve the "status quo" even against peaceful change if the change should be to Germany's benefit'. Thus, any conversations that were initiated would always stall on this fundamental point.[64]

The mantle of gloom that had descended upon the Foreign Office about the prospects of initiating any fruitful dialogue with Germany coincided somewhat unhappily with the assumption of the premiership by Neville Chamberlain who succeeded Baldwin on 28 May 1937. Chamberlain brought to his new office a desire and determination to explore the possibilities for a settlement with the dictators, especially Hitler. As he wrote to his sister shortly after assuming the premiership: 'If only we could get on terms with the Germans I would not care a rap for Musso'.[65] Eden, whose personal and professional relations with Chamberlain had hitherto been both cordial and productive, initially greeted the appointment, anticipating the new premier's 'energetic backing' for his policy.[66] As would soon become apparent, however, Chamberlain had his own ideas, and before long a rift began to develop between the two which had its roots in a fundamental disagreement over the wisdom of negotiating with the dictator states from a position of weakness. The Foreign Secretary could have had no quarrel with Chamberlain's basic approach which looked to 'the double policy of rearmament and better relations with Germany and Italy' to see Britain 'safely through the danger period'.[67] This, after all, had been the essence of the Foreign Office's own strategy since the DRC had delivered its report and one which, certainly in the case of Germany,

Eden had originally embraced. But for Eden, not only did Chamberlain wish to move too fast; his methods were also ill-chosen for his purpose. As Keith Middlemas notes, while the Foreign Secretary advocated a policy of 'keeping Germany guessing long enough to give Britain time to re-arm, so that he could negotiate from a position of strength, Chamberlain, conscious of time running out, preferred to settle the outstanding accounts at once, with Germany if possible but, if not, with Italy as a lever to open doors in Berlin'.[68]

For almost six months Chamberlain and Eden had no major disagreements in the sphere of Anglo-German relations, but matters came sharply to a head in the autumn of 1937 when Halifax, now Lord President of the Council, received an invitation from Goering to visit Germany. Although the ostensible reason for the visit was to enable Halifax to attend a hunting exhibition, it was inconceivable that he would not avail himself of the opportunity for political conversations with the German leaders. For Chamberlain this seemed to be precisely the kind of opening he had been seeking, not least, as he later reflected with misguided optimism, because it had created an atmosphere 'in which it was possible to discuss with Germany the practical questions involved in a European settlement'.[69] The Prime Minister's enthusiasm for the initiative was itself an implicit criticism of the Foreign Office which, he had written with obvious irritation only two months earlier, was devoid of imagination and courage.[70] Although he had initially cautiously approved the proposed visit, Eden soon had second thoughts, for while he and his advisers were still valiantly exploring ways of making a fresh start with Germany, there were clearly dangers inherent in the idea of an unofficial and essentially unmonitored exchange between a member of the British Cabinet and the German Chancellor. Moreover, without substantial preparatory discussions, it was difficult to see what positive issue might ensue. Speculation in the British press about the possible results of the initiative coupled with Hitler's insistence that Halifax should meet him at his mountain retreat in Southern Germany, a condition which made the visit 'look almost like a Canossa', vexed and angered Eden who was determined both to play down its significance and to avoid the impression that the British Government were 'in pursuit of the German Chancellor'.[71] The episode placed a severe strain on Eden's relationship with Chamberlain and, although he reluctantly consented to the visit, he did so without conviction, and on the not entirely satisfactory grounds that no genuinely compelling reason could be found to prevent Halifax from travelling.

The Hitler-Halifax meeting itself was a most curious affair, the gulf between the two individuals illustrated by Hitler's chilling remark that the British should rid themselves of the troublesome Gandhi by murdering him.[72] The German leader was sullen and uncooperative throughout what Eden would later justifiably term an 'aimless and therefore hazardous discussion'.[73] He attacked the democratic form of government and proved as intractable as ever on the question of a general settlement; such 'shibboleths', he declared, 'offered no practical prospect of a solution to Europe's difficulties'. The colonial question constituted the only problem between Britain and Germany and the responsibility for its solution rested firmly with the Western Powers. As far as Central Europe was concerned, settlements were possible over the Austrian and Czechoslovakian questions, but it remained to be seen whether satisfactory solutions would be achieved through the medium of 'higher reason' or what Hitler chose to term the 'free play of forces'. The Führer's advice that the British would be well advised to apply themselves to 'preparations through the diplomatic channels', a counsel that was so glaringly inconsistent with his oft-expressed preference for 'direct' diplomacy, signalled at the very least that there was no urgency attached to a solution of the colonial question. Of greater significance perhaps was what was left unsaid, for the insistence that the colonial question was the only stumbling block to an improvement in Anglo-German relations clearly implied that the Reich's European priorities were of no concern to Britain.[74] For his part, Halifax had acquitted himself well during a difficult conversation, although Eden, who had instructed the Lord President to 'confine himself to warning comment' on territorial issues, was later disturbed to learn that he had spoken of possible alterations in the status of Austria, Czechoslovakia and Danzig.[75]

The results of the initiative were naturally subjected to a close scrutiny in the Foreign Office. Predictably enough, the conclusions were less than encouraging. 'What strikes one in this conversation', noted Sargent:

> is that Hitler has on this occasion assumed a completely new attitude. Up until now he has given the impression of trying to justify his policy (e.g. his Peace Plan of March 1936) by concrete proposals for a general settlement, and of wishing in particular to come to a working arrangement on all outstanding questions with Great Britain.... On the present occasion he has adopted the line that a general settlement is not practical politics, that immediate negotiations between Great Britain and Germany are unnecessary,

but if all the same Great Britain really wants to improve Anglo-German relations she can do so by satisfying Germany's colonial claim.... Hitler gave Lord Halifax no indication that he is prepared to give anything in return for the colonies, except German goodwill. Disarmament and Germany's return to the League are completely impracticable, and he seems at the same time to have made it quite clear that he was not prepared as a quid pro quo to discuss with us, still less give us, any undertakings with regard to the German policy of expansion in Eastern Europe. Those were matters which Germany would settle for herself. She did not need to buy our consent.[76]

Eden subsequently pressed upon the Cabinet that the Halifax visit had made clear that the Germans would permit no linkage between their European priorities and the colonial question. 'It was important to realise this', he stressed, 'for if the Cabinet's attitude was, as his was, that Colonial concessions could only be contemplated in return for a general settlement, this was clearly not Germany's view.'[77]

Chamberlain, however, was undeterred. Convinced that the initiative had succeeded in breaking the ice, he now pressed ahead with a scheme to open discussions with Germany on the basis of colonial appeasement. For his part Eden did not fundamentally object to this idea, and, although he was becoming increasingly distracted by disagreements with the Prime Minister over other issues, he dutifully took the lead in working up the proposals that would eventually be presented to Germany. However, this was hardly because he was particularly enthusiastic about the scheme, still less due to confidence in a positive outcome, but because, short of hopeless drift, it was now the only constructive policy available towards Germany until British rearmament had made further significant progress. If nothing else, past experience alone suggested that Hitler was unlikely at this juncture seriously to engage with issues of disarmament or to contemplate a return of Germany to the League of Nations. In fact, although Eden sought to convey a positive impression of the prospects for European appeasement to the meeting of the Foreign Affairs Committee which convened in early December, his private views were clearly quite different.[78] Only days after Halifax's interview with Hitler, Eden had effectively registered his opposition to making any untimely approaches to the dictators in what one of his biographers considers 'the clearest statement he was ever to make while Foreign Secretary of the philosophy which lay behind his distinctive approach to foreign policy'.[79] Commenting on a paper submitted by the Chiefs of Staff which *inter alia* put forward the familiar view that the primary task of British diplomacy was to seek to reduce the number of potential enemies, the Foreign Secretary argued that it would be 'a mistake to try to detach any one member of the German-Italian-Japanese *bloc* by offer of support or acquiescence in the fulfilment of their aims', for 'a surrender to one might well be the signal for further concerted action on the part of all three powers to secure further sacrifices from ourselves'. While Britain might yet have to swallow further *faits accomplis*, the Foreign Secretary held that it would be:

> safer, and more in accordance with our honour and our interests, to tolerate for the time being at any rate, the present state of armed truce, unsatisfactory as it may be, and to trust that our own armed strength and that of our associates on the one side, and the natural hesitations and divergences of interest on the part of the three aggressive Powers on the other (which we would, of course, exploit whenever occasion offered), will maintain some kind of equilibrium and make it possible for international differences, as they arise, to be settled without war. In fact, in present circumstances, our best course is likely to [be] the unheroic policy of so-called 'cunctation'. For periods in the past, Europe has managed to exist, under armed truce, without a general settlement, but without war. If this is the best we can hope for, for some time to come, this is in some measure the price which we and other members of the League have to pay for our inability effectively to assert the principles of international order against the aggressor States since 1931.[80]

A tense state of uneasy co-existence waiting for the moment at which British rearmament would permit a stronger line with the dictators was clearly a far cry from Chamberlain's plans for the imminent opening of negotiations with Germany and Italy. Indeed, it seems fairly certain that by the close of 1937 Eden was more sceptical about the prospects of an Anglo-German dialogue than has sometimes been suggested.[81] The diaries of Sir Alexander Cadogan, for example, reveal that the Foreign Secretary had no faith whatsoever in Chamberlain's plans to initiate discussions with either Rome or Berlin.[82] Similarly, Oliver Harvey, one of Eden's closest friends and collaborators in Whitehall, wrote bleakly that the Foreign Office expected 'no real progress...from our own attempts at a "general settlement" with Germany and Italy. We only hope to gain time thereby pending our rearmament'.[83] Subsequent events, including the German administrative reshuffle in early February which saw the Anglophobe Ribbentrop replace Neurath, and the shameless intimidation of Schuschnigg at Berchtesgaden shortly afterwards, hardly augured well for the forthcoming approach to Hitler. Equally, as much as Chamberlain may have been buoyed by support from within the Cabinet for his colonial initiative, the signs from Berlin were palpably disheartening. In mid-February, for example, Goering assured Henderson that Germany would be prepared to give every guarantee of its good faith in any negotiations with Britain apart from renouncing the Anschluss. That, he asserted, neither Hitler nor any man in Germany could ever countenance 'even if we offered the whole of Africa in exchange'.[84] Sure enough, when on 3 March 1938 the British Ambassador finally broached the scheme with Hitler, the answer was unmistakably negative. A solution of the colonial question, the Führer announced coldly, could wait up to ten years; within ten days German troops were on the streets of Vienna.[85]

By that stage Eden was no longer Foreign Secretary. The details of the final breach with Chamberlain are known well enough and need not be recounted here.[86] Not surprisingly, his resignation was viewed both in Britain and overseas as an event of crucial significance for the future direction of British foreign policy. 'Wherever they may be', Churchill announced dramatically in the House of Commons on 22 February, 'the friends of England are dismayed and the foes of England are exultant'.[87] In Paris the French leaders were said to be 'gravely perturbed' by the development and anxious that it portended some radical change in the policy that had been agreed during their recent consultations in London. The French press went further, characterising the resignation as an event of 'first class importance' and one which was 'fraught with dangerous possibilities for France and for the cause of peace'.[88] Across the Rhine, however, it was an entirely different story. While Hitler and Goebbels gleefully celebrated the fall of Germany's 'most fanatical opponent', only Ribbentrop struck a cautionary note, predicting that Eden would return one day as Prime Minister.[89]

Between 1935 and 1938 Eden and his advisors in the Foreign Office had never been genuinely optimistic about the prospects of a satisfactory accommodation with Germany. Forced throughout to negotiate from a position of weakness due primarily to the parlous state of British defences and the impossibility of rapid and extensive rearmament, they had patiently but vainly pursued avenues of potential agreement with Hitler, first over the Rhineland and later over the Western Pact and the colonial question. As became increasingly apparent, however, the search for a 'general settlement' with the Nazi regime was a futile undertaking, not least because Hitler refused to be deflected from his goal of violent expansion in Eastern Europe. As Germany grew militarily stronger and acquired powerful friends in the shape of Italy and Japan, the Foreign Office was faced with ever dwindling possibilities in its attempts to bring Germany to terms. In consequence, Eden's calls for accelerated rearmament, solidarity with France and the cultivation of relations with the United States became ever more frequent and vociferous. By resigning his office Eden demonstrated his fundamental and unwavering commitment to the principle that it would be a fatal error to enter into negotiations with the dictators from a position of weakness and to make concessions without securing credible and binding guarantees in return. His policy between December 1935 and February 1938 had been determined by a simple but inviolable axiom: 'If we do not get: we shall not give'.[90] This basic formula had been at the core of the Foreign Office's concept of the 'general settlement' throughout the interwar years and had become the *sine qua non* of a satisfactory solution of the 'German problem' in the 1930s. But, as the fate of Chamberlain's colonial initiative demonstrated, by early 1938 any notion of a tolerable settlement with Hitler, 'general' or otherwise, unless it knowingly consigned the continent to Nazi domination, was little more than a fanciful delusion.

Notes

1. F.S. Northedge, *The Troubled Giant. Britain Among the Great Powers, 1916–1939* (London: LSE and Bell, 1966) p. 122.
2. See for example, The National Archives, London [hereafter UKNA], minute by Vansittart, 7 July 1933, FO 371/16726/C5963; E.L. Woodward, M.E. Lambert, W.N. Medlicott, et al. (eds), *Documents on British Foreign Policy 1919–1939* (London: HMSO, 1947–1984) [hereafter DBFP, 2], Ser. 2,vol. 5, no. 229.
3. Robert G. Vansittart, *The Mist Procession. The Autobiography of Lord Vansittart* (London: Hutchinson, 1958) p. 486.
4. On the deliberations of the DRC see W.K. Wark, *The Ultimate Enemy. British Intelligence and Nazi Germany 1933–1939* (Oxford: Oxford University Press, 1986) pp. 23ff.
5. See for example, UKNA, minutes by Wigram, Sargent, Vansittart and Stanhope, 8, 14, 15 and 17 October 1935 respectively, on FO memorandum (Central Department), 5 October 1935.
6. In this connexion see especially Hitler's speech to the Reichstag of 21 May 1935 in M. Domarus, *Hitler. Speeches and Proclamations, 1932–1945. The Chronicle of a Dictatorship, vol. II. The Years 1935 to 1938. Translated from the German by Chris Wilcox and Mary Fran Gilbert* (Wauconda, IL: Bolchazy-Carducci Inc, 1992) pp. 667ff.
7. Josef Henke, *England in Hitlers politischem Kalkül 1935–39* [England in Hitler's Political Calculation 1935–39] (Boppard am Rhein: Boldt, 1973) p. 33, n. 70.

8. The Earl of Avon, *The Eden Memoirs. Facing the Dictators* (London: Cassell, 1962) pp. 142–3.
9. UKNA, Loraine to Oliphant, 5 April 1935, FO 371/18837/C3379.
10. G. Martel, ed., *The Times and Appeasement. The Journals of A. L. Kennedy, 1932–1939* (Cambridge: Cambridge University Press, 2000) p. 171.
11. R.S. Churchill, *The Rise and Fall of Sir Anthony Eden* (London: MacGibbon & Kee, 1959) p. 110.
12. Avon, *Facing the Dictators*, p. 316.
13. R. Self, ed., *The Neville Chamberlain Diary Letters. Vol. 4. The Downing Street Years, 1934–40* (Aldershot: Ashgate, 2005) p. 166.
14. UKNA, Phipps to the FO, 13 December 1935, FO 371/18852/C8238; DBFP, Ser. 2, vol. 15, no. 383.
15. UKNA, minute by Sargent, 18 December 1935, FO 371/18852/C8329.
16. On Vansittart's attitude at the turn of 1935–6 see M.L. Roi, 'From the Stresa Front to the Triple Entente. Sir Robert Vansittart, the Abyssinian Crisis and the Containment of Germany', *Diplomacy and Statecraft*, 6, 1 (1995), pp. 61–90 and M.L. Roi, *Alternative to Appeasement. Sir Robert Vansittart and Alliance Diplomacy, 1934–1937* (Westport: Praeger, 1997) pp. 104ff.
17. Churchill College Archive, Cambridge [hereafter, CCAC] Vansittart to Phipps, 20 December 1935, Phipps Papers, PHPP I, 2/17. Emphasis in original.
18. On German views of the British Foreign Office see, for example, Bundesarchiv, Koblenz [hereafter BAK], Wassner to AA, 1 May 1935, ZSg 133/38; P.R. Sweet, M. Lambert, et al. (eds), *Documents on German Foreign Policy*, Series C, ed. (6 vols., London, HMSO, 1957–1983) [hereafter DGFP, C], vol. 3, no. 333; J von Ribbentrop, *The Ribbentrop Memoirs. Introduction by Alan Bullock* (London: Weidenfeld & Nicolson, 1954) p. 47.
19. Elke Fröhlich (ed.). *Die Tagebücher von Joseph Goebbels. Im Auftrag des Instituts für Zeitgeschichte und mit Unterstützung des Staatlichen Archivdienstes Russlands Teil I, Aufzeichnungen 1923–1941* [The Diaries of Joseph Goebbels. On behalf of the Institute of Contemporary History and with the Support of the National Archives Service of Russia. Part I, records 1923–1941] (9 vols., Munich: K.G. Saur Verlag, 1998–2005) [hereafter TJG, I], vol. 3/i, 24 December 1935.
20. Hoover Institution, Stanford University, Entrevue de Léni Riefenstahl avec Adolf Hitler (Notes personelles), 24 February 1936, Scapini Papers, Box 4. In February 1938, shortly before the storm broke over Eden's resignation, Goebbels referred to the outgoing Foreign Secretary as the 'travelling salesman of Bolshevism'. TJG, I, vol. 5, 9 February 1938.
21. See J.T. Emmerson, *The Rhineland Crisis, 7 March 1936. A Study in Multilateral Diplomacy* (London: Temple Smith, 1977) pp. 39ff.
22. DBFP, Ser. 2, vol. 15, no. 460.
23. DBFP, Ser. 2, vol. 15, no 509. On 13 February 1936 Eden told Harold Nicolson that the goal of his policy was 'to avert another German war'. To that end he was prepared to make 'great concessions' provided that Hitler agreed to a measure of disarmament and to bring Germany back to Geneva. See N. Nicolson, ed., *Harold Nicolson. Diaries and Letters 1930–1939* (London: Collins, 1966) p. 243.

24. Three weeks after the Italian invasion of Abyssinia Ralph Wigram informed Phipps that as the Stresa front had 'undoubtedly gone by the board...the wind seems to me to be setting towards some kind of accommodation with Germany'. CCAC, Wigram to Phipps, 25 October 1935, Phipps Papers, PHPP I, 2/25.
25. See especially DBFP, Ser. 2, vol. 15, app. I.
26. CCAC, Wigram to Phipps, 18 January 1936, Phipps Papers, PHPP I, 2/25.
27. On these developments see especially DBFP, Ser. 2, vol. 15, nos 520, 521 and app. IV (b). On 12 February 1936 Wigram told the Counsellor of the German Embassy in London in the strictest secrecy that the British were striving for a 'working agreement' between Britain, France and Germany. See DGFP, C, vol. 4, no. 562.
28. Brotherton Library, Leeds University [hereafter BLLU], memorandum by Eden, 8 March 1936, C.P. (73) 36, CAB 24/261.
29. For an account of the negotiations see Emmerson, *The Rhineland Crisis*, pp. 150ff.
30. UKNA, St Clair Gainer to Phipps, 31 March 1936, enclosed in Phipps to Eden, 6 April 1936, FO 408/66, lxxiv, no. 26. For an indication of Ribbentrop's brief for his conversations in London see J.L. Heineman, *Hitler's First Foreign Minister. Constantin Freiherr von Neurath, Diplomat and Statesman* (Berkeley: University of California Press, 1979) p. 140.
31. UKNA, Phipps to FO, 15 May 1936, FO 371/19905/C3677.
32. UKNA, Phipps to FO, 17 June 1936, FO 371/19907/C4376.
33. On this episode see T. Jones, *A Diary with Letters, 1931–1950* (London: Oxford University Press, 1954) pp. 194ff.
34. See E.L. Ellis, *T. J. A Life of Dr Thomas Jones CH* (Cardiff: University of Wales Press, 1992) pp. 403–4; Ribbentrop, *Memoirs*, pp. 44–5.
35. D. Dutton, *Anthony Eden. A Life and Reputation* (London: Edward Arnold, 1997) pp. 70–1.
36. BLLU, Cabinet minutes, 6 July 1936, CAB 23/85.
37. CCAC, minute by Vansittart, 1 June 1936, Vansittart Papers, VNST 2/26.
38. DBFP, Ser. 2, vol. 17, no. 84.
39. UKNA, Allen to Eden, 19 October 1936, FO 371/19914/C7613.
40. CCAC, Wigram to Phipps, 29 October 1936, Phipps Papers, PHPP I, 2/25. At the Cabinet meeting at which the preliminary Anglo-French-Belgian consultation on the 'new Locarno' had first been mooted, Eden warned his colleagues that while Hitler might accept an invitation to participate in subsequent discussions 'his only object would be to free his hands elsewhere than in Western Europe'. BLLU, Cabinet minutes, 6 July 1936, CAB 23/85.
41. See, for example, *The Times*, 12 August 1936; BAK, England. Stimmungsbericht, 23 October 1936, Reichskanzlei, R43II/1435a.
42. UKNA, Phipps to the FO, 2 November 1936, FO 371/19914/C7816.
43. Avon, *Facing the Dictators*, pp. 477–8. Emphasis in original.
44. UKNA, Secretary of State's Speech at Bradford, 14 December 1936, FO 371/19916/C8927.
45. UKNA, Phipps to Eden, 4 January 1937, FO 371/20709/C109.
46. UKNA, minute by Sargent, 29 December 1936, FO 371/19916/C9152.
47. UKNA, Chilston to Collier, 15 December 1936, FO 371/19916/C9043.

48. DBFP, Ser. 2, vol. 17, app. II. Emphasis in original.
49. Nicolson, *Harold Nicolson. Diaries and Letters 1930–39*, p. 288.
50. BLLU, Cabinet minutes, 13 January 1937, CAB 23/87.
51. See G.T. Waddington, ' "*Hassgegner*": German Views of Great Britain in the Later 1930s', *History*, 81, 261 (1996), pp. 22–39.
52. See CCAC, Vansittart to Phipps, 18 December 1936, Phipps Papers, PHPP I, 2/18; UKNA, Clerk to the FO, 8 February 1937, FO 371/20719/C1080; BAK, Dertinger Informationsbericht 55, 17 December 1936, ZSg 101/29; K. Hildebrand, *Vom Reich zum Weltreich. Hitler, NSDAP und koloniale Frage, 1919–1945* [From Empire to World Empire. Hitler, the Nazi Party and the Colonial Question, 1919–1945] (Munich, Fink, 1969) p. 501.
53. Sir Nevile Henderson summarised the evolution of German policy on the colonial question thus: 'In 1935 it was possible to perceive the smoke from the colonial dragon oozing from the mouth of the cave; in 1936 the head emerged, whilst in 1937 the whole animal came out into the open.' UKNA, Henderson to the FO, 10 January 1938, FO 371/21692/C250. On the tactical function of the German colonial claim in the mid-1930s see Hildebrand, *Vom Reich zum Weltreich*, pp. 441ff.
54. See, for example, UKNA, minute by Vansittart, 16 November 1935, on Phipps to FO, 7 November 1935, FO 371/18860/C7515.
55. D. Carlton, *Anthony Eden. A Biography* (London: Allen Lane, 1981) p. 115.
56. DGFP, C, vol. 6, no. 201.
57. UKNA, St Clair Gainer to Phipps, 5 February 1937, enclosed in Phipps to FO, 17 February 1937, FO 371/20732/C1429.
58. On Schacht's activities see A.J. Crozier, *Appeasement and Germany's Last Bid for Colonies* (Basingstoke: Macmillan, 1988) pp. 173ff.
59. See DGFP, C, vol. 6, no. 371; DBFP, Ser. 2, vol. 18, no. 495.
60. Office of the Historian, Department of State, *Foreign Relations of the United States. Diplomatic Papers 1937. Volume I. General* (Washington, 1954) pp. 84–5.
61. UKNA, Phipps to the FO, 2 May 1937, FO 371/20710/C3348.
62. DBFP, Ser. 2, vol. 18, no. 466, note 2.
63. R.J. Sontag, J.W. Wheeler-Bennett, et al. (eds), *Documents on German Foreign Policy*, Series D (13 vols, Washington: Government Printing Office, 1949–1964) [hereafter DGFP, D], vol. 1, no. 225.
64. DBFP, Ser. 2, vol. 18, no. 623. On the proposed Neurath visit see G.L Weinberg, *The Foreign Policy of Hitler's Germany. Starting World War Two, 1937–39* (Chicago: University of Chicago Press, 1980) pp. 99ff.
65. Self, *The Neville Chamberlain Diary Letters. Vol. 4*, p. 259.
66. Avon, *Facing the Dictators*, p. 445.
67. Self, *The Neville Chamberlain Diary Letters. Vol. 4*, p. 264.
68. K. Middlemas, *Diplomacy of Illusion. The British Government and Germany, 1937–39* (London: Weidenfeld & Nicolson, 1972) p. 128.
69. DBFP, Ser. 2, vol. 19, no. 349.
70. Self, *The Neville Chamberlain Diary Letters. Vol. 4*, p. 270. Chamberlain's criticisms of the Foreign Office intensified with the passage of time. On October 24, horrified at the initial opposition that had been aroused by the prospect of a visit by Halifax to Germany, he confessed that he was waiting for an opportunity to 'stir it up with a long pole'. Ibid., p. 279.

71. See respectively J. Harvey, ed., *The Diplomatic Diaries of Oliver Harvey, 1937–1940* (London: Collins, 1970) p. 59; Avon, *Facing the Dictators*, pp. 509–10.
72. A. Roberts, *'The Holy Fox'. A Biography of Lord Halifax* (London: Weidenfeld & Nicolson, 1991) p. 72.
73. Avon, *Facing the Dictators*, p. 515.
74. See BLLU, 'Visit of Lord Halifax to Germany, 17–21 November 1937', Papers of Edward Frederick Lindley Wood, 1st Earl of Halifax (1881–1959).
75. Avon, *Facing the Dictators*, pp. 509ff.
76. UKNA, minute by Sargent, 23 November 1937, FO 371/20736/C8161. Unbeknown to the British, virtually everything of substance that Hitler had said to Halifax had been vitiated by the monologue he had delivered two weeks earlier to his senior diplomatic and military advisors during the so-called 'Hossbach Conference'. See DGFP, D, vol. 1, no. 19.
77. BLLU, Cabinet minutes, 24 November 1937, CAB 23/90.
78. Nicolson, *Harold Nicolson. Diaries and Letters*, pp. 314–15.
79. Carlton, *Anthony Eden*, p. 115.
80. DBFP, Ser. 2, vol. 19, no. 348.
81. See, for example, A.R. Peters, *Anthony Eden at the Foreign Office 1931–1938* (Aldershot: Gower, 1986) p. 378.
82. D.N. Dilks (ed. and contributor), *The Diaries of Sir Alexander Cadogan O.M. 1938–1945* (London: Cassell, 1971) p. 37.
83. Harvey, *The Diplomatic Diaries of Oliver Harvey*, p. 69.
84. UKNA, Henderson to the FO, 16 February, FO 371/21655/C1119.
85. On Henderson's interview with Hitler see DGFP, D, vol. 1, no. 138; DBFP, Ser. 2, vol. 19, nos 609, 610.
86. See, for example, D.R. Thorpe, *Eden. The Life and Times of Anthony Eden. First Earl of Avon, 1897–1977* (London: Chatto, 2003) pp. 189ff; R. Rhodes James, *Anthony Eden* (London: Weidenfeld & Nicolson, 1986) pp. 172ff.
87. *Parliamentary Debates. Fifth Series. Volume 332. House of Commons Official Report* (London 1938) col. 242.
88. UKNA, Phipps to FO, 20 and 21 February 1938, FO 371/21590/C1192, C 1193 and C1300. The Italians, for whom Eden had long been a *bête noire*, were beside themselves with joy. On 20 February Ciano described the crisis over the resignation as 'perhaps one of the most important which has ever taken place'. See G. Ciano, *Ciano's Diary 1937–1938. Translation and notes by Andreas Mayor. With an introduction by Malcolm Muggeridge* (London: Methuen, 1952) p. 78.
89. TJG, I, vol. 5, 22 and 23 February 1938.
90. UKNA, undated annotation by Eden, 26 November 1937, FO 371/20736/C8161.

7
Harold Nicolson and Appeasement
John W. Young

Harold Nicolson is remembered for many aspects of a remarkably varied life. The son of a Permanent Under-Secretary of the Foreign Office, he became a successful diplomat himself, with a role in shaping the 1919 Paris peace settlement. He served as far afield as Constantinople, Tehran and, in the late 1920s, Berlin. He was a prodigious writer, his publication list including novels, a memoir of the Paris peace conference, the official biography of George V and two studies of diplomacy. Nicolson's life is peculiarly well documented thanks to his diaries, most of which have been published, and he has been the centre of attention too because of his unusual relationship with his wife, Vita Sackville-West – both were bisexual – with whom he created the gardens at Sissinghurst Castle, Kent. At different times he was a journalist, broadcaster, member of parliament and government minister, yet somehow his career never reached the heights he hoped. Under pressure from his wife, he gave up his diplomatic career in 1929, in favour of writing a column for the *Evening Standard*, but rapidly became disaffected with the triviality of the job and for a time was involved with Oswald Mosley, who later led the British Union of Fascists. Nicolson was a candidate for Mosley's New Party in the 1931 general election, but broke with him the following year when his fascist leanings became clear. Elected an MP in 1935 for West Leicester, Nicolson sat in the Commons for ten years but, as a member of the small National Labour group in the governing coalition, had limited long-term prospects. In his whole time as an MP he made barely two dozen speeches, while his ministerial career, as Parliamentary Secretary to the Ministry of Information, lasted little more than a year (1940–41).[1]

Yet Nicolson's time in parliament was significant. His diplomatic experience meant that he carried some weight in debates on foreign policy, he was an ally and admirer of Anthony Eden, and in 1938 spoke out strongly against Neville Chamberlain's policy of Appeasement. He has a reputation as an 'early and consistent warner of the dangers of appeasing the dictators'.[2] This chapter focuses on that period of his life to ask how he might fit into historiographical debates on the subject, especially in light of the questions David Dilks and others have raised about Chamberlain's critics. With the outbreak of World War II, accounts of the late 1930s became dominated by the 'guilty men' school, with its condemnation of the Prime Minister for his supposedly weak-kneed approach to the dictators. However, with the opening of official files around 1970, Dilks and other revisionists showed that Chamberlain's choices were limited. With an economy recovering only fitfully from the 'slump', a population who ideally wished to remain at peace, a paucity of allies and a potential risk of having to fight three aggressive powers – Germany, Italy and Japan – simultaneously, Britain was in an unenviable strategic predicament. In such circumstances it made sense to try to buy Adolf Hitler with concessions, especially since many people believed Germany had been treated harshly in the Treaty of Versailles and when there was no coherent, realistic alternative to Appeasement.[3] The issue of alternatives has been the focus of renewed interest in recent years, not least in the work of Andrew Stedman.[4] This chapter focuses on just one of Chamberlain's better-known critics – Nicolson – to ask how consistent and well-considered were his criticisms?

Abyssinia, the Rhineland and Spain

Nicolson's dislike of fascism was clear from an early date, even as he dabbled on its fringes. During his involvement with Oswald Mosley, Nicolson urged his friend 'not to get muddled up with the fascist crowd'.[5] And when Christopher Hobhouse, a New Party supporter, returned from a visit to Germany in early 1932, Nicolson's showed an instinctive dislike of fascist methods: 'Christopher... says that the Fuhrer contends that we British Hitlerites are trying to do things like gentlemen. That will never do. We must be harsh, violent and provocative. I do not care for this aspect of my future functions.'[6] Visiting Italy with Mosley, Nicolson was impressed by the efficiency of Mussolini's regime 'on paper', but feared 'it destroys individuality. It also destroys liberty.'[7] While in Germany soon afterwards he wrote of Nazism as a 'doctrine of despair'.[8] He later explained to his wife that 'my loathing for Fascism is due to the fact that I hate the type of mind that believes in brute force. It is not nobility on my part but a sort of physical loathing which I suppose is based on cowardice.'[9] Indeed, Nicolson's involvements of the early 1930s, gave him an insight into its methods that others lacked. So, when the threat of fascist aggression actually made itself evident a few years later, he was better prepared than most to understand its violent thirst for power and to resist this. Yet, for all that, his will to resist was diluted by an appreciation of diplomatic realities, a sense of loyalty to his political colleagues and an abhorrence of war, as well as by some personal weaknesses that sometimes led him to shun the parliamentary limelight.

Nicolson's maiden speech in the House of Commons, on 19 December 1935, coincided with growing concern about fascist aggression and involved the Hoare-Laval pact. This notorious agreement provoked public outrage because it revealed the willingness of Britain and France to strike a deal that rewarded Italy's Benito Mussolini for his recent invasion of Abyssinia (Ethiopia). As Nicolson said, 'Many of us on Monday last, when we read or heard of this new Paris plan, were filled with a feeling which I can only describe as bewildered despair'. But the novice MP, keen to make a name for himself as a parliamentarian, did not push his criticism of government policy too far. He welcomed a reassuring speech from the Prime Minister, Stanley Baldwin, and praised the former Foreign Secretary, Samuel Hoare, for 'his public-spirited act of self-sacrifice' in resigning once the national outrage became apparent. Nicolson also took a singularly unsympathetic view of the predicament of Mussolini's victim, declaring: 'I do not think the main object of the efforts of this Government or of this country should be the preservation of Abyssinian integrity.' He even said that he did not 'consider the terms of the Hoare-Laval pact unreasonable', which hardly suggested someone opposed in principle to handing small countries to dictators.

In fact, apart from regretting the damage done to the League of Nations by such a deal being struck behind its back, Nicolson's objections to Hoare's diplomacy were largely procedural and revolved around two points. First, there was the supposed danger of dealing with Italian diplomats, remarks that are worth repeating at some length because they reveal an oddly simplistic view of the significance of supposed national traits in international affairs:

> Members would agree with me if they had had my experience – that you must never negotiate with an Italian on his own level. It is impossible to do so, because he is much more ingenious and much more subtle than we are ourselves. It is essential, when dealing with an Italian, to adopt an entirely different level, the level of your own

integrity, and that level is so far removed from the Italian level that you will be perfectly certain of not getting inveigled into his coils.

Then there was another lesson learned from Nicolson's diplomatic career, the dangers inherent in personal diplomacy between politicians: 'It is a terrible mistake to conduct negotiations between Foreign Ministers'; international negotiations were best left to the professionals. 'Diplomacy is not the art of conversation. It is the art of the exchange of documents in a carefully considered and precise form and in such a way that they cannot be repudiated later...Diplomacy by conference is a mistake.'[10] Despite the praise he received for the speech, Nicolson realised that 'the matter was too thin'.[11]

In a way, there was a broad consensus within Britain's political leadership on the need for some measure of 'appeasement' in the mid-thirties, in the sense of making concessions to countries who had been treated unjustly in the past. Most accepted that Germany was harshly dealt with in the Treaty of Versailles and that it was worth offering something to Hitler if this would secure the peace. Nicolson met with Anthony Eden, the League of Nations minister, in February 1936 and the pair agreed that the key aim was to avoid war by striking a deal that involved making 'great concessions to German appetites provided they will sign a disarmament treaty and join the League of Nations'.[12] Whatever his dislike of Italian diplomatic methods, Nicolson soon focused his attention on the potential German menace. In his diary in late February 1936, the Conservative MP 'Chips' Channon recorded Nicolson giving to the Foreign Affairs Committee 'a brilliant address on Anglo-German relations. It was shrewd, but alarming and we almost heard the tramp-tramp of the troops. Harold predicted that trouble would come from the German source in 1939 or 1940.'[13] In this he may have been influenced by his old friendship with Robert Vansittart, Permanent Under-Secretary of the Foreign Office in 1930–37, with whom he continued to meet socially.[14] Vansittart, too, focused on the German menace though, in trying to create a strong anti-Nazi front, he may have been more ready than Nicolson to overlook Mussolini's misbehaviour. Indeed, the Permanent Under-Secretary had been a key advocate of the Hoare-Laval pact.[15]

On 7 March 1936, Hitler took his first step to overthrow the postwar settlement and expand German power via a sudden *fait accompli*, when he remilitarised the Rhineland. In doing so, he violated both the Treaty of Versailles and the 1925 Locarno Pact. Nicolson later recalled that, 'It was not pleasant during those weeks to be a Cassandra exposing weakness, indicating danger and prophesying disaster.'[16] But if this is intended as a reflection on his own role at the time, it exaggerates. True, at first he was deeply troubled and ideally wanted firm action. He told his wife, 'we should refuse to negotiate with Germany until she evacuates the Rhineland and should force her out of it. It is really essential to demonstrate that Treaties cannot be torn up by violence.' But, as on the Abyssinian question, he soon tempered his determination with a string of second thoughts. For one thing, British public opinion was 'terrified of war... And the result is that we shall give way to Germany and let down France.'[17] In the Commons too, he noted, the 'mood... is one of fear. Anything to keep out of war.'[18] By 12 March, he had doubts of his own about military action, though they were not entirely logical. On the one hand he felt an ultimatum unwise, because Hitler was unlikely to back down and there would be war. Nicolson was confident 'we shall win and enter Berlin. But what is the good of that? It would only mean communism in Germany and France.' (Quite why this followed was not explained.) In any case, Nicolson simultaneously argued that the British people would refuse to fight, so that, 'We must swallow this humiliation as best we may and be prepared to become the laughing-stock of Europe.' He argued this despite his realisation that, coming on top of the Abyssinian fiasco, it would 'mean the final end of the League' on which he had previously placed such hope.[19] Nicolson continued in his confused state for some time. At the Foreign Affairs Committee on 17 March, attended by more than two hundred MPs, he 'made an able and forceful speech reminding the meeting of the extent of the Locarno obligation' and urged that Britain should 'restrain France but not betray her'.[20] Then again, his position was far from unique. As James Emmerson remarked in his analysis of the Rhineland crisis, 'most persons who later came to be identified with anti-appeasement' – Nicolson, Vansittart, Robert Boothby, even Winston Churchill – accepted that the use of force was impossible at this point. And in this, of course, they were at one with the government, whose Foreign Secretary was another figure later identified as an anti-appeaser, Anthony Eden.[21]

In his second Commons' speech, on 26 March 1936 Nicolson revealed his admiration for Eden by praising a statement he had made as 'one of the most telling and effective... ever delivered in this House'. Nicolson also betrayed a feeling that Germany's case was not without merit, regretting that Britain had not been more willing to resuscitate her in the 1920s. 'When... Stresemann came into power and there was a real chance of being able to build up all that is best in German life and character, we did not give that encouragement which we should have tendered... Now, when Germany is strong, we fall upon our knees, we bow our foreheads in the dust, and we say "Heil, Hitler".' But, of course, his dislike of Nazism was reflected in the last remark and much of his speech was devoted to arguing the need for a policy of deterring German aggression, a policy to be carried out in close cooperation with France:

> Is there any Member in the House who believes that Germany is not a danger?...I do not advocate a definite practical alliance with France...But I advocate...the closest relationship with France during the critical months that are upon us...We must say, if the frontiers of Holland, Belgium or France are crossed by any country, especially by Germany, we will within such and such a time bring so many forces, ships and aeroplanes in their defence.

This was clearly much stronger than his approach to the Abyssinian crisis, even if Nicolson added the coda that cooperation with France should only apply 'to the West. It has nothing to do with the East.'[22]

Vansittart continued to influence Nicolson's thinking and recognised that, with the Rhineland secure, Hitler would now turn his attention eastwards. They lunched together in late April, when 'Van' argued that 'a German hegemony in Europe means the end of the British Empire' and that 'we have no right to buy Germany off...by offering here a free hand against the Slav countries.' But this came up against Nicolson's doubts about defending Eastern Europe – doubts already reflected in his Commons remark that cooperation with France should only apply in the West. He felt Vansittart 'is right in theory but in practice it would be quite impossible for us to get the British people to fight Germany for the sake of the Czechs'.[23] Nonetheless, a readiness to draw a line somewhere in the sand, over which the dictators should not cross, became a theme in Nicolson's speeches. In late June 1936, with the fall of Abyssinia to Italy, he was sympathetic to the government's predicament and argued that, 'We League people have been shown...by our ineptitude in this Abyssinian question that economic sanctions are not enough. We know, as has already been said, that aggressive violence can only be restrained by force. It is by the organisation, the co-ordination and the planning of force that the new League of Nations must be built.'[24] He did not provide, in any detail, a method to achieve such an aim and, in retrospect, it was clear that the League was a broken reed. But, in the Commons a few days later he came to the defence of the Secretary for War, Alfred Duff Cooper who, while on a visit to Paris, had seemed to advocate an alliance with France. The Opposition argued that this was out of step with official policy but it was clearly to Nicolson's taste.[25] Meanwhile, his expertise on international questions was recognised when he was asked to become Vice-Chair of the Foreign Affairs Committee, made up of MPs who supported the government coalition. And his views on the need for a strong stand against the dictators, backed by rearmament and an alliance with France, were evident in his writings at the time. In an article in the influential US journal, *Foreign Affairs*, in July he showed that he now recognised the need to protect Eastern European states: he rejected the idea 'that we surrendered Eastern Europe to German hegemony and thereby secured peace, perhaps only for a single generation, with the certainty of an eventually disastrous war'.[26]

Much of Nicolson's attention in late 1936 was absorbed by the abdication crisis and by November 1936, when he was asked to second the Address to the Throne, the international scene was more settled. On this occasion, when he was in any case expected to avoid controversy, Nicolson's views, apart from some jibes at Mussolini, seemed well in line with government policy.[27] During 1937 he made only a few speeches in the Commons. His most significant remarks were about the Spanish civil war, where he was pro-Republican ('If I were to say in the House what I think about Franco I should use the most turbulent language'[28]) yet opposed British intervention (partly because he feared that this would justify Italian and German intervention on a larger scale[29]). The war appalled him. After the bombing of Guernica by the German air force in April he wrote of his feeling 'that barbarism is creeping over the Earth again and that mankind is going backwards'.[30] Aside from Spain, the dictators created no crises but Nicolson's diary shows that he was concerned about their rising strength. In November he had a long talk with Winston Churchill about the balance of air power in Europe, which led to the conclusion that 'we are...not in a position to go to war without very active Russian assistance.'[31] Nicolson recognised – as the government, since May 1937 under Neville Chamberlain did – that 'we cannot fight Germany, Italy and Japan at the same moment'. But he was also impressed by the argument of Conservative MP Duncan Sandys that 'if Germany wishes to attack us, she will do so in any case, and her present policy is to get as much as she can meanwhile without war.'[32] Yet, the situation no longer seemed pressing. Addressing the Foreign Affairs Committee in December, Eden said there was 'no imminent likelihood of war and a far better prospect of appeasement than ever before'.[33] Major differences over appeasement – not a term that Nicolson himself used much – would only become obvious in the following year.

Chamberlain and Eden

The sense of calm did not last. The event that really seems to have turned Nicolson against the National government's foreign policy was not some action by the dictators but the resignation of Anthony Eden in February 1938, after differences with Chamberlain over how best to deal with Mussolini. As seen above, Nicolson had no liking for Italy's diplomatic style or its dictator; but the MP was an admirer of Eden and regularly praised him in the Commons. In July 1937 he told the Commons, 'I feel that our present Secretary of State for Foreign Affairs does represent in his person the greatest possible agreement that this country in foreign affairs could hope to achieve.'[34] Early in 1938, differences between Chamberlain and Eden came to a head when the Prime Minister was keen to enter into conversations with Mussolini and offer concessions – notably the recognition of Italian rule in Abyssinia – while Eden, who suspected that Mussolini was about to back a German invasion of Austria, argued that there should be no precipitate concessions. The Foreign Affairs Committee of 17 February, well aware of the differences within the Cabinet, was sympathetic to Eden. According to Leo Amery, Nicolson spoke 'vigorously and... pessimistically'. His line was that Hitler was fully in control in Germany and bent on adventurism, while Mussolini had sided with the German leader. Britain should 'keep a stiff upper lip... wait, and above all, arm'. Nicolson himself was delighted to find that the Committee, which was also addressed by Churchill, 'no longer believe[s] that we can buy Germany off with concessions'.[35] The potential for a political crisis only worsened on 20 February, when Eden resigned.

But the crisis was over almost as soon as it began. Before the Commons on 21 February, Eden, in Nicolson's own words, 'did not really make a good speech'. He made it seem as though, by insisting that the time was not quite right for talks with Italy, he had resigned on a point of detail. In the ensuing debate, an angry Nicolson proved more Edenite than Eden, insisting that in fact 'a great question of principle' was a stake. He returned to his old theme that Italian diplomats had to be handled carefully. 'It is the problem whether a country which has continuously, consistently, deliberately and without apology, violated every engagement into which she has ever entered can be taken back into the fold with a smile; or whether it is better to make a few concrete conditions before negotiations are resumed.' He talked of what he called the 'corkscrew' approach of the Italians: 'They have a perfect system of inventing something that they do not want, of clamouring for the thing they do not want, of saying they will die if they do not get it, and then when they get it, of asking for something else.' Thus, 'it would be foolish... to re-enter negotiations with Italy without first obtaining certain concrete guarantees.'

This time Nicolson did not pull his punches in attacking government policy. Instead he launched into a vitriolic attack on the Prime Minister, which had pre-echoes of what would be said after Munich: 'the Prime Minister comes here this evening and, with a gesture of triumph, produces Count Grandi's little note... The Prime Minister said that that document was a splendid bit of give-and-take. So it is. We give and they take.' All the Italian foreign minister had offered, argued Nicolson, was to withdraw some troops from Spain, 'where they ought never to have been in the first place'. Ultimately, he claimed, the Italians would ask for a share in controlling the Suez Canal. He risked losing his audience with reflections on Italian policy that went all the way back to 1882 but he ended on a high moral note:

> The late Foreign Secretary struggled hard to preserve the rule of law and order, the theory of the League of Nations, the belief in the sanctity of treaties, and the confidence of the world – which we may lose by this action. However weak we might be, however divided, however muddle-headed; although we might sometimes be frightened, and sometimes misled, we never definitely defended wrong with cool and planned deliberation as we are doing now.

Those who came up to congratulate him afterwards included Churchill and Lloyd George.[36]

Support for Eden could have proved costly for Nicolson, especially since he abstained on Labour's 22 February censure vote. Both the Conservative majority and his own National Labour colleagues condemned him; and there was opposition from within his Leicester constituency. 'Chips' Channon, a loyal Chamberlainite MP, considered that in his speech of 21 February Nicolson 'did the cause of peace as much harm as he could'.[37] At the Foreign Affairs Committee on 25 February, the atmosphere was 'most unpleasant'. Nicolson had heard that there would be an attempt to force the resignation of himself and the chair, Conservative MP, Paul Emrys-Evans, who had also abstained. The pair decided that, in the circumstances, they would be better off resigning on their own initiative, but – ironically – the pro-Chamberlain majority realised that this could embarrass the government and so urged them to wait.[38]

After these stressful events, Nicolson decided to 'lie low for the moment'. Such moderation upset a fellow anti-appeaser, Violet Bonham Carter, but Nicolson now argued, curiously, that 'Chamberlain must be given a chance.'[39] Nor, was he so much opposed to the Prime Minister as to want to join 'the Winston brigade', still preferring to hope for a lead from the more respectable Eden. Or so he told his wife.[40] But Nicolson remained deeply concerned about the international situation and he did sometimes meet with Churchill and the latter's supporters, such as Boothby.[41] On 9 March he was involved in a depressing meeting at the Royal Institute of International Affairs, where the feeling was that Britain and France together could not stand up to the German-Italian combination. Later he dined with another anti-appeasement MP, Edward Spears, and Vansittart, who now believed it impossible to prevent Germany dominating Eastern Europe. 'We are suddenly faced by the complete collapse of our authority, our Empire and our independence.'[42]

Any hope that Central Europe could escape Nazi domination was dented in mid-March when Hitler invaded Austria unopposed. On the 16th, Nicolson spoke during another debate about Spain, when he drew together a number of points in his thinking. He spoke of his 'very deep hatred' for Franco and accused Chamberlain of underestimating the dangers of the situation. Britain might soon see 'the establishment at vital strategic points of Italian and German batteries and submarine bases' in Spain, threatening the Royal Navy's control of the Mediterranean. Nicolson pressed the need to look at the situation, not in emotional terms, but from a strategic perspective and he again urged close cooperation with France. On the surface his arguments seemed hard-headed enough.[43] But, after he had finished, a note was passed along the benches from the Prime Minister. What, precisely, did Nicolson expect the government to do? 'Occupy Minorca', was the response. At this, Chamberlain flung 'back his head with a gesture of angered despair'.[44] The reaction is hardly surprising. Violent action by the British government at this point, would have justified similar action by the dictators, caused confusion at home and lost the moral high ground abroad. Nor is it clear what strategic gain would be made from seizing Minorca, when the Royal Navy already had a chain of Mediterranean bases. Nicolson's suggestion smacked of desperation when put on the spot by the Prime Minister. Yet it was the only precise proposal he could think of.

Chamberlain and his supporters now numbered Nicolson among 'the insurgents'.[45] But Malcolm Macdonald, the National Labour leader, worked to moderate Nicolson's opposition to the government[46] and, for a time, he became quiescent. In April, after weeks of pressure for him to do so, Nicolson resigned his position as co-chair of the Commons' Foreign Affairs Committee. Emrys-Evans resigned alongside him.[47] After that he avoided saying anything in Commons debates so that, by the summer, 'the general impression [is] that I have "dropped out".'[48] Meanwhile, Eden too showed no sign of taking a lead against Chamberlain. In conversation with Nicolson in May, the former Foreign Secretary seemed worried above all by the danger of splitting the country into hostile camps on foreign policy. 'He is himself determined to do everything to prevent such a split.'[49] Nicolson was encouraged by the so-called 'May Crisis' over Czechoslovakia, when Hitler seemed to back off from an invasion of the country (though actually he had no intention of acting at that point). Nicolson believed this showed 'strength and justice' could work and that war might be avoided if Britain rearmed. 'Hitler has for the first time been checked', Nicolson wrote, which might mean that Britain could 'negotiate with the Germans on equal terms'. It is significant that negotiation, not conflict, remained his hope.[50]

Nicolson's anti-appeasement activities went on away from the Commons chamber at this time. In the first half of 1938 he attended meetings of the so-called 'Salter's Soviet' at All Souls, Oxford. Arthur Salter, Professor of Political Theory, was a former civil servant who successfully stood as an anti-Chamberlain candidate in a 1937 by-election. A desire to resist the tide of dictatorship was central to the group but they fell out over how best to achieve this, with Nicolson taking a sceptical view of the possibility of negotiation with Hitler while others were reluctant to rule out talks.[51] There were similar disagreements within the National Labour leadership.[52] His anti-appeasement views were also reflected in his publications, as in a critique of the idea that German cooperation might be secured through colonial concessions.[53] In June 1938 Nicolson set out his private thoughts on the international situation in his diary. Chamberlain, he feared, was ready 'to give Germany all she wants at the moment, and cannot see that if we make this surrender we shall be unable to resist other demands.' He also feared that Germany and Italy aimed to divide Britain from France. However, if Britain stood up to Germany it could provoke a war that London would lose, so that perhaps a policy of buying time was the best course. An alliance with Russia was impossible because the British 'governing classes' had an intense 'hatred of the Reds'. Unsurprisingly, after such a circuitous argument, Nicolson retired to bed 'in gloom'.[54] His problem by now was clear: he recognised that the dictators could not be bought off with concessions; that, in other words, appeasement would fail. Yet he could not produce any coherent alternative to Chamberlain's policy.

Munich

In late August and early September 1938, Nicolson's thoughts were dominated by the looming Czechoslovakian crisis, as it became evident that Hitler might launch a military strike across the border. His earlier doubts about resisting Hitler in the East had now disappeared. He saw the new crisis as 'the final struggle between the principle of law and the principle of violence', and was increasingly concerned that Chamberlain would back down.[55] But when, on 14 September, it was announced that Chamberlain would make a personal visit to Hitler at Berchtesgaden, Nicolson wrote that the 'first feeling is one of enormous relief'.[56] With his wife arguing that the Sudeten Germans had a right to self-determination and the indecisive Eden insisting that he did not 'wish to lead a revolt or to secure any resignations from the Cabinet', it is not surprising that Nicolson felt heavy-hearted.[57] The Prime Minister flew off to Germany again on 22 September, as Churchill mounted an intense campaign against what he called 'the complete surrender of the Western democracies to the Nazi threat of force'.[58] At this point Nicolson was involved in a number of fraught meetings with other anti-appeasers. On the 22 September he was at Churchill's flat to discuss possible tactics against Chamberlain. Four days later, when it seemed there might yet be war – thanks to Hitler's increased demands in his second summit with Chamberlain – Nicolson was at the flat again along with Leo Amery, Boothby, Harold Macmillan and others, where it was agreed that, 'If Chamberlain rats again we shall form a united block against him.' Believing war to be imminent, the group wanted a coalition government, a blockade of Germany, national service and an approach to Russia.[59] But in the Commons on 28 September, Chamberlain announced his third and final visit to Germany for the Munich conference. Nicolson was one of the few MPs to refuse to rise as a tribute, drawing the remark from someone behind him, 'Stand up, you brute!' Once again, he felt a sense of relief in Chamberlain's summit diplomacy, 'But my moral anxieties are in no way diminished.'[60] At Munich the concession of the Sudetenland to Germany was finally settled. While the conference was underway, Nicolson attended the meetings at which Churchill tried to mobilise key MPs to sign a letter to the Prime Minister, warning him against any more concessions to Hitler. Eden and the Labour leader, Clement Attlee, refused to sign however, leaving

Churchill – and Nicolson – despondent.[61] Meanwhile, the BBC and the Foreign Office pressed Nicolson to avoid 'alarmist' warnings about war, and even criticisms of Nazism, in his broadcasts for *The Past Week*.[62]

While others lauded the Prime Minister for avoiding war at Munich, Nicolson nailed his colours to the anti-Chamberlain mast. At first he did so inadvertently, during a speech in Manchester on 1 October that caused a minor storm, because it – supposedly – contained a personal attack on the Prime Minister's key adviser, Horace Wilson. In fact the speech was misrepresented, because the newspapers based their reports on a draft version released by the National Labour party.[63] At the same time, Nicolson became more closely identified with 'Winston's dissentients', meeting with them to discuss tactics in the Commons.[64] His most famous contribution to the case against appeasement was his speech during the Munich debate of 5 October 1938. Here he rejected the idea that the crisis could somehow be blamed on Czechoslovakia itself or that the country was an 'artificial' creation of the Paris peace conference. He also rejected the argument that the question was solely a procedural one, to do with the fate of the Sudetenland (indeed, he conceded the case for separating the region): rather, 'it is essentially the problem whether...Germany is the dominant country in Europe.' His logic was that Germany had now achieved such dominance. 'That is the essential thing, the thing which we ought to have resisted, the thing which we still ought to resist' It was this point that led him to speak of 'this defeat, this humiliating defeat, this terrible Munich retreat'. Bulgaria, Rumania and Yugoslavia would, he argued, now strike deals with Hitler. He guessed that the whole of Eastern Europe would be at Hitler's feet in three months. Nicolson wrote off the 'piece of paper' Chamberlain had brought back as making 'friends with the strong against the weak'. For Nicolson it represented nothing less than the end of hundreds of years of balance of power diplomacy, designed 'to prevent by every means in our power the domination of Europe by any single Power or group of Powers'. He was not without some sympathy for 'all the excellent intentions, all the admirable courage and all the lonely dignity which the Prime Minister displayed', but he felt that Chamberlain had shown 'a lack of understanding of foreign mentality' and he ended the speech on an emotional note: 'I know that those of us who believe in the traditions of our policy...are accused of possessing the Foreign Office mind. I thank God that I possess the Foreign Office mind.'[65]

When it came to the vote Nicolson joined Churchill, Eden, Duff Cooper (who had just resigned from the government), Amery,

Macmillan and over 20 other Conservative MPs in abstaining. 'The House', he believed, 'knows that most of the above people know far more about the real issue than they do.' This was not mere vanity. In similar vein Oliver Harvey, Private Secretary to the Foreign Secretary, considered 'all the good speeches were against the government' and listed Nicolson's among them.[66] His behaviour caused renewed ructions within his Leicester constituency but Nicolson continued to identify with other anti-Chamberlainites.[67] In November, with a dozen Conservative MPs, including Amery, Duff Cooper and Macmillan, he attended a 'hush-hush meeting' with Eden where they finally agreed to form their own group – though they would not advertise it as such – meeting occasionally to discuss the international situation and 'organise ourselves for a revolt if needed'. Yet, even now, all was not as it seemed. Nicolson told his wife he was happy to be 'distinct from the Churchill group' and led by 'wise people' who 'do not mean to do anything rash or violent'.[68] But, once again, such moderation exposed a real weakness in his outlook. The Eden Group lacked robust leadership from the former Foreign Secretary, who continued to hope for a return to office. By the end of the month, Nicolson was complaining that, 'We still do not really constitute a group and Anthony still hesitates to come out against the government.'[69] Nicolson continued to state his own beliefs at public meetings.[70] But 1939 would see him retreat once more from an active role in the Commons, as he had retreated in the wake of his anger over Eden's resignation.

The coming of war

In early February 1939, Nicolson was predictably delighted with Chamberlain's announcement to the Commons of a closer relationship with France, amounting as this did to a military alliance. It seemed the Prime Minister had 'swung suddenly round to all that we have been asking for', he told his wife, 'I think it can only mean that he realizes that Appeasement has failed.' Chamberlain might even become an asset, because, 'No ordinary German or Italian will ever believe propaganda telling him that Chamberlain is a war-monger.'[71] In March, Nicolson even met his constituency chair's wish for a statement 'saying that I agree with the government's present policy. Which I do.' A letter to his wife, however, revealed that he had few illusions about why the 'ladies of Leicester' needed such a statement. They were worried by the world situation and eager to trust in Chamberlain, who 'has rendered cowardice and treachery respectable'.[72] With the collapse of the Munich agreement shortly afterwards, Nicolson could have driven home the point that the anti-appeasers had been proven right and the Prime Minister wrong. But, as Hitler marched on Prague, Nicolson felt it 'merely renders explicit facts that since Munich were implicit'[73] and his speech in the Adjournment debate of 3 April 1939 seemed a world away from his intervention of six months before. He began by declaring his wish 'to add my pebble to that great bastion of support which the Prime Minister must feel that he has now behind him' and could even find some retrospective praise for the events of the previous September. Nicolson believed that Chamberlain had convinced the Germans of his interest in peace and that they did not welcome the breech in the Munich agreement. He also felt that Hitler's anti-Semitic atrocities, with their 'cold and deliberate sadism', had alienated many Germans. He wanted a propaganda campaign to be pressed by the BBC and the British Council to explain the British case to the German people and convince them that peace was possible.[74] In this, as Drinkwater says, he missed 'the obvious point that, even if the majority of Germans and Italians regarded Chamberlain as a man of peace, they were ruled by men to whom this was irrelevant'.[75]

It was not that Nicolson ceased to have doubts about Chamberlain's policy, but he does seem to have been ready to accept that the Polish guarantee, given by Britain in the wake of Hitler's destruction of Czechoslovakia, marked a real change in foreign policy.[76] Behind the scenes he continued to associate with Churchill, joining the latter in a discussion with the Soviet ambassador, Ivan Maisky, to discuss a possible alliance.[77] And by mid-April Nicolson feared that Chamberlain, under the influence of Horace Wilson, might already be returning to his old belief in appeasement.[78] But in the Commons he said nothing to suggest such deep concern. Robert Boothby complained about his friend's weakness at this time, only to receive the reply that 'old queens like myself are capable of hysterical heroism but are not good at the constant fight.'[79] As his fears grew about 'another Munich over Danzig', any desire Nicolson might have to put his head above the parapet was probably deflated by Eden, who continued to miss 'every boat with exquisite elegance' when it came to criticising the Prime Minister.[80]

On 31 July 1939, in his last Commons speech before the outbreak of war, Nicolson seemed bent on securing peace both at home and abroad. His logic was that 'the way of appeasement... is dead' and that 'the way of peace' had now become the 'proper focus'. He began by defending Eden: 'seldom in the history of any political controversy, any political disagreement, has such moderation been shown, such extreme consideration been displayed, such reticence, almost, been exercised, as has been shown by my right honourable Friend in the unhappy controversy that arose after his retirement.' At home Nicolson hoped to abolish 'this ridiculous duality between appeasers and resisters', building an 'agreement that there must be the maximum of resistance first, and thereafter the maximum of conciliation'. Abroad, he feared that such conciliation could prove difficult because 'war has become a vested interest in Germany' and the whole economy had become geared to armaments production. The solution was to make 'it clear to Hitler that victory is a physical impossibility and that peace is a physical possibility'. And as part of this policy Nicolson specifically urged that Britain should offer loans to help Germany through a process of disarmament. He wanted an inspection regime to oversee such disarmament and he wanted the Nazis to withdraw from Czechoslovakia.[81] It was another odd display, as high on moral principle as it was thin on practicalities. It showed that he still hoped for a negotiated settlement, albeit from a position of strength. Yet, as war approached over the following weeks he reverted to his belief that a deal with Hitler was impossible, that Chamberlain's attempts at maintaining the peace were wrong and that war had to be faced.[82]

The outbreak of war saw Nicolson in a gloomy mood. He admitted, 'there is a little timid, selfish side of myself that tempts me by still murmurings to hope that we shall reach a form of appeasement after the Germans have conquered Poland'; but he immediately added that 'the real thing in me loathes and detests any such capitulation.'[83] During the phoney war he continued to criticise Chamberlain's performance – 'no gift for inspiring anybody' and 'one feels the confidence and spirits of the House dropping inch by inch' were just two comments on the Prime Minister's speeches[84] – and remained part of the Eden Group (though Eden himself had now rejoined the government). His criticism of Chamberlain's diplomacy was evident once more to the public when he authored a Penguin Special: *Why Britain is at War* in December 1939. Here he likened the Prime Minister and Horace Wilson on the international stage to 'two curates entering a pub for the first time; they did not observe the difference between a social gathering and a rough house'.[85] Nicolson also continued to exchange views with Vansittart[86] and recognised Churchill's gifts as a potential leader. By late September 1939, with the prospect of defeat heightened by the Soviet invasion of eastern Poland, he wrote that 'Churchill might be our Clemenceau or our Gambetta' and in October was involved in a discussion in the Eden Group about his replacing Chamberlain.[87] In the vote of May 1940, when Chamberlain's majority crashed to only 81, Nicolson was among those who voted against him, helping bring Churchill into office.

Conclusion

What might be said by way of an overall interpretation of Nicolson's approach to appeasement? He gained an early reputation as an anti-appeaser and his public line certainly embraced a certain logic. He had a visceral dislike of dictators and saw Italian and German policy as an ideological menace as well as a threat to British security. He hated the Spanish civil war and was appalled by the results of Nazi anti-Semitism in Austria. 'We stand for tolerance, truth, liberty and good humour. They stand for violence, oppression, untruthfulness and bitterness.'[88] He also wanted to see the government make a stand at some point. In his speech following the remilitarisation of the Rhineland he insisted that, 'It is no use merely to express virtuous intentions. We must act in such a way that the countries of Europe – Germany above all – must say, "This time they really mean it".' He always deeply believed in cooperation with France, at least in terms of security in Western Europe. In his Commons speeches, he said nothing specific about some of the problems that concerned the government, such as the threat from Japan or Britain's economic weakness. But it is clear from his diaries and other sources that he thought about such problems. In 1937 he considered that an agreement between Britain, the US, Germany and Japan to develop China would provide business for those factories that were diverted from arms production, neatly combining the desire for peace, the problems of East Asia, the need to stimulate the world economy and, it must be said, the potential for 'economic appeasement'.[89] He was not a firm advocate of a Soviet alliance in 1936–38, but he was friends with the Soviet ambassador, Ivan Maisky; he complained about Chamberlain's anti-Russian outlook[90] and in 1939 he saw the logic of Churchill's arguments in favour of a Soviet alliance. He was also willing to run risks for his beliefs, alienating other members of National Labour, their Conservative allies and his constituency party with his criticisms of Chamberlain.

Nonetheless, a chronological look at Nicolson's thoughts and statements on British foreign policy in 1935–39 shows that, whatever his dislike of the dictators, his attitude towards appeasement was volatile. Down to February 1938 he did not differ substantially with government policy. Nicolson's rejection of military action during the Rhineland crisis led David Carlton to refer to him merely as 'a so-called anti-appeaser'.[91] Nicolson was not alone in being a critic of Munich, having earlier refused to stand up over the Rhineland. David Dutton has highlighted Eden's desire, as Foreign Secretary, for a *modus vivendi* with Hitler while simultaneously pursuing rearmament: 'If this was appeasement through strength, it was appeasement nonetheless.' It was a policy supported by another of Nicolson's influences, Robert Vansittart.[92] Of course, it is possible to defend those who took such views at a time when Hitler did no more than 'march into his own backyard'. Norman Rose has argued that, in 1936, Nicolson was reluctant to march ahead of public opinion, reluctant to distance himself from the government (especially with Eden as Foreign Secretary) and 'at a loss' to know how to deal with Hitler.[93] And, again, in this he was not alone. Besides, surely his opposition to appeasement in 1938 is what matters? By the time of Munich, Nicolson came to see appeasement as meaning one-sided concessions in a vain attempt to buy off the dictators and he was prepared even to stand up for Eastern European countries. He made his position clear in April 1939 when appeasement seemed to have collapsed: 'I have always contended that Germany wanted only one thing and that was power. Now, power is an expanding ambition and it is impossible to fix its frontiers. Chamberlain and the appeasement folk imagined that you could.'[94] Yet, even during 1938 itself he showed signs, during the middle of the year, before the Munich crisis loomed, of withdrawing from the front line, even if he remained very active behind the scenes. Again, during the first seven months of 1939 – though he remained active as a speaker, writer and broadcaster – Nicolson's few parliamentary speeches suggest a backing away from his earlier attacks on the Prime Minister, a readiness to value him as a 'Man of Peace' and, perhaps more significant, a willingness to use economic concessions to wean Hitler from his wish for war. But for the most part he seemed to withdraw again from parliamentary life, having nothing to say in the Commons during the crisis over Poland, even if his dislike of Chamberlain was clear enough to those around him.

As Derek Drinkwater has argued, Nicolson had a 'liberal realist philosophy of international relations', rejecting utopian solutions to the world's problems but also appreciating the dangers of power politics. His belief in the League of Nations in 1935–37 was based on a desire to avoid dividing Europe into alliance blocs, such as had occurred before 1914. But, within this liberal idealist outlook, his views could range quite widely.[95] Aside from an inevitable evolution in his thinking over time, this chapter has also shown that he was influenced by events and individuals around him. These included not only the actions of the dictators or the behaviour of his own government, but also the attitudes of his wife and his friends, the carping from his constituency party, the criticism of his fellow MPs and the behaviour of the less-than-heroic Eden. Nicolson was determined to work with the Eden Group rather than with Churchill and this may be one reason why he never became close to the wartime Prime Minister. In mounting a campaign against appeasement, Nicolson was also affected, in a negative sense, by his own self-doubt and feelings of depression, by his decency and moderation, perhaps by his Englishness, which he once summed up as implying a 'habit of compromise, gradualness and the middle path between extremes'.[96] As one of his biographers has written, Nicolson lacked the 'spirit of leadership... He was too soft and sentimental.'[97]

Criticisms from without and self-doubt within: these explain his withdrawals from the political fray in mid-1938 and after October 1938. He did not have the nerve or commitment necessary for the long haul, while the same sensitivity that made him an anti-fascist made him long for peace. 'What I need', he told his wife in the wake of the Rhineland crisis, 'is a feeling that we shall avoid war'.[98] This desire, somehow, to avoid war made him feel powerless, as reflected in another, highly sentimental letter to her a few months before war came: 'We wish only to do good on earth. We are not vulgar in our tastes or cruel in our thoughts. Why is it that we are impotent to prevent something that we know to be evil and terrible?'[99] In analysing world affairs he could be lucid and intelligent, but equally he had an almost naïve belief in the significance of national traits, as in his attack on Italian diplomatic methods after the Hoare-Laval pact.[100] Above all, while confident of the need to resist aggression, re-arm and cooperate with other nations, he never could produce a coherent alternative to appeasement. Neither, it might be said, did Eden or Churchill. But after his suggestion that Britain had best occupy Minorca, it is probably understandable that Chamberlain did not see Harold Nicolson as a source of sound advice on how best to deal with the fascist menace.

Notes

1. For biographies see: James Lees-Milne, *Harold Nicolson, A Biography* (2 vols, London: Hamish Hamilton, 1988); and Norman Rose, *Harold Nicolson* (London: Jonathan Cape, 2005). Also valuable is Denis Drinkwater, *Sir Harold Nicolson and International Relations: The Practitioner as Theorist* (Oxford: Oxford University Press, 2005). Excellent as these are, they are all, to my mind, rather too generous to Nicolson when it comes to dealing with his opposition to appeasement. I am grateful to my colleague Dr Nick Thomas for comments on an earlier version of this paper.

2. Thomas Otte, 'Nicolson', in G.R. Berridge, M. Keens-Soper and T. Otte (eds), *Diplomatic Theory from Machiavelli to Kissinger* (Basingstoke: Macmillan, 2001) p. 171.
3. For a review of the literature see Sidney Aster, 'Appeasement: Before and After Revisionism', *Diplomacy and Statecraft*, 19, 3 (2008), pp. 443–80. David Dilks' key contribution was 'Appeasement Revisited', *University of Leeds Review*, 15 (1972), pp. 51–64.
4. Andrew David Stedman, *Then What Could Chamberlain Do, Other Than What Chamberlain Did? A Synthesis and Analysis of the Alternatives to Chamberlain's Policy of Appeasing Germany* (PhD, University of Kingston, 2007).
5. Nigel Nicolson, ed., *Harold Nicolson: Diaries and Letters, 1930–39* (London, Collins, 1966) p. 97, entry of 24 November 1931.
6. Nicolson to Sackville-West, 3 January 1932, in Nigel Nicolson, ed., *Vita and Harold: The Letters of Vita Sackville-West and Harold Nicolson* (New York, Putnam's, 1992) p. 231. See also Nicolson, ed., *1930–39*, p. 108, 24 January 1932, for further comments, including 'Hitlerism ... is a doctrine of despair.'
7. Nicolson, ed., *1930–39*, p. 106, 6 January 1932.
8. Nicolson, ed., *1930–39*, p. 108, 24 January 1932.
9. Nicolson to Sackville-West, 4 August 1938, in Nicolson, *Vita and Harold*, pp. 304–6.
10. *HC Deb.* 5s, vol. 307, cols 2076–81, 19 December 1935. Similarly, in June 1936, he argued that 'the personal mission of a Minister abroad is the most dangerous form of diplomacy which can possibly exist': *HC Deb.* 5s, vol. 314, col. 131. All quotes from Hansard are via http://hansard.millbanksystems.com/commons [accessed 6 June 2009].
11. Nicholson, ed., *1930–39*, p. 233, 19 December.
12. Nicholson, ed., *1930–39*, p. 243, 13 February 1936.
13. Robert Rhodes James, ed., *Chips: The Diaries of Sir Henry Channon* (London: Weidenfeld and Nicolson, 1967) p. 59, 27 February.
14. At some points these became quite frequent, as in early 1938: Nicholson, ed., *1930–39*, p. 322 (17 February), 327 (28 February), 330 (9 March) and 334 (11 April).
15. For a recent discussion see Keith Neilson and Thomas Otte, *The Permanent Under-Secretary for Foreign Affairs* (Abingdon: Routledge, 2009) ch. 7.
16. Harold Nicolson, *Why Britain is at War* (Harmondsworth: Penguin, 1939) p. 56.
17. Nicolson to Sackville-West, 11 March 1936, in Nicolson, *Vita and Harold*, pp. 280–1.
18. Nicolson, ed., *1930–39*, p. 248, 9 March.
19. Nicolson, ed., *1930–39*, pp. 249–50, Nicolson to Sackville-West, 12 March.
20. John Barnes and David Nicholson (eds), *The Empire at Bay: The Leo Amery Diaries, 1929–45* (London: Hutchinson, 1988) p. 411, entry of 17 March 1936; Nicolson, ed., *1930–39*, p. 252, 17 March.
21. J.T. Emmerson, *The Rhineland Crisis* (London: Temple Smith, 1977) p. 145.
22. *HC Deb* 5s, vol. 310, cols. 1468–72, 26 March; Nicolson, ed., *1930–39*, p. 254, 26 March 1936. Nicolson pursued similar points about the Rhineland in talking at Chatham House: Rose, *Nicolson*, pp. 196–7.

23. Nicolson, ed., *1930–39*, p. 259, reproducing Nicolson to Sackville-West, 28 April.
24. *HC Deb.* 5s, vol. 313, cols. 1663–8, 23 June.
25. *HC Deb.* 5s, vol. 314, cols. 131–5, 29 June.
26. Harold Nicolson, 'Has Britain a Policy?', *Foreign Affairs*, 14, 4 (1936), p. 561.
27. *HC Deb.* 5s., vol. 317, cols. 17–21, 3 November.
28. *HC Deb.* 5s, vol. 326, col. 1892, 19 July.
29. *HC Deb.* 5s, vol. 322, col. 1095, 14 April.
30. Nicolson to Sackville-West, 29 April, in Nicolson, *Vita and Harold*, pp. 294–5.
31. Nicolson, ed., *1930–39*, pp. 312–13, 15 November.
32. Nicolson, ed., *1930–39*, p. 313, 18 November.
33. Nicolson, ed., *1930–39*, pp. 314–15, 9 December.
34. *HC Deb.* 5s, vol. 326, col. 1893, 19 July.
35. Nicolson, ed., *1930–39*, p. 323, 17 February 1938; Barnes and Nicholson, *Amery Diaries*, p. 455, entry of 17 February; Earl of Avon, *The Eden Memoirs: Facing the Dictators* (London: Cassell, 1962) pp. 579–80.
36. Nicolson, ed., *1930–39*, pp. 323–5, 22 February; *HC Deb.* 5s, vol. 332, cols. 99–104, 21 February.
37. James, ed., *Chips*, 145, 21 February.
38. Nicolson to Sackville-West, 25 February 1938, in Nicolson, ed., *1930–39*, pp. 325–7; Barnes and Nicholson, *Amery Diaries*, p. 458, entry of 24 February; and on Emrys-Evans as an anti-appeaser see Lynne Olson, *Troublesome Young Men: The Rebels who Brought Churchill to Power* (New York: Farrar, Straus and Giroux, 2007) pp. 101–3.
39. Nicolson, ed., *1930–39*, p. 327, 28 February.
40. Nicolson to Sackville-West, 2 March, in Nicolson, ed., *1930–39*, pp. 327–8.
41. Nicolson, ed., *1930–39*, p. 332, 16 March.
42. Nicolson to Sackville-West, 9 March, in Nicolson, *Vita and Harold*, pp. 297–8.
43. *HC Deb.* 5s, vol. 333, cols. 521–4, 16 March. And see Nicolson, ed., *1930–39*, p. 332, 29 March 1938.
44. Nicolson, ed., *1930–39*, pp. 331–2, 16 March.
45. James, ed., *Chips*, p. 153, 22 March.
46. Nicolson, ed., *1930–39*, p. 333, 29 March.
47. Nicolson, ed., *1930–39*, p. 333, 7 April.
48. Nicolson, ed., *1930–39*, p. 348, 30 June.
49. Nicolson, ed., *1930–39*, p. 339, 11 May.
50. Nicolson to Sackville-West, 30 May, reproduced in Nicolson, *Vita and Harold*, p. 301; Nicolson, ed., *1930–39*, p. 344, 23 May.
51. See A.L. Rowse, *All Souls and Appeasement* (London: Macmillan, 1961) pp. 59–60; Sidney Aster, ' "Salter's Soviet": Another View of All Souls and Appeasement', in M.G. Fry (ed.), *Power, Personalities and Policies: Essays in Honour of Donald Cameron Watt* (London: Frank Cass, 1992) pp. 144–74; Rose, *Nicolson*, pp. 209–11.
52. N.A. Rose, ed., *Baffy: The Diaries of Blanche Dugdale, 1936–47* (London: Vallentine Mitchell, 1973) p. 65, 2 November 1937.
53. Harold Nicolson, 'The Colonial Problem', *International Affairs*, 17, 1 (1938), pp. 32–51.

54. Nicolson, ed., *1930–39*, pp. 345–6, 6 June.
55. See, for example, Nicolson, ed., *1930–39*, p. 359, 11 September.
56. Nicolson, ed., *1930–39*, pp. 359–60, 14 September.
57. Nicolson, ed., *1930–39*, pp. 360–1, 15 and 19 September.
58. Churchill press statement, 21 September, reproduced in Martin Gilbert, *Winston S. Churchill, vol. V, 1922–39* (London: Heinemann, 1976), pp. 978–9.
59. Nicolson, ed., *1930–39*, pp. 363–8, 22 and 26 September; Barnes and Nicholson, *Amery Diaries*, p. 517, entry of 26 September.
60. Nicolson, ed., *1930–39*, pp. 368–71, 28 September.
61. Nicolson, ed., *1930–39*, pp. 371–2, 29 September.
62. Lees Milne, *Nicolson, volume 2*, 109–10.
63. Nicolson, ed., *1930–39*, pp. 359–60, 1 October.
64. Nicolson, ed., *1930–39*, p. 375, 5 October; Barnes and Nicholson, *Amery Diaries*, p. 526, entry of 5 October.
65. *HC Deb* 5s, vol. 339, cols. 426–34, 5 October.
66. Nicolson, ed., *1930–39*, pp. 375–6, 6 October; John Harvey, ed., *The Diplomatic Diaries of Oliver Harvey, 1937–40* (London: Collins, 1970) p. 210.
67. Nicolson to Sackville-West, 10 October, in Nicolson, *Vita and Harold*, pp. 307–8.
68. Nicolson to Sackville-West, 9 November, in Nicolson, ed., *1930–39*, pp. 377–8.
69. Nicolson, ed., *1930–39*, pp. 380–1, 24 November.
70. See, for example, his remarks to the Junior Constitutional Club: Nicolson, ed., *1930–39*, pp. 359–60, 30 November.
71. Nicolson to Sackville-West, 7 February 1939, in Nicolson, *Vita and Harold*, pp. 308–9.
72. Nicolson to Sackville-West, 29 7 March, in Nicolson, *Vita and Harold*, pp. 310–11.
73. Nicolson, ed., *1930–39*, p.392, 14 March.
74. *HC Deb* 5s, vol. 345, cols. 2524–9, 3 April.
75. Drinkwater, *Nicolson*, p. 155.
76. Nicolson, ed., *1930–39*, p. 393, 17 March, with pp. 393–4, 31 March.
77. Nicolson, ed., *1930–39*, p. 394, 3 April.
78. Nicolson, ed., *1930–39*, pp. 397–8, 11 and 19 April.
79. Nicolson, ed., *1930–39*, pp. 402–3, Nicolson to Boothby, 6 June, and for the reply, 9 June, Olson, *Troublesome Young Men*, pp. 195–6.
80. Nicolson, ed., *1930–39*, pp. 405–6, 18 July.
81. *HC Deb* 5s, vol. 350, cols. 2080–4, 31 July.
82. See especially Nicolson, ed., *1930–39*, pp. 411–22, 23 August–3 September.
83. Nigel Nicolson, ed., *Harold Nicolson: Diaries and Letters, 1939–45* (London, Collins, 1967), pp. 31–2, 11 September; and see p. 30, 5 September, for similarly pessimistic thoughts.
84. Nicolson, ed., 1939–45, p. 35, 20 September, and p. 37, 26 September.
85. Nicolson, *Why Britain is at War*, p. 106, but see pp. 130–1 for a more sympathetic line on Chamberlain's predicament and the danger of harsh retrospective judgments.
86. For example, Nicolson, ed., *1939–45*, pp. 33, 60 and 96.
87. Nicolson, ed., *1939–45*, pp. 34–5, 17 September, and p. 38, 3 October.

88. Nicolson, ed., *1930–39*, p. 273, 20 September.
89. Nicolson, ed., *1930–39*, p. 302, 16 June.
90. For example, Nicolson, ed., *1930–39*, p. 329, 7 March.
91. David Carlton, *Anthony Eden: A Biography* (London: Allen Lane, 1981) p. 81.
92. David Dutton, *Anthony Eden: A Life and Reputation* (London: Edward Arnold, 1997) p. 60.
93. Rose, *Nicolson*, pp. 198–9.
94. Nicolson, ed., *1930–39*, p. 401, 29 April.
95. Drinkwater, *Nicolson*, p. 15 and see ch. 6 on the inter-war period.
96. Harold Nicolson, 'British Public Opinion and Foreign Policy', *Public Opinion Quarterly*, 1, 1 (1937), pp. 53–63.
97. Lees-Milne, *Nicolson*, vol. 2, p. 85.
98. Nicolson, ed., *1930–39*, p. 259, reproducing Nicolson to Sackville-West, 28 April 1936.
99. Nicolson, ed., *1930–39*, p. 404, Nicolson to Sackville-West, 19 June 1939.
100. The same outlook is evident in, for example, his 'What France Means to England', *Foreign Affairs*, 17, 2 (1939), esp. pp. 351–3.

8
Another Jewel Forsaken
The Role of Singapore in British Foreign and Defence Policy, 1919–68

Malcolm H. Murfett

Size doesn't always matter. Singapore may have been tiny, devoid of mineral resources and with an insufficient water supply for its own residents, but its sheltered position in Southeast Asia, one degree north of the equator on the trade routes to Australasia and East Asia, made it another precious economic jewel in the British crown for roughly a century and a half in the late modern period. While it could never claim to be as illustrious as India – which country could? – Singapore had nonetheless developed into an increasingly alluring entrepôt by the turn of the twentieth century. Once World War I had been mercifully brought to an end in late 1918, however, Singapore's value as a promising economic hub became subordinated to that of its increasing geostrategic significance in the eyes of HMG policymakers in Whitehall. This enhanced military potential arose directly from the abandonment of the Anglo-Japanese Alliance in 1921 and the somewhat begrudging acceptance of the Washington treaty system that streamlined naval establishments around the world and supposedly brought a new reality to bear in international relations.[1]

Sacrificing an alliance of 20 years to curry favour with the Americans didn't do the British any favours whatsoever. Worst of all it played into the hands of those Japanese nationalists like Katō Kanji who saw in its rejection a haughty and contemptuous Caucasian response towards their treaty partners and one which could be used in future to justify a set of anti-western policies.[2] While the Anglo-Japanese Alliance may not have been quite the diplomatic coup that some claimed it to be, a strategic partnership – however shallow it may have been – was still notably better than a mutual relationship of hostility and aggression.[3]

After the abrogation of that alliance at the Washington Conference, the plain fact emerged that policing the waters of the Far East could no longer in theory, much less in practice, be entrusted to the Imperial Japanese Navy (IJN) on behalf of their erstwhile British allies. From February 1922 onwards, therefore, the British were faced by an undeniable new reality: if they wished to protect their overseas investments in the littoral states washed by these seas, they would have to find ways and means of doing so themselves. This wouldn't be easy and it would be expensive. Could they afford to do so? Even if the answer was no, what was the alternative? In a sense this was the acute British dilemma of the entire interwar period for all those possessions east of Madras. HMG was obliged to protect the empire its predecessors had established in the past, but truthfully it didn't really have the means to do so any longer. As a result, wishful thinking often bridged the gap between ways and means. It shouldn't have done so since strategic planning ought not to be based on hyperbolic best-case scenarios. Unfortunately, they tended to be *de rigueur* in the Far Eastern theatre for far too long.

This regrettable situation gave rise to one of the most painful myths of the modern era. Some naval scholars still persist in seeing merit in the 'Singapore Strategy' even though it was Micawberish in theory and abjectly failed in practice. A marriage of convenience bequeathed by a robust Admiral Jellicoe and a subdued British government, the 'Singapore Strategy' became a political football between Tory and Labour administrations in the 1920s; the former supporting investment in imperial defence as opposed to the latter's belief in financial restraint and disarmament.[4] In essence, the Washington Conference had left the Japanese in a very favourable monopoly position in the Western Pacific since the United States had agreed not to build any first class naval base closer to Japanese shores than Pearl Harbor in Hawaii and the British had accepted a similar restriction as far as Singapore was concerned. So the United States would not be able to use Subic Bay in the Philippines as their main forward base in the region while the British would be similarly denied the use of their existing naval base in Hong Kong.[5]

After undertaking a grand inspection mission east of Suez two years before the leading naval powers gathered in Washington and the Anglo-Japanese Alliance was sacrificed, Admiral Jellicoe had boldly issued a series of recommendations to the dominion governments he had visited and to his paymasters at the Board of Admiralty. His trenchant and undiplomatic reports were notable for their sagacity, foresight, and staggering cost. If the vexatious Jellicoe could be believed, the Asia-Pacific was unlikely to remain quiescent in future and the Japanese would ultimately pose a distinct threat to Western interests in the region. These were conclusions that the stunned Board of Admiralty didn't wish to receive. Typically his own man, Jellicoe had exceeded his instructions, but could the Admiralty reject his report solely on the basis of it being *ultra vires*? This was annoyingly unlikely as his reports to the dominions had ensured that the cat was out of the bag. In this case, the cat happened to be the proposal for the stationing of a major naval force in the Far East to deter the IJN from executing any aggressive policy deep into Southeast Asia. Jellicoe had stirred up a hornet's nest; the Australasian dominions, in particular, could hardly feel sanguine about the future if the Japanese decided to build up their navy and widen their imperialist focus beyond mainland China.[6]

In the rather febrile atmosphere generated by the Versailles peace conference, Lloyd George's coalition government passed a pious Cabinet resolution in August 1919 stating that for planning purposes Britain could reliably work on the notion that it would avoid engagement in any major war for the next ten years.[7] Whether accurate or not, how did this prediction square with Jellicoe's warning about the preparations needed to meet a future threat from Japan? It didn't. Something had to give and basic economics determined that Jellicoe's scheme for a substantial Far Eastern Fleet would not come to pass. Nonetheless, even if the former First Sea Lord's warnings fell on deaf ears in London they were unlikely to be dismissed as wildly exaggerated by either the Australians or New Zealanders who might find themselves in direct line of fire if the Japanese decided that the time had come to embark upon their long anticipated *nanshin-ron*. To assuage the concerns of the empire, therefore, something would have to be done. Quite what ought to be done was the problem that the British government had to deal with in the following years.

Whatever the Admiralty thought of Jellicoe's crystal ball gazing, future defence requirements in the Far East seemed to point to the establishment of a naval base in the region. Where this might be best situated was a matter of lively debate in the newly reformed Committee of Imperial Defence. Hong Kong and Sydney were touted as possible locations but both were ultimately ruled out because they were either too close and intensely vulnerable (Hong Kong) or too far away (Sydney) from any likely scene of confrontation with a determined Japanese foe in the indeterminate future. In the end, Singapore won the location vote by geographical default.[8]

Nonetheless, developing a naval base on the diamond shaped island lying immediately to the south of the Malayan hinterland was a good deal easier said than done. First of all the existing maritime port in Keppel Harbour was not physically large enough to cope with both the mercantile fleet and its naval counterpart. Without a massive land reclamation scheme, the like of which was only resorted to from the 1970s onwards, the existing Keppel resources could only serve the needs of one or other of these fleets but not both. It had been geared for the red ensign and that was what it ended up by continuing to serve. By ignoring Keppel, the Admiralty advisors (surveyors and engineers) had few realistic alternatives. Short of creating an artificial base in the Singapore roads (Selat Sinki) that would cause more problems than it was worth and cost a king's ransom to build and then support on an annual basis, the advisors limited themselves to four possibilities along the NNE coastline of Singapore. Ultimately Sembawang, situated less than a mile from the shore of the Malayan mainland, was chosen as the site of the new base, but its defensive vulnerability was obvious to the War Office from the outset. Apart from anything else, it would need a 30-mile defensive perimeter to protect it from artillery assault or infantry encroachment.[9] Would it ever get this perimeter? Judging from the fudged size of the naval base itself, the answer was always likely to be no.

If Sembawang was to become a first class naval base in both peace and war it would need to be able to handle the requirements of a substantial capital ship fleet. Unquestionably, the 'Green Scheme' that Leopold Savile, the Admiralty's leading civil engineer, designed for the naval base would have met that objective, but the cost of doing so was considered by the Treasury mandarins as being far too high to be economically sustainable. Their concerted opposition ensured that Savile's proposal was summarily rejected in March 1923 in favour of a much inferior alternative – the 'Red Scheme'. Instead of being able to service the needs of a full battle fleet as Savile's original 'Green Scheme' would have done, the much cheaper 'Red Scheme' was supposed to only ever cater for a peacetime force roughly one-fifth the size of the full battle fleet.[10] Why 20 per cent is a moot point. It made no sense whatsoever if Jellicoe's prediction should ever come to pass and the IJN did eventually sweep south seeking its date with destiny.

Surely under these circumstances, a relatively small British peacetime fleet was more likely to serve as a magnet rather than as a deterrent to the Kidō Butai and its accompanying forces? Admiralty war planners were not fazed by such complications because they had a compelling way of cutting the Gordian knot. In essence it lay in persuading the British government to send its Main Fleet to Singapore in the event of war with

Japan. While the 'Singapore Strategy' became the ubiquitous answer to the perennial strategic question of the day in the Far East, what the Main Fleet was supposed to do once it had reached Southeast Asia was one of the great imponderables of the age. Apart from anything else, the naval base would never be large enough to receive the full complement of British warships that were supposedly being sent to it! Quite what those elements of the fleet that couldn't be accommodated within the naval base were supposed to do while they waited for a wharf in the dockyard to be vacated was not obvious in the original script.[11]

Should this surprise one? I suppose the answer should be a categorical yes, but the closer one looked at the 'Singapore Strategy' the more porous it became. So much was unclear and open to change depending upon the circumstances of the war that the Japanese would be waging at the time. Reactive rather than proactive, the entire British strategic doctrine left much to be desired. Spontaneity may on occasion be extremely desirable but like many things it can be massively overdone. It was in this case.

Accountants and economists have much to answer for when it comes to strategic planning; cheaper options often carry the day politically but not where it matters most on the battle front if war results. Looked at in terms of its location and projected size, therefore, one does not need to be a Cassandra to assess the choices relating to the Singapore naval base as being at best strategically injudicious and at worst fatally flawed. Singapore was not destined to be another Malta. Expecting it to hold out for weeks or months at a time was unreasonable unless the British were prepared to lavish substantial sums on defensive preparations in Johor and had sufficient forces throughout Malaya to thwart the ambitions of a determined enemy intent on territorial aggrandizement.

General Jan Smuts was never a fan of the 'Singapore Strategy' and always remained a sceptic. He couldn't see how the British government could afford to let its Main Fleet steam off to a base more than 8,000 nautical miles away for perhaps months at a time if the situation in Europe, the Mediterranean or the Middle East was unsettled and threatening.[12] He was right. Why so few other leading statesmen and politicians couldn't see the wisdom in his opposition to the 'Singapore Strategy' almost defies belief. Whatever the reason – perhaps a mix of complacency, overconfidence and wishful thinking – the support of the conservative political/diplomatic establishment for the 'Singapore Strategy' remained typically vibrant both at home and around the Commonwealth long after the honeymoon of Locarno had been replaced by the eerie 1930s when extremism often trumped moderation in international relations. For some supporters of the equatorial strategy apparently ignorance was bliss.

Accordingly, money was stumped up for the construction of the base from a variety of sources and some preparatory drainage work began in the mid-1920s. Despite the fact that progress on the Sembawang base was glacial over the next few years, the project still managed to survive all efforts to sabotage it. Ramsay MacDonald tried and failed to sink it in both his stints at the head of a Labour administration in Downing Street (1924 and 1929–31), and Winston Churchill, in his unlikely capacity as Chancellor of the Exchequer, damaged it still further by slashing expenditure on the inferior 'Red Scheme', thereby ensuring the future naval base would bear little or no relation to the first class structure that the Washington Treaty had allowed HMG to construct in 1921.[13]

Once the Japanese had begun to fulfil Jellicoe's predictions by renouncing Taishō democracy and embracing a militant imperialism in the early 1930s, the 'Singapore Strategy' that had been designed to thwart those ambitions was still years away from being a credible proposition. Work on the Sembawang base accelerated somewhat in the post-Manchukuo phase, but much still needed to be done to enable it to receive a fraction of the Main Fleet should it ever be sent east of Suez in an emergency.[14] This fact was of singular importance once disarmament was seen to have shot its bolt by 1934 and the world began witnessing a more assertive foreign policy by Italy and Germany, the leading dictatorial powers of Europe. When Spain threatened to be added to that list from 1936 onwards, the British government was confronted by a potentially hostile coalition of forces on its continental doorstep with a barren League of Nations and few realistic options at its immediate disposal to tackle the problem. Collective security was by now a broken reed and the French, who had never really trusted the concept in any case, showed precious little interest in mounting anything other than a defensive posture hitherto in international relations. If the French couldn't be lured out from behind their Maginot Line, what other friends could be expected to help pick up the slack on the United Kingdom's behalf? Expecting active assistance from the Americans who had spent the postwar years disengaged from Europe and the wider world in an isolationist frame of mind was unlikely to say the least and legislatively complicated by the neutrality legislation it had wrapped itself in from 1935 onwards.[15] Commonwealth states had their own problems to deal with and those lying to the east of Suez were focused upon the increasingly bellicose activities of the Japanese who after the Marco Polo Bridge incident of July 1937 were intent on subjugating the Chinese and seemingly anyone else who came in their way. As for linkage with the Soviet Union, the Baldwin and Chamberlain governments were deeply suspicious of socialism in all of its forms – a view echoed by the French Far Right in 1936: 'Better Hitler than Blum'.[16]

Despite sterling efforts by Anthony Eden, the British Foreign Secretary, to interest the Americans in a joint naval demonstration of force against the Japanese in the aftermath of the *Panay* incident of 12 December 1937, President Roosevelt preferred to keep his powder dry. Talks between naval representatives of the two sides were arranged but they neither amounted to much nor plugged the gap in dealing with the Japanese threat in the Far East.[17] It didn't surprise the experienced diplomat Sir Ronald Lindsay in the least. He observed tellingly a few months before: 'Anglo-American relations are fool-proof and are only in danger when attempts are made to improve them.'[18]

Forestalled on one front, the British fell back upon their own limited resources. On 15 February 1938 – exactly three years to the day before the fall of Singapore to the Imperial Japanese Army – the King George VI dry dock at Sembawang was opened by Sir Shenton Thomas, Governor of the Straits Settlements. While still not fully operational, the naval base (a truncated version of the 'Red Scheme') was now basically in place.[19] Ironically, as it came on stream the commitment to the 'Singapore Strategy' became increasingly endangered by the crises now surfacing in Europe. Prime Minister Neville Chamberlain responded to these threats by promoting the policy of appeasement. He hoped that consensual diplomacy would trump military aggression and that Hitler and Mussolini would see reason if the democracies showed good faith and indulged them to some extent. An expedient policy, appeasement may have bought Chamberlain et al. a little time, but it did so at considerable cost to the Czechs and subsequently to the Slovaks as well. By March 1939 the architect of this deeply flawed policy went before his own constituents in Birmingham and admitted that all had not gone according to plan.[20] Herr Hitler's promises had proven as bankrupt as the Austrian Creditanstalt had been in the Great Depression.

While appeasement was manifestly dead, what could replace it short of a resort to war? If there was another alternative, Chamberlain, for one, didn't know how to grasp it. Confronted by what FDR described as the three bandit nations (Germany, Italy and Japan), the United Kingdom was left with little option other than to prepare for the worst and hope for the best.[21] Where Singapore now figured in this strategic equation was anyone's guess. Once described as a keystone of imperial defence, the supposed fortress of Singapore had seen better days. In June 1939 the official 'period before relief' was raised to 90 days. It would be doubled to 180 days once the Germans, buoyed up by the signing of the Nazi-Soviet Pact on 23 August, poured across the Polish border eight days later to start the European phase of World War II.[22]

It was all very well having a 'period before relief' set at 6 months, but how realistic was it to expect that the British would be able to accomplish what could easily turn out to be a formidable military objective in that time frame? Was the defensive structure in place to ensure that Singapore could survive that long without adequate reinforcements? Judging from the relative inadequacy of the Sembawang base and the failure to make good the defensive limitations in Johor exposed by Major-General Sir William Dobbie when he was GOC Malaya from 1935 to 1939, the prospects were not propitious.[23] Even if the Royal Navy or a large part of it could be sent off to the Far East when the United Kingdom was at war in Europe – a seminal question in itself given the fact that the war at sea had been anything but phoney from the outset – could the Main Fleet be certain of defeating the IJN wherever it was in the region and be successful in raising the siege of the island fortress from those intent upon its destruction? What if the IJN was conspicuous by its absence and the danger to Singapore was posed by significant elements of the Imperial Japanese Army? How long would the Main Fleet be expected to remain in the region if it couldn't bring the IJN to battle and subdue it? These and a whole range of other sobering questions about the 'Singapore Strategy' needed to be addressed by those advocating the policy since they cut to the heart of its feasibility. Frustratingly, however, many of these probing questions simply couldn't be answered in advance regardless of how many Far East Appreciations were drawn up by the Chiefs of Staff in London. As such, the 'Singapore Strategy' remained in abeyance with no resolution on whether it was practical or impractical, possible or impossible. This didn't stop people from all walks of life in Singapore and beyond putting their trust in it, but their faith in the implementation of this strategy would be severely put to the test in the coming months.

Once the phoney war was over with the German attack on Denmark and Norway in April 1940, the chances of the British government implementing the 'Singapore Strategy' appeared to get slimmer by the day. After the attack on France and the Low Countries on 10 May and the Italian declaration of war a month later, the prospect of a Far Eastern demarche was profoundly unlikely. By the time the French had called for an armistice later in June the likelihood of the Main Fleet going anywhere beyond Alexandria was so remote as to be unworthy of contemplation save by the foolhardy. Churchill's government hoped that this point would become self-evident to those members of the Commonwealth who were relying upon the British to fulfil their earlier strategic promises and come to their rescue if need be.[24] Somehow, however, the penny didn't drop. Those needing help continued to assume it would be forthcoming and the British wouldn't turn their back on them.[25]

If the strategic picture in continental Europe looked bleak in the summer of 1940, the global picture proceeded to get a good deal worse as the autumn drew on. Japanese aggression extended beyond mainland China into Tonkin on 22 September and the announcement five days later of the Tripartite Pact linking the governments in Tokyo with those in Berlin and Rome seemed even more ominous.[26] Clearly the dictatorships were on the march and the war looked set to widen and assume an Asian dimension in the not too distant future.

That epochal event was still more than 14 months away, however, and within that time frame the isolated British, aided and abetted by a partial but non-belligerent United States, just about held their own against the Germans in home waters and the North Atlantic and did more than that to the Italians in the Mediterranean and Red Sea.[27] Providing this situation continued to prevail, the Admiralty hoped that something might be done further afield in the spring of 1942, such as the build-up of a balanced force east of Suez. Winston Churchill, who had never been to Southeast Asia in his life and yet professed to believe he understood the strategic picture better than his military advisors, did not want to wait that long. Although he still regarded Singapore as a military fortress and one that the Japanese would refrain from attacking, he sensed that he couldn't pin his long-term hopes for the Far East on the Americans unless the British were prepared to show President Roosevelt and the Commonwealth leaders that they honoured their commitments and were prepared to show the flag in the Far East. For this reason, Churchill returned from the 'Atlantic Charter' meeting with Roosevelt in August 1941 determined to show his hand and warn the Japanese that the British meant business in the region. Rejecting the cautious approach in the Indian Ocean offered by First Sea Lord Admiral Sir Dudley Pound and the Admiralty, he revived the Drax-Backhouse scheme of 1938–39 of sending a 'flying squadron' of two fast capital ships and a carrier escort to Singapore.[28] Churchill was wrong about the Japanese; he was wrong about Singapore; and worst of all he was wrong about the deterrent value of Force G. To make matters far worse, HMS *Indomitable*, the carrier assigned to Force G, didn't even survive the journey out east. She ran aground in the Caribbean and no replacement carrier was sent in her stead.[29] If that was not bad enough, Churchill also had his hand in the appointment of T.S.V. Phillips as the commander of the Eastern Fleet. 'Titch' Phillips had been a trusted, but desk bound, figure for many years as director of plans and subsequently VCNS. He was short of operational experience and showed it badly when the Pacific War began in December 1941. Within two days of the attack on Pearl Harbor and the first bombing attacks on Singapore, the Royal Navy's latest battleship *Prince of Wales*, the veteran battle cruiser *Repulse* and 840 of their officers and men of the 'flying squadron' were no more.[30] It was another tragic misstep in a catalogue of misadventures concerning Singapore. Sadly, it wouldn't be the last.

Over the past 70 years a sub-school of modern military history has been devoted to the defence and fall of Malaya and Singapore, but this is not the place to plough that familiar furrow again. Suffice it to say that whereas the Japanese planned their invasion systematically and kept their eyes steadfastly on the main prize, the British devised their countermeasures in an indecisive, disputatious and incoherent manner. Brian Farrell sums up the position witheringly: 'Singapore was all but lost before a shot was fired.'[31] Seventy days after battle was joined and 20 days earlier than the Japanese had planned, Singapore fell to General Yamashita's 25th Army on 15 February 1942.[32]

Watching the mighty British Empire humiliated by the Japanese was a lasting shock for the citizens of Malaya and Singapore. This was not supposed to happen and yet it had. Lee Kuan Yew who was to become one of the most perceptive and indomitable statesmen of the twentieth century was an impressionable adolescent when he witnessed the unthinkable happening, namely, thousands of Commonwealth servicemen trudging off wearily to Changi to begin their period of captivity at the hands of an Asian power. It made him lose respect for the British who had promised much to the Malays and Singaporeans and yet had demonstrably failed to deliver when the going got rough. A tough lesson in life had been swiftly learnt by the 18-year old; don't rely upon others to save you. Self-defence was of paramount importance. Caucasians often talked loud and long but, ultimately, action counted far more than mere words. For a young man little interested in religion, this might have been a Calvinistic epiphany. While it didn't appear to stir his interest in faith, it certainly caused him to re-think his mindset about the dominance of the 'white man' and feel a certain continental pride in the Asian people who evidently weren't going to be the footstool of the Europeans any longer.[33]

Unhappily, trading British stewardship for that of the Japanese brought profound misery for many Chinese and Eurasian people during the occupation of Singapore. This accentuated the sense of betrayal felt by the local population towards their former British rulers. It also didn't do anything for Anglo-Australasian relations either. Whatever Churchill might have said and felt about the scale of the military disaster that had overtaken the British Empire, the sad fact about HMG's dereliction of duty couldn't be hidden. Churchill's unfamiliarity with the region and its peoples notwithstanding, he sensed that much had to be done to repair the poor image of the United Kingdom in the eyes of the Commonwealth. It was for this reason that he was determined to recover the Malayan peninsula and Singapore from the Japanese in the last weeks of the war. Operation *Zipper* and its Singaporean equivalent (Operation *Tiderace*) didn't succeed in doing that. Launched five days after the Japanese had signed the instrument of surrender on the heavy cruiser HMS *Sussex* on 4 September 1945, *Zipper* became nothing more than a massive propaganda exercise that would be faithfully recorded on film reels and shown in cinemas throughout the Commonwealth.[34] Since these PR opportunities couldn't take away the despair and violence of the Japanese Occupation, neither the operations nor the media bombast convinced the locals (and especially not the burgeoning nationalists) on either side of the Causeway that the British deserved another chance to return as the dominant colonial authority once again. And who could blame them?

Yet return they did. After a graduated beginning overseen by the British Military Administration and subsequently by South East Asia Command (SEAC), the colonial administration assumed power once again with more forces on the ground than before the war but with the same kind of strategic problems of imperial and financial overstretch dogging their continued existence east of Suez. How Churchill would have dealt with this problem is unknown. He wasn't given the chance of restoring British power in the region because the UK electorate opted for a radical alternative to Conservatism with both a big and a small c in July 1945. To the incredulity of the victorious war leader, Churchill was replaced as British Prime Minister by Clement Attlee at the head of a Labour administration pledged to bring about substantial change across the board in the immediate future.[35]

Attlee may have been wickedly lampooned by Churchill as 'a sheep in sheep's clothing', but the British people were inclined at the end of the war to trust someone who wouldn't say one thing and do another.[36] Attlee may not have been a terribly charismatic fellow – he would have admitted that himself – but he was sincere and far more able than most of his detractors were prepared to admit. He saw value in the British Empire but unlike many of his Conservative opponents, he didn't see it as being an end in itself. Unlike Churchill, in particular, Attlee sensed that the time for selective decolonization was nigh and that former promises about independence needed to be kept. He didn't need reminding that the British were facing a stark economic climate in the immediate post-war world and wasn't given to sentimentality over ends and means. He acknowledged that Malaya and Singapore needed to be retained because they were good dollar earners, but the cost of doing so must not become prohibitive.[37] Attlee's problem was complicated because of the recent history of the territories. Could a classic cost-benefit analysis be ruthlessly applied in this case? Surely other factors were at work here? Even if Malaya was big enough to let go at some stage in the future, Singapore looked far too small and vulnerable to be cast adrift on its own and so was duly established as a Crown Colony in April 1946.[38] Thereafter, devising a suitable means of keeping the scattered British territories in Southeast Asia together once they had outlived their immediate usefulness to HM Treasury became an increasingly important issue for the colonial authorities in London.

Apart from the staggering cost of implementing its radical social legislative agenda, Attlee's Labour administration soon found itself in highly penurious circumstances. Six years of war had left the United Kingdom in economic disarray with a reserve currency that was overvalued and under pressure. Much needed to be done to rehabilitate the basic fabric of the state. At every level from housing and factories to roads and rolling stock, the United Kingdom needed massive investment.[39] Where was it to come from? Unfortunately, President Truman's immediate ending of Lend-Lease didn't do the United Kingdom any favours whatsoever. An urgent loan sought from the US Treasury by John Maynard Keynes rather inadequately plugged the gap and actually caused more convertibility problems than it solved. A fierce winter (it turned out to be the worst of the century) didn't help a government already stretched too thin to take any further economic body blows, but they came anyway.[40]

It was recognized that major cuts would have to be made in public expenditure but Cabinet ministers knew they couldn't be applied across the board. Some ministries would have to absorb far more than others if the celebrated Labour manifesto of *'Let Us Face the Future'* was going to mean anything. Essentially, it would have to be a case of 'robbing Peter to pay Paul', of course, but it wouldn't be the first time this classic device was resorted to by a government nor would it be the last; it just had to be done. Financial inadequacy proved to be the stimulus the government needed to tackle some of the Tory Party's 'sacred cows' – namely, empire and defence – in order to make substantial savings on an annual basis in the medium to long term. Divesting themselves of Burma, Ceylon, India, and Palestine, however, proved to be far from painless or free of bloodshed. There was little applause and much acrimony. Labour was accused (with considerable justification in the case of both India and Palestine) of abandoning the principles of equity, freedom and justice as it sought an undignified and scrambled exit from the subcontinent and the Levant.[41] It wouldn't be the last time the charge of 'cutting and running' would be levelled against a Labour government in the post-war world.

If relinquishing parts of the empire was fraught, consolidating foreign and defence policy across the globe at the outset of the Cold War had its own restless dynamic. Defence Review – whether ministerial appreciations or working parties of invited experts – revealed much to be concerned about east of Suez. According to the Harwood Report (1949), substantial on-going savings could be made by closing both the naval bases at Aden and Singapore.[42] Attlee wasn't a nostalgic individual. Accepting the rhythm of Harwood's proposals, he worked on the basis that if it made economic sense to close a famous base and wouldn't adversely impact the UK's position in the region, he was inclined to do it. Almost perversely, however, just when the Labour administration was looking to cut men and materiel in the Gulf and Southeast Asia, the Malayan Emergency arose to concentrate the minds of the COS and defence experts in Whitehall with what they believed was a new Cold War reality. It now seems clear that what was thought to have been a subversive communist plot funded from Moscow was actually more of a nationalist uprising to expel the despised colonial authorities from the peninsula and one that was unaided by comrade Stalin. At the time, however, it was interpreted very differently. French problems in grappling with Ho Chi Minh and the *Viet Minh* did much to confuse the issue and make what appeared to be happening in Malaya seem part of a regional struggle for ideological supremacy.[43] It was this kind of mentality that gave rise to President Eisenhower's 'domino theory' a little later in the 1950s. By then, of course, Mao's communists had triumphed in the Chinese Civil War and the Korean War had confirmed that Asia was in turmoil.[44]

Attlee's government seemed to be subject to a case of Murphy's Law. Despite needing to get its financial house in order and seeking a cut in defence spending and the shedding of some of its former territories and surplus imperial possessions to help accomplish that goal, the Cabinet found itself immediately buffeted by a rapidly deteriorating geo-strategic picture in East Asia which forced it to abandon all of those plans. Instead of shrinking its defence establishment east of Suez, therefore, it was required to beef up its already fairly substantial resources on the equator. By the time Malcolm MacDonald became the commissioner-general in South-East Asia in 1948, a tri-service combined headquarters had already been located on the island along with thousands of servicemen and even more tons of equipment. Into the Singapore mix was also poured the top secret British Defence Coordination Committee Far East (BDCCFE) – a multipurpose regional COS think tank whose brief was to examine and plan defence strategy.[45] It was a heady military brew and one unlikely to be constrained by financial considerations when recommending an appropriate defence posture for the region. One didn't need to be in the BDCCFE to appreciate that a global Cold War was way beyond the military capability of the United Kingdom. American help in Europe had already been delivered in multiple ways during the years 1945–49 in the shape of the Truman Doctrine and Marshall Plan; the defeating of Stalin's blockade of Berlin and the formation of NATO.[46] It would be needed in all other theatres as well. In the Far East – or the 'near north' as the Australasian dominions were concerned – a pressing case for military assistance was also required from the governments in Canberra and Wellington. This ultimately found expression in the establishment of the ANZAM (Australia, New Zealand and Malaya) agreement in 1950; the signing of the ANZUS Pact in 1951 which committed American military support to the defence of the Australasian dominions; founding membership in the South East Asia Treaty Organization (SEATO) in 1954; and the creation of a Commonwealth Strategic Reserve based at Butterworth in Malaya from 1955 onwards.[47]

It is difficult to imagine these expansive military demands coming at a worse time for the Labour administration. Sticking with an overvalued pound had done no favours for the British in the immediate post-war years, but devaluing it as savagely as Sir Stafford Cripps, the aesthetic Chancellor of the Exchequer, did in October 1949, however, hurt all those countries holding sterling balances.[48] Once again, the United Kingdom was accused of letting down its friends. It couldn't do so again once Kim Il Sung's troops had made their military presence felt on the Korean peninsula with an invasion of the south on 25 June 1950. Although the possibility of such a violent demarche had been foreseen by the British defence community, Attlee was nonetheless horrified by the attack. Even so, he recognized from the outset, however, that this distant and most undesirable commitment couldn't be ignored. His government was obliged with others to respond.[49] Thereafter whether Labour or Conservative governments were in power in London the focus on being a part of the UN effort to resolve the North Korean problem developed into a wider policy of containing the communists wherever they sought to push the envelope and endanger the territorial integrity of independent states or colonial possessions.[50]

By the time an armistice was signed on 27 July 1953 to bring the active phase of the Korean War to an end, the United Kingdom had changed its government ushering in another Churchill-led administration in October 1951 but had continued its predecessor's undertaking committing more than 90,000 troops to the conflict. An uneasy peace may have come to Korea, but it was in many ways an unsatisfactory stalemate and few intimately involved in attempting to resolve the conflict doubted that it had the potential to flare up again at any stage in the future.[51] A nuclear power in its own right (Bevin had been adamant that the British should acquire such a capability and their first atomic bomb had been successfully exploded in October 1952), the United Kingdom was beginning to become wedded to a new geo-strategic orientation. In 1952 a COS review of global defence strategy had recommended that in future there should be less emphasis on the building up of conventional forces in bases around the world and much greater reliance placed upon the nuclear option and its value as a deterrent.[52] This would have profound consequences for the British in the Middle East – particularly in Egypt – as well as in Southeast Asia in the years to come.[53]

Unlike the British decision to quit their bases in the Suez Canal zone, withdrawal from Singapore was not an option in the early to mid-1950s. Too much instability in the region and beyond dictated a wholly different response since the Cold War couldn't be wished away from either Europe or Asia and Churchill's pro-American rhetoric dictated that a close alignment with Washington be maintained without being sycophantic towards the Eisenhower administration. This was not an easy manoeuvre to bring off and helps to explain the somewhat problematic birth of SEATO (South-East Asia Treaty Organization) the mutual defence pact linking the United States with Australia, France, New Zealand, Pakistan, the Philippines, Thailand and the United Kingdom in 1954.[54] Churchill's loathing for John Foster Dulles was real and this complicated an already unusual relationship between the prime minister and the president who had formerly been his military subordinate during World War II.[55] While the British needed the Americans more than the other way round, the United States expected the United Kingdom to hold the fort in other areas of Southeast Asia while it was engaged in Vietnam. Quite what that meant in practical terms was at the heart of the complicated relationship between SEATO and its individual member states. None more so that the British whose forces operated independent of SEATO command unless a major conflict arose when they would be expected to be an integral part of its force structure! It looked like a messy arrangement – a bit like the tortured relationship with the EEC/EU in the years to come – but it served its purpose for the time being. It also ensured that Singapore would be retained as a base since it was the only British base large enough in the region to handle and sustain any major operational redeployment of SEATO forces.[56]

In laying out a radical new approach for British defence policy, the 1952 Global Strategy Paper was always likely to be controversial.[57] It proved to be all of that and more as the Suez Crisis demonstrated so vividly in the summer and autumn of 1956. Eden's initiative in pushing for a withdrawal of British conventional forces from the Suez Canal zone unintentionally coincided with the rise of the opinionated Egyptian nationalist Gamal Abdul Nasser; it was a 'shotgun marriage' but one in which convenience rarely featured. Already unsettled, this partnership worsened perceptively once Eden had become premier in April 1955. Thereafter, Eden began seeing the Egyptian colonel as both a 'cad' and another Mussolini.[58] This in turn triggered the uncompromising revival of his default anti-appeasement attitude from the late 1930s, thereby ensuring that meaningful cooperation between the two leaders became increasingly unlikely. Manipulation of this tragic discord both from within and without made the Suez Crisis worse and led inexorably to the ill-fated invasion of October-November 1956 from which the United Kingdom emerged with a deeply sullied reputation.[59] In many ways the 'ghost of Suez' would only be lifted by British success in the Falklands War 26 years later. Meanwhile, Eden paid the immediate price for mishandling the crisis; giving up the premiership he had striven so long to secure. Into his place in Downing Street came Harold Macmillan, the Cabinet colleague who had done so much to encourage Eden's belligerence in the first instance and yet who had been the first minister to defect when the Americans began to play rough by threatening a run on the pound.[60]

Despite his less than winning performance on Suez, Macmillan for a time became an inspired prime minister. His short spell at the Treasury had been sufficient to convince him that the United Kingdom was living well beyond its means, but he didn't need reminding that imposing grim austerity packages on the British taxpayer would make the Tories even more unpopular with the electorate than they already were. Macmillan's answer was to provide the public with the means of obtaining previously scarce consumer items through the easing of credit while making major cuts in overseas expenditure. It became known as the 'you've never had it so good' era and for many it was.[61] Quite whether the defence establishment felt similarly on the subject was, however, a moot point. In seeking a radical overhauling of the nation's defence expenditure without surrendering its military capability, Macmillan evidently wanted the best of all worlds. He aimed to get it by masterfully passing the buck to Duncan Sandys, a rather imperious member of the party's right-wing who also happened to be Churchill's son-in-law.[62]

Sandys was an intemperate fellow who knew his own mind and judged it to be far sharper than any of his opponents on either side of the political divide. His 1957 Defence White Paper, which the press dubbed 'the Sandys Axe', did all that Macmillan desired of him and then some. Apart from phasing out the commitment to national service, Sandys sought to elevate the nuclear option at the expense of conventional forces and the RAF over the Royal Navy; overseas bases were naturally vulnerable to this kind of strategic thrust and many were considered expendable.[63] In the end, however, for all the bombast from Whitehall, the strategic requirements of the Far East – with a Cold War that showed no signs of disappearing and every likelihood of escalating in intensity in the future – dictated that a British military presence would be preserved in Singapore for some time to come. Quite how long into the future that would be was, of course, the key question, but as long as there was a need for a supply and logistics centre in the region Singapore looked to be the safest and best choice of all the available options to assume that role.[64]

So 'the Sandys Axe' was not ruthlessly applied to the British territories in Southeast Asia. Instead Macmillan's government found itself more involved than ever. While Malaya was given its independence on 31 August 1957, the British were still linked militarily with the new state. Apart from the existence of the Commonwealth Strategic Reserve, the Anglo-Malayan Defence Agreement (AMDA) added a level of bi-lateral security on 12 October 1957 (which was further enhanced by the addition of Australia and New Zealand a couple of years later and Singapore in November 1961), but it still didn't persuade Tunku Abdul Rahman, the Malayan Prime Minister, to join SEATO at any price. He didn't trust the organization's combative style and with good reason.[65]

He was rather inclined to see Singaporean politicians in much the same way. In this he wasn't entirely alone. Back in Whitehall the problem of what to do about Singapore had caused successive British governments' some passing concern. It seemed too small and resourceless to become fully independent; the internal threat posed by Chinese communists appeared palpably real – a matter of no small significance to its northern neighbour across the Johor Strait – and to complicate matters still further the desire for self-government from leading political figures of the island state was growing shriller as time passed.[66] Since the British needed to retain their military presence in Singapore to complement their regional defence policy and satisfy the Americans that they were whistling the same tune when it came to the Cold War, a compromise solution had to be arranged with the Singaporean politicians. A measure of limited self-government had been fashioned in 1955, but not enough to satisfy David Marshall, the mercurial Chief Minister appointed under that constitution, who resigned in the following year describing the British offer to increase local power without yielding full internal self-government as 'Christmas pudding with arsenic sauce'.[67]

Marshall's brinkmanship was not imitated by his resourceful successor Lim Yew Hock, whom the British found distinctly more to their taste when it came to negotiating a way forward. Despite this advantage, Lim wouldn't become the beneficiary of the constitutional change he had overseen as Chief Minister. By 1959 the tough line he had taken against the local Chinese communists had backfired upon him and his hold on power had been wrenched aside at the national elections by Lee Kuan Yew, another bright and argumentative lawyer about whom the British, fearing another Marshall, were distinctly less enamoured.[68] Could the brash, populist Lee, who saw union with Malaya as his preeminent goal, be trusted to navigate the domestic shoals wherein the communists lurked? Neither the urbane Tunku nor the resilient Macmillan was certain about the young and gifted Singaporean Prime Minister and yet if he couldn't be trusted both would suffer. What couldn't be allowed to happen, of course, was the growth of another Cuba in Southeast Asia.[69]

They needn't have worried. Lee was no Fidel Castro. He knew what he wanted and it wasn't close engagement with, let alone loyal servitude towards, Beijing or Moscow. His objectives were not shared, however, by either the left-wing activists of his party or by a vociferous Chinese-language educated student body that eschewed any desire for union with Malaya – the Tunku's bastion of anti-communism lying disconcertingly a short distance away to the north. From the outset, therefore, Lee had been forced to be Machiavellian in the pursuit of his goals.

It was a high stakes game of risk which could easily have gone wrong. It didn't because he was adept at playing it, but at times Lee's hold on power within his own party looked distinctly fragile.[70] Viewed from Kuala Lumpur, the potential for disruption from Singapore looked disconcertingly real if Lee's left-wing rivals triumphed for they looked even more menacing than he did. This may help to explain the Tunku's eventual decision to put aside his initial reservations about Lee and begin to offer him some encouragement on the prospect of a constitutional merger as a means of bolstering the young prime minister's position within Singapore.[71]

As the months passed, Lee's grasp of internal politics and external realism was sufficient to convince the British government that, after all, he was a man with whom they could do mutually satisfactory business. Veteran statesman though he was, Macmillan seemed to prefer to negotiate with much younger leaders. He found the charismatic President Kennedy more appealing than Dwight Eisenhower and Lee's energy and enthusiasm, if tapped properly, could be another force for good.[72] Despite his growing influence, Lee was not the crucial figure for the British to cultivate. His fellow Cambridge graduate the Tunku was the vital cog in this particular wheel. Without his support, the idea of some 'Grand Design' linking the former British territories in Southeast Asia together under an expanded Malaysia wouldn't materialize. This concept had been floated back in the late 1940s by Malcolm MacDonald when he was commissioner-general for Southeast Asia, but it didn't have much traction with the authorities in Whitehall because the suffocating economic climate in the United Kingdom at that time was such that Malaya's primary products – an important source of foreign exchange earnings – were considered too important to lose. By the early 1960s, however, the allure of rubber and tin had lost some of its early appeal and Macmillan, looking for ways of saving significant sums on overseas expenditure, had come to see the virtues of a 'Greater Malaysia'.[73]

In supporting this concept the British prime minister was noticeably ahead of many of his own officials and some of those intimately involved in the plan. Negotiating such a constitutional outcome was, therefore, always likely to be a long drawn out and vexatious affair (and so it proved to be), but it would be made far worse because both Indonesia and the Philippines, large and important neighbours, regarded 'Greater Malaysia' as anathema to their own schemes for territorial acquisition in the region.[74] While the Tunku and Lee settled uneasily on a plan for merger, the Sultan of Brunei wavered and the British were left hoping for the best but well aware that the worst was never likely to be far away. It was a sentiment borne out by a series of upheavals on the regional stage beginning with an armed revolt in Brunei in December 1962. Although the anti-Malaysia rebels, facilitated by covert Indonesian support, were swiftly routed by the British military operating out of Singapore in its new guise as Far East Command, the attempted coup did nothing to convince the Sultan of the oil rich territory to put his faith in the Tunku or his dream of an enlarged Malaysian federation.[75]

Another formidable obstacle to circumvent on the road to a 'Greater Malaysia' was President Sukarno. A complex individual of many discordant parts, he loathed the concept as an overt expression of neo-colonialism, even though he himself entertained grandiose ideas of forming a 'Greater Indonesia' at some stage in the future.[76] If he saw any inconsistency in his approach to these matters, Sukarno never let it bother him. After the uprising in Brunei had been suppressed, therefore, his focus turned towards confronting those forces that were underpinning the move towards a 'Greater Malaysia'. Despite Subandrio's announcement of *Konfrontasi* on 20 January 1963, the British couldn't be certain whether it was a rhetorical flourish from the Indonesian foreign minister or something more ominous.[77] As the weeks went by they discovered that it wasn't merely grandstanding. Several acts of aerial provocation were the precursor for cross border raids from Kalimantan into Sarawak that began in April on the island of Borneo. This came as a severe blow to Macmillan's government which had hoped to save money rather than spend a vast amount more on defending its territories in Southeast Asia from hostile forces. *Konfrontasi* ensured that any kind of frugality remained a pipedream for another three years. Instead the British decided that it wasn't sufficient merely to parry the Indonesian thrusts but to engage and inflict collateral damage on Sukarno's forces in ways that might give the president and his Cabinet pause for thought.[78]

While Indonesia's guerrilla forces were stirring the pot on the ground, its government was flirtatiously engaged in a series of diplomatic negotiations with the Tunku and Diosdado Macapagal, the President of the Philippines, about the establishment of a proposed regional confederation. Supported by the Americans and the Australians as a progressive means of keeping the peace, *Maphilindo* became all the rage for a few weeks in mid-summer.[79] Despite the clamour for consensus, *Maphilindo* held no appeal for the British who saw it as some kind of Trojan horse, and the scheme swiftly outlived its usefulness to the Indonesians as well when the Tunku finally set his reservations aside and brought the

Federation of Malaysia into being on 16 September 1963. It was not all that he and the British had hoped for originally since it didn't include oil-rich Brunei, but it did give the hard-bargaining Lee much of what he wanted to the exasperation of many in Kuala Lumpur.[80]

Malaysia's confinement had not been trouble-free and its birth was even more problematic. Whether a rent-a-mob or not, 10,000 activists appeared magically on the streets of Jakarta when news broke of the emergence of the new constitutional state in their midst and it was very apparent that they were not deliriously happy about this latest regional development. Frustrated even more once they discovered that the Malaysian ambassador was out of town, the assembly swiftly became riotous and took their fury out on the newly-built British Embassy nearby which swiftly became a building site again with every window pane smashed beyond redemption and any sense of diplomatic immunity ignored. In the aftermath of this shambles, Malaysia broke off diplomatic relations with both Indonesia and the Philippines on 17 September and the frenzied mob returned again to the British Embassy to burn and ransack it.[81] Thereafter, *Konfrontasi* couldn't be disputed and would need to be addressed. Once again either ironically or perversely, just when the United Kingdom wanted to cut overseas expenditure the opposite happened. For over two years another vast stream of money would flow into Singapore and Malaysia to combat the Indonesian menace.[82] Although the British war effort was remarkably successful in coping with *Konfrontasi*, the problem of dealing with the mercurial Sukarno on a long-term basis left the Macmillan government bereft.[83]

By the time Major-General Soeharto strode onto the stage to supply the answer in the last quarter of 1965, much had changed both in the United Kingdom as well as in Southeast Asia. Macmillan, whose premiership had collapsed into a sorry heap tainted by sleaze and permissiveness, had resigned in the autumn of 1963 fearing he had a terminal health condition (he didn't, it was shamefully misdiagnosed); his successor – the Earl of Home – relinquished his peerage to secure the premiership but lasted less than a year before having to give it up again when the General Election of October 1964 brought 13 years of Tory rule to a timely end. Barely victorious, the Labour Party took over the reins of government from the retreating Conservatives and was immediately confronted by a stunning balance of payments deficit that was far larger than Harold Wilson and his colleagues had feared it would be.[84] Determined not to devalue even though it should have made the most sense to the former Economics don at Oxford, Wilson sought a series of solutions elsewhere. None of them provided the Treasury with the answer it was seeking and they ended up costing the UK a billion pounds over the course of the next three years before Callaghan et al. reached the forlorn conclusion that devaluation could no longer be postponed.[85]

Long before the bell tolled for the overvalued pound and at some 8,000 miles distance from the City of London, Malaysia had its own cathartic moment in early August 1965 when the Tunku expelled Singapore from the Federation.[86] Somehow British intelligence became more than a little oxymoronic by failing to warn Wilson's government in advance of this possibility.[87] Appalled by the banishment of Singapore and the precipitous decline of the 'Grand Design', Wilson's Cabinet was forced to re-examine its regional defence policy. What this meant in effect was that Denis Healey, the robust secretary of state for Defence, was required to make sense out of the chaotic mess that had suddenly fallen into his lap. It's not immediately clear that he knew the answer to that riveting question. For a start, the United Kingdom had to take into account the views of the Americans who were incontrovertibly on the front line against communism in Vietnam and whose money the British needed to shore up their faltering economy. President Johnson was always known to drive a hard bargain and the least he expected from Wilson's government – a SEATO partner after all – was a commitment to hold the fort in the rest of Southeast Asia if he couldn't persuade it to send troops to assist the United States in the war itself. This obviously meant remaining an active presence in the region based in Singapore and not one that replicated the interwar pattern of promising from afar what in reality it couldn't provide.[88] In addition, of course, the British had obligations to the Commonwealth states directly involved in the regional conflict whether in Malaysia or Vietnam. This appeared to leave Healey with very little room to manoeuvre until a very murky episode in Indonesian politics changed the dynamic fundamentally.

Who knew in advance about the Untung coup in Jakarta on 1 October 1965 remains shrouded in mystery more than four decades later. What is emphatically clear, however, is that Major-General Soeharto became the major beneficiary of the coup at Sukarno's expense, while the forces of anti-communism in Indonesia slaughtered the PKI and as many of their personal rivals as they could in the weeks and months to come.[89] Although this savagery definitely helped Healey since it led to the scaling down of *Konfrontasi* and ultimately its end in August 1966, no 'smoking gun' has ever been found linking the UK's Ministry of Defence to the coup. In an age in which conspiracy theories are a growth industry, it's still too much of a stretch to believe that the British acted as an *agent provocateur* to the plotters or counter plotters.

While the diminishing influence of the mercurial Sukarno and the marked reduction in military costs resulting from the winding up of *Konfrontasi* left the Wilson government much better off than before, it didn't solve the Cold War equation that the Johnson administration had posed for its trans-Atlantic partners the year before. In receiving $1.4 billion from the United States to tide it over its latest economic crisis in the summer of 1965 the British had consented to a 10-year defence commitment east of Suez.[90] Pre-Untung it looked a good deal and infinitely preferable to joining the Americans and their ANZUS allies in fighting the communists in Vietnam. After the rise of Soeharto, however, the deal with Washington looked decidedly different from London's perspective. By then Wilson's precarious wafer-thin majority government had already been transformed into a secure and dominant presence by its commanding performance in the British General Election of March 1966, but a costly seamen's strike and further damaging attacks on sterling by speculators over the summer months had left Callaghan and the Treasury needing to adopt harsh deflationary measures including major cuts in public expenditure to restore some semblance of stability to economic affairs and lessen the suffocating air of crisis that enveloped both the City and sterling.[91] Within the £500 million Treasury reduction target was a sum of £100 million which was to be pruned from the defence budget. Those on the left-wing of the Labour Party had few doubts as to where those cuts should be administered and weren't shy in articulating their disdain for a military presence east of Suez. Healey and Wilson had already told an anxious Lee Kuan Yew in late April 1966 that while they were prepared to keep troops in Singapore they wouldn't outstay their welcome in the region.[92] When Healey next met Lee three months later he was less coy about the future and told his Singaporean host that the economic pressures at home dictated that military cutbacks were essential and significant troop withdrawals would proceed now that *Konfrontasi* was over to all intents and purposes.[93] Unfortunately that wasn't the end of the matter because the Treasury – now in the ascendancy – revisited the defence estimates shortly thereafter and demanded further cuts of £200 million to £300 million. Healey could neither hold out against these demands nor find the extra sums easily. Since piecemeal economies would no longer apply, radical solutions were required. Working closely with the choleric George Brown at the Foreign Office seems to have brought about some kind of 'Eureka' moment for the far from sanguine Healey and as a result of their engagement the defence secretary began to recommend a series of steep cuts in British forces overseas (including a 50 per cent cut in Far East Command). He even went so far as to suggest that a total withdrawal from the Far East might also be on the cards in the not too distant future.[94]

By the time a Defence Review had been hastily completed in March 1967, Healey had become a zealous new convert to the cause of withdrawal. He let Wilson know that in order to match the savings insisted upon by the Treasury, British force levels in Malaysia and Singapore would have to be halved by 1970–71 and all troops withdrawn from the two states by 1975–76.[95] While this might appease the Treasury, it was unlikely to be popular in Singapore where 25 per cent of its GDP was dependent upon British military investment in the republic or with the Johnson administration whose recent financial aid had been conditional on the British maintaining an active presence east of Suez.[96] Early signs that a 50 per cent cut back in force levels was unlikely to be hugely contentious in foreign capitals were, therefore, welcome to the emissaries sent to pass on this information, but could the same be said about a total withdrawal from the region? Although Brown was uncharacteristically phlegmatic about the task ahead, his confidence that all would be well was seriously misplaced. Lee Kuan Yew and his combative ministerial colleague Goh Keng Swee were not alone in seeing a total British withdrawal from one degree north of the equator as being a step too far. They came to London to dispute the pull out describing the intended withdrawal as a reckless abandonment of the UK's Cold War obligations to the free world, but found that they had precious few bargaining chips at their disposal.[97] Timing is a political art and for once the Singaporeans had got it wrong. By the time they undertook their mission to make the British think again, the Six-Day War had been waged in the Middle East disrupting international trade and heaping further pressure on sterling.[98]

Against the backdrop of a rather febrile economic environment, Healey calmly left the Singaporean delegation in no doubt as to what was being planned. He revealed that by 31 March 1971 there would only be 32,000 British troops left in Singapore and all of these would have departed over the course of the next four years.[99] Shorn of ground troops, military aircraft and anything larger and more dynamic than small-scale naval amphibious units to protect his nation, Lee was not surprisingly furious. His complaints were anticipated and gravely acknowledged (save by those left-wingers like Richard Crossman who trenchantly proclaimed that the United Kingdom couldn't be expected to pull the chestnuts out of the fire for Singapore any longer), but the high-octane anger and strident appeals to conscience from Lee didn't change the overall plan even if it may have increased the compensation that HMG was willing to provide in lieu of its exit from the equator.[100]

It appeared that the die had been irretrievably cast, but there were further dramatic twists in this sad tale to come from the British side. After an autumn bedevilled with further industrial unrest and a set of wretched trade figures for October, the pressure on sterling returned with a vengeance in November. This time there would be no escape. Callaghan and Wilson were left with little recourse other than to devalue – the very thing they had been determined not to do for the past three years.[101] It was a shattering blow to their morale and the chancellor felt duty bound to resign. His premier did not. Into the Treasury was parachuted another Balliol man – Roy Jenkins – who had never been wistfully drawn to the east of Suez policy entertained for so long by his college contemporary Denis Healey.[102] Deflationary policies were the order of the day; ministries with large budgets, such as defence, were obvious targets for a radical chancellor seeking to balance the books. Jenkins didn't disappoint. By the middle of December he had reached the conclusion that the United Kingdom couldn't afford an east of Suez policy that stretched into the middle of the next decade. Instead he wished to see the withdrawal of all British forces from Southeast Asia brought forward by several years to 1970–71. Healey and Wilson were rapidly converted to this new timeframe as was the Cabinet, but few doubted that the other powers most affected by this earlier withdrawal would be as amenable to change.[103]

They were right. George Thomson and George Brown were deputed to take the disagreeable message to the Commonwealth states east of Suez and to the US administration respectively in January 1968 and both suffered at the hands of their hosts who let them know in no uncertain terms that the United Kingdom had reverted to type and was disgracefully letting its friends down yet again. Thomson found his reception in Kuala Lumpur frosty enough; it proceeded to get much worse when he flew down to Singapore.[104] A tortuous evening – the worst and most sustained diplomatic assault Thomson could ever remember – was spent with Lee's Cabinet lambasting the secretary of state for his government's dereliction of duty, but Brown's hostile reception at the State Department in Washington a few days later was little better.[105] Dean Rusk didn't bother to hide his true feelings about the many shortcomings of the feeble Wilson government. Brown, who loathed being lectured to by anyone, found the entire experience 'bloody unpleasant'.[106]

How could it not have been? American dismay that the Wilson government had connived and dissembled in order to get financial aid only to backtrack from its promises once it had obtained the money was felt by the entire Johnson administration.[107] A quid pro quo is what it is or at least should be. By ignoring it, the Wilson government was imperilling the 'Special Relationship' which Macmillan had resurrected with Eisenhower and Kennedy from 1957 to 1963. Who could trust Wilson's word any longer? It was a question that was being posed on both sides of the Atlantic as well as in Southeast Asia.

Lee, having dispensed with Thomson on his home ground, now sought to tackle his old friend, the talented but flawed, Wilson away in London. One may see this as a variation on the familiar theme of the organ grinder and the monkey. His visit was not the best New Year's present that Wilson had received in 1968, not least because the resolute Singaporean prime minister meant business and would cause a great fuss if he didn't get his own way. In the end, to quell the Lee storm and to satisfy the needs of his own Cabinet, Wilson hit upon a compromise solution – the military withdrawal would be put back nine months to 31 December 1971.[108]

Lee departed with both the pregnant concession and the knowledge that the delay meant another General Election would have to be fought in the United Kingdom before the military deadline had been reached. Since Wilson's policy wasn't in any sense bi-partisan, Lee could still hope that the British electorate might come to his aid by abandoning Labour at the polls. If that was to happen a new Conservative government under Edward Heath might cancel the east of Suez withdrawal and retain a military foothold on the equator for years to come.[109] It would prove to be a fanciful but vain hope. Despite much sound and fury from the Opposition front bench with talk of 'scuttle' and 'ratting' on commitments in the debate following Wilson's announcement of the military withdrawal in January 1968, the Tories spent the next two years edging ever closer to Healey's plan without ever actually endorsing it.[110] By the time that Labour did fall out of favour with the electorate and lost the General Election of June 1970, Lee and his Cabinet were well aware that the Tories were not going to put the clock back to where it was before devaluation. Far from it – it soon became clear that the rundown of Far East Command (40 per cent less than it had been in April 1968) would continue.[111] Moreover, Lord Carrington, Healey's successor at the Ministry of Defence, seemed intent on scrapping the AMDA (Anglo-Malayan Defence Agreement) and sharing the burden of defence among the five Commonwealth powers that had a direct or abiding interest in the continued security of Malaysia and Singapore.[112] This manoeuvre looked in tune with the Tory precedent adopted by Sir Robert Peel more than a century before and practiced often since of one political party stealing its opponent's ideas and claiming them as their own![113] Whatever Carrington might say about the unique features of his plan, they looked remarkably like those that Healey had been promoting to the same set of disgruntled Commonwealth statesmen only a few months before!

Realists rather than romantics, the Malaysians and Singaporeans grudgingly accepted the fait accompli that had been given them and sought to make the best of it, driving as hard a bargain as possible to gain the maximum concessions out of the new security deal that was being offered to them by the Heath government and its companion in arms the Australian and New Zealand administrations. A tough series of protracted negotiations and some ill-temper preceded a final agreement, but ultimately the various powers accepted that both time and economic costs had finally caught up with the AMDA and Far East Command. In their place would come a Five Power Defence Agreement (FPDA) that would begin operations on a far more modest basis from 1 November 1971.[114]

In conclusion, in late 1967 when the British decided to quit Singapore in the aftermath of the devaluation crisis, they did so not to empower the emerging Commonwealth state but in order to save money for their own beleaguered economy. When the Wilson government revealed they were leaving the metropolitan city state within three years there was no guarantee that the island republic would survive the withdrawal unscathed. On the contrary, few, if any, of the leading experts in London could have imagined it would have done as well economically as it has done in moving from a tiny Third World Commonwealth dependency in the early 1970s to joining the behemoths of the First World in the following four decades. It says much for the resourcefulness and resilience of the people and the vibrant forward-thinking policies enacted by Lee, Goh and the other old guard leadership in what has become colloquially known as 'one north'. Whatever one feels about the political rigour of the PAP government and the manner of their control over Singapore since they came to power in 1959, their story is still an astonishing one.[115]

Unfortunately, the same cannot be said of the British who for the second time in less than three decades had been proved wanting as a Commonwealth partner. On the first occasion they had been comprehensively defeated by the Japanese military; on the second they had been decisively beaten by their own economic fragility. In 1942 they had surrendered to force majeure; in 1967 all the force had been applied from within the United Kingdom. Despite the radically differing circumstances prevailing in war and peace, a distressingly similar result had occurred – Singapore had been essentially left to fend for itself. It's no wonder, therefore, that after being let down twice within a generation by the same foreign power, Lee and his colleagues subsequently shared a deeply-held conviction that in future they couldn't count upon anyone else to save them other than themselves.[116] As for the British political establishment, the hand-wringing embarrassment of 1941 was not much in evidence 30 years later and it had disappeared completely by the time the last British soldier left Singapore in 1976.[117] By then a harder edge was evident in its foreign and defence policy; dictated by the bottom line, there was precious little room for old world sentimentality when it came to balancing the books.

From henceforth, therefore, any burnishing of the old jewel of Singapore would have to come from the locals and those expatriate businessmen who possessed the foresight to work closely with them. Their combined success has been remarkable and underlines the fact that under favourable influences old jewels can still gleam anew!

Notes

1. Malcolm H. Murfett, 'Look Back in Anger: The Western Powers and the Washington Conference of 1921–22', in B.J.C. McKercher (ed.), *Arms Limitation and Disarmament: Restraints in War, 1899–1939* (Westport, CT: Praeger, 1992) pp. 83–103.
2. David C. Evans and Mark R. Peattie, *Kaigun: Strategy, Tactics, and Technology in the Imperial Japanese Navy, 1887–1941* (Annapolis, MD: Naval Institute Press, 1997) pp. 185–87, 197; Hosoya Chihiro, 'Britain and the United States in Japan's View of the International System', in Ian Nish (ed.), *Anglo-Japanese Alienation 1919–1952* (Cambridge: Cambridge University Press, 1982) pp. 3–10; Sadao Osada, 'From Washington to London: the Imperial Japanese Navy and the Politics of Naval Limitation, 1921–30', in Erik Goldstein and John Maurer (eds), *The Washington Conference, 1921–22: Naval Rivalry, East Asian Stability and the Road to Pearl Harbor* (London: Frank Cass, 1994) pp. 151–6.
3. D.N. Dilks, 'Appeasement Revisited', in *The University of Leeds Review*, 15, (1972), pp. 28–56; Ian Nish, 'Echoes of Alliance, 1920–30', in Ian Nish and Yoichi Kibata (eds), *The History of Anglo-Japanese Relations 1600–2000: Volume I: The Political-Diplomatic Dimension, 1600–1930* (Basingstoke: Macmillan, 2000) pp. 255–78.
4. Malcolm H. Murfett, 'Living in the Past: A Critical Re-Examination of the Singapore Naval Strategy, 1918–41', *War & Society*, 11, 1 (1993), pp. 73–103.

5. Malcolm Murfett, *Naval Warfare 1919–1945: An Operational History of the Volatile War at Sea* (Abingdon: Routledge, 2009) pp. 4–5.
6. Malcolm H. Murfett, 'A Keystone of Imperial Defence or a Millstone around Britain's Neck? Singapore 1919–1941', in Malcolm H. Murfett, John N. Miksic, Brian P. Farrell and Chiang Ming Shun, *Between Two Oceans: A Military History of Singapore from 1275 to 1971* (2nd edn) (Singapore: Marshall Cavendish, 2011) pp. 148–50; Ian Hamill, *The Strategic Illusion: The Singapore Strategy and the Defence of Australia and New Zealand* (Singapore: Singapore University Press, 1981) p. 286.
7. UK National Archives (UKNA), War Cabinet 'A' Minutes, 616A, 15 August 1919, Cab 23/15
8. Murfett, 'A Keystone', pp. 148–50, 152–5.
9. Ibid., pp. 154–5; UKNA, Committee of Imperial Defence (CID) 165th meeting (30 November 1922) & 165th meeting (14 December 1922), CAB 2/3.
10. Murfett, 'A Keystone', pp. 155–7.
11. Ibid., p. 157; Hamill, *The Strategic Illusion*, pp. 271–315; Paul Haggie, *Britannia at Bay: The Defence of the British Empire against Japan 1931–1941* (Oxford; Clarendon Press, 1981).
12. Murfett, 'A Keystone', p. 158.
13. Ibid., pp. 158–60, 162–3.
14. Ibid., pp. 164–5; UKNA, CID 256th mtg. (9 June 1932), CAB 2/5; CIC Paper 370C, 'Report of the Coastal Defence Committee', (24 May 1932), CAB 2/5.
15. R.A. Divine, *The Illusion of Neutrality* (Chicago: Chicago University Press, 1962); Malcolm H. Murfett, *Fool-Proof Relations: The Search for Anglo-American Naval Cooperation during the Chamberlain Years, 1937–1940* (Singapore: Singapore University Press, 1984) pp. 14–16.
16. Ronald Tiersky, *Francois Mitterand: A Very French President* (Lanham, MD: Rowman & Littlefield, 2003) p. 47.
    Leon Blum was the first Jewish politician to become prime minister of France. He was also the first socialist to hold that position. A moderate politician, he headed the Popular Front government that survived for just over a year from June 1936. It was detested by the French conservatives who did everything they could to destroy it. Piers Brendon, *The Dark Valley: A Panorama of the 1930s* (New York: Alfred A. Knopf, 2000) pp. 338–42, 344–5, 347–50, 581–4, 596.
17. Murfett, *Fool-Proof Relations*, pp. 88–161.
18. UKNA, Sir Ronald Lindsay to Foreign Office, 22 March 1937, No. 247, A2378/38/45, FO371/20651.
19. Murfett, 'A Keystone', p. 171.
20. *The Times*, 18 March 1939, p. 14.
21. Robert Dallek, *Franklin D. Roosevelt and American Foreign Policy, 1932–1945* (Oxford: Oxford University Press, 1995) p. 148.
22. Murfett, 'A Keystone', p. 171.
23. Ibid., pp. 169–71.
24. Lord Caldecote to Sir Geoffrey Whiskard, 17 June 1940, No. 406 in H. Kenway, H.J.W. Stokes and P. G. Edwards (eds), *Documents on Australian Foreign Policy 1937–49. Vol. III January–June 1940* (Canberra: Australian Government Publishing Service, 1979) p. 460; Malcolm H. Murfett, 'When

Trust is Not Enough: Australia and the Singapore Strategy', in Carl Bridge and Bernard Attard (eds), *Between Empire and Nation: Australia's External Relations, 1901–39* (Melbourne: Australian Scholarly Publishing, 2000) pp. 230–50.

25. They might have been less confident in this outcome had they taken cognizance of the wryly satirical aphorism attributed to both Thomas Brown (1663–1704) and Jonathan Swift (1667–1745) but used commonly thereafter: 'Promises, like pie-crust, are made to be broken.'
26. Murfett, 'A Keystone', p. 174.
27. Murfett, *Naval Warfare*, pp. 66–134.
28. Malcolm H. Murfett, 'Phillips, Sir Tom Spencer Vaughan', in Brian Harrison (ed.), *Oxford Dictionary of National Biography*, vol. 44 (Oxford: Oxford University Press, 2004) pp. 150–4; Ian Cowman, *Dominion or Decline: Anglo-American Naval Relations in the Pacific, 1937–1941* (Oxford: Berg, 1996) pp. 244–63; Brian P. Farrell, 'Too Little, Too Late: Preparing for War, 1941–1942', in Murfett et al., *Between Two Oceans*, pp. 187–8, 201–2.
29. Force G was re-designated as Force Z once it had arrived in Singapore in early December 1941. Murfett, 'Phillips', pp. 150–4; Malcolm H. Murfett, 'Reflections on an Enduring Theme: The 'Singapore Strategy' at Sixty', in Brian Farrell and Sandy Hunter (eds), *A Great Betrayal? The Fall of Singapore Revisited* (Singapore: Marshall Cavendish, 2010) pp. 1–18.
30. Murfett, *Naval Warfare*, pp. 125–6, 135, 138–40; Martin Middlebrook and P. Mahoney, *The Sinking of the Prince of Wales and the Repulse: The End of the Battleship Era* (Barnsley: Leo Cooper, 2004).
31. Farrell, 'Too Little, Too Late', p. 176.
32. Ibid., pp. 175–244; Brian P. Farrell, *The Defence and Fall of Singapore 1940–1942* (Stroud: Tempus, 2005).
33. Han Fook Kwang, Warren Fernandez and Sumiko Tan (eds), *Lee Kuan Yew: The Man and His Ideas* (Singapore: Times Editions, 1998) pp. 21–2, 31; Lee Kuan Yew, *The Singapore Story: Memoirs of Lee Kuan Yew* (Singapore: Times Editions, 1998) pp. 50–3, 55.
34. Murfett, *Naval Warfare*, pp. 452–3.
35. Kenneth O. Morgan, *Britain since 1945: The People's Peace* (Oxford: Oxford University Press, 2001) pp. 29–70; Malcolm H. Murfett, *In Jeopardy: The Royal Navy and British Far Eastern Defence Policy 1945–1951* (Kuala Lumpur: Oxford University Press, 1995) pp. 22–4.
36. William Manchester, *The Last Lion: Winston Spencer Churchill 1874–1932* (Boston: Little, Brown & Co., 1983) p. 34; Robert D. Pearce, *Attlee's Labour Governments 1945–51* (London: Taylor & Francis, 2006) p. 1.
37. Murfett, *In Jeopardy*, p. 15.
38. C.M. Turnbull, *A History of Modern Singapore 1819–2005* (Singapore: NUS Press, 2009) pp. 225–8, 233.
39. David Kynaston, *Austerity Britain 1945–51* (New York: Walker & Co., 2008) pp. 19–39.
40. Murfett, *In Jeopardy*, pp. 41–2, 49–50.
41. Kenneth O. Morgan, *Labour in Power 1945–1951* (Oxford: Clarendon Press, 1984) pp. 188–231.

42. UKNA, 'Report of the Inter-Service Working Party on Shape and Size of the Armed Forces', Annex, 28 Feb.1949, CAB 131/7; Murfett, *In Jeopardy*, pp. 86–97, 106, 118, 152, 154.
43. Cheah Boon Kheng, 'The Communist Insurgency in Malaysia, 1948–1989: Was it Due to the Cold War?', in Malcolm H. Murfett (ed.), *Cold War Southeast Asia* (Singapore: Marshall Cavendish, 2012) pp. 31–49.
44. Malcolm H. Murfett, 'What's in it for Us? Rethinking the British Defence Commitment to Singapore and Malaysia from Macmillan to Wilson', in Malcolm H. Murfett (ed.), *Cold War Southeast Asia* (Singapore: Marshall Cavendish, 2012) pp. 252, 258.
45. Brian P. Farrell, 'Old Wine in a New Bottle', in Murfett et al, *Between Two Oceans*, pp. 290–92.
46. Murfett, *In Jeopardy*, pp. 42, 63, 94, 109, 113–14, 123–4.
47. Farrell, 'Old Wine in a New Bottle', pp. 293–302.
48. Murfett, *In Jeopardy*, pp. 81–2, 96–8.
49. Ibid., pp. 114–24, 129, 131–3, 136, 138–40, 147, 153–4.
50. Morgan, *Labour in Power*, pp. 422–31; Klaus Larres, *Churchill's Cold War: The Politics of Personal Diplomacy* (New Haven, Yale University Press, 2002) pp. 125, 134, 136, 146, 158, 167, 181, 187, 189, 201, 212, 222, 238, 241, 289.
51. Farrell, 'Old Wine in a New Bottle', pp. 288–9, 292, 294, 307.
52. Ibid., p. 295.
53. Keith Kyle, *Suez: Britain's End of Empire in the Middle East* (London: I.B. Taurus, 2011).
54. Brian Farrell, 'Alphabet Soup and Nuclear War: SEATO, China and the Cold War in Southeast Asia', in Murfett (ed.), *Cold War Southeast Asia*, pp. 81–131.
55. Roy Jenkins, *Churchill: A Biography* (New York: Farrar, Straus and Giroux, 2001) 848, 874.
56. Farrell, 'Old Wine in a New Bottle', p. 297.
57. Eric J. Grove, *Vanguard to Trident: British Naval Policy since World War Two* (Annapolis, MD: Naval Institute Press, 1987) pp. 78–126.
58. Eden was not alone in depicting Nasser as a most unsavoury dictator. He had support from President Eisenhower who thought him demonic; Dag Hammarskjöld and Selwyn Lloyd who saw him as Hitlerian; and Hugh Gaitskell who saw him as deplorable and cast from the same cloth as Hitler and Mussolini. Peter Wilby, *Eden* (London: Haus Publishing, 2006) p. 92; Kyle, *Suez*, pp. 106, 159, 164, 179, 519.
59. Kyle, *Suez*, pp. 291–563.
60. Alistair Horne, *Macmillan, Vol.II of the Official Biography: 1957–1986* (London: Macmillan, 1989) pp. 2–21.
61. Ibid., pp. 138–71; Morgan, *Britain since 1945*, pp. 158–94.
62. Murfett, 'What's in it for Us?', p. 254.
63. Ibid., pp. 254–5.
64. Farrell, 'Old Wine in a New Bottle', pp. 294–6.
65. Chin Kin Wah, *The Defence of Malaysia and Singapore: The Transformation of a Security System 1957–1971* (Cambridge: Cambridge University Press, 1983).

66. Murfett, 'What's in it for Us?', pp. 256–8.
67. Ronald Hyam, *Britain's Declining Empire: The Road to Decolonization 1918–1968* (Cambridge: Cambridge University Press, 2006) pp. 201–2.
68. Turnbull, *A History of Modern Singapore*, pp. 254–71.
69. In April 1956 the Eden government had indicated to David Marshall that it was determined to ensure that Singapore wouldn't ever become an outpost of the PRC or a colony of Beijing. These concerns remained in vogue for several years until Lee launched Operation *Cold Store* in February 1963. As late as 1966 the Australasian dominions were still somewhat fearful of what might happen in the future. Ibid., pp. 264, 281–2, 285, 332; Murfett, 'What's in it for Us?', p. 278.
70. Turnbull, *A History of Modern Singapore*, pp. 272–82.
71. Tan Tai Yong, 'The Cold War and the Making of Singapore', in Murfett (ed.), *Cold War Southeast Asia*, pp. 132–64; Murfett, 'What's in it for Us?', pp. 264–6.
72. Horne, *Macmillan, II*, pp. 281–90, 292–7, 303–8, 323, 337–8, 438–9, 525–6, 576–8.
73. Tan Tai Yong, *Creating 'Greater Malaysia': Decolonization and the Politics of Merger* (Singapore; Institute of Southeast Asian Studies, 2008) pp. 3–4; Hyam, *Britain's Declining Empire*, p. 293.
74. UKNA, Foreign Office contribution to Joint Intelligence Committee Report on 'Future Indonesian Intentions', forwarded by A.S. Fair to E.V. Vines (Canberra), F.R.39/2 (10 Oct.1962), DO 169/67; Murfett, 'What's in it for Us?', pp. 259–61.
75. Brian P. Farrell, 'End of Empire; From Union to Withdrawal', in Murfett et al., *Between Two Oceans*, p. 317; David Easter, *Britain and the Confrontation with Indonesia 1960–1966* (London: Tauris Academic Studies, 2004) pp. 22–44.
76. Matthew Jones, *Conflict and Confrontation in South East Asia, 1961–1965* (Cambridge: Cambridge University Press, 2002) pp. 31–60.
77. UKNA, Background Memos on Indonesia for Talks Between Lord Home and Dean Rusk (14 Sept.1963), FO 371/169906; Murfett, 'What's in it for Us?', pp. 262–4.
78. Easter, *Britain and the Confrontation with Indonesia*, pp. 45–89; Farrell, 'End of Empire', pp. 317–21.
79. Murfett, 'What's in it for Us?', pp. 262–3, 267–8.
80. Tan, *Creating 'Greater Malaysia'*, pp. 172–82.
81. Murfett, 'What's in it for Us?', pp. 266–7.
82. *Konfrontasi* was costing the British taxpayer £1M a day in early 1965. John Subritzky, *Confronting Sukarno: British, American, Australian and New Zealand Diplomacy in the Malaysian-Indonesian Confrontation, 1961–6* (Basingstoke: Macmillan, 2000) pp. 198–9.
83. Murfett, 'What's in it for Us?', p. 268, n. 50; Easter, *Britain and the Confrontation with Indonesia*, pp. 31, 69–71.
84. David Reynolds, *Britannia Overruled: British Policy and World Power in the Twentieth Century* (London: Longman, 1991) pp. 226–31; Morgan, *Britain since 1945*, pp. 243–6.
85. Diane B. Kunz, ' "Somewhat Mixed Up Together": Anglo-American Defence and Financial Policy during the 1960's', in Robert D. King and Robin

Malcolm H. Murfett 191

W. Kilson (eds), *The Statecraft of British Imperialism. Essays in Honour of Wm. Roger Louis* (London: Frank Cass, 1999) pp. 213–32; Murfett, 'What's in it for Us?', p. 271.
86. Turnbull, *A History of Modern Singapore*, pp. 282–95.
87. Murfett, 'What's in it for Us?', p. 275.
88. Ibid., p. 274; Peter Lowe, *Contending with Nationalism and Communism: British Policy towards Southeast Asia, 1945–65* (Basingstoke: Palgrave Macmillan, 2009) pp. 82, 150–7, 231.
89. Merle C. Ricklefs, *A History of Modern Indonesia since c.1200* (4th edn) (Basingstoke: Palgrave Macmillan, 2008) pp. 318–21, 327; John D. Legge, *Sukarno: A Political Biography* (Singapore: Archipelago Press, 2003) pp. 431–58.
90. Kunz, ' "Somewhat mixed up together" ', pp. 216–18; Saki Dockrill, *Britain's Retreat from East of Suez: The Choice between Europe and the World?* (Basingstoke: Palgrave Macmillan, 2002) pp. 114–24.
91. Morgan, *Britain since 1945*, pp. 239, 254–5, 263–6.
92. UKNA, 'Record of Meeting between Denis Healey and Lee Kuan Yew, London', (22 April 1966), PREM 13/1832.
93. Murfett, 'What's in it for Us?', p. 282.
94. Ibid., pp. 282–3; Harold Wilson, *The Labour Government 1964–70* (London: Pelican, 1974), p. 381.
95. 'Report of the OPD (Official) Committee's Defence Review Working Party', OPDO (DR) (67)16 (20 March 1967), FCO 24/25; Minutes of OPD(67) 14th Mtg. (22 March 1967), CAB 148/30; Memorandum by George Brown and Denis Healey, 'Defence Expenditure Studies', C(67)40 (31 March 1967), CAB 129/128.
96. Malcolm H. Murfett, ' "The Times They are A-Changin"': Britain's Military Commitment to Singapore, 1967–1971', in Brian P. Farrell (ed.), *Churchill and the Lion City: Shaping Modern Singapore* (Singapore: NUS Press, 2011), p. 151.
97. Murfett, 'What's in it for Us?', pp. 285–7
98. Wilson, *The Labour Government 1964–70*, p. 513.
99. UKNA, Note of a Meeting at the Commonwealth Office (22 June 1967), PREM 13/1832.
100. Richard Crossman, *The Diaries of a Cabinet Minister. Vol. II* (London: Hamish Hamilton & Jonathan Cape, 1976) pp. 399–400; Lee Kuan Yew, *From Third World to First: The Singapore Story, 1965–2000* (Singapore: Times Media, 2000) p. 55.
101. Kenneth O. Morgan, *Callaghan: A Life* (Oxford: Oxford University Press, 1997) pp. 268–76.
102. Roy Jenkins, *A Life at the Centre* (London: Macmillan, 1991), pp. 222–3.
103. P.L. Pham, *Ending 'East of Suez': The British Decision to Withdraw from Malaysia and Singapore 1964–1968* (Oxford: Oxford University Press, 2010) pp. 207–36.
104. UKNA, Thomson to Wilson, Telegrams nos. 21–23 (7–8 January 1968), C(68)13 (9 January), CAB 129/135.
105. UKNA, Thomson to Wilson, Tel. nos. 26 (8 January 1968); no.32 (9 January 1968); Memo by Michael Stewart, C(68)15 (11 January 1968); Memo by Thomson, C(68)13 (15 January 1968), CAB 129/135.

106. UKNA, Brown to Stewart, Tel. no. 54 (11 January 1968), attachment to 'Singapore and Malaysia: Far East', C(68)22 (12 January 1968), CAB 129/135.
107. Dockrill, *Britain's Retreat*, pp. 204–5; Murfett, 'What's in it for Us?', pp. 291–3.
108. UKNA, Note of a meeting between Lee and Wilson (14 January 1968), PREM 13/2081; Correspondence between the two leaders (15–16 January 1968), FCO 46/43; Lee, *From Third World*, pp. 58–62.
109. Ibid., pp. 64–5; Karl Hack, *Defence and Decolonisation in Southeast Asia: Britain, Malaya and Singapore 1941–1968* (Richmond: Curzon, 2001) pp. 287–8; Murfett, 'What's in it for Us?', pp. 293–4.
110. Murfett, ' "The Times They are A-Changin" ', pp. 145–55.
111. UKNA, British High Commission (BHC), Singapore to Foreign & Commonwealth Office (FCO), Tel. no. 516 (23 June 1970), DEFE 68/2; BHC, Singapore to FCO, Tel. no. 515 (23 June 1970), DEFE 25/245.
112. UKNA, Memos by Carrington, 'UK Military Presence in South East Asia after 1971', DOP(70)10 (17 July 1970), CAB 148/101; 'UK Military Presence in South East Asia after 1971', DOP(70)26 (1 October 1970), CAB 148/102; Murfett, ' "The Times They are A-Changin" ', pp. 156–7.
113. In the course of a rancorous debate that took place in the House of Commons on 28 February 1845 Benjamin Disraeli, the backbench Tory MP, viciously attacked Sir Robert Peel, the British prime minister, for seeking to abolish the Corn Laws and did so using language that would be remembered long after the prime minister had left office: 'The Right Honourable Gentleman caught the Whigs bathing and walked away with their clothes. He has left them in the full enjoyment of their liberal position and he is himself a strict conservative of their garments.' *The Times*, 1 March 1845. It was a device resorted to by other political leaders in the years to come. Modern exponents of this trend of 'political acquisition' include both Bill Clinton and Tony Blair.
114. While the FPDA celebrated its fortieth birthday in 2011, foreign troop levels in the two equatorial republics began falling away with the withdrawal of the Australian units in 1974 and the British in March 1976. Finally, the New Zealanders pulled out their remaining troops in 1989. Farrell, 'End of Empire', pp. 332–5.
115. Turnbull, *A History of Modern Singapore*, pp. 299–375.
116. Ibid., p. 312; Lee, *From Third World*, pp. 19–20, 33–7, 41–2, 44, 47–65, 69–73, 416.
117. It is instructive that neither the leading British players in this drama nor their biographers commented upon this last phase of the troop withdrawal. It was not as it would be in Hong Kong 21 years later. John Flowerdew, *The Final Years of British Hong Kong: The Discourse of Colonial Withdrawal* (Basingstoke: Palgrave Macmillan, 1998) pp. 171–90, 214–21.

9
Quadruple Failure?
The British-American Split over Collective Security in Southeast Asia, 1963–66

Brian P. Farrell

David Dilks devoted a lifetime to exploring the history of British foreign policy, especially during the twentieth century. Naturally that led him to consider the historical experience of dismantling the British overseas empire, formal and informal. The other side of that coin was the decline, relative and absolute, of British power in the world. Dilks began one of his more influential volumes by citing celebrated public comments made by Dean Acheson, retired former American Secretary of State, on 5 December 1962. Acheson asserted that 'Britain has lost an empire and not yet found a role', a dilemma aggravated by the fact that the British effort to maintain their role as a global power by leveraging 'based on a "special relationship" with the United States... is about to be played out'.[1] The controversy this speech provoked, especially in the United Kingdom, was quickly addressed by President John Fitzgerald Kennedy's (JFK) administration, which two days later formally declared 'US-UK relations are not based only on a power calculus, but also on deep community of purpose and long practice of cooperation... "Special relationship" may not be a perfect phrase, but sneers at Anglo-American reality would be equally foolish.'[2] The very next day, 8 December 1962, Acheson's assertion, and the quick 'clarification', were challenged by an event in Southeast Asia that severely tested British power and policy, and the British-American strategic relationship.

On 8 December 1962, units of the *Tentara Nasional Kalimantan Utara* (TNKU) [North Kalimantan National Army] launched coordinated attacks against government, police and oil industry facilities in the British protectorate of Brunei. The TNKU was the military wing of the *Partai Rakyat Brunei* (PRB) [Brunei People's Party], the largest

193

political organisation in a Sultanate still governed autocratically by Sultan Omar Ali Saifuddien III. A.M. Azahari, leader of the PRB, launched the armed revolt mainly to prevent the consummation of a plan to merge the British protected and administered territories in Borneo – Brunei, Sarawak, and British North Borneo – with Malaya and Singapore, to create a new federal state, Malaysia. This 'Grand Design' had evolved as British policy for managing political change and decolonisation in Southeast Asia. The larger federation was intended to establish a stronger and thus more viable post-colonial state – one that would secure each individual territory in a larger critical mass, remain within the Commonwealth, preserve British economic interests, enable the British to continue supporting Western collective security in the region from their existing military facilities within Malaysia, but at the same time allow them to pass on a heavy internal security burden to this new ally. The populations of the three Borneo territories were at best ambivalent about this new federation, many preferring to foster closer relations between themselves before considering any merger with Malaya and Singapore. But the British were managing the political process of 'selling' Malaysia to the peoples involved – until the TNKU revolted.[3]

The PRB and TNKU saw themselves as leading an anti-colonial liberation struggle. To them the British 'Grand Design' was a neo-colonial plot to preserve British dominance in the territories. They turned for help to a neighbour presenting itself to the world as a leader in the Afro-Asian struggle to decolonise: Indonesia, by now a 'Guided Democracy' led by its charismatic President, Sukarno. Azahari personally fostered close ties with leading figures in the Indonesian government, military high command and intelligence agencies. Those ties helped him persuade Indonesian government and military agencies to provide training, equipment and even recruits, as well as sympathy and moral support. The British Far East Command (FEC) had little trouble putting down the TNKU revolt, chasing the survivors into the jungle, and restoring the Sultan's government.[4] But the revolt helped detonate a much greater problem.

The TNKU uprising reinforced fundamental changes in attitude taking shape in Jakarta. Indifferent at first to the Malaysia project, the Indonesian government now turned against it. On 20 January 1963, Subandrio, Indonesian Foreign Minister and head of the *Badan Pusat Intelijen* (BPI) [Central Intelligence Agency], publicly declared Indonesia would follow a policy of 'Confrontation' against Malaya, to retaliate for its behaving 'as the henchman of Neo-Imperialism and Neo-Colonialism pursuing a policy hostile to Indonesia'.

Senior Indonesian military officers made similarly bellicose statements. British intelligence reported that the *Tentara Nasional Indonesia* (TNI) [Indonesian National Army] was deploying combat forces in Borneo, and providing training and other support to the TNKU, as well as dissident groups from Sarawak who opposed the Malaysia project. This convinced the British government that Indonesia would try to abort the consummation of Malaysia, by methods including force of arms.[5] This transformed the situation.

Indonesia was the fifth most populous country in the world, with a population of 98 million, and by far the largest state in Southeast Asia. Indonesian territory pressed on the British protected and administered territories all the way from northern Malaya to the southeastern border of British North Borneo. No lasting political or security arrangements could be made in the region against determined Indonesian opposition. And Indonesia was governed by a regime that saw itself as the champion of national liberation and anti-colonialism, the leader of the so-called Non-Aligned Movement, also referred to as the Afro-Asian bloc, and an exponent of radically different approaches to international relations and the states system. Indonesian hostility turned the Malaysia project from a British exit strategy into a major threat to British power and policy in Asia.[6] What made this potentially much worse was that the British and American governments struggled to see eye to eye about how to handle this grave new problem.

Confrontation with Indonesia from 1963 to 1966 became a major test of the British-American strategic partnership, and of the UK's ability to leverage that relationship in order to sustain a larger strategic role, beyond Europe. British-American discussions about Confrontation led to larger four power discussions, bringing in Australia and New Zealand, about how best to maintain effective Western-led collective security in Southeast Asia. More acutely than anywhere else, the problems of decolonisation and Cold War merged in Southeast Asia into a fundamental challenge to Western efforts to manage change and contain communism. Too long eclipsed in scholarship by the giant shadow cast by the war in Vietnam, it was the problem of dealing with a hostile Indonesia that actually exposed a cardinal fact: the British and American governments did not in fact agree about how to wage Cold War, and manage change, in Asia.

Confrontation forced the British to consider, earlier and more intensively than they expected, whether or not they could still remain a military power on a wider stage. When American military intervention in Vietnam coincided with a Commonwealth military commitment to defend Malaysia against escalating Indonesian pressure, the combination forced the British to also consider just how strong any 'deep community of purpose' really was, regarding collective security in Southeast Asia. Those investigations played out through a recurring series of reviews, assessments, decisions and debates both within and between the British government and one, two, or often all three of its closest Western allies committed to the region: the United States of America, Australia and New Zealand. Both military burdens and political discussions revealed how completely the British now depended on American support to play any meaningful strategic role in the region, if not indeed anywhere at all. This dependency prompted the British to try to navigate through drastic changes in their global defence policy and grand strategy by persuading the Americans to underwrite arrangements whereby a four power 'inner circle' of Western allies could concert policies, and pool resources, to prosecute a very different approach to collective security in Southeast Asia. This tested the 1962 claims that when push came to shove a 'deep community of purpose and long practice of cooperation' would keep such allies working together effectively as strategic partners. This chapter will explain how and why Confrontation presented this test; indicate why 'quadrilateral' discussions indicated, in 1966, that for Southeast Asia at least the answer was 'no'; and discuss why any of this mattered, to the British or anyone else.

This problem in Southeast Asia really began in spring 1954. The two great geopolitical forces shaping the post-war world order were decolonisation and the Cold War. One pit declining European overseas empires against rising post-colonial national feeling and aspiration, in Africa and Asia. The other became a global struggle to define the trajectory of world politics between two inveterately hostile ideological blocs, the communist bloc led by the Soviet Union and the liberal democratic or Western bloc led by the United States. Both profound forces collided in Vietnam, in a war that began as a struggle between Vietnamese nationalism and a desire by France to restore colonial rule. That war was transformed by one of the decisive events of the Cold War: communist victory in civil war in China and the establishment of the People's Republic of China (PRC), which 'tilted to one side' and lined up alongside the Soviet Union in a now global Cold War. The PRC also recognised the Vietnamese forces fighting France for independence, the Democratic Republic of Vietnam (DRV), led by Ho Chi Minh and what was in fact, if no longer in name, the Communist Party of Indochina.[7] Those developments provoked two crucial American reactions. First, American politics at home became poisoned by the accusation that the Democratic Party and the

Truman administration 'lost' China, and were soft and unreliable in what was now seen as an existential challenge to American security: to contain the global expansion of malignant aggressive communism. This made American decision makers very sensitive to charges of failing to stand firm against the 'red menace', adding greatly to the burdens of making American strategic foreign policy in a more highly charged situation at home. Second, and in that context, the Truman administration decided France was now fighting not an imperial but an anti-communist war in Vietnam, and committed the United States to underwriting that struggle, to draw the line of containment in Southeast Asia. The outbreak of the Korean War, and Chinese intervention in that conflict, only deepened this new American commitment to using military force to halt the threat posed to the Western position in Asia by 'Red China'.[8] Things went well in Korea – but not in Vietnam.

Despite formidable American financial and equipment support, the French lost control of their war in Vietnam. By 1954 a French plan to bait their *Viet Minh* enemy into a set-piece battle backfired when superior communist forces besieged the French garrison in the valley of Dien Bien Phu. This dramatic military showdown led towards a summit conference of the great powers arranged for Geneva, bringing the Americans, Soviets, British, French and communist Chinese together to discuss the problems of both Korea and Indochina. The Eisenhower administration reluctantly agreed to attend a conference with their Chinese adversary, and became gravely concerned at the prospect of a spectacular French defeat at Dien Bien Phu. That April, President Dwight Eisenhower publicly discussed two themes which, for the next 15 years, shaped American policy towards Southeast Asia. At a press conference on 7 April, Eisenhower declared that the West could not lightly accept defeat by communist forces in Vietnam, because it would set off a chain reaction throughout the rest of the region, compromising efforts to build stable non-communist states. Eisenhower coined the now notorious 'domino theory': 'You have a row of dominoes set up, you knock over the first one, and what will happen to the last one is that it will go over very quickly. So you have a beginning of a disintegration that will have the most profound influences.' Combining external aggression with internal subversion, communist forces would push forward from their new base in Vietnam to overrun the rest of the region, local communist parties drawing support and direction from the PRC. The President also, however, accepted a condition already spelt out by Congress regarding any military intervention to rescue the French at Dien Bien Phu: the United States would not take on such a burden by itself. Other Western allies must also participate, in what came to be called 'united action'. That meant, in practice, the British, the only other Western power with appreciable military strength in the region. But the British government refused to participate in any military intervention in Vietnam, so no such action ensued.[9] The British reaction exposed, instead, ominous disconnection between British and American approaches towards the region.

The disconnect started with China. Whereas the United States treated 'Red China' as a menace beyond the pale and refused to recognise the PRC or its government, the British pragmatically decided to accept an accomplished fact and recognise both. London agreed the communist Chinese were a major new Cold War threat to Western interests in Asia, but strongly disagreed with the 'emotional' American reaction to the new threat, and became concerned that American strategy would provoke an avoidable wider war with China. The British preferred to approach containment in Asia by a more varied strategy. The line had to be held militarily in Korea, but the British drew from that conflict the conclusion that the Western allies should avoid committing ground forces to any conflict on the mainland of Asia in which the Chinese could readily intervene. British forces were of course at that time heavily committed to a counterinsurgency campaign against a communist challenge in Malaya, but geography allowed them to isolate this war from outside military interference. The campaign was going well by 1954, but was also expensively pinning down large British military forces. The government led by Winston Churchill agreed that communist China posed a serious threat to Western interests in Southeast Asia, but did not think treating China as an enemy with whom a major war was unavoidable was the right way to contain that threat. They also felt the French position in Vietnam was beyond rescue, and the best the Western allies could now do was regroup and reorganise, using diplomacy to work out a position on the mainland from where China could still be contained. Senior American officers and officials became irritated by British reluctance to 'stand up to China'; senior British officers and officials became worried by American readiness to do so. This however posed a truly grave problem for the British, because they agreed the communist bloc did pose an existential global threat to British and Western interests, and knew that containment could not work, either in Europe or Asia, without determined American commitment and leadership. How then to manage this disagreement with the Americans over how to handle 'Red China', define British and Western vital interests in Southeast Asia, and secure American commitment to protect such interests?[10]

The answer in 1954 was to accept the American warning expressed by the 'domino theory', and use diplomacy both to regroup in mainland Southeast Asia and anchor an American commitment to lead collective security in the region. That however required the British to make commitments of their own. The French lost both Dien Bien Phu and Vietnam, losses confirmed in Geneva by the conclusion, in July, of a series of Agreements. Laos and Cambodia were recognised as independent states. Vietnam was temporarily partitioned at the 17th parallel. The northern region was handed over to the *Viet Minh*, the southern region placed under the administration of the French-created State of Vietnam. Arrangements were made for population transfers, military withdrawals, international supervision, and for nationwide elections to reunify the country to be held in two years. The American delegation refused to engage the Chinese, glowered sullenly at the Agreements, did not sign but 'took note' of them, and reserved full freedom to act if any party violated any of them. The Soviet Union and the United Kingdom agreed to act as supervising Co-Chairmen of the Conference, the Agreements, and their implementation. The difference between British and American positions was very thinly veiled indeed: the British regarded the Agreements as a way to ease the Western Powers out of Vietnam so as to regroup more effectively elsewhere, whereas the Americans regarded the partition line drawn at the 17th parallel as the front line on which to contain communism from spreading any further in Southeast Asia. To help conceal and manage this difference, the British added to their commitments by spearheading the negotiation of a new, formal collective security alliance to defend Southeast Asia.[11]

The price for refusing to intervene in Vietnam was the Manila Pact, leading to the Southeast Asia Treaty Organization (SEATO). While this formalised an American commitment to leading collective security in Southeast Asia, it did so by adding further hostages to fortune to a disconnect between the British and the Americans. SEATO was expressly aimed to prevent the spread of communism in Southeast Asia, to prevent it from being dragged into other disputes such as the feud between Pakistan, which joined, and India, which did not. At American insistence the organisation was loosely structured and members' commitment to respond to any challenge left vaguely defined, to preserve maximum freedom of action. But the Americans also insisted on adding a Protocol to the Pact which designated Vietnam, Laos and Cambodia as Protocol States, which SEATO would consider defending if they suffered any communist aggression, direct or indirect. Through SEATO, the United States thus declared it would resist communist expansion into

Southeast Asia by drawing the line at the partition line of Vietnam, but would not make advance commitments as to how it might respond to any situation, nor consider itself bound to respond to any non-communist threat to Western interests. It also pledged to support its allies, but clearly expected this to be reciprocal.[12] That, for the British, was the nub of the problem.

The United Kingdom needed SEATO. It was the only instrument that linked the Americans to all other Western Powers with continuing interests in the region; it thus cut across the exclusion of the British from the ANZUS Pact by which the signatories pledged to help defend Australia and New Zealand from external aggression; it amplified a recent but emphatic Australian and New Zealand shift in strategic priority towards a strategy of 'forward defence' in Southeast Asia; it provided some assurance the United States would not stand aloof if such challenges as the Malayan Emergency got out of hand. But it also signalled American intent to contain communism in mainland Southeast Asia by force if necessary, and underlined the American diagnosis that Chinese-led and inspired expansionism was the principal threat to the region. This threatened to pull the British into any future trouble in Vietnam, an area they were inclined to write off as compromised. It also challenged a growing British view that the strongest political force in the region was nationalism, not communism. It was a force they tended to define as an irresistible rise in feelings of national aspiration or irredentism. This force had to be handled very carefully, as its principal target was to remove what was left of the European colonial presence in the region. But it could also admittedly be exploited and hijacked by communism, as happened in Vietnam. The British felt they were fending off just such a threat in Malaya, where the Emergency officially came to an end in 1960. But British authorities concluded that victory in Malaya against the communists relied heavily on their willingness to accept fundamental political change: to appease national feeling by decolonising Malaya and granting independence to the country in order to win the war, not after the fact. The UK thus turned Malaya into an ally, one which, with Singapore, remained the principal host of the continued British military presence in the region. Willingness to bend before such 'winds of change' made the British more disposed to focus on managing change as their most vital interest in Southeast Asia. When armed struggle resumed in Vietnam in 1960, the British government worried that the Americans were more determined to prevent rather than guide change – and that American policy might push the Western Powers onto the wrong side of emerging national feelings in the region, thereby playing into communist hands. The 'common purpose' was still defined as containing communist China by protecting Southeast Asia from further communist expansion – but it now seemed very vulnerable to this potential disconnect between the two principal Western Powers as to how best to manage communism, nationalism, decolonisation and collective security.[13]

One final British conclusion only deepened the problem. The British government entered the 1960s determined to dismantle what was left of their formal empire in an orderly manner, one that left behind friendly successor states staying inside the Commonwealth and aligning with the West in the Cold War – yet also to remain a military power with global reach. But this was now dangerously expensive. Despite 'never having had it so good' the British taxpayer's economy struggled to adjust to changing times while still supporting a triple burden in defence: an independent nuclear deterrent; significant contributions to NATO and collective security in the West; and strong forces deployed overseas, protecting British and Western interests. British officials reminded themselves that the United States was the only other nation managing such a triple burden, which it did with far greater resources. Searching inquiries concluded by 1961 that British economic interests in Southeast Asia were too small to warrant the large and expensive military forces stationed in the region to protect them, and by the end of the decade the government would have to reduce this burden. The same inquiries also indicated that changing political conditions in the region would further undermine the British military presence, which might perhaps become so unpopular to emerging nationalism as to become a liability. This prompted preliminary considerations of possible alternative bases, such as Australia. But finally, inquiries also indicated that the most vital British interest of all, globally, was to preserve as much influence on American policy and strategy as possible. This clinched decisions in 1961 and 1962 to maintain military forces in Southeast Asia and remain committed to SEATO – indeed, to deploy nuclear weapons to the region to enhance that commitment.[14] In this context, the British 'Grand Design' to reduce burdens by midwifing Malaysia provoked trouble with Indonesia – just as the Americans found themselves pulled more deeply into the war in Vietnam.

The strategic partnership became strained by Indonesia's decision to 'confront' Malaysia when important American officials, especially in the State Department, blamed the British for provoking what they thought was an avoidable and dangerous conflict. The threats of January escalated from April 1963 onwards into cross-border incursions by armed men into the Borneo territories, especially Sarawak. Indonesian authorities denied their regular armed forces were involved, but openly supported these operations by 'the forces of liberation', which emanated from their province of Kalimantan. Summit diplomacy in June and July then produced what appeared to be room for possible rapprochement. The Prime Ministers, Presidents and Foreign Ministers of Malaya, Indonesia and the Philippines agreed to stop publicly denouncing each other, and to establish a loose confederation, called *Maphilindo*. The three states would remain fully sovereign but, within this larger grouping, they would strive to operate by consultation and consensus, to harmonise policies and stabilise the region. In return, Indonesia and the Philippines would agree to accept the mergers that would create Malaysia, provided 'an independent and impartial survey' confirmed this was what the peoples of the Borneo territories wanted.[15] However, these agreements threatened to solve old problems by creating new ones.

One provision of these Manila Agreements annoyed the Americans and alarmed the British, by declaring that the three states would shoulder responsibility for 'peace and security in the region', would 'abstain from the use of arrangements of collective defence to serve the particular interests of any of the big powers', and that foreign military bases in the region could not be allowed to subvert national independence, and must be regarded as 'temporary in nature'. Such claims seemed aimed directly at SEATO, and could be taken to indicate that sooner rather than later Malaya/Malaysia would demand the British abandon their extensive military facilities, especially in Singapore – the facilities that enabled significant British and Commonwealth military forces to operate in the region.[16] And the Agreements themselves threatened to expose some very real internal fault lines which made the whole Malaysia project so delicate in the first place. The most serious was the awkward relationship between Malay and Chinese communities in Malaya and Singapore.

The Chinese were a commanding majority in Singapore and, if combined alone with Malaya, would make that community the plurality in a larger Malaya. The threat of radical subversion in Singapore persuaded Tunku Abdul Rahman, Prime Minister of Malaya, that it was safer to include rather than exclude Singapore from the post-colonial state – but this troubling ethnic and ideological friction also made it necessary to include the Borneo territories and turn Malaya into Malaysia, in order to contain communal friction by ensuring the Chinese did not become numerous enough to challenge Malay political ascendancy. The Chinese-dominated government of Singapore, led by Lee Kuan

Yew and his People's Action Party (PAP), could accept this, in return for compensating economic and other advantages from merger into Malaysia. *Maphilindo*, however, was a very different story. The Singapore government adamantly rejected the concept, fearing that any such confederation of the whole Malay archipelago would atomise scattered Chinese diaspora minorities and compromise the very nature of Singapore. There were also legitimate concerns about lukewarm public opinion in the Borneo territories, which certainly went no further than reluctantly being willing to accept Malaysia if the British insisted on leaving. In this volatile situation the Singapore and British governments insisted they would brook no delay, demanding Malaysia must be consummated as and when planned. Rightly concluding it was bound to provoke a serious backlash whichever choice it made, the Malayan government gave in to intense British pressure and agreed to consummate Malaysia as planned, in order to establish the entity before any additional strains could arise. This however clearly reneged on the Malayan commitment to confirm the wishes of the people of Sarawak and British North Borneo before Indonesia and the Philippines agreed to recognise Malaysia.[17] When Malaysia duly declared itself on 16 September, before the Secretary General of the United Nations, U Thant, could submit his report about public opinion in Borneo, Sukarno immediately denounced this as a slap in the face to Indonesia. The Indonesian government refused to recognise Malaysia, severed relations with the government in Kuala Lumpur, and palpably escalated confrontation on all fronts, military, diplomatic, economic, propaganda and political. It was this turn of events which provoked some senior American – and Australian – officials to react in exasperation, and blame the British government for at the very least giving Sukarno a good excuse to stir up trouble, if not for provoking the whole conflict by being impatient and abrasive.[18] These American reactions were also fuelled, however, by considerations that did much to complicate this new and most unwelcome challenge.

Those considerations revolved around American views of Indonesia, and its role in international relations. The American government knew it would be difficult if not impossible to secure and stabilise a decolonising Southeast Asia without a friendly or at least benign Indonesia. Sheer size of population, territory, and potential economic wealth dictated this, even without considerations of politics, ideology or Cold War. Such considerations only made things more complicated. Separatist stresses and strains provoked two regional rebellions in Indonesia in 1958 which the American Central Intelligence Agency (CIA), assisted by their British counterparts, unwisely supported. When these covert operations were outed, Sukarno denounced them as proof the Western Powers opposed his most important goal: to complete the territorial unification of the archipelago, to cement Indonesia as a unified and fulfilled state that would step forward to play a leading role in the region. Sukarno's 'Guided Democracy', announced in 1957, emphasised from 1959, looked like a turn away from democracy towards authoritarianism at home, just as his leadership in what the Americans considered the 'so-called' Non-Aligned Movement looked like a dangerous tilt towards the Communist bloc abroad. The Indonesian government emphasised the 'national revolution' and national unity, to consolidate the sprawling archipelago and its diverse populations into a unified and dynamic state. Sukarno reinforced this vehement nationalism by emphasising the need for social revolution at home, which brought him closer to the growing *Parti Kommunis Indonesia* (PKI) [Communist Party of Indonesia], and international revolution abroad – pitting 'new emerging forces', led by Indonesia, against the 'old established forces' of the imperial and colonial powers. This all looked and sounded distinctly anti-Western.[19]

Indonesian irredentism and revolution now focused on the former colonial master. Dutch economic interests were expelled. The Indonesian government then demanded the transfer of the last remaining Dutch controlled area in the archipelago, Western New Guinea, to Indonesian sovereignty, and openly adopted a strategy of 'Confrontation' to pressure the Dutch to withdraw. The strategy included large scale purchases of sophisticated modern weaponry from a very willing Soviet Union, to increase Indonesian naval, air and military power. This turn to the Soviets alarmed the Western Powers, as did this new strategy of 'Confrontation'. The British FO defined the strategy as combining 'public invective, economic blockade, piracy, subversion, and direct armed aggression'.[20] Throw in relentless diplomatic pressure, in all forums ranging from the UN to direct discussions with the adversary, and this defined very well the *modus operandi* Sukarno and his colleagues used to try to drive a wedge between the Dutch and their American allies – and then later to try to disrupt the formation of Malaysia. The Kennedy administration finally decided, in autumn 1961, to lean on the Dutch, to accept what in practice would become Indonesian annexation of the territory. JFK signed off on this policy because his administration was now very worried that Sukarno would drift completely into the communist camp, at home and abroad, and turn Indonesia into a major new Cold War adversary. This would be bad enough in its own right. Meanwhile, however, the DRV resumed the armed struggle in Vietnam, and the American government found itself pulled into a political and military commitment to defend the partition line of 1954 and its ally the Republic of Vietnam (ROV). The communist 'insurgency' in South Vietnam coincided with renewed outbreaks of military and political trouble in Laos. By the end of 1961 the situation in Indochina was serious enough to become the focal point of American Cold War concerns in Asia. Should Indonesia now turn hostile, the combination seemed likely to jeopardise the entire Western strategic position in Southeast Asia.[21]

Two prominent considerations rounded off the American approach to this new regional problem. One was a widespread tendency to see China as playing a driving role in both Vietnam and Indonesia, working through communist parties on the ground. The other was a pretty strong feeling that Indonesian nationalism could be reinforced strongly enough to head off this apparent turn towards communism, at home and abroad. The American government decided to support the creation of Malaysia, as a legitimate expression of regional opinion – and a probable Western ally. This recognised the fact that the Americans wanted continued British support in the region, and the British were committed to Malaysia. Not surprisingly the British complained about continued American miscellaneous economic and military support for Indonesia, after it escalated Confrontation. Such considerations limited how far the Kennedy administration could go to try to mollify Sukarno and his government. American officials duly warned the Indonesian government, in increasingly blunt terms, that if it continued to 'Confront' Malaysia aggressively there would be serious consequences for Indonesian-American relations.[22] However, because many American officials in Washington and Southeast Asia, especially the American Ambassador in Jakarta, Howard Jones, believed the British had provoked Sukarno, they felt he could still be prevented from drifting into a communist embrace, at home and abroad, by continued political engagement and economic inducement. Close professional and personal ties between the TNI and the American Army also fuelled optimism in American military circles that Indonesia could be kept 'on side', because the TNI saw the PKI as a grave threat to their future vision for Indonesia. This all made continued American engagement with Indonesia seem necessary.[23]

Unfortunately for Jones in particular, Jakarta did not respond as desired. Judging by their public statements and actions, senior Army officers seemed just as committed to Confrontation with Malaysia as Sukarno, Subandrio, and the PKI, if perhaps for different reasons.

Sukarno was not impressed by economic considerations, tilted closer to the PKI, and continued to complain about the 1958 intervention, as well as the Malaysia 'slap in the face'. And the PKI leaned towards the PRC in the ever more obvious feud between the Soviet Union and the PRC – a feud defined to a large degree by Chinese calls for more aggressive policy towards the West, especially in Asia. It thus seemed, by late 1963, that Confrontation with Indonesia had the potential to provoke real trouble between an American government, that now had a Cold War crisis in Vietnam on its hands, and a British government that it might blame for provoking Indonesia to turn hostile in that same Cold War.[24] But fate then intervened, as it often does.

On 19 October 1963 Alec Douglas-Home became Prime Minister of the UK, when Harold Macmillan retired. On 2 November, Ngo Dinh Diem was toppled by a coup in Saigon and murdered in the process. On 22 November, JFK was assassinated in Dallas. These leadership changes brought confusion to Southeast Asia and Lyndon Baines Johnson (LBJ) to the White House. They also provoked reassessments of British and American policy. After a false start, the British achieved what they saw at the time as a real breakthrough, an agreement that cleared the air and redefined a solid 'common purpose' between the allies in Southeast Asia. All too soon, however, events exposed British policy for the dangerous calculated risk it really was.

LBJ did not share his predecessor's desire to be gentle with Sukarno and Indonesia, but at first was not inclined to rock that boat until he could settle in and test the waters. To do just that, he agreed to State Department suggestions to send a high level emissary to try to broker a ceasefire between the warring parties in Confrontation, to allow negotiations to resume. Playing the emotional card, the new administration sent the Attorney General, Robert F. Kennedy, the late President's brother, to Asia in January 1964. Grinding their teeth behind closed doors, the Malaysian and British governments agreed to a ceasefire – but the agreement contained a crucial flaw that both made it unworkable and opened a door for LBJ. The Malaysians, understandably, wanted the ceasefire to be conditional on the withdrawal back across the border of all groups of armed men who had penetrated into their territory. The Indonesians refused. Weeks of bickering over the issue ran both the ceasefire and a subsequent round of negotiations between Foreign Ministers into the ground.[25]

As the initiative visibly faltered, Douglas-Home visited Washington. On 12 February 1964, the British delegation conferred with the President and senior advisers at the White House. Secretary of State Dean Rusk told the President that 'good progress had already been made by representatives of the two governments in a common approach to Southeast Asian problems'. The two heads of government then endorsed a pivotal agreement. The British would publicly support American policy in Vietnam, which now included escalating military support to the new government in Saigon. In return, the Americans would publicly support British efforts to defend Malaysia against Indonesia. The public communique duly made the references, which in fact sealed a larger strategic bargain. LBJ accepted the British argument that Indonesia posed a threat to larger Western interests, which must be met by containment more than engagement. He also agreed that because Malaysia was a British responsibility, the Americans would regard its defence as the principal British contribution to the collective Western effort to contain Cold War aggression in Southeast Asia. In return, they would regard British public support for American efforts in Vietnam as sufficient.[26]

This bargain did relieve some pressure on the British in their efforts to defend Malaysia. But it also helped provoke Sukarno and Subandrio into stepping up Confrontation, not backing away. And it created a very dangerous situation. The agreement with LBJ to define the conflicts in Southeast Asia as one connected and common problem, and to tackle that problem by a division of labour and leadership, made British policy a hostage to fortune in both Indonesia and Vietnam. And things did not go as hoped in either situation. Worse, this all began to expose an underlying British premise that ran dangerously contrary to the bargain made in the White House.

The outline of the problem publicly appeared that same month, February 1964, but from a different quarter. French President Charles De Gaulle grandly announced that the only realistic solution to the Cold War in Southeast Asia was to 'neutralise' the region. His rather broad but emphatic argument rested on two rationales: that China was indeed the root of the problem from the Western point of view; and that in mainland Southeast Asia at least, if not all over the region, the combination of national feeling and proximity to China meant that using Western military power as the primary instrument of containment ultimately could not succeed, and might well backfire. China should be engaged diplomatically, to at least try to orchestrate wider agreements that would expand on the 1962 Geneva Agreements to 'neutralise' Laos.[27] The New Zealand government dismissed the arguments as naïve. The Australian government angrily reacted the same way. The American government summed up a consensus: De Gaulle might well be expressing French resentment at being pushed out of the region, and at best was naïve about the ability of governments in the region to survive any political compromises with communists, both internally and with the PRC. The Commonwealth governments' reactions were heavily influenced by grave concern that any such change in Western strategy would shatter their whole strategy of 'forward defence'. The American government regarded the Laos agreements as at best a holding action to freeze an exposed position they could not easily maintain, not an example on which to expand. After the sobering experience of Soviet political aggression through coalition manipulation and subversion in Eastern Europe, in the late 1940s, precious few senior American decision makers were prepared to agree that neutralising Southeast Asia might actually be a viable strategy to contain communism – at best, the PRC would provide enough support to local communist parties to help subvert and shatter one state after another, from within. Shades of Czechoslovakia, Poland and the whole Eastern bloc.[28] In London, however, some people in high places thought De Gaulle had a point.

By 1964 British governments, particularly permanent officials, were closing in on two decades of continuous political decolonisation. That accumulated experience persuaded many, especially in the Foreign Office (FO), that the real force behind the 'winds of change' so famously identified by Macmillan was the force of nationalism, especially aspirations for national independence. National feeling, if not addressed, could easily be channelled in hostile directions. The argument that true and profound change could come only through expelling the economic and social system built by the colonial power, as well as by regaining control of government and administration, seemed all too attractive all too often. Ho Chi Minh and the DRV might have been the poster boy for this argument, but many British officials feared that this awkward combination of a European overseas colonial presence, resting on market economics, played all too readily into communist propaganda. There was a palpable sense, certainly within the FO, that in the battle for rhetorical appeal the communist position was dangerously attractive to the emerging states of the Afro-Asian bloc, certainly as long as European colonial interests were seen to be dominating aspiring nations. This was the very dynamic Sukarno addressed with his rhetoric about 'old established' against 'new emerging' forces. Turbulent transitions in India, Malaya, Kenya, Cyprus and now Malaysia all fed these developing British views. Southeast Asia seemed to stand out. The British decision in 1954 to reject 'united action' rested on the diagnosis that the French position in Indochina was doomed. Subsequent experience only expanded this view. By 1964, the British 'official mind' was clearly sceptical that direct Western military intervention was a viable way to contain communist pressure in Southeast Asia. Local governments seemed too fragile, communist pressures too strong. While not expressing this view as loudly as De Gaulle, a consensus slowly evolved in Whitehall. In essence, the West was strategically off balance and overstretched in the region – at the very least north of Malaysia – and would have to find another way to contain China and communism.[29]

The question was obvious: was there a realistic alternative? Events on the ground now made this issue acute, in both Vietnam and Confrontation. By August 1964 the Johnson administration was committed to open-ended military intervention to help protect the ROV from the communist onslaught, internal and external. The commitment was sealed by the Tonkin Gulf Resolution, securing strong Congressional support for what amounted to a free hand for LBJ to wage war in Vietnam.[30] As for Indonesia, Sukarno now seemed ready to jump into the Cold War against the West. Trying to salvage something from the Kennedy ceasefire mission, Sukarno claimed that Kennedy told him the United States would not support the British if they waged open war against Indonesia. When it became clear this was not correct, and that American policy was stiffening, Sukarno lashed out, publicly telling the Americans in March 'you can go to hell with your aid'. TNI combat units reinforced border areas in Kalimantan, leading to increased cross-border incursions into Sarawak in particular. Disturbed by such escalation, the British not only sent their own reinforcements but authorised ground forces in Borneo to carry out carefully controlled counter-incursions. The aim was to maintain the initiative on the ground at the border by disrupting Indonesian movements, and keeping the enemy off balance. In this dangerous climate, Sukarno delivered a particularly incendiary Independence Day speech on 17 August, calling for greater efforts to 'crush Malaysia', telling his people it was time to 'live dangerously'. He then launched the new campaign by bitterly denouncing American behaviour in Southeast Asia as leading the hated 'old established forces', and announcing the formation of an 'axis' aligning Indonesia with the PRC, North Korea, and the DRV.[31]

That same evening, miscellaneous forces controlled by the BPI launched seaborne incursions against the west coast of Malaya itself, crossing the Straits of Melaka by small groups travelling in sampans. This launched *Operation A*, a campaign aimed to destabilise Malaya and Singapore by internal subversion, stoked by external infiltration. These raids were followed by an audacious airborne raid in which infiltrators were dropped by parachute into northern Johor state on 2 September;

another seaborne raid on the west coast followed on 29 October. Indonesian agents also stirred up already tense communal feelings in Singapore – possibly helping provoke race riots in July, certainly doing so in a second round in September. Such pressure not only prompted the British to send still larger reinforcements of ground, air and naval forces, they also induced more concrete discussions, with the Americans and Australians, about what now seemed to be a serious threat of open war with Indonesia.[32]

These discussions indicated that the American government now realised the Commonwealth allies might have to escalate military operations against Indonesia, if Indonesian provocations did not abate. Rusk actually encouraged contingency planning, advising the British that if open war did erupt 'we would be much better advised to do so in a positive manner rather than to rely on defensive and long drawn out scrapping in the jungle'.[33] But what seemed arguably justified in the disputed territories of Borneo looked like naked aggression against the established sovereignty of Malaya and Singapore. The raids backfired badly by alienating world opinion, undermining Indonesia's diplomatic campaign to denounce Malaysia as a neo-colonial front. This made Sukarno even angrier. Combining his stronger rhetoric with the new front opened by *Operation A*, Far East Command argued that it must be prepared to face a possible surprise Indonesian strike against their vital air and naval bases in Singapore and Malaya. A much larger war, one the British government and its military advisers emphatically did not want to fight, seemed dangerously close.[34]

This escalation in both Vietnam and Indonesia fostered a sense of crisis in the region, which to some degree drew the British and their Western allies closer together, at least regarding contingency planning. But the strain of sending such powerful forces to Southeast Asia provoked concerns that cut across department lines in Whitehall. The Treasury blanched at the increased cost. The FO fretted at the greater danger of war in the region. And the newly unified Ministry of Defence worried about the need to drain both the strategic reserve, and forces committed to NATO, just to be able to deter, or if necessary defeat, Indonesian armed forces that could now deploy sophisticated Soviet-produced weapons. Did the danger of wider war offset any gain from greater American sympathy? Before these new problems could be closely evaluated, however, fate once again chose October to intervene.

On 15 October the Labour Party returned to government in the UK, after 13 years in opposition. The next day, the PRC successfully detonated its first nuclear weapon. The British election brought to power a government hanging on by the precarious majority of four seats in the House of Commons, leading a party hungry for innovation at home but divided over how to relate to the rest of the world. The Chinese nuclear test, coming earlier than expected, helped focus the Johnson administration's growing concern over the struggle to contain communism in Southeast Asia. The result was a collision between the efforts of a new British government to maintain a smaller, yet still effective, strategic role for Britain beyond Europe and NATO, and the Johnson administration's decision to wage war in Vietnam, as the focal point for collective security and containment in Southeast Asia. The British government resorted to quadripartite discussions to try to persuade their allies to underwrite a smaller, yet still acceptable, British military presence in the region. They failed.

The new British government led by Harold Wilson took office determined to stand firm in Confrontation, and maintain Britain's wider role in the region and the world. Wilson and his Defence Secretary, Denis Healey, both championed this agenda. But Wilson also initiated, not unreasonably for a party so long out of office, a full scale review and reconsideration of British policies, defence, economic and foreign. From these discussions between ministers, officials and departments in London, as well as diplomats and military advisers abroad, there emerged what became an annual effort to resolve a cardinal problem: how to harmonise effective policies to reinvigorate the economy, and erase the current account deficit in the balance of payments in trade, yet still meet British strategic commitments. The central theme became a recurring Defence Review, which evolved in stages. Departments battled over how to forge an overall British policy. That policy was then discussed with the UK's closest allies, to try to persuade them to accept and align accordingly. The main problem was clear: the connection between the current account deficit and the strength of the currency on the one hand, and strategic commitments on the other.[35] This could not be resolved without working out effective agreements with the Americans. And it became most acute over Southeast Asia.

By spring 1965 the British government was ready to start selling its changing defence policy to its closest allies. Three fundamental principles were identified, as the basis for this revised policy. First in importance was cost. The Treasury successfully argued that the best way to reduce burdens the British economy should no longer bear was to impose a flat absolute ceiling on total defence spending. That ceiling was expressed as annual defence spending not more than £2 billion by 1970 as calculated in current value, a reduction from the previous government's readiness to spend £2.4 billion every year. This arbitrary approach, based on total financial capability rather than overall strategic need, had the virtue of being very clear. But it also forced Whitehall to decide just what to cut, and why. And such decisions could not be made without arguing about strategic priorities. That led to the second fundamental principle: henceforth, the United Kingdom would no longer accept any unilateral military commitment against any other power that could deploy sophisticated weapon systems. British armed forces would only fight alongside capable allies. The third principle was that British bases would no longer be maintained in places where the local political climate did not support their presence.[36] All three principles were heavily influenced by Confrontation with Indonesia, and all bore directly on any future British military role in Southeast Asia.

The real problem posed by Confrontation was not so much the military strain of fighting this low intensity undeclared war against a volatile but disorganised foe, but rather the military deterrent required to prevent the conflict from escalating to open war. British military strategy for the war at hand called for maintaining the initiative and keeping the enemy off balance by aggressive covert cross-border counter-incursions into Kalimantan. This required larger and more intensively trained and prepared ground forces, as well as an extensive and expensive array of support to keep them mobile and responsive, drawing heavily for example on helicopter and transport aircraft units. But in order to cope with the credible danger of escalation to open war, against a TNI whose sheer size – including some 132 infantry battalions – posed a real threat, as well as an air force equipped with modern Soviet-supplied jet bomber and fighter aircraft, and a navy that deployed Soviet-supplied submarines, frigates and missile patrol craft, the British government felt compelled to reinforce FEC strongly enough to allow it to prevail in any scenario. This amounted, by spring 1965, to more than 63,000 personnel deployed in theatre, a larger force than the supposedly higher priority British Army of the Rhine forces committed to NATO. By that time – counting only British and Gurkha units committed to the Confrontation theatre of operations, thus excluding the Hong Kong garrison plus Australian and New Zealand units operating under its direction – FEC had under its operational control 12 infantry battalions, 15 RAF combat and transport squadrons, five Army and Navy helicopter squadrons, and 13 major surface combat vessels, including two aircraft carriers. By comparison, the combined total of units then committed to NATO or in reserve in the United Kingdom amounted to 21 infantry battalions, 47 combat and transport squadrons, four Army and Navy helicopter squadrons – none left in Germany – and 32 major surface combat vessels, including only one aircraft carrier. FEC had more than doubled in size, in order to deter Indonesian escalation.[37]

Such expensive concentration of force turned FEC into the most financially costly British overseas military commitment, as well as draining the strategic reserve and drawing important resources, such as helicopter squadrons, away from NATO forces. This compromised the UK's ability to take on any other serious military commitment, as long as it was required to maintain such a strong deterrent to protect Malaysia. And it all happened as a result of Indonesia's reaction to the 'Grand Design' exit strategy meant to reduce the British military burden in Southeast Asia, while at the same time securing British military facilities in the region in friendly territory. The best laid plans.... So something now had to give. The plan was to use the palpable consequences of Confrontation to persuade the allies the British military role in the region must change and they must help, not just agree – whether they liked it or not.

The persuasion campaign really began when Wilson led a large delegation to Washington, DC, in December 1964, to consult in person with a safely re-elected LBJ. The British Prime Minister got straight to the point: 'Our main purpose was to make clear our defence problems and to prepare the ground for further more detailed discussions; this was established.' This was correct – but. Wilson made the connection between defence spending overseas and the current account balance of payments problem, stressed the need to revitalise the British economy and keep the pound sterling strong, and made the point about Britain's strategic overstretch. Reporting after the fact to his New Zealand counterpart, Keith Holyoake, Wilson then spelt out the crux of the matter:

> I said that we wanted to secure the necessary reductions in our overall defence expenditure in cooperation with the United States and our other allies, by a rather more equitable sharing of the burden than there is at present. We wanted, therefore, to discuss with them how they might contribute in such a cooperative enterprise.

The British Prime Minister summarised his report optimistically, noting 'This was only the first stage in a continuing process of consultation, and I feel very satisfied that we have opened up a fruitful dialogue with the Americans.'[38] The optimism was however at best premature. Wilson certainly got the American President's attention, establishing three points in the process: the British needed American help to make necessary changes in defence and economic policy; because these changes affected American interests they expected support; but in order to make such changes effective they would consult in detail with the American government, before making final decisions. Wilson was right to assume the Americans were sympathetic about British economic and fiscal concerns, but badly misread the real American concern regarding defence.

At the White House, Rusk pressed Wilson hard to maintain Britain's global military role and presence, calling it a force multiplier that helped the United States project its own power. Wilson's ready agreement that he intended to do so suggested the basis of a good consensus. But when LBJ cautiously suggested it would be helpful if the British could deploy a token military force to help the war effort in South Vietnam, Wilson parried the request by making two points. The British were fully pinned down by Confrontation, which, as agreed, was their principal contribution to collective security in the area. And as regards Vietnam, the British position as Co-Chair of the Geneva Agreements had to be preserved, so that it might be useful should negotiations become possible or desirable. To avoid conflict of interest, the United Kingdom should refrain from even token official involvement. The public communique of 9 December seemed satisfactory:

> the President and the Prime Minister recognised the particular importance of the military effort which both their countries are making in support of legitimate governments in South-East Asia, particularly in Malaysia and South Vietnam, which seek to maintain their independence and resist subversion.

But the message concealed more than it revealed. LBJ was by now personally committed to breaking the communist effort to destroy South Vietnam, but, responding to growing domestic political pressures, sought ever more earnestly to legitimise the increasing American military burden there by securing visible coalition military support. The President was carefully briefed by his advisers, who informed him that while Wilson's government was eager to find ways to maintain a British military role east of Suez, early indications suggested they were thinking more of an arms-length role emphasising naval and air forces – whereas what the American government most needed was tangible proof of 'united action' on the ground, at the sharp end. Wilson did not oppose American policy in Vietnam, but realised there was neither public nor official support in the United Kingdom for sending in ground forces, and worried that American escalation might put his government in a difficult political position at home. Johnson kept his patience, which lulled Wilson into thinking the President was not really distressed by either the British refusal to send a token force or their effort to shield behind the Co-Chair role, to keep the request at bay.[39] All the Prime Minister really did was alert the Americans to the fact that this new British government was going to be making major changes they did not really like, but probably not offering anything they wanted in return. And if Confrontation either escalated, as then seemed possible, or ended, which sooner or later had to happen, what then?

Because the answer to that question depended so heavily on the war in Vietnam, it was just as well for that first summit meeting that Wilson did not spell out, in any detail, the underlying political rationale now guiding British deliberations regarding Southeast Asia. That rationale was summarised in a memorandum presented by the FO to the Defence and Overseas Policy Committee (OPD), the inner circle of senior Cabinet ministers which steered defence and foreign policy, in mid-November. The paper represented the distilling of years of deliberations by officials, both anticipating and responding to events, over what to do regarding Southeast Asia. Traces of 1954, let alone the reviews of 1961, stand out sharply in its paragraphs. That underlines an important point: what the Wilson government went on to overhaul for the next two years relied heavily on themes already well-crafted before it came into office. When the OPD accepted the paper as written, the FO justifiably construed this to indicate broad agreement. The paper was used accordingly as a basis for subsequent discussions, in London and Southeast Asia, about 'British Policy Towards South-East Asia', its title. The 13 page paper was summarised by a ten-part conclusion. The real message however was two-fold: the United Kingdom could not abandon a strategic role in Southeast Asia, but the Western allies must drastically change their approach to collective security in the region – and the conjunction of these two points should shape changes in British policy and strategy.[40]

The paper summarised the argument that the British must remain committed to Southeast Asia as follows: (*my paraphrasing as well as direct quotes*)

> Southeast Asia did not matter economically to the UK but did matter politically, for three reasons: it was threatened by communist aggression and subversion, which if successful would compromise Western global security; Australia and New Zealand would be compromised

by any collapse in the region, and as 'old Commonwealth allies' they remained a vital British interest; but above all, because the region mattered to the Americans the British absolutely must 'make a respectable contribution', in order to retain any influence on American policy. Retaining such influence was essential, otherwise the UK could not 'keep our position as a world power and the United States' principal partner'. And that role underpinned UK security itself. Britain could not lose American confidence.

But the whole Western approach to collective security in the region must change. That argument went as follows:

In the long run the only way to keep communism at bay from the region was to neutralise it within the Cold War, by either tacit or formal agreement. Relying on Western military forces would alienate local nationalism sooner or later; but regional Non-Alignment would orient local political feeling against communism, or at the very least against Chinese dominance, just as predictably.

The problem must however be nuanced, otherwise changes in Western policy could do more harm than good. The gist of that final argument was:

The French were right about the long run, but not about the moment; Western military power must stand firm until the correlation of forces stabilised. Once they did, Western policy should distinguish between Continental and Archipelago Southeast Asia, for strategic purposes. Continental Southeast Asia was too vulnerable to Chinese intervention, so Western military commitment there would ultimately backfire; the aim should be to see the eventual emergence of governments non-threatening to both Cold War blocs. Island Southeast Asia was less vulnerable, but must still become more cohesive in order to withstand communist subversion. To help make that happen, Western military forces and bases must sooner or later withdraw.

The paper could not, however, persuasively apply its ultimate rationale to the crises of the moment. On Confrontation there was reasonable clarity: the fight must be seen through to success, before British forces could withdraw from the region; but once it was, they should go. But on Vietnam it was helpless. Noting that a head on collision had developed between American commitment and communist aggression, it could only conclude, pathetically, 'but it is not at all impossible that, with time, this situation could change'. Once it did, the region should be neutralised and Western military forces withdrawn.

De Gaulle would have been as receptive to this paper as LBJ would have been infuriated by it. But the only new or even recent considerations it contained were the nuances regarding the situations in Vietnam and Confrontation. The 'big ideas' were all familiar: Indochina, or at least Vietnam, could no longer be saved; but the region could not be abandoned; so Western policy must change, by agreement and in lockstep, as soon as possible. Familiar too were other principles now emerging through British discussions at home and abroad. As early as February 1959 the Macmillan government reviewed a lengthy paper discussing 'The Prospects of Retaining our Present Bases in South-East Asia'. Much of it could have been recycled in 1964: military planning must be coordinated and improved, through ongoing quadripartite discussions with the Americans, Australians and New Zealanders; British military forces should plan and prepare to operate only as part of a coalition, not on their own or even necessarily in the lead; the British strategic role in the region should stress naval, air and nuclear forces over ground forces; American confidence must be retained; local political conditions would sooner or later jeopardise British bases in Malaya and Singapore; the logical alternative was to relocate British forces and facilities to Australia, to underpin a reoriented collective security commitment to the region. Clearly, the Wilson defence overhaul was now being sifted through ideas long percolating in Whitehall, brought closer to boiling point by the strains of Confrontation and the stress of Vietnam.[41]

Australian Prime Minister Sir Robert Menzies grew concerned about indications the new British government was considering major changes to collective security in Southeast Asia. Such indications seemed all the more worrying given developments in January 1965. Sukarno ostentatiously withdrew Indonesia from the UN, celebrating his 'axis' with Beijing; less dramatically but of more direct concern, more TNI combat units deployed within striking distance in both Kalimantan and Sumatra. The military moves provoked the British government to authorise FEC to conduct more aggressive covert cross-border incursions in Borneo, and approve contingency plans for destroying Indonesian air and seapower by sustained strategic bombing, should open war break out. They also provoked the Australian and New Zealand governments to commit combat forces to Borneo, to reinforce their Commonwealth allies; their forces had already engaged Indonesian raiders in Malaya. Meanwhile Menzies and his government were seriously considering committing Australian combat forces to Vietnam. This spike in tension prompted Menzies to suggest the four Western allies should urgently review the situation 'on the political level', in order to 'get the balance and priorities right in Southeast Asia'. Quiet discussion along the sidelines of the state funeral for Winston Churchill at the end of January pointed towards the SEATO Council meeting, scheduled for London in early May. The Foreign Ministers and Secretary of State could hide behind this wider gathering to have their own private discussions, unobtrusively.[42]

Subsequent events made such a meeting seem useful. At the policy level, British deliberations moved along. But in the region, communist attacks on American installations in South Vietnam provoked President Johnson to initiate, in March, Operation *Rolling Thunder*, a strategic bombing offensive involving systematic air strikes on multiple targets in North Vietnam. This was significant escalation from the retaliation strikes the Americans had already delivered. Its aim was to make it impossible for North Vietnam to continue sending men and materiel south to wage its war to destroy South Vietnam.[43] This direct attack on North Vietnam provoked instant and lasting controversy in many countries, including the United Kingdom. For the British this turned out in fact to be a game changer, although such a judgment can really only be made in retrospect. Both the Labour Party and the country as a whole were so aroused by the American bombing campaign against North Vietnam that this feeling imposed, henceforth, a political live wire regarding Vietnam, one Wilson dared not cross. LBJ provided what looked like some wiggle room in April, when he publicly declared that the American war aim was to convince the DRV government the United States would not allow the ROV to be destroyed, and therefore to resume negotiations about a political settlement. This allowed the Wilson government to hold out the prospect of playing some useful role in such negotiations, as a basis for British policy regarding Vietnam. On the other hand the Australian government stepped up the pressure by declaring, on 29 April, that it would commit an Australian infantry battalion to military operations in Vietnam.[44] All this made quiet quadripartite talks seem timely indeed. Wilson helped confirm the meeting by urging LBJ, in late April, to support 'a greater degree of four-power planning in relation to the defence of Asia and the Far East generally'. The President's broad agreement enabled just such 'informal' discussions to take place in London in early May, covered by the SEATO Council meeting.[45]

This gathering was the first of five rounds of high level but quiet quadripartite discussions, stretching from May 1965 into October 1966, through which the four Western allies tried, and failed, to weave changes in British policy into that 'deep community of purpose and long practice of cooperation' that JFK publicly hailed in 1962. From this first quiet four-cornered gathering in London the roots of the problem could clearly be seen. The British wanted to step back militarily from Southeast Asia as soon as possible – their allies however were doing the opposite.

The discussion in London on the evening of 2 May reached only two agreements: that the strategic challenges in Southeast Asia were indeed one connected problem that should be treated as such, and that four cornered discussions about the matter, especially its military aspects, should continue – but very unobtrusively and informally. The by now long-standing concern that such discussions would suggest there was a 'white man's club' in which the real decisions about collective security were made, hiding behind SEATO for concealment, was duly minuted. But so was the now open disagreement. George Ball, American Under Secretary of State, put it directly: 'Mr. Ball refuted the Walter Lippmann thesis that China would inevitably come one day to control all South-East Asia and it would be better for the United States to recognize this sooner than later.' Ball was responding to Foreign Secretary Michael Stewart's comment that the longer-term problem was how to handle China. The aim should be to bring about some normalisation of the Cold War confrontation with the PRC, to engineer 'the kind of relationship between China on the one hand and the rest of the world on the other as now existed between the USSR and the rest of the world'. While everyone agreed this could not be done until after China was persuaded that communism could not prevail in Vietnam or Indonesia, the Americans believed this must be done by force, in Vietnam, and wanted allied support.[46] This discussion, which of course underlined the fact that the American and British governments were quietly working through a Western 'inner circle' to reconsider collective security in Southeast Asia, left the big issue hanging in the air: should military intervention in Southeast Asia remain the basis on which to build collective security, or should it instead be used in order to bring about a wider diplomatic reorientation in the region?

The hard facts of the matter now pressed in very roughly indeed on the British government. Grand visions of economic growth and transformation made no progress, faced by persistent problems in the current account deficit and heavy pressure on the pound sterling. Commonwealth military support in Borneo only underlined the strain of that ongoing commitment. And American escalation in Vietnam threatened to detonate the whole politically combustible mixture. This was underlined by Stewart's predecessor, Patrick Gordon Walker, in a report he submitted on 7 May after an intensive three week tour of the region, trying to drum up support for British efforts to extend the neutralisation solution beyond Laos to Cambodia – in hopes this might prompt still wider political discussions, which the United Kingdom, in its role as Geneva Co-Chair, could promote. Walker's conclusions were chilling. Because defeat in southern Vietnam would be disastrous, the British should continue to support American military operations there. But because the conflict could only end in a political settlement, they should also 'search for a policy which, while backing America loyally, allows us a certain more apparent independence of view'. Domestic pressures were one reason to seek such finesse, but longer-term strategic considerations were also relevant:

> The white man cannot indefinitely support one set of Asians against another. (This applies to Malaysia as well as to South Viet-Nam). There is no solid Asian bloc and many Asian countries (especially India) are frightened of China. Nonetheless we must not underrate the feeling that is growing in Japan and India and perhaps elsewhere that white men have no military place in Asia.[47]

What Stewart tried to put across after dinner on 2 May was the strategic rationale for the reconsideration now taking shape in Whitehall. The central conclusion was clear: British military power should cease to play any independent role in collective security in Southeast Asia as soon as possible, not just because they could no longer afford to but because it was also becoming counterproductive. This meant that the whole Western approach to the region should also change, before it was too late. Events then intervened, so dramatically the British went so far as to suggest it might already be.

On 9 August 1965 Malaysia and Singapore formally separated, the latter established by agreement, implemented through Malaysian legislation, as an independent and sovereign republic. Having been deliberately kept in the dark, Western governments, the British in particular, reacted indignantly. But no manner of protest could undo the damage, and some senior British officials suggested that this dramatic fracture within Malaysia might provide the necessary occasion for the United

Kingdom to convince its allies that British strategic foreign policy in the region must be drastically redesigned. Three concerns came together: the strain of battling to keep the pound sterling healthy; the view that in the long term Western military intervention in Southeast Asia must prove counterproductive; and the more widely held view that sooner rather than later local political conditions would make it impossible to maintain military forces and facilities in Malaysia and Singapore. On 15 August Wilson, Healey, and several other senior Cabinet ministers and officials discussed how to handle the repercussions of the Singapore separation. They reached three important conclusions. First, the search for alternatives to the facilities in Malaysia and Singapore must now accelerate. Second, and more important, the separation called into question the very reasons for defending Malaysia against Indonesia in the first place. Confrontation must be reexamined. Finally, and as a matter of great urgency, the British must again consult their allies regarding the whole question of a continued role for the United Kingdom in effective collective security in the region. The minutes of this ad hoc meeting precisely captured the British dilemma: 'In the longer term we must seek to reduce our own commitments in the Far East without, however, prejudicing our *bona fides* and our relations with Australia, New Zealand and the United States.'[48]

Quiet discussions at the senior official level were hastily organised for the first week of September, in London. All three allies came to the talks very concerned about reports the British would suggest a radical change to their policy for Southeast Asia, on the grounds that the expulsion of Singapore compromised the effort to defend Malaysia. Menzies went further when he read the British draft paper, warning Wilson on 3 September that British proposals 'exhibit a general attitude towards the probable development in that part of Asia which we would require to examine and, if necessary, challenge'. The suggestion that provoked the Australian Prime Minister was that Confrontation was now pointless as well as too expensive, and that Singapore could no longer be relied on as the platform for British, and Commonwealth, military projection in the area, so an accelerated redeployment should be considered forthwith. Menzies took no chances, directly warning Johnson that any such radical change in British policy would be 'of historic significance... for the political and military balance in Southeast Asia, and certainly for the United States in view of your own positive policies for containment of communist expansion and preservation of small free countries'.[49] Johnson did not need the warning, and he had greater leverage.

Exploiting the coincidence that the talks between officials coincided with a prearranged 'secret meeting without attracting attention', to discuss the obviously related issues of the British Defence Review on the one hand, and American efforts to support the pound sterling on the other, Ball brought his President's message directly to Wilson on 8 and 9 September. Ball declared that four power talks on the British leaving Singapore were 'premature and hazardous', insisting that if the fact the British were even considering leaving got out this would encourage Sukarno and the PKI, and undermine the American campaign in Vietnam. He then bluntly reminded Wilson that the British were pledged to consult the Americans in advance before making final decisions in their Defence Review, something made necessary by the fact that American efforts to help the British economic position must be related to the global defence burdens they both shouldered. Wilson insisted the British were in no position to make any contribution in Vietnam but he also backpedalled, arguing that British proposals regarding Singapore were only contingencies aimed to provoke a timely conversation about choices, ideas based on what they saw as the unpredictable future of Lee Kuan Yew, his government and its policies. Notably, he had to deny the British had decided to give up on Confrontation and pull out of the region.[50]

Many British officials were taken aback by how strongly all three allies condemned the suggestion that Singapore might now be untenable, and Confrontation therefore unwinnable, and that this made a larger conversation timely. This allied criticism definitely influenced how Whitehall decided to resolve both British policy and how to sell it to their allies. The New Zealand High Commission spotted and spelt out the principal reason for such an apparent misstep: Wilson and Healey were using American, Australian and New Zealand reactions to help sway both what the British finally decided, and how they moved forward. Senior officials who wanted to accelerate major changes in British strategic foreign policy in the region could not deny such changes would be fraught if they went ahead against American opposition in particular; these talks forced them to agree the British must both accept a more measured pace and present a somewhat different case. It was clear how difficult it would be to persuade the allies to accept any British argument regarding the wisdom of broader neutralisation in Southeast Asia.[51] Yet again, however, fate chose October to intervene dramatically.

On the night of 30 September/1 October the TNI was nearly decapitated by an attempted coup in Jakarta. The plotters unaccountably failed to target General Soeharto, commanding KOSTRAD, the strategic reserve forces concentrated around the capital. Soeharto restored order and the coup fell apart. This set off months of violent political confusion in Indonesia, which led to the destruction of the PKI, massive loss of life, and by spring 1966 the de facto ousting of Sukarno, replaced by a new coalition led by Soeharto and supported by the Army high command. In retrospect this marked the definitive turning point in Confrontation; the British and their allies outlasted the regime that unleashed the conflict on them in the first place.[52] But this was only clear in retrospect, and in the British case the margins were narrow. For the remainder of 1965, the strain did not abate at all.[53]

No one could be certain whether the Indonesian Army would come out on top in the political struggle unfolding mainly in Java, and meanwhile the expensive concentration of British forces remained in place – and the pound sterling continued to struggle. By October FEC was arguing that plans to compel the Indonesian leadership to terminate Confrontation, by escalated military pressure, should be moved forward.[54] The next round of quiet four party discussions, held at the officials level in London on 1–2 December 1965, concentrated on the immediate situation in Indonesia, and how best to tackle it. Without much difficulty, all parties agreed it was too soon to send any sort of 'peace feelers' to whoever might now be in charge in Jakarta. This reflected the most interesting change these talks revealed: the British now agreed to set aside any idea of making concessions to terminate Confrontation, and see the conflict through to a successful resolution that did not compromise Malaysia or Western interests. That was a direct result of allied pressure exerted at the discussions in September, and in subsequent exchanges. All agreed the only action would be to signal quietly to Jakarta that Commonwealth forces would not try to take any military advantage if the Indonesians withdrew front line forces from the Borneo border for 'internal security duties'. The policy was to ride out the Indonesian storm.[55]

This quadripartite consensus was shaped very much by wider developments, as well as allied pressure. Australian and New Zealand military forces were now committed to action in both Vietnam and Borneo. The war in Vietnam escalated sharply, including heavy engagements between American and communist ground forces. The American bombing campaign against North Vietnam provoked growing international criticism, including in the United Kingdom. And serious friction between Malaysia and the new Republic of Singapore threatened to disrupt the united front against Indonesia. This all helped persuade the British government to agree by January 1966 that 'judicious use of military action might incline the Indonesians to look somewhat more favourably on negotiation than they otherwise would of their own accord', and endorse FEC plans to compel an end to Confrontation should it prove necessary.[56]

This hard line reflected the by now massive strain imposed on British global policy by the clash between ongoing economic difficulty and the acrimonious Defence Review. The decision to bend to allied pressure and see Confrontation through was part and parcel of trying to finalise, and sell, a revamped defence policy and grand strategy. The Americans increased the pressure by declaring repeatedly that they regarded a continued significant British military commitment to Southeast Asia as essential; indeed, McNamara went so far as to say that if cuts must be made it would be better to make them from NATO commitments.[57] This all shaped the new defence policy which, by December, the Wilson Cabinet was ready to present to its allies. The British government proposed to connect immediate commitments to the longer-term desire for change by changing the tone and manner by which they presented British intentions. Tough talk about seeing Confrontation through replaced any hint of the desire to pull out; but that tough talk must be linked to careful spin regarding how to make necessary and major changes in the region once the conflict ended. That involved two things: redefining the region, and embedding British policy and forces squarely within a coordinated allied framework.

The British diplomatic offensive began, predictably, with another Wilson visit to Washington in December 1965. Wilson sought Johnson's support for the conclusions of his government's Defence Review. Given that, he was confident the new policy could be sold to the other inner circle allies and to public opinion. British strategy rested on three lines of persuasion: to assure the Americans that the British would continue to play an extra-European role in collective security even after making necessary reductions in overseas defence commitments; to demonstrate that in the Far East this could only be done, after Confrontation ended, through some concrete integration of British forces and commitments within larger allied capabilities; and to redesign the region, and therefore the British presence, transforming the 'Far East', an area really amounting to Southeast Asia, to the 'Indo-Pacific theatre', an area that could stretch from the east coast of Africa to the Pacific Islands. Such a redesign could not only allow the British to consider relocating their forces away from the apparently unstable hub of Singapore, it might also allow them to do three other things: piggyback off allied capabilities, economising on their own costs; count British forces deployed well away from Southeast Asia and the SEATO theatre as being available for both; and draw the Americans into taking on greater responsibilities for leading collective security in the larger region encompassing both the Indian Ocean and the SEATO area. Johnson settled for the assurance that the British would continue to play a wider military role outside Europe. But Wilson's direct hint about specific changes intended to transform the Far East into the Indo-Pacific pointed towards real trouble. To replace Singapore, the British were 'considering the possibility of an alternative base in northern Australia'.[58]

In order to reduce their military commitment to Southeast Asia without annoying their allies, the British had to convince them that not only was the redesign of the region strategically reasonable, but that a very different configuration of British forces would, if integrated within allied frameworks, make a contribution to collective security important enough to persuade them to adjust their own policies, and expectations. The floating element was of course Confrontation; whether it ended sooner or later, when it did, not only would reductions in British forces committed to the region have to begin, the British would also have to look for a way to relocate whatever forces they retained away from Singapore without destabilising the region. The only real alternative, one under some sort of consideration from 1957, appeared to be Australia.[59] But such a relocation would not only require really major changes in British policy, strategy, and deployment, it would also by necessity transform Australian policy. The range of difficulties in making such changes, and the extent to which they would involve passing British burdens onto other shoulders, provoked obvious questions about British intentions. Those questions came out very directly when Denis Healey followed up Wilson's lead by taking on the difficult challenge to persuade the Australians and New Zealanders to help underwrite this very different British policy east of Suez.

On 1 and 2 February 1966, Healey met the Australian government, now led by Harold Holt, and New Zealand Defence Minister Dean Eyre. The New Zealanders saw most clearly the key challenges facing each of their three allies: to persuade the British not to be pessimistic about the prospects of remaining in Singapore for some time to come; to persuade the Australians to consider in good faith the viability of relocating British forces from Singapore to an alternative hub, presumably Australia; and above all to persuade the Americans to agree to implement much more closely harmonised four power coordination of defence policies in the region, which we may take as a euphemism for de facto integration of plans and forces.[60] The last was the really crucial point. The Australians were very willing to support British appeals for quadripartite harmonisation of regional defence, led by the Americans – but most reluctant to support moving British forces out of Singapore.

Healey briefed his Antipodean colleagues on the Defence Review decisions, then made the key points. Some £50 million in savings still must be found; any allied reluctance to accept British proposals might yet push the Cabinet, which had not yet made its final decision, to seek the economy in the Far East. The British would see Confrontation through to a successful outcome. But after that, their continued military engagement would rest on three conditions. They would not again be able to fight on their own – which also meant in the lead role – a 'sophisticated opponent', defined as an enemy with advanced weaponry. Nor would they be able to take the lead in any prolonged counterinsurgency operations. Finally, they would not base in or operate from any position where local opinion did not strongly support their presence and operations. Healey concluded by trying to leverage the Americans, pointing out they were pleased to hear the British would not leave the region after Confrontation but would instead stay in Singapore as long as practicable under their stipulations above, and agreed basing alternatives to Singapore should be examined. The Australians replied robustly. They argued that only American engagement could prevent communist China from subverting Southeast Asia, and that a continued British military presence within the region was a vital stabilising factor. It would help keep the Americans committed, whereas withdrawal would discourage them and provoke trouble in the region. Healey replied by expressing the new British narrative: 'there was no difference of view between us and our Allies on the desirability of deploying as far north as possible for as long as possible', but in the long-term neutralising the area might be the only way to keep China at bay. Because sooner or later that would require redeployment, the British needed to know if the Australians were willing to consider whether moving Far East Command from Singapore to Australia was feasible economically and politically, and would be effective militarily.

The message was clear: the British felt that by the 1970s Western military forces could only effectively underpin containment by redeploying from the mainland to the periphery of Southeast Asia. This amounted to writing off South Vietnam, which directly contradicted American policy, and assuming the worst in Malaysia and Singapore. Both conclusions provoked the allies. Paul Hasluck, Australian Minister for External Affairs, argued that neutralisation would only open the door to China; withdrawal from the mainland was more likely to force the West one day to enforce containment by nuclear weapons. Forward defence required military engagement; sheer American weight set its own logic. Dean Eyre agreed, arguing bases in Australia would be 'beyond the fringe'; any real British disengagement from the region would push the Australians and New Zealanders to 'change their strategy from forward defence to home defence, and to greater dependence on the United States'. But Healey stuck to his brief. The British agreed to maintain a smaller but still potent Far East Command as long as the Americans fought on in Vietnam; in return the Americans agreed the British could search for an alternative base. The Australians reverted to a fallback position, based on their clear priority: to entangle the Americans and British together in any military decision that affected containment in Southeast Asia; if British forces did move, the four powers must adjust policies accordingly and coherently. A difficult bargain finally took shape. The Australians agreed to explore, without commitment, the practicalities of relocating British forces. Healey would make the strongest statement in public about British intentions to remain in Singapore that he could persuade his colleagues to accept. Most important, all three governments would press for continuing quadripartite official and ministerial discussions, to consider 'the prospects of working together militarily in the 1970s'.[61] This last point was the issue on which continued military cooperation with the British in the region would stand or fall. The Americans were the key factor. If they agreed to accept British force reductions and redeployment and take the lead in a *de facto* four power military bloc, the British could carry on. On those terms, the Australians and New Zealanders could consider British relocation. The consequences of British withdrawal from Singapore could be offset by the larger fact of close four power coordination of collective security.

The critical problem with this agreement, however, was that it rested on a non-starter. Upon investigating the practicalities of relocating British forces and even FEC itself to Australia, the Australian planners found what they expected to find: quite a few reasons why it would not work or should not be tried, none in favour. To single out the most critical problems: the Australians baulked at the sheer cost of the proposal – more than their annual defence budget – most of which they were expected to fund; they expressed no interest in basing British forces in Western Australia to allow them to operate in East Africa and the Indian Ocean, dismissing the British effort to redesign the Far East as the Indo-Pacific theatre; they concluded that when the project became public, as it must, this would compromise the important British position in Malaysia and Singapore; and perhaps most poignantly, they saw political catastrophe beckoning should British ground forces sit in garrison in Australia, as an ostensible but dormant SEATO commitment, while Australian conscript soldiers fought and died in Vietnam.[62] This clear rejection prompted Hasluck to try to reorient the whole problem. Two weeks after the Healey talks he urged his department to reconsider the whole question of quadripartite cooperation. Hasluck forensically picked apart the loose thinking dogging the issue. Australia wanted a real voice in Western policy in the region but must abort 'the danger that one ally, alongside whom we were fighting, might have different views from those of the other great ally, alongside whom we were also fighting'. The only way to do that would be to stop pressing for quadripartite 'arrangements'. That suggested concrete policy steps and public commitments sure to expose, not heal, British-American divergence, especially on Vietnam, but also on the question of eventual regional neutralisation. Australia should instead promote quadripartite 'discussions'. Provided they kept the Americans and British talking in a group of four, the Australians might persuade them to focus on what brought them together: the fundamental goal, to contain China, and the need to share that burden. Plans and forces might be at least reconciled if shared grand strategy kept all four together. It might still be possible to entice British and American policies to coexist.[63]

This was the most thoughtful proposal about making quadripartite cooperation really effective in Southeast Asia that emerged during this entire long effort to try to manage changes in British defence policy, without compromising collective security in the region. And even it exposed the fault line. Cooperation without formal commitment and integration was precisely what the Americans wanted; but de facto commitment to integration under American leadership was now the only way the Wilson government would be able to maintain any significant British presence east of Suez. Nor did the march of events bring any relief. Confrontation wound down, to the point where by May it was clear that the new regime in Jakarta led by Soeharto was seeking the political resolution that did in fact emerge in August, through the Bangkok Agreement. But that compelled the British to begin their draw down of forces, and effectively ended the agreement whereby their commitment to Confrontation kept them too busy to make any contribution in Vietnam.[64] A general election in March brought Wilson a comfortable majority but that included a more vocal left wing, which increased the pressure on the Prime Minister over both his reluctance to condemn the American bombing of North Vietnam and the whole east of Suez commitment. The Defence White Paper released on 22 February barely lasted beyond a news cycle. Further economic pressure compelled Healey to agree to search for yet more economy in defence spending. In due course the COS decided that any further economies should be sought east of Suez.[65] All these developments challenged one last high-level four-cornered discussion at which the British sought to 'sell' their repackaged commitment to regional collective security. Appropriately, it came during confidential quadripartite meetings on 30 June, hidden inside SEATO Council meetings in Canberra.

Foreign Secretary Stewart took the British lead, but he was playing with a weak hand. The British remained convinced that the most effective Western approach to the region, in the vaguely defined 'longer term', would be to redeploy military forces to its periphery and try to arrange some broader agreement on strategic neutralisation. That of course also best suited their own revamped strategic intentions, driven by the combination of economic pressure at home and their evaluation of the politics of the region. But given the now tense situation in Vietnam, the Australian and New Zealand commitment to it and to the policy of 'forward defence', and the outbreak of a very loud internal Labour Party confrontation over policy towards Vietnam back in London, this was not a theme they could stress in Canberra. The more important discussion had in fact already taken place in London, three weeks earlier, when Rusk and Wilson failed so completely to find any common ground over what kind of contribution the British might make to collective security on the mainland in Southeast Asia that the American openly talked of how to 'wind up SEATO', once Vietnam was secure. Taking the only viable approach, Stewart replied in kind to Hasluck's effort to find common ground on strategic priorities as a way to bind the four powers together. Both were clearly hoping for the same outcome, if for different reasons: hoping that a comprehensive discussion of strategic problems presented by the region would demonstrate so conclusively the need for close four power cooperation, led by an obliging United States, that some way would be found to reconcile British refusal to engage in mainland Southeast Asia with American determination to do so. The 'white man's club' agreed to direct officials to study the political and strategic situation in Southeast Asia country by country; each delegation would then present a report on a given country for the others to discuss. Rusk readily agreed to exchange views and papers 'in a discreet way'.[66] With that decision, the effort to use quadripartite discussions to embed a drastically different British strategy for Southeast Asia within a larger allied framework quietly petered out.

By the time a lower level meeting of officials finally convened in London, from 3 to 5 October, it was clear that the so-called London Study Group discussions would in fact indicate conclusively why there would be no quadripartite collective security front in Southeast Asia. Confrontation was over, and the British draw down had begun. Relations between Wilson and Johnson were at a low ebb over Vietnam; Wilson felt himself caught between the rock of American expectations and the hard place of domestic criticism. British officials relied on the London Study Group exercise to demonstrate why their desire to neutralise the region and redesign it as the Indo-Pacific made sense for all concerned. Such hopes foundered on the rocks of American determination to draw the line in mainland Southeast Asia and Australian determination not to allow the Western presence in the region to wobble. The papers and discussions underlined the dilemma. The New Zealand paper on Thailand was in fact based almost entirely on information provided by the Americans, and pointedly argued that a visible SEATO commitment to that country was essential to regional security. The American paper on Vietnam insisted South Vietnam could and would be salvaged. The British papers on Malaysia and Singapore argued that notwithstanding Lee Kuan Yew's growing support for the Western military presence in general, the unstable politics of the region added too much to the already serious financial strain of maintaining FEC. The search for changes to begin from 1970 must therefore continue. This all but drowned out an Australian paper, driven by Hasluck, on how to rally support for the Western military and political presence in the region, rather than assume that presence was counterproductive.[67] The British decision to withdraw militarily from the region would not in fact be made until spring 1967. But both the turn towards Europe, and the split with the Americans over how to prosecute collective security in Asia, were already there for all to see.

Money mattered, very much. It made it very difficult to maintain British military forces in Southeast Asia, as well as prompting questions about why the British should keep trying to do so. But it did not determine the fate of allied collective security in the region. The British-American clash of policy over Southeast Asia was in fact fundamental. The global need to work in step with the Americans, strategically and economically, meant the British could never stop trying to make sure the Americans at least did not condemn any changes in British policy. Regarding Asia, shared interest in containing China and managing change kept them talking, and trying to work together, in Southeast Asia. But truly fundamental disagreement about how to contain China in mainland Southeast Asia drew a hard line that emerged after the Americans intervened militarily in Vietnam. That hard line was reinforced by British calculations about emerging political and profound forces within the region, as well as the need to make hard choices about managing their own overstretched military capabilities. Confrontation with Indonesia was both a turning point and a pyrrhic victory. The effort required to prevail convinced the British that they could not continue to act as a leading or even significant military power in the region, and directly prodded them onto the reconsideration of policy that led to clear divergence from the Americans. That breach, revealed through quiet four power discussions, ruled out four power military harmonisation, short of full scale war against China. Useful as a British commitment to the region was, the Americans would not pay for it. Forced to choose, the Australians, and to a lesser extent the New Zealanders, clung to forward defence, under American leadership, for as long as they could.

The collapse of Western efforts to maintain collective security in Southeast Asia did not come until the mid-1970s, when the Vietnam War ended. And by then the grand strategies of all four powers were very different, as was the Cold War. There is even a retrospective case to make for the British claim that in the long run Western withdrawal from the region would do more good than harm. But what stood out at the time was how long, and how hard, British governments tried to maintain a major role for the United Kingdom in collective security in Asia even when it could no longer pay for it, or convince allies to pick up the slack on its behalf. Successive British governments never really strayed from the 1954 diagnosis that the partition of Vietnam was untenable, and should not be defended. But they also found themselves trapped between the need to piggyback on American strength all over the world and the growing American determination to defend the line of 1954. The British-American split over Southeast Asia did no fatal or even lasting damage to their strategic relationship. Personalities change, and concrete vital interests trump hard feelings. But it was real nonetheless. The 'deep community of purpose' did not hold fast, and the 'long practice of cooperation' buckled accordingly. This shed important light on the mindset of a generation of British decision makers, trapped between recognising the need for changes but trying nevertheless to avoid paying any real price to make them. This made reducing Britain's world role more costly, controversial, and consequential than it could have been. Acheson's aphorism was not in fact far from the mark. David Dilks recognised as much when he evaluated the problem in 1981. His can be the last words: 'The aphorism was much resented. At a distance of twenty years, we may have the grace and humility to admit that it held a good deal of substance.'[68]

Notes

1. David Dilks, *Retreat from Power: Studies in Britain's Foreign Policy of the Twentieth Century*, Vol. II: *After 1939* (London, 1981), p. 35. Acheson made the remarks during a speech delivered at the US Military Academy, West Point NY, on the subject of strengthening NATO, and singled out British confusion as a problem in this regard: DGA to General Maxwell Taylor, 30 July 1962. Series I, box 30, folder 385, DGA-Yale. Dean G. Acheson, 'Our Atlantic Alliance: The Political and Economic Strands', in *Vital Speeches of the Day*, 24, 6 (1 January 1963) pp. 162–6.
2. David Reynolds, *From World War to Cold War: Churchill, Roosevelt, and the International History of the 1940s* (Oxford: Oxford University Press, 2006) p. 329.
3. Brian P. Farrell, 'What Do They Want and How Can We Respond? Commonwealth Intelligence and Confrontation with Indonesia 1963', in Malcolm H. Murfett (ed.), *Imponderable but Not Inevitable: Warfare in the 20th Century* (Santa Barbara, CA: Praeger, 2011) p. 78; Tan Tai Yong, *Creating Greater Malaysia: Decolonization and the Politics of Merger* (Singapore: Institute of Southeast Asian Studies, 2008) ch. 1.
4. Australian War Memorial (AWM), 125, Item 2, CBB4/12/1, Report by Maj-Gen. W.C. Walker, Director of Operations Borneo, on The Operations in Borneo 22 December 1962 to 15 March 1963; H.A. Majid, *Rebellion in Brunei: The 1962 Revolt, Imperialism, Confrontation, and Oil* (London: I.B. Tauris, 2007); Nicholas van der Bijl, *The Brunei Revolt 1962–1963* (Barnsley: Pen and Sword, 2012).
5. National Archives Australia (NAA), A1209/1962/1010, Commonwealth Relations Office (UK) (CRO) to British High Commission Canberra, 35, 12 December 1962; NA, CO1035/164, JICFE Weekly Review of Current Intelligence, 24 January 1963; CAB158/48, Joint Intelligence Committee (JIC) (63)8, Indonesian Involvement in the Borneo Territories in the Next Three Months Short of Overt Aggression, 17 January, JIC(63)14, Indonesian Military Capabilities Against the Borneo Territories up to the End of 1963, 31 January 1963; CAB158/46, JIC(62)58(Final), Indonesian Aims and Intentions, 28 January 1963.
6. Important studies include: H. Crouch, *The Army and Politics in Indonesia* (Singapore: Equinox Publishing, 2007 (1978)); J.S. Djiwandono, *Konfrontasi Revisited: Indonesia's Foreign Policy under Soekarno* (Jakarta: Centre for Strategic and International Studies, 1996); J.D. Legge, *Sukarno: A Political Biography* (Singapore: Archipelago Press, 2003 (1972)); C.L.M. Penders and U. Sundhaussen, *Abdul Haris Nasution: A Political Biography* (St Lucia, QD: University of Queensland Press, 1985); U. Sundhaussen, *The Road to Power: Indonesian Military Politics 1945–1967* (Oxford: Oxford University Press, 1982); F.B. Weinstein, *Indonesian Foreign Policy and the Dilemma of Dependence: From Sukarno to Soeharto* (Singapore: Equinox Publishing, 2007 (1976)).

7. Fredrik Logevall, *Embers of War: The Fall of an Empire and the Making of America's Vietnam* (New York: Random House, 2012).
8. Odd Arne Westad, *The Global Cold War: Third World Interventions and the Making of Our Times* (Cambridge: Cambridge University Press, 2007); John Lewis Gaddis, *The Cold War: A New History* (London: Penguin, 2006).
9. United States Government, *Public Papers of the President of the United States: Dwight D. Eisenhower, 1954* (Washington: USGPO, 1958), Press Conference, 7 April 1954; Office of the Historian, Department of State, *Foreign Relations of the United States* (FRUS), *1952–54, Vol. XII, Part 1, East Asia and the Pacific* (Washington, USGPO), Documents 137, 150, 164; James Cable, *The Geneva Conference of 1954 on Indochina* (Basingstoke: Macmillan, 2000); Mark Moyar, *Triumph Forsaken: The Vietnam War 1954–1965* (Cambridge: Cambridge University Press, 2009); John Prados, *Operation Vulture* (New York: IBooks, 2002).
10. David Goldsworthy (ed.), *British Documents on the End of Empire, Series A Volume 3: The Conservative Government and the End of Empire 1951–1957*, Part I (London: HMSO, 1994, Documents 61–62 [hereafter *BDEE Conservative Government*]; Karl Hack, *Defence and Decolonisation in Southeast Asia: Britain, Malaya and Singapore 1941–68* (Richmond: Curzon, 2001) pp. 110–13; Nicholas Tarling, *Britain, Southeast Asia, and the Impact of the Korean War* (Singapore: NUS Press, 2005) chs. 3–5.
11. Tarling, *Britain, Southeast Asia, and the Impact of the Korean War*, chs. 3–5; Damien Fenton, *To Cage the Red Dragon: SEATO and the Defence of Southeast Asia 1955–1965* (Singapore: NUS Press, 2012) ch. 1.
12. Archives New Zealand (ANZ), EA1, W2668, Department of External Affairs (Australia and New Zealand) (DEA) Brief, *Relations between SEATO, CENTO and NATO*, 3 April 1963; FRUS, *1952–54, Vol. XII, Part 1, East Asia and the Pacific*, Documents 250–261; *BDEE Conservative Government*, Part I, Documents 63–65; Brian P. Farrell, 'Alphabet Soup and Nuclear War: SEATO, China and the Cold War in Southeast Asia', in Malcolm H. Murfett (ed.), *Cold War Southeast Asia* (Singapore: Marshall Cavendish, 2012) pp. 84–6; Fenton, *To Cage the Red Dragon*, ch. 1; Hack, *Defence and Decolonisation in Southeast Asia*, chs. 5–6.
13. A.J. Stockwell (ed.), *British Documents on the End of Empire, Series B Volume 3: Malaya*, Part 3 (London: HMSO, 1995) Documents 341–343, 356, 394, 404–406, 409, 411–412, 421, 426, 438–439, 448, 467; Leon Comber, *Malaya's Secret Police 1945–60: The Role of the Special Branch in the Malayan Emergency* (Melbourne: Monash Asia Institute, 2008) chs. 9–12; Anthony Short, *In Pursuit of Mountain Rats: The Communist Insurrection in Malaya* (Singapore: Cultured Lotus, 2001 [1975]) ch. 19. See also the essays by Hack and Kumar in Richard J. Aldrich et al (eds.), *The Clandestine Cold War in Asia 1945–65: Western Intelligence, Propaganda and Special Operations* (London: Frank Cass, 2000) chs. 10–11.
14. National Archives UK (UKNA), CAB134/555, CPC(57)6, Future Constitutional Development in the Colonies, 28 January 1957; CAB134/1644, DSE(60)9, United Kingdom Economic and Financial Interests in South and South East Asia, 1 July 1960; CAB134/1645, DSE(60)30(Final), Final Report, 3 November 1960; CAB163/22, COS(62)131, Nuclear Strike Planning in the Far East, 27 March 1962.

15. UKNA, CO1035/164 JICFE Weekly Review of Current Intelligence, 14 June 1963; M. Dee (ed.), *Australia and the Formation of Malaysia 1961–1966* (Canberra: Department of External Affairs, 2005); Matthew Jones, *Conflict and Confrontation in Southeast Asia, 1961–1965: Britain, the United States and the Creation of Malaysia* (Cambridge: Cambridge University Press, 2002) ch. 6; John Subritzky, *Confronting Sukarno: British, American, Australian and New Zealand Diplomacy in the Malaysian-Indonesian Confrontation 1961–65*, (Basingstoke: Macmillan, 2000) ch. 3.
16. UKNA, CO1035/164, JICFE Weekly Review of Current Intelligence, 9 August 1963; Jones, *Conflict and Confrontation in South East Asia*, ch. 6; Subritzky, *Confronting Sukarno*, ch. 3.
17. UKNA, Foreign Office (UK) FO371/169703, Note of Meeting between the Commonwealth Secretary and Malayan High Commissioner to London, 24 June 1963; NAA, A1209, 1963/6637 Part 2, Australian Mission Singapore to DEA, 421, 8 August 1963; David Easter, *Britain and the Confrontation with Indonesia 1960–66* (London: Tauris Academic Studies, 2004) ch. 3; Lee Kuan Yew, *The Singapore Story: Memoirs of Lee Kuan Yew* (Singapore: Prentice-Hall, 1998); Tan Tai Yong, *Creating Greater Malaysia*.
18. UKNA, DO169/67, British High Commission Canberra to CRO, 5 July 1963; NAA, A4940, C3389, DEA to Australian High Commission London, 3067, 4 August 1963; FRUS, 1961–63, *Vol. XXIII, Southeast Asia*, Documents 309–315; Roger Hilsman, *To Move a Nation: The Politics of Foreign Policy in the Administration of John F. Kennedy* (New York: Dell publishing Co., 1967 [1964]); Stig Aga Aandstand, *Surrendering to Symbols: United States Policy Towards Indonesia 1961–1965* (Oslo: Self-published revised PhD thesis, 2006 (1999)) ch. 3.
19. Farrell, 'What Do They Want and How Can We Respond?', pp. 76–7; see also note 6 above.
20. UKNA, PREM11/4907, INTEL Report 39, FO to HM Representatives Abroad, 20 March 1964.
21. FRUS, 1961–63, *Vol. XXIII, Southeast Asia*, ably documents the Kennedy administration effort to manage simultaneous escalating challenges in Vietnam and Indonesia; Hilsman, *To Move a Nation*; Subritzky, *Confronting Sukarno*, ch. 1; Aandstand, *Surrendering to Symbols*, ch. 2; Lawrence Freedman, *Kennedy's Wars: Berlin, Cuba, Laos and Vietnam* (Oxford: Oxford University Press, 2000).
22. FRUS, 1961–63, *Vol. XXIII, Southeast Asia*, Documents 297–318; Aandstand, *Surrendering to Symbols*, ch. 3.
23. FRUS, 1961–63, *Vol. XXIII, Southeast Asia*, Documents 316–323; Jones, *Conflict and Confrontation*, chs. 5–7; Howard Jones, *Indonesia: The Possible Dream*, New York, 1971; Aandstand, *Surrendering to Symbols*, ch. 3
24. UKNA, CO1035/165, JICFE Weekly Review of Current Intelligence, 6 September 1963; ANZ, AAFD-811-W3738, 235/1/2, Part 1, JIC Intelligence Review, 4 September 1963; Rex Mortimer, *Indonesian Communism under Sukarno: Ideology and Politics 1959–1965* (Singapore: Equinox Publishing, 2006 (1974)); Crouch, *The Army and Politics*; Sundhaussen, *The Road to Power*; Lorenz M. Luthi, *The Sino-Soviet Split: Cold War in the Communist World* (Princeton: Princeton University Press, 2008).
25. UKNA, PREM11/4906, DH103145, Record of Conversation between Butler and Kennedy, 24 January 1964; CAB21/5075, Record of Conversation

between Douglas-Home and Kennedy, 26 January 1964; FRUS, 1964–68, *Vol. XXVI, Indonesia, Malaysia-Singapore, Philippines*, Documents 1–32; Easter, *Britain and the Confrontation*, ch. 4; Jones, *Conflict and Confrontation*, ch. 9.
26. National Archives and Records Administration, USA (NARA), RG59, POL 7UK, 2/1/64, Box 2777, State Dept. to many posts, Talks with Douglas-Home and Butler, 14 February 1964; POL Indon-UK, 1/1/64, Box 2326, State Dept to Embassy Jakarta, 6 and 10 February, Embassy Jakarta to State Dept, 9 February 1964; UKNA, CAB128/38, Cabinet Minutes, 13 February 1964; Easter, *Britain and the Confrontation*, ch. 4; Jones, *Conflict and Confrontation*, ch. 9; FRUS, 1964–68, *Vol. XII, Western Europe*, Document 225.
27. FRUS, 1964–68, *Vol. XXVII, Mainland Southeast Asia, Regional Affairs*, Documents 46–53; Dee, *Australia and the Formation of Malaysia;* Subritzky, *Confronting Sukarno*, ch. 5.
28. FRUS, 1964–68, *Vol. XXVII, Mainland Southeast Asia, Regional Affairs*, Documents 1–2, 46–53; Dee, *Australia and the Formation of Malaysia*.
29. UKNA, FO371/175070, Brown to Gordon Walker, 27 November 1964; FO371/180205, Bottomley to Gordon Walker, 30 December 1964, Callaghan to Gordon Walker, 1 January 1965; Jones, *Conflict and Confrontation*, ch. 10; Easter, *Britain and the Confrontation*, ch. 6.
30. FRUS, 1964–68, *Vol. I, Vietnam, 1964*, Documents 255–308; E.E. Moise, *Tonkin Gulf and the Escalation of the Vietnam War* (Chapel Hill: University of North Carolina Press, 1996).
31. NARA, RG59, POL Indon-UK, 1/1/64, Box 2326, Memorandum of Conversation, 17 April, State Dept to Embassy Ottawa, 3 July 1964; NAA, A1209/1963/6668, JIB(A) Report No. 5/1/64, January 1964; AWM, 121/25/J/1, JIC(Aust)(64)50 Final, September 1964; Jones, *Conflict and Confrontation*, chs. 9–10; Subritzky, *Confronting Sukarno*, chs. 5–6.
32. UKNA, DEFE5/154, COS273/64 [covering CINCFE88/64], 8 October 1964; 5/156, CINCFE117/64, 7 January 1965; DEFE4/174, COS minutes, 1, 4, 7 September 1964; DEFE5/161, CINCFE54/65, 26 May 1965; CAB148/10, DO(O)(S)(64)43, 21 October 1964; 148/17, OPD(64)8, 12 November 1964; NAA, A1209/1964/6647 Part 3, Australian High Commission (HC) London to DEA, Inward, 7993, 20 November 1964.
33. AWM, 121/233/D/1, Secretary to COSC, 23 July 1964; UKNA, CAB21/5075, Mountbatten to Thorneycroft, 14 July, Trend to Home, Butler to Home, 21 July 1964; PREM11/4908, British Embassy Washington to FO, 2361, 26 June 1964; Brian P. Farrell, 'Escalate to Terminate: Far East Command and the Need to End Confrontation', in Peter Dennis and Jeff Grey (eds.), *Entangling Alliances: Coalition War in the Twentieth Century* (Canberra: Australian Military History Publications, 2005).
34. UKNA, DEFE4/175, COS minutes, 29 September, 15, 20 October 1964; DEFE32/14, COS minutes, Secretary's Standard File, 9 September 1964; DEFE5/154, COS286/64 [covering CINCFE 96/64], 14 October 1964; NAA, A1209/1964/6647 Part 3, British High Commission to Lawler, 18 November 1964; AWM, 121/233/D/1, JIC(Aus) note Indonesia: Confrontation Policy, 23 September 1964; Farrell, 'Escalate to Terminate'.
35. The rich literature analysing this lengthy British Labour government effort to combine economic stimulus with strategic foreign policy divides over the most basic question: in the end, was it all because of the

236   Quadruple Failure?

economy? Different arguments are presented by Jeffrey Pickering, *Britain's Withdrawal from East of Suez* (London: Macmillan, 1998); Saki Dockrill, *Britain's Retreat from East of Suez: The Choice between Europe and the World?* (Basingstoke: Palgrave Macmillan, 2002; and P.L. Pham, *Ending 'East of Suez': The British Decision to Withdraw from Malaysia and Singapore 1964–1968* (Oxford: Oxford University Press, 2010). For an analytical summary, see Malcolm H. Murfett, ' "The Times They Are A-Changin": Britain's Military Commitment to Singapore, 1967–1971', in Brian P. Farrell (ed.), *Churchill and the Lion City: Shaping Modern Singapore* (Singapore: NUS Press, 2011).

36. UKNA, CAB130/213, MISC17/1, Future Size of the Defence Budget, 20 November 1964; PREM13/214, Minutes of Healey-McNamara meeting, 30 May, CAB130/213, MISC17/8, Defence Expenditure Review, 13 June, and CAB128/39, Cabinet Minutes, 15 June 1965, sum up months of discussion, debate, revisions, and reconsideration; Dockrill, *Britain's Retreat from East of Suez*, chs. 3–4; Pham, *Ending 'East of* Suez', ch. 1.
37. See the global summary presented to the new Labour government in UKNA, DEFE5/155, COS295/64, Appendix 1, Disposition of UK Fighting Units on 29 Oct 64; see also Denis Healey, *The Time of My Life* (New York: W.W. Norton, 1989).
38. ANZ, LONB106/7, Part 1, Wilson to Holyoake, 14 December 1964.
39. UKNA, PREM13/692, Suggested Line if President Johnson Requests More British Aid for Vietnam, 4 December 1964; CAB133/266, Minutes of Meetings at the British Embassy and the White House, 7–8 December 1964; CAB128/39, Cabinet Minutes, 11 December 1964; NARA, RG59, POL7UK, Johnson to Wilson, 9 December 1964; FRUS, 1964–68, *Vol. XII, Western Europe*, Documents 234–237; J. Colman, *A 'Special Relationship'? Harold Wilson, Lyndon B. Johnson and Anglo-American Relations 'At the Summit', 1964–68* (Manchester: Manchester University Press, 2004) ch. 2.
40. UKNA, CAB148/17, OPD(64)10, British Policy Towards Southeast Asia, 19 November 1964; FO371/181490, Peck to HM Ambassadors and High Commissioners in Southeast Asia, 31 December 1964.
41. UKNA, CAB21/5128, The Prospects of Retaining our Present Bases in South-East Asia, 3 February 1959.
42. UKNA, PREM13/889, Stewart to Wilson, Four Power Talks During SEATO Meeting, 30 March 1965; Dee, *Australia and the Formation of Malaysia*.
43. Ronald B. Frankum, *Like Rolling Thunder: The Air War in Vietnam 1964–1975*, (Lanham, MD: Rowman & Littlefield, 2005).
44. The British government had ample warning of President Johnson's growing determination to take the war to the enemy in Vietnam and the Australian government's preparations to contribute. Both developments only made them more determined to revamp British policy in the region before they found themselves caught between the proverbial rock of allied pressure and hard place of domestic public opinion: UKNA, PREM13/692, Harlech to FO, No. 4229, 31 December 1964; UKNA, CAB148/18, OPD minutes, 5 February 1965; 148/21, OPD(65)97, 14 June 1965; NAA, A1838/3024/2/1/1 Part 1, Australian HC Singapore to DEA, Saving 2, 15 March 1965; NARA, RG59, POL 7UK, 12/12/64, Wilson-President Discussions re Malaysia, 17 December 1964.

45. ANZ, ABHS7148-W4628, LONB106/5A Part 1, Wilson to Holyoake, 26 April 1965; UKNA, DEFE25/105, Record of a discussion held after dinner at 1 Carlton Gardens, 2 May 1965.
46. UKNA, DEFE25/105, Record of a discussion held after dinner at 1 Carlton Gardens, 2 May 1965.
47. NAA, A1209/1965/6263, Report by the Right Honourable Patrick Gordon Walker on his Fact-Finding Tour of South-East Asia as Special Representative of the Foreign Secretary, 7 May 1965.
48. UKNA, CAB130/239, Misc.76/1st Meeting, Minutes of Meeting at Culdrose RN Air Station, 15 August 1965; NARA, RG59, POL16Singapore, 1/1/65, American Embassy London to State Dept, 16 August 1965.
49. NAA, A1209/1965/6595 Part 1, Australian HC London to DEA, 7578–79, 2 September, Menzies to Wilson, 3 September 1965; NARA, RG59, DEF6UK, 1/1/64, Box 1691, Menzies to Johnson, 6 September 1965; ANZ, ABHS-7148-W4628, LONB106/5A Part 1, New Zealand HC London to DEA, 2 September 1965.
50. NARA, RG59, DEF6UK, 1/1/64, Box 1691, State Dept. to American Embassy London, 23 August, American Embassy London to State Dept., 7 September, 9 September, 1965; NAA, A1209/1965/6595 Part 1, DEA to Washington, 2558, 2565, 6 September, Australian HC London to DEA, 7756, 7 September, Summary of Main Points in Verbal Report to FADC Following Quadripartite Meetings in London, 8 September, Copy of Telegram from President Johnson to Wilson, 13 September 1965; ANZ, ABHS-7148-W4628, LONB106/5A Part 1, New Zealand HC London to DEA, 4, 7, and 13 September, DEA to New Zealand HC London, 6 September 1965.
51. ANZ, ABHS-7148-W4628, LONB106/5A Part 1, New Zealand HC Kuala Lumpur to DEA, New Zealand Embassy Washington to DEA, 16 September, New Zealand HC London to DEA, 4 and 13 October 1965; LONB106/5A Part 2, DEA Wellington to New Zealand HC London, 27 January 1966; NARA, RG59, DEF6UK, 1/1/64, Box 1691, American Embassy Wellington to State Dept., 11 September 1965.
52. It remains unclear who orchestrated the coup and why such an obvious target as Soeharto was not attacked. The roles and knowledge of Sukarno and the PKI remain especially controversial, driven by the very heavy loss of life that ensued, in Java especially, over the next months, as army units dismantled the PKI. Subsequent political changes in Indonesia only added to the controversy, there and abroad. Significant studies include: Benedict R. O'G Anderson and Ruth T. McVey, *A Preliminary Analysis of the October 1, 1965 Coup in Indonesia* (Singapore: Equinox Publishing Ltd, 2009 (1971, 1965)); J. Hughes, *The End of Sukarno: A Coup that Misfired, A Purge that Ran Wild* (Singapore: Archipelago Press, 2002 (1967)); John Roosa, *Pretext for Mass Murder: The September 30th Movement and Suharto's Coup d'état in Indonesia* (Madison: University of Wisconsin Press, 2006); Helen-Louise Hunter, *Sukarno and the Indonesian Coup* (Westport, CT: Praeger Security International, 2007); Jusuf Wanandi, *Shades of Grey: A Political Memoir of Modern Indonesia 1965–1998* (Singapore: Equinox Publishing, 2012).
53. As late as spring 1966 Far East Command remained nearly as strong as British NATO forces in manpower: UKNA, DEFE5/166, ANZAM Defence Cttee minute 1/1966, Review of UK Defence Policy, 22 March 1966.

54. UKNA, DEFE25/105, CINCFE Call on CDS, 19 October 1965; DEFE4/190, COS2442/13/10/65, Proposals by the C-in-C Far East to end Indonesian Aggression, 13 October, COS minutes, 19 October 1965; CAB158/59, JIC(65)44(Final), 19 August 1965; CAB158/57, JIC(65)29(Final), 23 August 1965; Farrell, 'Escalate to Terminate'.
55. UKNA, FO371/181502, Stanley to Pritchard, 1 November 1965; CAB158/60, JIC(65)89(Final), 16 December 1965; DEFE4/192, COS minutes, 7 December 1965; DEFE5/164, COS219/65, 30 December 1965; NARA, RG59, DEF6UK, 1/1/64, Box 1691, American Embassy London to State Dept, 18 November, 1–2 December 1965; NAA, A1209/1964/6647 Part 5, Australian Embassy Washington to DEA, Inward 3828, 1 November, Australian HC London to DEA, Inward 9783, 1 November, Bailey to Bunting, 2 November 1965; A1209/1965/6595 Part 2, Bailey to Menzies, 11 November 1965; ANZ, ABHS-7148-W4628, LONB106/5A Part 1, NZ HC in London to DEA, 8 November, 1 and 3 December, Short Term Policy Towards Indonesia, 3 December 1965.
56. UKNA, DEFE4/192, COS minutes, 7 December 1965; 4/193, COS minutes, 21 December 1965; DEFE5/164, COS219/65, 30 December 1965; CAB148/24, OPD(65)191, 14 December 1965; 148/18, OPD minutes, 22 December 1965; NARA, RG59, POL7UK, 11/1/65, Box 2778, Memorandum for the President: Visit of Prime Minister Wilson, 13 December 1965; Farrell, 'Escalate to Terminate'.
57. NARA, RG59, DEF6UK, 1/1/64, Box 1691, American Embassy London to State Dept, 9 September 1965.
58. NARA, RG59, POLUK-US, 1/1/66, Notes on Johnson-Wilson Conversation, 17 December 1965.
59. See Brian P. Farrell, 'What Do We Do Now? British Commonwealth and American Reactions to the Separation of Malaysia and Singapore', in *Australian Defence Force Journal*, 170 (2006).
60. ANZ, ABHS-7148-W4628, LONB106/5A Part 1, New Zealand Embassy Washington to DEA, 16 September, New Zealand HC London to DEA, 4 and 13 October 1965; LONB106/5A Part 2, DEA Wellington to New Zealand HC London, 27 January 1966.
61. NAA, A1209/1965/6595 Part 6, Defence Consultations: Summary of discussions 1–2 February 1966 and *ANZ*, ABHS-7148-W4628, LONB106/5A Part 2, Report of the New Zealand Delegation, 3 February 1966. See also the account in P.G. Edwards, *A Nation at War: Australian Politics, Society and Diplomacy during the Vietnam War 1965–1975* (Sydney: Allen & Unwin, 1997) pp. 89–91.
62. AWM, 121, 31/B/1, Joint Planning Committee (JPC) note 19/66, 8 March, report 14/66, British Bases in Australia, 24 February and 14 March, COS Minute, 16 March 1966; NAA, A1209/1965/6595 Part 6, Defence Committee minute 7/1966, 17 February 1966; 25/J/1, JIC(Aust)(66)50 (Final), The Threat to Australia and her Territories, April, 1966; ANZ, ABHS-7148-W4628, LONB106/5A Part 2, New Zealand HC Canberra to DEA, 1 March 1966.
63. NAA, A1209/1965/6595 Part 3, Hasluck to Plimsoll, 16 February 1966; A1209/1965/6595 Part 6, Australian HC Wellington to DEA, 105, 16 February, Defence Committee minute 7/1966, 17 February, DEA to Australian Embassy Washington, 175, 3 March, Hasluck to Holt, 11–12 April 1966; ANZ, ABHS-7148-W4628, LONB106/5A Part 2, New Zealand HC London to DEA, 22 and 26 April, DEA to New Zealand Embassy Washington, 27 April, Notes

of Discussion Between Holyoake and Hasluck, 7 May, Notes of Meeting with Plimsoll, 9 May, DEA to New Zealand Embassy Washington, 10 May 1966; AAFD-811-W3738, 222/3/1 Part 1, Note for File on Hasluck Visit, 11 May 1966.
64. UKNA, CAB158/63, Note re JIC(66)45 and JIC(66)46, 13 June 1966; CAB148/28, OPD(66)68, 14 June 1966; PREM13/1454, Healey and Razak Meeting, Minutes, 7 July, Healey to Wilson, 19 July 1966; CAB164/19, Wilson and Lee Kuan Yew Meeting, Minutes, 25 April 1966; DEFE5/171, COS140/66 [Covering CINCFE42/66], 2 January 1967; NAA, A1838, TS682//22/1 Part 7, CINCFE Meetings with High Commissioners, February through July 1966.
65. UKNA, DEFE4/202, COS Minutes, 12 July 1966; DEFE4/205, COS1893/31/8/66, 31 August, COS Minutes, 8 September 1966; DEFE4/206, COS1969/23/9/66, 23 September, COS Minutes, 27 September 1966.
66. UKNA, DEFE5/169, COS78/66, 27 June 1966; NAA, A1209/1965/6595 Part 7, Defence Committee Minute 43/1966 and Memorandum, Quadripartite Talks, 22 June, DEA to Australian Embassy Washington, 1950, 2 July, Hasluck to Holt, 5 and 14 July, Australian Embassy Washington to DEA, 9 August 1966; ANZ, ABHS-7148-W4628, LONB106/5A Part 2, New Zealand HC London to DEA, 13 July, DEA to New Zealand Embassy Washington, 2 August 1966.
67. NAA, A1209/1965/6595 Part 7, UK FO Memorandum London Study Group: Singapore, 2 October, Australian HC London to DEA, 9846, 6 October 1966; ANZ, AAFD-811-W3738, 222/3/1 Part 1, CP(66)782, 8 September 1966; ABHS-7148-W4628, LONB106/5A Part 1, Memorandum, The Australian View of Southeast Asia, 5 September 1966; LONB106/5A Part 2, DEA to New Zealand Embassy Washington, 9 and 16 August, 28 September, New Zealand Embassy Washington to DEA, 16 and 18 August, 6 September 1966; New Zealand HC London to DEA, 6 and 13 October, 23 November 1966 [the last document contains the full but 'unofficial' British transcript of the October meetings].
68. Dilks, *Retreat from Power*, 35.

10
GCHQ and UK Computer Policy
Teddy Poulden, ICL and IBM
Richard J. Aldrich

Government Communications Headquarters or 'GCHQ' is Britain's largest intelligence agency. Currently commanding some 6,000 employees, it moved to new premises in Cheltenham in 2003 which for the previous few years constituted the largest building project in Europe and which is known locally as the 'Doughnut'. GCHQ, together with its defensive arm, the Communications-Electronics Security Group and their various historical predecessors have presided over the complex matter of gathering intelligence from the ether and also attempting to protect the security of British codes and ciphers for more than a century.[1] In GCHQ's distinctive new building international relations meets big science. Deep below the offices of the linguists and the analysts are vast computer halls. The exact size and type of these computers are secret but GCHQ is rumoured to have several machines each with a storage capacity of 25 petabytes (25,000 terabytes) equipped with over 20,000 cores to provide rapid parallel processing. Such computers are required for only a few specialist scientific tasks: simulating complex weather systems, mapping the human genome, designing nuclear weapons and of course cryptography – the science of making and breaking ciphers.[2]

Cryptography is one of the core activities of all signals intelligence organisations. For many years signals intelligence was a serious lacuna in our understanding of post-war international history. This problem has been addressed over the last ten years, albeit the subject still remains problematic for historians to attack on anything other than a piecemeal basis.[3] What we have so far failed to address is the history of interface between GCHQ and Britain's post-war research, education and science base. We know a great deal about Bletchley Park's wartime contribution to early computing and about important figures such as Alan Turing, but we know less about what happened after 1945.[4]

Unlike, MI5 and MI6, which were 'tiddlers' in terms of the scale of their activity, GCHQ had an impact on various aspects of national life ranging from space programmes to language teaching. Typically, when the University Grants Committee was considering the future of Chinese language provision in British Universities, the committee was steered by Arthur Cooper, GCHQ's eminent sinologist and brother of Josh Cooper who had headed the Air Section at Bletchley Park. This chapter seeks to illustrate the way in which GCHQ had the potential to impact on wider aspects of national life by examining one small aspect: the role of a single GCHQ officer, Commander Teddy Poulden, in the context of British government policy towards the computer industry in the early 1970s.[5]

In the 1970s, GCHQ enjoyed access to excellent computers. Whereas other areas of British government were continually under pressure to take under-performing machines from the ailing British computer industry, GCHQ could always play the trump card of Anglo-American compatibility. The need to be able to work with its American partner, the United States National Security Agency (NSA) meant that they were allowed to buy from the world-leader in computers, America's IBM. By the mid-1960s, IBM was in a position that British officials described as 'oligopoly', enjoying 70–80 per cent of the world's market and spending £30 million a year on research and development. IBM easily recovered these costs through production runs of thousands of machines. GCHQ bought IBM computers not only because of the need for NSA compatibility but also because its machines were cutting edge and delivered outstanding performance.[6]

In 1977 GCHQ was also one of the first organisations to acquire one of the fabled CRAY supercomputers, designed by Seymour Cray at his Chippewa Falls plant in Minnesota which delivered fantastic parallel processing power. This helped GCHQ in its struggle to stay in the premier league of cryptography. At Cheltenham a special supply of chilled water has to be arranged to cool this new suite of equipment.[7] Partly because GCHQ tended to buy American, it is sometimes assumed that it had less impact upon the UK computer industry in the 1970s than its American counterpart. While this is true to some extent, GCHQ nevertheless exerted some influence since it was called in to look at the British computing industry during the 1970s in an advisory capacity rather than as a consumer. This came largely in the form of one person, Teddy Poulden, who was lent by GCHQ to the Cabinet Office as an adviser. Poulden was, in many ways, an unlikely figure for this role. He was a general signals intelligence manager rather than a computer specialist. Poulden had been born in 1915 and had joined the Navy as a cadet. An adept signals officer, he had been the communications officer on the latest British battleship HMS *Prince of Wales* when Churchill had steamed to Placentia Bay to meet Roosevelt in August 1941. In 1942 he served as the signal staff officer on HMS *Anson*, the flagship of Vice Admiral Fraser then second in command of the Home Fleet.[8]

Poulden had cut his teeth on signals intelligence while helping Commander Bruce Keith to run the vast British naval Sigint station on Ceylon during the war called HMS *Anderson*. *Anderson* mostly served the needs of Admiral Lord Louis Mountbatten and South East Asia Command, together with the East Indies Fleet.[9] Poulden's first postwar job had been to develop the nascent Australian Sigint organisation, the Defence Signals Bureau (DSB).[10] Four Australian applicants for the directorship were rejected in favour of Britain's Poulden, who filled the senior posts with 20 GCHQ staff and communicated with GCHQ in his own special cipher.[11] When New Zealand joined UKUSA, the world-wide post-war Sigint alliance of English speaking nations, Australia's DSB initially signed on New Zealand's behalf, and so the signature of the fabled UKUSA agreement is that of Teddy Poulden.[12]

Along with John Somerville and John Borough, Poulden was one of several naval officers who were important to the development of GCHQ in the two decades following World War II. In the 1950s and 1960s, he occupied key posts, succeeding Bill Bonsall as Head of J Division (the large and prestigious Soviet section) and served as SUKLO, the GCHQ liaison officer in Washington. The latter posting allowed him insight into the enormous effort that NSA was making to harvest the possibilities of advanced technology for intelligence gathering and processing, including the early use of satellites. Poulden liked computers and after his spell as liaison at NSA at a time of increasing automation, he returned to GCHQ to occupy the post of Co-ordinator of Technical Services with a brief to watch over the computer section known as X Division.[13]

Dick White, the new go-ahead Intelligence Co-ordinator in the Cabinet Office, was another computer enthusiast. In 1968, White had been appointed to the new post of Cabinet Office Intelligence Coordinator as part of the Trend reforms of the UK central intelligence machinery.[14] White was expected to exercise a coordinating role and assist Burke Trend, the Cabinet Secretary, in the increasingly vexed matter of preparing budgets for the secret service. White believed that computers might well deliver not only better performance but also cost savings.[15]

In February 1969, White was chatting to Joe Hooper, the [
GCHQ, about new technologies. Hooper happened to menti
American system called COINS (Community On-line Intellig
tem) that was intended to provide a shared database across the wnole
US intelligence community. White was excited and asked him for a
detailed appraisal. Hooper rather relished giving White the doleful story.
Begun in 1965 as a presidential initiative by Lyndon Johnson, who
was an intelligence enthusiast, after four years and vast expense it was
still not working. Led by NSA, COINS was a packet-switched network
intended to connect organizations across the US intelligence community. The idea was to allow access by all the agencies to each other's
computerised files, together with 'read-only' access for the Pentagon and
the State Department. However, it exhibited many of the classic problems of larger networks. There were 'major difficulties' with different
file formats and divergent terminologies. There was also vast duplication but the committee set up to address this had 'got nowhere'. There
were constant technical failures and so 'less than 20% of the enquiries
receive answers'.[16]

Dick White was not deterred. A huge fan of new technology, by early
1970 he had persuaded the Joint Intelligence Committee to get busy in
this area. Brian Stewart, Secretary of the Joint Intelligence Committee,
arranged for a new group to be created on Automatic Data Processing which also comprised MI5, SIS, the Defence Intelligence Staff and
the Foreign Office. Poulden from GCHQ was given the task of chairing
it.[17] GCHQ and NSA had just completed a shared computer project to
standardise geographical locations in Russian and their spelling.[18] What
GCHQ really thirsted for was progress on machine translation, but so far
this had failed on grounds of high costs and complexity. The Defence
Intelligence Staff had looked at storing more of its material on computer but had been horrified by the sheer labour required to keep such
databases current.[19]

Despite these early disappointments, they all recognised that NSA's
growing use of computers for data-storage and the arrival of automatic
message switching meant this was the shape of the future. 'Most Sigint
end-product already contained simple machine symbols' a result of
its journey through the communications system. As a consequence,
'NSA already maintained an almost complete file of Sigint end-product
for retrieval' on computer. By June 1971, Poulden was predicting that
these changes would spread through the entire Western intelligence
community over the next ten years, although like Hooper, he regarded
COINS as a complex and costly failure.[20] A few years later, Dick White's

successors as Intelligence Co-ordinator, Joe Hooper and then Brooks Richards, were looking more closely at Automatic Data Processing in a desperate effort to cut staff numbers in the face of swingeing cuts to the intelligence and defence budgets during the early 1970s.[21]

The very largest computers were effectively seen as strategic weapons that could be deployed for both high-grade cryptography and also for the design of nuclear weapons. Inevitably, by the early 1970s, computers for Sigint and nuclear weapons had acquired a sensitive European dimension. Vice-Admiral Louis Le Bailly, the Director-General of Defence Intelligence, explained that they raised the spectre of what was called 'the Trojan Horse syndrome'. This meant international corporations buying up strategically important national industries and then subjecting them to external control. The French computing industry was a classic case. In 1972 Machines Bull, the leading French manufacturer of mainframe computers, was taken over by the US international corporation General Electric. Bull was the only company in France capable of supplying the enormous 'number crunching computers essential for the development of the French independent nuclear programme' known as the 'Force de Frappe'. As part of an American combine it was subject to American regulation. This forbade the supply of such computers to the French government under the Non-Proliferation Treaty. Accordingly, although the technology that Paris required was available from a French company, it could not access it. Much the same issues applied to machines required for cryptanalysis.[22] Teddy Poulden confirmed that they could not work with France on computer security issues because GCHQ made use of American expertise which was 'subject to stringent regulations precluding disclosure to third parties'.[23]

In the early 1970s, Poulden was co-opted into a high-level government task-force on the future of the troubled British computer industry. In the past, Britain had arguably indulged in too many small-scale computer ventures. Absurdly, at one time the UK was producing more different models of computer than the United States. In the late 1960s, Harold Wilson's government had addressed this through a government assisted 'Computer Mergers Scheme' that combined the many ailing companies into a Frankenstein creation called International Computers Limited (ICL).[24] This had involved pulling together elements of companies such as International Computers and Tabulators, Elliott Automation and English Electric-Leo-Marconi Computers (who had bought the computer element of J. Lyons). The Ministry of Technology acted 'as both marriage broker and godfather'. Tony Benn at the Ministry of Technology had presided over this exercise.[25] This was part of the same government strategy of modernization through intervention and merger that created British Leyland.[26]

The important connections between computing, defence and intelligence had already been made clear to ministers from the first days of ICL's existence. In 1968, Tony Benn had developed a scheme to allow ICL to export to the Soviet Union, but this was vetoed by the Pentagon and his own Foreign Office. In April of that year, Moscow wanted to sign a deal with a UK trade delegation to Moscow that would have allowed the bulk purchase of ICL's System 4 and Series 1900 mid-range computers. Soviet officials tempted the British with the offer of a complete British monopoly of the Soviet market, which was then thought to be worth £200 million – almost ten times the annual government subsidy to ICL. American opposition, channelled through the Foreign Office, prevented the deal from going ahead. Prime Minister Harold Wilson was told in no uncertain terms that such an agreement would be seen as a breach of 'Cocom', the Western regime of export restrictions designed to slow Soviet strategic weapons development. The US threatened to stop exports of computer components to Britain, including supplies to ICL. Wilson initially planned to stand firm against Washington. But when UK diplomats were prevented from attending defence and trade discussions, Wilson backed down. Thereafter, ICL focused on the British home market.[27]

As late as April 1971, to all outward appearances, ICL looked in good shape. However, in reality the financial position of the company was deteriorating fast and by the autumn of that year, the Department of Trade and Industry had asked worried Treasury officials for subsidies amounting to £25 million over a five year period.[28] Ted Heath's new think tank, the Central Policy Review Staff (CPRS) led by Lord Rothschild, was chosen to undertake an investigation of the problem.[29] It was asked to look at overall government strategy on computers including what they called the 'problem of lame ducks', direct subsidies, the role of government purchasing of computers (which was recognised as an important source of indirect subsidy) and finally European co-operation.[30] The CPRS were looking for a big brain to help them and Sir Alan Cottrell, the senior defence scientist, recommended Teddy Poulden. Poulden was initially worried that participating in this review would disturb his good relations with the Department of Trade and Industry, who supplied some of GCHQ's equipment. However, after some negotiation with Joe Hooper, it was agreed that Poulden would be released to the CPRS on a part-time basis for the computer study. The project leader at CPRS was Peter Carey and they were joined by William Plowden, James Joll and Sir Brian Flowers.[31]

Teddy Poulden instantly warmed to Lord Rothschild who asked him to prepare an overview paper drawing on the experience of his GCHQ colleagues.[32] Poulden confessed that GCHQ was an 'atypical' user of computing resources. So he talked broadly about GCHQ and its American partner the US National Security Agency, while also trying to think of the typical user's point of view. In summary, Poulden did not think that Britain needed to control the supply of its computer resources or maintain a separate computer industry as a strategic asset. Nor was the balance of payments an issue given ICL's modest exports. Instead Poulden argued that the dominant factor in their considerations should be what is now known as Moore's Law.[33] This law states that processor power was doubling every two years affecting both communications and computers:

> The remarkable thing about communications technology is that, in many respects, it has shown such unimpeded growth over decades and with no regard to national boundaries... In its much shorter life computer technology has followed the same sort of pattern, but the growth rates have been greater... The 'size' and 'power' of the most powerful computer to date is increasing at a rate of 10 times in 5 years.

What did this mean for the future of ICL? Quite simply, it meant that research in information and communications technologies was racing ahead. Poulden asserted, research time-cycles had to be kept short and this demanded serious investment that only high volume manufacturers would be able to afford. In short, he concluded 'computing is costly' and needed higher volumes of manufacturing to support the intense research and development activity. In his opinion, the upshot of this was that ICL would only achieve adequate volume as part of a bigger combine, perhaps with European firms.[34]

Poulden narrated GCHQ's own experience with ICL for the benefit of the Cabinet Office. GCHQ had a current contract for an ICL 4–70 system. They had been asked to buy this for what Poulden politely described as government policy reasons, and Cheltenham had quickly allocated it to a peripheral task (since their central computer group which undertook mainstream cryptanalysis would not even look at it). Because ICL knew they had a captive customer, their performance had been poor in every respect. The machine had eventually worked because GCHQ had expended endless time and talent on it. However, Poulden added, there were very few customers in either the public or private sectors who were willing to do ICL's work for them in this way or indeed who had the expertise close at hand to tinker endlessly with a problematic system.[35]

In recent years, GCHQ had been put under some duress to buy some 'very large computers' for central computing from ICL. GCHQ had resisted the 'pressure' since this meant ICL's dreadful 'Project 52' machine which Poulden regarded as notoriously weak. 'No-one would buy it given a free choice' he sneered. Other parts of government had found that their 'arms had been twisted' and had given in to pressure.[36] One of Poulden's greatest pleasures was taking 'a formidable party' from GCHQ to listen to a presentation by ICL on the 'Project 52' machine. Poulden took five specialists including the renowned Professor Robert Churchhouse. In the early 1960s, Churchouse had helped to set up the Atlas Computer Laboratory at the Atomic Energy Research Establishment at Harwell, one of largest computer projects in Britain. He had then transferred to GCHQ as a systems analyst and had followed the troubled history of 'Project 52' at a distance. Poulden explained with relish that Churchhouse knew more about the past mistakes of ICL's component elements than did its current management.[37]

In the summer of 1971, ICL's 'Project 52' was several years behind IBM, whose comparable model was already on the market. Absurdly, ICL management were determined to make it non-compatible with IBM, despite the fact that their own scientists had warned them this would ensure that it would 'fall flat on its face'.[38] Poulden explained that even the recent Russian RYAD system was designed to take IBM software as one of the easiest ways of increasing performance. No-one, Poulden complained, seemed to understand the importance of software.[39] Poulden derided ICL's 'Project 52' as a projection of a pompous desire for national independence, akin to the precarious French nuclear deterrence system known as the 'Force de Frappe'.[40] GCHQ could always escape the pressure to purchase from ICL by citing the need for compatibility with the American code-breakers at NSA, but their masters at the Foreign Office did not have the same privilege and were being browbeaten into buying ICL. So miserable were the Foreign Office about this that they were resisting computerisation *per se* because of their deep fear of under-performing ICL machines.[41]

Looking to the future, Poulden predicted that government would have to pump £50 million over five years into ICL if its planned 'New Range' of computers were to stand a chance of competing in world markets. Poulden's judgements were harsh but accurate and reflected inside information because GCHQ's X Division, which provided central computing, worked so closely with IBM. Poulden told government frankly that the subsidy would be required simply to bring down the costs of the 'New Range' to a point where it could compete with IBM. Meanwhile he suggested that it would certainly take five years 'to correct management failings in ICL'.[42] In October 1971, Poulden had invited key players for a day of so-called 'rambunctious interchanges' with X Division at Cheltenham. Douglas Nicoll of the Department of Trade and Industry was there and argued for closer collaboration with the French. However, X Division had explained that this would not work – since they would still not have large enough economies of scale and yet would have the increased costs of working across two countries.[43] Officials were exasperated because they knew that to simply throw in the towel completely on ICL was not an adequate solution: there would be 'massive expense' incurred by all their current British customers who would lose systems support. A high proportion of these customers were British government departments.[44]

ICL was visibly in trouble by February 1972, underlined by the resignation of its chairman Sir John Wall.[45] Poulden continued to assist during 1972, sending in another technical team from GCHQ led by Paul Foster, a bright P-Division staffer, to probe ICL's so-called 'New Range' on which government ministers were pinning considerable hopes.[46] Poulden also brought insider intelligence on IBM. One of the reasons that he was downbeat about the British industry was that he had been able to obtain information on new breakthroughs by IBM. Early in 1972, he had warned that IBM were bringing forward radical new changes in technology and pricing that would make it difficult for their competitors around the world, whom officials increasing referred to as 'the remaining dwarfs'. This included a marked reduction in the price of memory, innovations in software writing and a major upgrade of their current 370 range. On 31 July 1972, Poulden rang the Cabinet Office with a tip-off that many of these changes would be announced in the coming week. IBM's intention was to 'put a spoke in the wheel of a Japanese competitor', by which he probably meant Fujitsu, but Poulden observed that it would also damage ICL's so-called 'New Range' machines. The Cabinet Office agonised over how to respond to this piece of confidential commercial intelligence, observing: 'Poulden has come by it in his GCHQ capacity' and could not give it directly to Trade and Industry.[47] Even at that moment, ICL were using Sir Arnold Weinstock to try to persuade

Ted Heath that although ICL required 'massive government support' at present – it might be able to stand on its own two feet within two years. However, Poulden's intelligence on 'the latest IBM moves' convinced Cabinet Office officials that such hopes were 'chimeral' (sic) and that the ICL 'New Range' was doomed.[48]

By May 1973, Britain was facing some tough choices. All this was set against a general deterioration in the UK economic situation which presented the government with an unprecedented level of difficulty. Plowden had even begun to talk to Lord Rothschild about the possibility of 'dropping ICL'. Although, Plowden fundamentally believed that supporting ICL was a worthwhile cause, the problem was how to do this 'without forcing public sector users to buy unsuitable ICL systems'.[49] ICL finally introduced its 'New Range' in October 1974 after some £25 million in government aid. ICL continued to struggle on through the 1970s, attempting to address many of the structural problems that Poulden had identified and making losses of £10–20 million a year. However, Poulden was probably wrong about the ICL 'New Range' – later known as the 2900 series – which did better than expected. The computer was a truly radical design and used a unique Virtual Machine Environment (VME) software which delivered decent performance. The down-side was that it was not IBM compatible which made foreign customers nervous of investing in it on any scale. Nonetheless, there were significant contracts from government including the Post Office, the Inland Revenue, the Department of Pensions and the Ministry of Defence. ICL also had a strong customer base with local authorities. By the late 1970s, however, ICL was once again in financial trouble as it sought to create a successor to the 2900 series.[50]

In 1981, Robb Wilmot, managing director of ICL, concluded an agreement with Fujitsu to help create the next generation of computers to replace the 'New Range' 2900 series machines. Some criticised this deal, but at this point the only other alternative was probably to build IBM clones. Paying Fujitsu some £17 million, it bought chip technology that allowed them to develop new machines that ran the VME software written for 2900, but faster and more efficiently.[51] Fujitsu was one of the world's best semiconductor manufacturers and eventually became a strong manufacturer of desk top PCs. ICL's relationship with Fujitsu began in a limited way because ICL needed a cheaper source of technology, but in November 1990 Fujitsu bought all of the company and dropped the ICL brand. In this respect, the structural observations of Teddy Poulden and X Division about the need for merger and higher volumes of production and investment were probably correct.[52]

Acknowledgements

I am indebted to the British Academy for funding some of the research for this chapter. Parts of it were read at the Cambridge Intelligence Seminar at Corpus Christi College Cambridge in April 2012 and at the Centre for the History of Science, Technology and Medicine seminar at the University of Manchester in April 2013 and I am grateful for the questions and comments received. Errors remain the responsibility of the author.

Notes

1. The history of British communications security is an especially important area that has long been neglected. For a path-breaking essay on cipher and document security see, D. Dilks, 'Flashes of Intelligence: The Foreign Office, The SIS and Security Before the Second World War', in C. Andrew and D. Dilks (eds), *The Missing Dimension: Governments and Intelligence Communities in the Twentieth Century* (London: Macmillan, 1982), pp. 101–25. More recently see J. Ferris, 'The British "Enigma": Britain, Signals Security and Cipher Machines, 1906–1946', *Defense Analysis*, 3, 2 (1987), pp. 153–63 and also R.A Ratcliff, *Delusions of Intelligence: Enigma, Ultra, and the End of Secure Ciphers* (Cambridge, Cambridge University Press, 2006).
2. R.J. Aldrich, 'The Ultimate Spy: Why the Real James Bond is a Supercomputer', *BBC Science Magazine*, 248 (November 2012), pp. 55–9.
3. See for example Matthew Aid, *Secret Sentry: The Top Secret History of the National Security Agency* (New York: Bloomsbury 2009); Matthew Aid and Cees Wiebes (eds), *Secrets of Signals Intelligence During the Cold War and Beyond* (London: Frank Cass, 2001); D. Ball and D. Horner, *Breaking the Code: Australia's KGB Network* (Sydney: Allen and Unwin, 1988); J. Bamford, *The Puzzle Palace: America's National Security Agency and Its Special Relationship with GCHQ* (London: Sidgwick & Jackson, 1983); J. Bamford, *Body of Secrets: How NSA and Britain's GCHQ Eavesdrop on the World* (London: Doubleday, 2001).
4. However see S. Lavington, 'In the Footsteps of Colossus: A Description of Oedipus', *IEEE Annals of Computing*, (2006), pp. 44–55. On wartime and the emergence of computers there is a vast literature. See especially B.J. Copeland, *Colossus: The Secrets of Bletchley Park's Codebreaking Computers* (Oxford: Oxford University Press, 2006); P. Gannon, *Colossus: Bletchley Park's Greatest Secret* (London: Atlantic Books, 2006); A. Hodges, *Alan Turing: The Enigma* (London: Burnett Books, 1992); W.W. Chandler, 'The Installation and Maintenance of Colossus', *IEEE Annals of the History of Computing*, 5, 3 (1983), pp. 260–2; A.W. Coombs, 'The Making of Colossus', *IEEE Annals of the History of Computing*, 5, 3 (1983), pp. 253–9; T. Sale, 'The Colossus of Bletchley Park – The German Cipher System', in R.H. Rojas (ed.), *The First Computers: History and Architecture* (Cambridge, MA: The MIT Press 2000) pp. 351–64.
5. Correspondence in the papers of Arthur Cooper (presently in private hands). On Josh Cooper, see A. Bonsall, 'Bletchley Park and the RAF Y Service: Some Recollections', *Intelligence and National Security*, 23, 6 (2008), pp. 827–41.

6. Laver (T) to Lees (T), 4 Jan. 1965, T 224/1127, UK National Archives (UKNA). See also Couzens (T) to Henley (DEA) memo, 'The Government and the British Computer Industry', 4 Jan. 1965, ibid.
7. Burnett, Tate & Partners, 'GCHQ Phase II, Benhall Site, Cheltenham', 9 Sept. 1976, CM 23/133, UKNA.
8. Barrie H. Kent, *Signal! A History of Signalling in the Royal Navy* (East Meon: Hyden, 2004) pp. 140–2.
9. R.J. Aldrich, *Intelligence and the War Against Japan: The Politics of Secret Service* (Cambridge: Cambridge University Press, 2000) p. 236. See also D. Ford, *Britain's Secret War Against Japan, 1937–1945* (London: Routledge, 2006) p. 210; P. Elphick, *Far Eastern File: The Intelligence War in the Far East 1930–1945* (London: Hodder & Stoughton, 1998) pp. 94–105; M. Smith, *The Emperor's Codes: Bletchley Park and the Breaking of Japan's Secret Ciphers* (London: Bantam, 2000) pp. 207–16; M. Smith, 'An Undervalued Effort: How the British Broke Japan's Codes', in M. Smith and R. Erskine (eds), *Action this Day* (London: Bantam, 2001) pp. 127–51; A. Stripp, *Codebreaker in the Far East* (London: Frank Cass, 1989).
10. Ball and Horner, *Breaking the Codes*, pp. 167–9, 314.
11. C.M. Andrew, 'The Growth of the Australian Intelligence Community and the Anglo-American Connection', *Intelligence and National Security*, 4, 2 (1989), pp. 213–57.
12. N. Hager, *Secret Power: New Zealand's Role in the International Spy Network* (Nelson: Craig Potton, 1996), pp. 61–3.
13. 'Obituaries: Lt-Cdr Teddy Poulden', *Daily Telegraph* (London), 20 November 1992. Poulden's period of service as SUKLO in Washington was somewhat truncated on account of some local difficulties. After retiring from GCHQ in the 1970s he became the first head of computing at SIS.
14. J.W. Young, 'The Wilson Government's Reform of Intelligence Co-ordination, 1967–68', *Intelligence and National Security*, 16, 1 (2001) pp. 133–51. The Trend reforms echoed a wider review of government under Fulton.
15. R.J. Aldrich, 'Counting the Cost of Intelligence: The Treasury, National Service and GCHQ', *English Historical Review*, 128, 532 (2013), pp. 596–627.
16. Hooper (D/GCHQ) to White (CAB), D/7873/1802/13, 3 March 1969, CAB 163/119, UKNA.
17. Poulden (GCHQ) to Stewart (Sec. JIC), D/8987/1402/37, 'JIC (A) Sub-Committee on Automatic Data Processing', 29 September 1969, CAB 163/119, UKNA. This initiative was strongly steered by GCHQ since Poulden was in the chair, the GCHQ representative was H. Long and the secretary, also provided by GCHQ, was J.R. Cheadle.
18. JIC (A) (ADP) (71) 1st mtg., 15 February 1971, CAB 182/81, UKNA.
19. JIC (A) (ADP) (70) 2nd mtg., 3 August 1970, CAB 182/75, UKNA.
20. JIC (A) (ADP) (71) 2nd mtg., 14 June 1971, CAB 182/81, UKNA.
21. COS (73) 13th mtg. (4), 'The Intelligence Co-ordinator's Annual Review of Intelligence 1975 and His Report on Reductions in Intelligence Expenditure', 15 May 1975, DEFE 32/22, UKNA.
22. MoD memo. 'The Impact of the International Corporation UK Defence Policy', 1972, File 7, Box 5, Le Bailly papers, Churchill Archives, Churchill College Cambridge.
23. JIC (A) (ADP) (72) 2nd mtg., 19 Jun. 1972, CAB 182/81, UKNA.

24. The definitive history of ICL is Martin Campbell-Kelly, *ICL: A Business and Technical History* (Oxford: Clarendon Press, 1989).
25. Minitech, 'A History of the Computer Mergers Scheme, 1964–1969', 9 June 1969, T 325/161, UKNA.
26. Glen O'Hara, 'Attempts to Modernize: Nationalization and the Nationalized Industries in Post-War Britain', in Franco Amatori, Robert Millward and Pier Angelo Toninelli (eds), *Reappraising State-Owned Enterprise: A Comparison of the UK and Italy* (London: Routledge, 2011) pp. 50–67.
27. 'Uncle Sam's Nyet to ICL Deal', 6 January 2000, Computing.co.uk, online at: http://www.computing.co.uk/ctg/news/1853985/uncle-sams-nyet-icl-deal [accessed 8 april 2014] On the wider effects of Cocom see, M. Mastanduno, *Economic Containment: CoCom and the Politics of East-West Trade* (Ithaca: Cornell University Press, 1992).
28. Plowden (CPRS) to Rothschild (CPRS), 'Government and ICL', 26 April 1972, CAB 184/63, UKNA.
29. Campbell-Kelly, *ICL*, pp 284–6. On CPRS see Christopher Pollitt, 'The Central Policy Review Staff 1970–1974', *Public Administration*, 52, 4 (1974), pp. 375–92 and also Rodney Lowe, *The Official History of the British Civil Service: Reforming the Civil Service, Vol. 1: The Fulton Years, 1966–81* (London: Routledge, 2011) pp. 155–90. The functions of the CPRS were mostly transferred to the Downing Street Policy Unit in the 1980s.
30. CPRS mtg., 'Computers', Q 19/1, 19 May 1971, CAB 184/13, UKNA.
31. 'The UK Computer Industry: CPRS Action Programme', draft May 1971, CAB 184/12, UKNA. See also Armstrong (CAB) to Part (DTI), 18 March 1971, CAB 184/13, UKNA.
32. Poulden (GCHQ) to Rothschild (CPRS), 18 March 1971, CAB 184/13, UKNA; Poulden (GCHQ) to Rothschild (CPRS), 'UK Computer Industry', D/2281/1801/9/4, 2 April 1971, CAB 184/12, UKNA.
33. Gordon E, Moore, the co-founder of Intel stated in a 1965 paper that the number of transistors that could be inexpensively placed on an integrated circuit or 'chip' was increasing exponentially and was doubling approximately every two years. See Mark Lundstrom, 'Moore's Law Forever?', *Science*, 299, 5604 (10 January 2003), pp. 210–11.
34. Poulden (GCHQ) to Carey (CPRS), 'Central Policy Review of the British Computing Industry' and Attachment, D/2728/1801/9/4, 29 June 1971, CAB 184/12, UKNA.
35. Poulden (GCHQ) to Carey (CPRS), D/3466/1801/9/4, 12 November 1971, CAB 184/15, UKNA.
36. CPRS mtg., 'Computers', Q 19/1, 19 May 1971, CAB 184/13, UKNA.
37. Poulden (GCHQ) to Carey (CPRS), D/3193/1801/9/4, 17 September 1971, CAB 184/14, UKNA.
38. Plowden (CPRS) Memo. 'Computers: "The Whole Future of ICL Depends on Project 52" Discuss', 11 August 1971, CAB 184/14, UKNA.
39. Note of a mtg. between Poulden (GCHQ) and Carey (CPRS), 22 Apr. 1971, CAB 184/12, UKNA.
40. Poulden (GCHQ) to Carey (CPRS), enclosing 'The British Computer Industry: the Requirement', D/3191/1801/9/4, 17 September 1971, CAB 184/14, UKNA.

41. Poulden (GCHQ) to Carey (CPRS), D/3466/1801/9/4, 12 November 1971, CAB 184/15, UKNA.
42. Ibid.
43. Poulden (GCHQ) to Carey (CPRS), D/3337/1801/9/4, 14 October 1971, ibid.
44. Plowden (CPRS), 'Computer', 15 Oct. 1971, ibid.
45. Campbell-Kelly, *ICL*, p. 265.
46. Poulden (GCHQ) to Plowden (CPRS), D/4272/1801/9/4, 4 April 1972, CAB 184/63, UKNA. P-Division was Planning Division and a place where young potential managers were often sent to get a sense of future policy at GCHQ.
47. Ridley (CAB) to Rothschild (CPRS), 'Innovations by IBM', 31 July1972, CAB 184/64, UKNA.
48. Plowden (CPRS) to Rothschild (CPRS), 'Meeting with ICL: 1 August', 31 July 1972, ibid.
49. Plowden (CPRS) to Rothchild (CPRS), 'ICL', 8 May 1973, CAB 184/186, UKNA.
50. Campbell-Kelly, *ICL*, p. 265.
51. John Lamb, 'Britain's New Mainframe has a Japanese Heart', *New Scientist*, 25 April 1985, p. 24.
52. Martin Campbell-Kelly, 'The ACE and the Shaping of British Computing', in B. Jack Copeland (ed.), *Alan Turing's Electronic Brain: The Struggle to Build the ACE, the World's First Computer* (Oxford: Oxford University Press, 2005) pp. 149–72.

Select Bibliography

Primary sources: Archival

Australian War Memorial
AWM 121   Army Office Operations Branch records
AWM 125   Written Records, Southeast Asian Conflicts

National Archives of Australia
A1209   Prime Minister's Department records
A1838   Department of External Affairs, correspondence files
A4940   Menzies and Holt Ministries – Cabinet files

Archives New Zealand
AAFD   Cabinet Office records
ABHS   Ministry of Foreign Affairs and Trade records

Bundesarchiv, Koblenz, Germany
ZSg   Zeitgeschichtliche Sammlungen
Reichskanzlei

National Archives, United Kingdom
CAB 2   CID minutes and memoranda
CAB 16   Ad-hoc Sub-Committees of Enquiry
CAB 21   Cabinet Office registered files
CAB 23   Cabinet minutes
CAB 24   Cabinet memoranda
CAB 27   Committees: General Series
CAB 29   Anglo–French staff conversations
CAB 64   Minister for Coordination of Defence: Registered files
CAB 128   Post-War Cabinet minutes
CAB 129   Post-War Cabinet memoranda
CAB 130   Miscellaneous Committees minutes and papers
CAB 131   Cabinet Defence Committee Meetings
CAB 133   Commonwealth and International Conferences and Ministerial Visits
CAB 134   Miscellaneous Committees minutes and papers
CAB 148   Defence and Overseas Policy Committee and Subcommittees minutes and papers
CAB 158   Joint Intelligence Committee memoranda
CAB 163   Joint Intelligence Committee Secretariat files
CAB 164   Cabinet Office subject files

CO 1035	Colonial Office: Intelligence and Security Departments: Registered files
DEFE 4	Chiefs of Staff Committee minutes
DEFE 5	Chiefs of Staff Committee memoranda
DEFE 25	Chief of Defence Staff registered files
DEFE 32	Chiefs of Staff Committee Secretary's standard files
DEFE 68	Ministry of Defence registered files
DO 169	Commonwealth Relations Office and Commonwealth Office: Far East and Pacific Department: Registered files
FCO 24	Foreign & Commonwealth Office: South West Pacific papers
FCO 46	Foreign & Commonwealth Office: Defence & Disarmament papers
FO 371	Foreign Office Political Departments: General correspondence 1906–66
FO 408	Papers relating to Germany and Austria
PREM 1	Correspondence and papers to 1940
PREM11	Prime Minister's Office correspondence and papers 1951–64
PREM13	Prime Minister's Office correspondence and papers 1964–70
T 161	Treasury: Supply files
T 175	Sir Richard Hopkins papers
T 224	Department of Trade & Industry
T 325	Treasury files

National Archives and Records Administration, United States of America

RG59 General Records of the Department of State

Primary sources: Printed

Acheson, Dean 'Our Atlantic Alliance: The Political and Economic Strands', speech delivered at the United States Military Academy, West Point, New York, 5 Dec. 1962. Reprinted in *Vital Speeches of the Day*, 24, 6 (1 January 1963). DGA to General Maxwell Taylor, 30 July 1962. Series I, box 30, folder 385, DGA-Yale.

Anderson, Benedict R.O'G and McVey, Ruth T., *A Preliminary Analysis of the October 1, 1965 Coup in Indonesia*. Singapore: Equinox Publishing Ltd, 2009 (1971, 1965).

Dee, M., (ed.), *Australia and the Formation of Malaysia 1961–1966*. Canberra: Department of External Affairs, 2005.

Goldsworthy, David (ed.), *British Documents on the End of Empire, Series A, Vol. 3: The Conservative Government and the End of Empire 1951–1957, Part I*. London: HMSO, 1994.

Kenway, H., Stokes, H.J.W. and Edwards, P.G. (eds), *Documents on Australian Foreign Policy 1937–49. Vol. III January–June 1940*. Canberra: Australian Government Publishing Service, 1979.

Office of the Historian, Department of State, *Foreign Relations of the United States*. Washington: US Government Printing Office (USGPO) [various volumes; much of this series may also be researched online at http://history.state.gov/historicaldocuments].

Parliamentary Debates. Fifth Series, Vols 307, 310, 313–14, 317, 322, 326, 332–33, 339, 345, 350. House of Commons Official Report. London: HMSO, 1938.

Sontag, R.J., Wheeler-Bennett, J.W. et al (eds), *Documents on German Foreign Policy*, Series D. 13 vols. Washington: US Government Printing Office, 1949–1964.

Stockwell, A.J. (ed.), *British Documents on the End of Empire, Series B Vol. 3: Malaya, Part 3*. London: HMSO, 1995.

Sweet, Paul R., Lambert, Margaret, et al. (eds), *Documents on German Foreign Policy*, Series C, 6 vols. London: HMSO, 1957–1983.

United States Government, *Public Papers of the President of the United States: Dwight D. Eisenhower, 1954*. Washington: US Government Printing Office, 1958.

Woodward, E.L., Lambert, M.E., Medlicott, W. et al (eds), *Documents on British Foreign Policy 1919–1939*, Series 1A, 2, 28 vols. London: HMSO, 1947–1984.

Private Papers

Bodleian Library, Oxford
Rumbold papers
Toynbee papers

British Library, London
Curzon papers

British Library of Economics and Political Science, LSE London
Webster papers

Brotherton Library, University of Leeds
Edward Frederick Lindley Wood, 1st Earl of Halifax papers

Churchill College Archive Centre, Cambridge
Inskip papers
A.L. Kennedy papers
Le Bailly papers
Noel-Baker papers
Phipps papers
Vansittart papers
Weir papers

Hoover Institution, Stanford University
Scapini papers

Library and Archives Canada
Kirkwood papers
Laurier papers

Liddell Hart Centre for Military Archives, King's College London
Hamilton papers

National Library of Australia, Canberra
Clunies Ross papers
Piesse papers

National Archives, Kew Gardens
J Ramsay MacDonald papers

National Archives of Scotland, Edinburgh
Lothian papers

National Library of Scotland, Edinburgh
James Stewart Lockhart papers,

Parliamentary Archives, London
Lloyd George papers

Times Newspaper Limited Archive, News International Limited, London
Harold Williams papers

University of Birmingham Library
Neville Chamberlain papers

University of Toronto Archives
Massey papers

Yale University
Dean Acheson papers

Memoirs, Diaries and Speeches

Avon, The Earl of, *The Eden Memoirs: Facing the Dictators*. London: Cassell, 1962.
Barnes, John and Nicholson, David (eds), *The Empire at Bay: The Leo Amery Diaries, 1929–45*. London: Hutchinson, 1988.
Bond, Brian (ed.), *Chief of Staff: The Diaries of Lieutenant–General Sir Henry Pownall, Vol.I*. London: Leo Cooper, 1972.
Bonsall, Arthur, 'Bletchley Park and the RAF Y Service: Some Recollections', *Intelligence and National Security*, 23, 2008.

Ciano, Galeazzo, *Ciano's Diary 1937–1938*. London: Methuen, 1952.
Crossman, Richard, *The Diaries of a Cabinet Minister, Vol. II*. London: Hamish Hamilton & Jonathan Cape, 1976.
Dalton, Hugh, *Call Back Yesterday*. London: Muller, 1953.
Dilks, David N. (ed. and contributor), *The Diaries of Sir Alexander Cadogan O.M. 1938–1945*. London: Cassell, 1971.
Domarus, Max, *Hitler. Speeches and Proclamations, 1932–1945. The Chronicle of a Dictatorship, Vol. II, The Years 1935 to 1938*. Wauconda, IL: Bolchazy-Carducci Inc, 1992.
Fröhlich, Elke (ed.), *Die Tagebücher von Joseph Goebbels*. 9 vols. Munich: K.G. Saur Verlag, 1998–2005.
Harvey, John (ed.), *The Diplomatic Diaries of Oliver Harvey, 1937–1940*. London: Collins, 1970.
Healey, Denis, *The Time of My Life*. New York: W.W. Norton, 1989.
James, Robert Rhodes (ed.), *Chips: The Diaries of Sir Henry Channon*. London: Weidenfeld and Nicolson, 1967.
Jenkins, Roy, *A Life at the Centre*. London: Macmillan, 1991.
Jones, Howard, *Indonesia: The Possible Dream*. New York: Harcourt, Brace, Jovanovich, 1971.
Jones, Thomas, *A Diary with Letters, 1931–1950*. London: Oxford University Press, 1954.
Lee Kuan Yew, *From Third World to First: The Singapore Story, 1965–2000*. Singapore: Times Media, 2000.
Lee Kuan Yew, *The Singapore Story: Memoirs of Lee Kuan Yew*. Singapore: Prentice-Hall, 1998.
Martel, Gordon (ed.), *The Times and Appeasement: The Journals of A.L. Kennedy, 1932–1939*. Cambridge: Cambridge University Press, 2000.
Minney, R.J., *The Private Papers of Hore-Belisha*. London: Collins, 1960.
Montgomery, Viscount, *The Memoirs of Field-Marshal the Viscount Montgomery of Alamein*. London: Collins, 1958.
Nicolson, Nigel (ed.), *Harold Nicolson: Diaries and Letters, 1930–39*. London: Collins, 1966.
Nicolson, Nigel (ed.), *Harold Nicolson: Diaries and Letters, 1939–45*. London, Collins, 1967.
Nicolson, Nigel (ed.), *Vita and Harold: The Letters of Vita Sackville-West and Harold Nicolson*. New York: Putnam's, 1992.
Redesdale, Lord, ' "Old and New Japan" Lecture to the Japan Society of London, 14 November 1906, in H. Cortazzi (ed.), *The Memoirs and Recollections, 1866–1906, of Algernon Bertram Mitford, the First Lord Redesdale*. London: Athlone Press, 1985.
Ribbentrop, Joachim von, *The Ribbentrop Memoirs*. London: Weidenfeld & Nicolson, 1954.
Rose, Norman (ed.), *Baffy: The Diaries of Blanche Dugdale, 1936–47*. London: Vallentine Mitchell, 1973.
Self, Robert (ed.), *The Neville Chamberlain Diary Letters. Vol.4. The Downing Street Years, 1934–40*. Aldershot: Ashgate, 2005.
Vansittart, Robert G., *The Mist Procession: The Autobiography of Lord Vansittart*. London: Hutchinson, 1958.

Wanandi, Jusuf, *Shades of Grey: A Political Memoir of Modern Indonesia 1965–1998*. Singapore: Equinox Publishing, 2012.
Wilson, Harold, *The Labour Government 1964–70*. London: Pelican, 1974.

Secondary sources

Aandstad, Stig Aga, *Surrendering to Symbols: United States Policy towards Indonesia 1961–1965*. Oslo: Self-published (revision of University of Oslo PhD thesis), 2006 (1999).
Adas, Michael, *Machines as the Measure of Man: Science, Technology, and Ideologies of Western Dominance*. Ithaca: Cornell University Press, 1989.
Aid, Matthew, *Secret Sentry: The Top Secret History of the National Security Agency*. New York: Bloomsbury, 2009.
Aid, Matthew and Wiebes, Cees (eds), *Secrets of Signals Intelligence during the Cold War and Beyond*. London: Frank Cass, 2001.
Aldrich, Richard J., 'Counting the Cost of Intelligence: The Treasury, National Service and GCHQ', *English Historical Review*, 128, 2013.
Aldrich, Richard J., *Intelligence and the War Against Japan: The Politics of Secret Service*. Cambridge: Cambridge University Press, 2000.
Aldrich, Richard J., 'The Ultimate Spy: Why the Real James Bond is a Supercomputer', *BBC Science Magazine*, 248, 2012.
Aldrich, Richard J. et al (eds), *The Clandestine Cold War in Asia 1945–65: Western Intelligence, Propaganda and Special Operations*. London: Frank Cass, 2000.
Andrew, Christopher M., 'The Growth of the Australian Intelligence Community and the Anglo-American Connection', *Intelligence and National Security*, 4, 1989.
Aster, Sidney, 'Appeasement: Before and After Revisionism', *Diplomacy and Statecraft*, 19, 2008.
Aster, Sidney, ' "Guilty Men": The Case of Neville Chamberlain', in Robert Boyce and Esmonde Robertson (eds), *Paths to War: New Essays on the Origins of the Second World War*. London: Macmillan, 1989.
Aster, Sidney, ' "Salter's Soviet": Another View of All Souls and Appeasement', in M.G. Fry (ed.), *Power, Personalities and Policies: Essays in Honour of Donald Cameron Watt*. London: Frank Cass, 1992.
Ball, Desmond and Horner, David, *Breaking the Code: Australia's KGB Network*. Sydney: Allen and Unwin, 1988.
Bamford, James, *Body of Secrets: How NSA and Britain's GCHQ Eavesdrop on the World*. London: Doubleday, 2001.
Bamford, James, *The Puzzle Palace: America's National Security Agency and Its Special Relationship with GCHQ*. London: Sidgwick & Jackson, 1983.
Bell, Peter, *Chamberlain, Germany and Japan, 1933–34*. New York: St Martin's Press, 1996.
Bell, Peter, 'The Foreign Office and the 1939 Royal Visit to America: Courting the United States in an Era of Isolationism', *Journal of Contemporary History*, 37, 2002.
Bennett, E.W., *Germany and the Diplomacy of the Financial Crisis, 1931*. Cambridge, MA: Harvard University Press, 1962.

Bennett, Gillian H., *British Foreign Policy during the Curzon Period*. Basingstoke: Macmillan, 1995.
Best, Antony, 'British Intellectuals and East Asia in the Interwar Years', in Wm Roger Louis (ed.), *Yet More Adventures with Britannia*. Austin: IB Taurus/University of Texas Press, 2005.
Best, Antony, *British Intelligence and the Japanese Challenge in Asia, 1914–41*. Basingstoke: Palgrave, 2002.
Best, Antony, 'Economic Appeasement or Economic Nationalism?: A Political Perspective on the British Empire, Japan and the Rise of Intra-Asian Trade, 1933–37', *Journal of Imperial and Commonwealth Studies*, 30, 2002.
Best, Antony, 'Race, Monarchy and the Anglo-Japanese Alliance, 1902–1922', *Social Science Japan Journal*, 9, 2, 2006.
Best, Antony, 'The Anglo-Japanese Alliance and International Politics in Asia, 1902–23', in Antony Best (ed.), *The International History of East Asia, 1900–1968: Trade, Ideology and the Quest for Order*. London: Routledge, 2010.
Best, Antony, 'The "Ghost" of the Anglo-Japanese Alliance: An Examination into Historical Mythmaking', *Historical Journal*, 49, 2006.
Bickers, Robert, *Britain in China: Community, Culture and Colonialism, 1900–1949*. Manchester: Manchester University Press, 1999.
Bijl, Nick van der, *Confrontation: The War with Indonesia 1962–1966*. Barnsley: Pen and Sword Ltd, 2007.
Bijl, Nick van der, *The Brunei Revolt 1962–1963*. Barnsley: Pen and Sword, 2012.
Blumenthal, Henry. *Illusion and Reality in Franco-American Diplomacy, 1914–45*. Baton Rouge: Louisiana State University Press, 1986.
Bond, Brian, *British Military Policy between the Two World Wars*. Oxford: Clarendon Press, 1980.
Bond, Brian, *Liddell Hart: A Study of His Military Thought*. London: Cassell, 1977.
Boyle, Andrew, *Trenchard, Man of Vision*. London: Collins, 1962.
Brendon, Piers, *The Dark Valley: A Panorama of the 1930s*. New York: Alfred A. Knopf, 2000.
Cable, James, *The Geneva Conference of 1954 on Indochina*. Basingstoke: Macmillan, 2000.
Campbell-Kelly, Martin, *ICL: A Business and Technical History*. Oxford: Clarendon Press, 1989.
Campbell-Kelly, Martin, 'The ACE and the Shaping of British Computing', in B. Jack Copeland (ed.), *Alan Turing's Electronic Brain: The Struggle to Build the ACE, the World's First Computer*. Oxford: Oxford University Press, 2005.
Carlton, David, *Anthony Eden. A Biography*. London: Allen Lane, 1981.
Carlton, David, *MacDonald Versus Henderson*. London: Macmillan, 1970.
'Cato', *Guilty Men*. London: Victor Gollancz, 1940.
Chandler, W.W., 'The Installation and Maintenance of Colossus', *IEEE Annals of the History of Computing*, 5, 1983.
Charmley, John, *Chamberlain and the Lost Peace*. London: Hodder & Stroughton, 1989.
Cheah Boon Kheng, 'The Communist Insurgency in Malaysia, 1948–1989: Was it Due to the Cold War?', in Malcolm H. Murfett (ed.), *Cold War Southeast Asia*. Singapore: Marshall Cavendish, 2012.

Chihiro, Hosoya, 'Britain and the United States in Japan's View of the International System', in Ian Nish (ed.), *Anglo-Japanese Alienation 1919–1952*. Cambridge: Cambridge University Press, 1982.

Chin Kin Wah, *The Defence of Malaysia and Singapore: The Transformation of a Security System 1957–1971*. Cambridge: Cambridge University Press, 1983.

Chirol, Sir Valentine, *Fifty Years in a Changing World*. London: Jonathan Cape, 1927.

Churchill, Randolph S., *The Rise and Fall of Sir Anthony Eden*. London: MacGibbon & Kee, 1959.

Churchill, Winston S., *The Second World War: Vol. 1, The Gathering Storm*. New York: Houghton Mifflin, 1948.

Clifford, Nicholas, *'A Truthful Impression of the Country': British and American Travel Writing in China, 1880–1949*. Ann Arbor: University of Michigan Press, 2001.

Colman, J., *A 'Special Relationship'? Harold Wilson, Lyndon B. Johnson and Anglo-American Relations 'at the Summit', 1964–68*. Manchester: Manchester University Press, 2004.

Comber, Leon, *Malaya's Secret Police 1945–60: The Role of the Special Branch in the Malayan Emergency*. Melbourne: Monash Asia Institute, 2008.

Coombs, Allen W., 'The Making of Colossus', *IEEE Annals of the History of Computing*, 5, 1983.

Copeland, B. Jack, *Colossus: The Secrets of Bletchley Park's Codebreaking Computers*. Oxford: Oxford University Press, 2006.

Cowman, Ian, *Dominion or Decline: Anglo-American Naval Relations in the Pacific, 1937–1941*. Oxford: Berg, 1996.

Crouch, Harold A., *The Army and Politics in Indonesia*. Singapore: Equinox Publishing, 2007 (1978).

Crozier, Andrew J., *Appeasement and Germany's Last Bid for Colonies*. Basingstoke: Macmillan, 1988.

Dallek, Robert, *Franklin D. Roosevelt and American Foreign Policy, 1932–1945*. Oxford: Oxford University Press, 1995.

Davidann, Jon Thares, *Cultural Diplomacy in U.S.-Japanese Relations, 1919–1941*. Basingstoke: Palgrave/Macmillan, 2007.

Delmas, Jean, 'La perception de la puissance militaire française', in René Girault and Robert Frank (eds), *La Puissance en Europe 1938–1940*. Paris: Publications de la Sorbonne, 1984.

Dennis, Peter J., *Decision by Default: Peacetime Conscription and British Defence 1919–39*. London: Routledge and Kegan Paul, 1972.

Dilks, David N., *A View on Two Squares: John Holmes in London and Moscow, 1944–48*. London: Canadian High Commission, 1992.

Dilks, David N., 'Allied Leadership in the Second World War: Churchill', *Survey*, 21, 1–2, 1975.

Dilks, David N., 'Appeasement and Intelligence', in David N. Dilks (ed.), *Retreat from Power: Studies in Britain's Foreign Policy of the Twentieth Century, Vol. I: 1906–1939*. London: Macmillan, 1981.

Dilks, David N., 'Appeasement Revisited', *The University of Leeds Review*, 1972.

Dilks, David N., 'Baldwin and Chamberlain', in Lord Butler (ed.), *The Conservatives: A History from their Origins to 1965*. London: Allen & Unwin, 1977.

Dilks, David N. (ed. and contributor), 'Britain and Canada: A Colloquium held at Leeds in October, 1979', Commonwealth Foundation Occasional Paper XLIX.

Dilks, David N., 'Britain and Europe, 1948–1950: The Prime Minister, the Foreign Secretary and the Cabinet', in R. Poidevin (ed.), *Origins of European Integration*. Brussels: Bruylant, 1986.

Dilks, David N., 'Britain and Germany, 1937–1939: A Context for British Reactions to the German Resistance', in Adolf M. Birke, Magnus Brechtken and Alaric Searle (eds), *An Anglo-German Dialogue: The Munich Lectures on the History of International Relations*. Munich: K.G. Saur Verlag, 2000.

Dilks, David N., 'Britain: No New Jerusalem', in Barrie Pitt (ed.), *History of the Second World War*. London: Purnell Publishing, 1968.

Dilks, David N., *Britain, the Commonwealth and the Wider World in the Second World War*. Hull: University of Hull Press, 1998.

Dilks, David N., 'British Political Aims in Central, Eastern and Southern Europe, 1944', in Jonathan Chadwick, Elisabeth Barker and F.W. Deakin (eds), *British Political and Military Strategy in Central, Eastern and Southern Europe in 1944*. London, Macmillan, 1988.

Dilks, David N., 'British Reactions to Italian Empire Building, 1936–39', in Christopher Seton-Watson and Enrico Serra (eds), *Italia e Inghilterra nell'eta dell'Imperialismo*. Milan: Franco Angeli, 1990.

Dilks, David N., *Churchill and Company: Allies and Rivals in War and Peace*. London: I.B. Tauris, 2012.

Dilks, David N., 'Churchill as Negotiator at Yalta', in Paola Brundu Olla (ed.), *Yalta: Un Mito che Resiste*. Rome: Edizioni dell'Ateneo, 1988.

Dilks, David N., 'Collective Security: 1919 and Now', in Samuel F. Wells and Paula Bailey Smith (eds), *New European Orders, 1919–1991*. Baltimore, MD: Johns Hopkins University Press, 1996.

Dilks, David N., *Communications, the Commonwealth and the Future*. Hull: University of Hull Press, 1994.

Dilks, David N., *Curzon in India*. 2 vols. London: Rupert Hart-Davis, 1969–70.

Dilks, David N., *De Gaulle and the British*. Hull: University of Hull Press, 1996.

Dilks, David N., 'Deakin. Sir (Frederick) William Dampier (1913–2005)', in *Oxford Dictionary of National Biography*, 94863, 2009.

Dilks, David N., 'Flashes of Intelligence: The Foreign Office, The SIS and Security Before the Second World War', in Christopher Andrew and David Dilks (eds), *The Missing Dimension: Governments and Intelligence Communities in the Twentieth Century*. London: Macmillan, 1984.

Dilks, David N., 'Great Britain and Scandinavia in the "Phoney War"', *Scandinavian Journal of History*, 2, 1977.

Dilks, David N., 'La Grande-Bretagne et Le Monde Extérieur en 1945', in Maurice Vaïsse (ed.), *8 mai, 1945: La victoire en Europe*. Brussels: Éditions Complexe, 2005.

Dilks, David N., *Mackenzie King and the British*. London: Canadian High Commission, 1985.

Dilks, David N., *Neville Chamberlain: Vol. I. Pioneering and Reform, 1869–1929*. Cambridge: Cambridge University Press, 1984.

Dilks, David N., 'New Perspectives on Neville Chamberlain', *The Listener*, 11 November 1976.

Dilks, David N., 'Parker, Sir (Arthur) Douglas Dodds- (1909–2006)', in *Oxford Dictionary of National Biography*, 97431, 2010.

Dilks, David N., 'Public Opinion and Foreign Policy: Great Britain', in *Opinion Publique et Politique Extérieure, Vol. 2, 1915–1940*. Rome: Ecole Française de Rome, 1984.

Dilks, David N. (ed. and contributor), *Retreat from Power: Studies in Britain's Foreign Policy of the Twentieth Century*, 2 vols. London: Macmillan, 1981.

Dilks, David N., 'Rumours and Threats of War: Responses in Western and Northern Europe, 1931–39', in S. Hietanen et al (eds), *The Road to War: Essays in Honour of Professor O. Vehvilainen*. Tampere: Tampere University Press, 1993.

Dilks, David N., 'The British Foreign Office between the Wars', in B.J.C. McKercher and D.J. Moss (eds), *Shadow and Substance in British Foreign Policy 1895–1939*. Edmonton: University of Alberta Press, 1984.

Dilks, David N., 'The British View of Security: Europe and a Wider World, 1945–1948', in Olav Riste (ed.), *Western Security: The Formative Years*. New York: Columbia University Press, 1985.

Dilks, David N., 'The Conference at Potsdam, 1945', in Gill Bennett (ed.), *The End of the War in Europe 1945*. London: HMSO, 1996.

Dilks, David N., ' "The Great Dominion": Churchill's Farewell Visits to Canada, 1952 and 1954', *Canadian Journal of History*, 23, 1, 1988.

Dilks, David N., *The Great Dominion: Winston Churchill in Canada 1900–1954*. Toronto: Thomas Allen Publishers, 2005.

Dilks, David N., ' "The Great Game" and "A Most Superior Person" ', in *The British Empire*. London: BBC/Time Life Books, 48 & 60, 1972–73.

Dilks, David N., *The Office of Prime Minister in Twentieth Century Britain*. Hull: University of Hull Press, 1993.

Dilks, David N., 'The Queen and Mr. Churchill', *Finest Hour*, 135, 2007.

Dilks, David N., 'The Twilight War and the Fall of France: Chamberlain and Churchill in 1940', *Transactions of the Royal Historical Society*, 5th Series, 28, 1978.

Dilks, David N., ' "The Unnecessary War": Military Advice and Foreign Policy in Great Britain, 1931–39', in Adrian Preston (ed.), *General Staffs and Diplomacy before the Second World War*. London: Croom Helm, 1978.

Dilks, David N., *Three Visitors to Canada: Winston Churchill, Stanley Baldwin, and Neville Chamberlain*. London: Canadian High Commission, 1985.

Dilks, David N., ' "We Must Hope for the Best and Prepare for the Worst": The Prime Minister, the Cabinet and Hitler's Germany, 1937–1939', *Proceedings of the British Academy*, 73, 1987.

Dilks, David N., 'Youth Exchanges in the Commonwealth', *Journal of the Royal Society of Arts*, 121, August, 1973.

Dilks, David N. with Beattie, Alan J. and Pronay, Nicholas, *Neville Chamberlain*. Leeds: Inter-University History Film Consortium Archive Series, 1978.

Dilks, David N., Davies, R.R., Davis, R.H.C. and Moore, R.I., 'University Historians and the 18+', *History*, 62, 205, 1977.

Dilks, David N. and Erickson, John (eds), *Barbarossa: The Axis and the Allies*. Edinburgh: Edinburgh University Press, 1994.

Dilks, David N. with Manley, R., 'The Commonwealth Youth Exchange Council – A New Arm at Work', in *Commonwealth*, 15, 6, 1971.

Dilks, David N. and Müller, K.J. (eds), *Grossbritannien und der deutsche Widerstand 1933–1944*. Paderborn: Munich: Schöningh, 1994
Dilks, David N. and Pronay, Nicholas, 'Communications and Politics in the 20th Century', *Studies in Higher Education*, 1, 1, 1976.
Divine, Robert A., *The Illusion of Neutrality*. Chicago: Chicago University Press, 1962.
Djiwandono, J.S., *Konfrontasi Revisited: Indonesia's Foreign Policy under Soekarno*. Jakarta: Centre for Strategic and International Studies, 1996.
Dockrill, Saki, *Britain's Retreat from East of Suez: The Choice between Europe and the World?* Basingstoke: Palgrave Macmillan, 2002.
Drinkwater, Denis, *Sir Harold Nicolson and International Relations: The Practitioner as Theorist*. Oxford: Oxford University Press, 2005.
Dutton, David, *Anthony Eden. A Life and Reputation*. London: Edward Arnold, 1997.
Dutton, David, *Neville Chamberlain*. London: Edward Arnold, 2001.
Easter, David, *Britain and the Confrontation with Indonesia 1960–1966*. London: Tauris Academic Studies, 2004.
Edwards, E.W., *British Diplomacy and Finance in China 1895–1914*. Oxford: Clarendon Press, 1987.
Edwards, Peter G., *A Nation at War: Australian Politics, Society and Diplomacy during the Vietnam War 1965–1975*. Sydney: Allen & Unwin, 1997.
Edwards, Peter G., *Prime Ministers and Diplomats: The Making of Australian Foreign Policy 1901–1949*. Melbourne: Oxford University Press, 1983.
Ellis, Edward L., *T. J.: A Life of Dr Thomas Jones CH*. Cardiff: University of Wales Press, 1992.
Elphick, Peter, *Far Eastern File: The Intelligence War in the Far East 1930–1945*. London: Hodder & Stoughton, 1998.
Emmerson, James T., *The Rhineland Crisis, 7 March 1936. A Study in Multilateral Diplomacy*. London: Temple Smith, 1977.
Evans, David C. and Peattie, Mark R., *Kaigun: Strategy, Tactics, and Technology in the Imperial Japanese Navy, 1887–1941*. Annapolis, MD: Naval Institute Press, 1997.
Farrell, Brian P., 'Alphabet Soup and Nuclear War: SEATO, China and the Cold War in Southeast Asia', in Malcolm H. Murfett (ed.), *Cold War Southeast Asia*. Singapore: Marshall Cavendish, 2012.
Farrell, Brian P., 'End of Empire; From Union to Withdrawal', in Malcolm H. Murfett, John N. Miksic, Brian P. Farrell and Chiang Ming Shun. *Between Two Oceans: A Military History of Singapore from 1275 to 1971* (2nd edn). Singapore: Marshall Cavendish, 2011
Farrell, Brian P., 'Escalate to Terminate: Far East Command and the Need to End Confrontation', in Peter Dennis and Jeff Grey (eds), *Entangling Alliances: Coalition Warfare in the Twentieth Century*. Canberra: Australian Military History Publications. 2005.
Farrell, Brian P., *The Defence and Fall of Singapore 1940–1942*. Stroud: Tempus, 2005.
Farrell, Brian P., 'Too Little, Too Late: Preparing for War, 1941–1942', in Malcolm H. Murfett, John N. Miksic, Brian P. Farrell and Chiang Ming Shun. *Between Two Oceans: A Military History of Singapore from 1275 to 1971* (2nd edn). Singapore: Marshall Cavendish, 2011.

Farrell, Brian P., 'What Do They Want, and How Can We Respond? Commonwealth Intelligence and Confrontation with Indonesia, 1963', in Malcolm H. Murfett (ed.), *Imponderable but Not Inevitable: Warfare in the 20th Century*. Santa Barbara, CA: Praeger, 2011.

Farrell, Brian P., 'What Do We Do Now? British Commonwealth and American Reactions to the Separation of Malaysia and Singapore', *Australian Defence Force Journal*, 170, 2006.

Feiling, Keith, *The Life of Neville Chamberlain*. London: Macmillan, 1946.

Fenton, Damien, *To Cage the Red Dragon: SEATO and the Defence of Southeast Asia 1955–1965*. Singapore: NUS Press, 2012.

Ferris, John, 'The British "Enigma": Britain, Signals Security and Cipher Machines, 1906–1946', *Defense Analysis*, 3, 1987.

Flowerdew, John, *The Final Years of British Hong Kong: The Discourse of Colonial Withdrawal*. Basingstoke: Palgrave Macmillan, 1998.

Ford, Douglas, *Britain's Secret War Against Japan, 1937–1945*. London: Routledge, 2006.

Frankum, Ronald B., *Like Rolling Thunder: The Air War in Vietnam 1964–1975*. Lanham, MD: Rowman & Littlefield, 2005.

Freedman, Lawrence, *Kennedy's Wars: Berlin, Cuba, Laos and Vietnam*. Oxford: Oxford University Press, 2000.

French, David, *Raising Churchill's Army*. Oxford: Oxford University Press, 2000.

Gaddis, John Lewis, *The Cold War: A New History*. London: Penguin Press, 2006.

Gannon, Paul, *Colossus: Bletchley Park's Greatest Secret*. London: Atlantic Books, 2006.

Gibbs, Norman H., *Grand Strategy*. London: HMSO, 1976.

Gilbert, Martin, *Winston S. Churchill, Vol. V, 1922–39*. London: Heinemann, 1976.

Grayson, R.S., *Austen Chamberlain and the Commitment to Europe*. London: Frank Cass, 1997.

Grove, Eric J., *Vanguard to Trident: British Naval Policy since World War Two*. Annapolis, MD: Naval Institute Press, 1987.

Hack, Karl, *Defence and Decolonisation in Southeast Asia: Britain, Malaya and Singapore 1941–68*. Richmond: Curzon, 2001.

Hager, Nicky, *Secret Power: New Zealand's Role in the International Spy Network*. Nelson: Craig Potton, 1996.

Haggie, Paul, *Britannia at Bay: The Defence of the British Empire Against Japan 1931–1941*. Oxford; Clarendon Press, 1981.

Hamill, Ian, *The Strategic Illusion: The Singapore Strategy and the Defence of Australia and New Zealand, 1919–42*. Singapore: Singapore University Press, 1981.

Han Fook Kwang, Warren Fernandez and Sumiko Tan (eds), *Lee Kuan Yew: The Man and His Ideas*. Singapore: Times Editions, 1998.

Harris, J.P., *Men, Ideas and Tanks*. Manchester: Manchester University Press, 1995.

Harrison, Austin, 'Great Prospects', *English Review*, August 1921.

Hart, Basil Liddell, *Europe in Arms*. London: Faber and Faber, 1937.

Heineman, John L., *Hitler's First Foreign Minister. Constantin Freiherr von Neurath, Diplomat and Statesman*. Berkeley, CA: University of California Press, 1979.

Henke, Josef, *England in Hitlers politischem Kalkül 1935–39*. Boppard am Rhein: Boldt, 1973.

Henning, Joseph M., *Outposts of Civilization: Race, Religion and the Formative Years of American-Japanese Relations*. New York: New York University Press, 2000.

Hevia, James L., *English Lessons: The Pedagogy of Imperialism in Nineteenth Century China*. Durham, NC: Duke University Press, 2003.
Hildebrand, Klaus, *Vom Reich zum Weltreich. Hitler, NSDAP und koloniale Frage, 1919–1945* [From Empire to World Empire. Hitler, the Nazi Party and the Colonial Question, 1919–1945]. Munich: Fink, 1969.
Hilsman, Roger, *To Move a Nation: The Politics of Foreign Policy in the Administration of John F. Kennedy*. New York: Dell Publishing Co., 1967.
Hodges, Andrew, *Alan Turing: The Enigma*. London: Burnett Books, 1992.
Hohler, Thomas, *Diplomatic Petrel*. London: John Murray, 1942.
Holmes, Colin, 'Sidney Webb and Beatrice Webb and Japan', in Hugh Cortazzi and Gordon Daniels (eds), *Britain and Japan 1859–1991: Themes and Personalities*. London: Routledge, 1991.
Holmes, Colin and Ion, A. Hamish, 'Bushidō and the Samurai: Images in British Public Opinion, 1894–1914', *Modern Asian Studies*, 14, 1980.
Horne, Alistair, *Macmillan, Vol. II of the Official Biography: 1957–1986*. London: Macmillan, 1989.
Howard, Michael, *The Continental Commitment*. London: Temple Smith, 1972.
Hughes, John, *The End of Sukarno: A Coup that Misfired: A Purge that Ran Wild*. Singapore: Archipelago Press, 2002 (1967).
Hunter, Helen-Louise, *Sukarno and the Indonesian Coup*. Westport, CT: Praeger Security International, 2007.
Hyam, Ronald, *Britain's Declining Empire: The Road to Decolonization 1918–1968*. Cambridge: Cambridge University Press, 2006.
Iikura, Akira, 'The Anglo-Japanese Alliance and the Question of Race', in Phillips O'Brien (ed.), *The Anglo-Japanese Alliance*. London: Routledge, 2004.
Iriye, Akira, *Across the Pacific: An Inner History of America—East Asian Relations*. New York: Harcourt, Brace and World, 1967.
James, Harold, 'The Causes of the German Banking Crisis of 1931', *Economic History Review*, 37, 1984.
James, Robert Rhodes, *Anthony Eden*. London: Weidenfeld & Nicolson, 1986.
Jenkins, Roy, *Churchill: A Biography*. New York: Farrar, Straus and Giroux, 2001.
Jones, Matthew, *Conflict and Confrontation in South East Asia, 1961–1965*. Cambridge: Cambridge University Press, 2002.
Kasza, Gregory C., 'Fascism from Above? Japan's Kakushin Right in Comparative Perspective', in Stein Ugelvik Larsen (ed.), *Fascism Outside Europe: The European Impulse against Domestic Conditions in the Diffusion of Global Fascism*. New York: Columbia University Press, 2001.
Kennedy, Greg C., *Anglo-American Strategic Relations and the Far East, 1933–1939*. London: Frank Cass, 2002.
Kennedy, Greg C., 'Neville Chamberlain and Strategic Relations with the US during his Chancellorship', *Diplomacy & Statecraft*, 13, 1, 2002.
Kennedy, Greg C., ' "Rat in Power": Neville Chamberlain and the Creation of British Foreign Policy, 1931–39', in T.G. Otte (ed.), *The Makers of British Foreign Policy From Pitt to Thatcher*. Basingstoke: Palgrave Macmillan, 2002.
Kennedy, Sir John, *The Business of War*. London: Hutchinson, 1957.
Kent, Barrie H., *Signal! A History of Signalling in the Royal Navy*. East Meon, Hants: Hyden, 2004.
Kent, Bruce, *The Spoils of War: The Politics, Economics, and Diplomacy of Reparations, 1918–32*. Oxford: Clarendon Press, 1989.

Kimball, Warren F., *Forged in War: Churchill, Roosevelt and the Second World War*. New York: William Morrow, 1997.
Kirby, William C., 'Images and Realities of Chinese Fascism', in Stein Ugelvik Larsen (ed.), *Fascism Outside Europe: The European Impulse against Domestic Conditions in the Diffusion of Global Fascism*. New York: Columbia University Press, 2001.
Koh, D.S.J. and Tanaka, K., 'Japanese Competition in the Trade of Malaya in the 1930s', *Southeast Asian Studies*, 21, 1984.
Kowner, Rotem, ' "Lighter Than Yellow", But Not Enough: Western Discourse on the Japanese "Race" 1854–1904', *Historical Journal*, 43, 2000.
Kunz, Diane B. ' "Somewhat Mixed Up Together": Anglo-American Defence and Financial Policy During the 1960s', in Robert D. King and Robin W. Kilson (eds), *The Statecraft of British Imperialism. Essays in Honour of Wm Roger Louis*. London: Frank Cass, 1999.
Kyle, Keith, *Suez: Britain's End of Empire in the Middle East*. London: I.B. Taurus, 2011.
Kynaston, David, *Austerity Britain 1945–51*. New York: Walker & Co., 2008.
Lamb, John, 'Britain's New Mainframe has a Japanese Heart', *New Scientist*, 25 April 1985.
Larres, Klaus, *Churchill's Cold War: The Politics of Personal Diplomacy*. New Haven, Yale University Press, 2002.
Lavington, Simon H., 'In the Footsteps of Colossus: A Description of Oedipus', *IEEE Annals of Computing*, 2006.
Lees-Milne, James, *Harold Nicolson, A Biography*, 2 vols. London: Hamish Hamilton, 1988.
Legge, John D., *Sukarno: A Political Biography*. Singapore: Archipelago Press, 2003.
Liu, Lydia H., *The Clash of Empires: The Invention of China in Modern World Making*. Cambridge, MA: Harvard University Press, 2004.
Logevall, Fredrik, *Embers of War: The Fall of an Empire and the Making of America's Vietnam*. New York: Random House, 2012.
Lowe, Peter, *Britain and Japan, 1911–15: A Study of British Far Eastern Policy*. London: Macmillan, 1969.
Lowe, Peter, *Contending with Nationalism and Communism: British Policy Towards Southeast Asia, 1945–65*. Basingstoke: Palgrave Macmillan, 2009.
Lowe, Peter, 'The Round Table, the Dominions and the Anglo-Japanese Alliance 1911–1922', in Andrea Bosco and Alex May (eds), *The Round Table: The Empire/Commonwealth and British Foreign Policy*. London: Lothian Foundation Press, 1997.
Lowe, Rodney, *The Official History of the British Civil Service: Reforming the Civil Service, Vol. 1: The Fulton Years, 1966–81*. London: Routledge, 2011.
Lundstrom, Mark, 'Moore's Law Forever?', *Science*, 299, 10 January 2003.
Luthi, Lorenz M., *The Sino-Soviet Split: Cold War in the Communist World*. Princeton: Princeton University Press. 2008.
Magee, Frank, 'Conducting Locarno Diplomacy; Britain and the Austro-German Customs Union Crisis, 1931', *Twentieth Century British History*, 11, 2000.
Magee, Frank, 'Limited Liability? Britain and the Treaty of Locarno', *Twentieth Century British History*, 6, 1995.
Majid, H.A., *Rebellion in Brunei: The 1962 Revolt, Imperialism, Confrontation, and Oil*. London: I.B. Tauris, 2007.

Manchester, William, *The Last Lion: Winston Spencer Churchill 1874–1932*. Boston: Little, Brown & Co., 1983.
Mastanduno, M., *Economic Containment: CoCom and the Politics of East-West Trade*. Ithaca: Cornell University Press, 1992.
Maurice, Sir Frederick, 'The Chances of War in the Pacific', *Empire Review*, January 1926.
McKercher, Brian J.C., 'Deterrence and the European Balance of Power: The Field Force and British Grand Strategy, 1934–1938', *English Historical Review*, 123, 2008.
McKercher, Brian J.C., *Transition of Power: Britain's Loss of Global Pre-eminence to the United States, 1930–1945*. Cambridge: Cambridge University Press, 1999.
Meaney, Neville, *The Search for Security in the Pacific 1901–14*. Sydney: University of Sydney Press, 1976.
Messerschmidt, Manfred, 'German Military Effectiveness Between 1919 and 1939', in Allan R. Millett and Williamson Murray (eds), *Military Effectiveness, Vol. II*. Boston: Unwin Hyman, 1988.
Middlebrook, Martin and Mahoney, P., *The Sinking of the Prince of Wales and the Repulse: The End of the Battleship Era*. Barnsley: Leo Cooper, 2004.
Middlemas, Keith, *Diplomacy of Illusion. The British Government and Germany, 1937–39*. London: Weidenfeld & Nicolson, 1972.
Moise, E.E., *Tonkin Gulf and the Escalation of the Vietnam War*. Chapel Hill, NC: University of North Carolina Press, 1996.
Morgan, Kenneth O., *Britain since 1945: The People's Peace*. Oxford: Oxford University Press, 2001.
Morgan, Kenneth O., *Callaghan: A Life*. Oxford: Oxford University Press, 1997.
Morgan, Kenneth O., *Labour in Power 1945–1951*. Oxford: Clarendon Press, 1984.
Mortimer, Rex, *Indonesian Communism under Sukarno: Ideology and Politics 1959–1965*. Singapore: Equinox Publishing, 2006 (1974).
Moyar, Mark, *Triumph Forsaken: The Vietnam War 1954–1965*. Cambridge: Cambridge University Press, 2009.
Murfett, Malcolm H., 'A Keystone of Imperial Defence or a Millstone Around Britain's Neck? Singapore 1919–1941', in Malcolm H. Murfett, John N. Miksic, Brian P. Farrell and Chiang Ming Shun (eds), *Between Two Oceans: A Military History of Singapore from 1275 to 1971* (2nd edn). Singapore: Marshall Cavendish, 2011.
Murfett, Malcolm H., *Fool-Proof Relations: The Search for Anglo-American Naval Cooperation During the Chamberlain Years, 1937–40*. Singapore: Singapore University Press, 1984.
Murfett, Malcolm H., *In Jeopardy: The Royal Navy and British Far Eastern Defence Policy 1945–1951*. Kuala Lumpur: Oxford University Press, 1995.
Murfett, Malcolm H., 'Living in the Past: A Critical Re-examination of the Singapore Naval Strategy, 1918–41', *War & Society*, 11, 1993.
Murfett, Malcolm H., 'Look Back in Anger: The Western Powers and the Washington Conference of 1921–22', in B.J.C. McKercher (ed.), *Arms Limitation and Disarmament: Restraints in War, 1899–1939*. Westport, CT: Praeger, 1992.
Murfett, Malcolm H., *Naval Warfare 1919–1945: An Operational History of the Volatile War at Sea*. Abingdon: Routledge, 2009.
Murfett, Malcolm H., 'Phillips, Sir Tom Spencer Vaughan', in Brian Harrison (ed.), *Oxford Dictionary of National Biography*,44. Oxford: Oxford University Press, 2004.

Murfett, Malcolm H., 'Reflections on an Enduring Theme: The "Singapore Strategy" at Sixty', in Brian Farrell and Sandy Hunter (eds), *A Great Betrayal? The Fall of Singapore Revisited*. Singapore: Marshall Cavendish, 2010.
Murfett, Malcolm H., ' "The Times They Are A-Changin": Britain's Military Commitment to Singapore, 1967–1971', in Brian P. Farrell (ed.), *Churchill and the Lion City: Shaping Modern Singapore*. Singapore: NUS Press, 2011.
Murfett, Malcolm H., 'What's in it for Us? Rethinking the British Defence Commitment to Singapore and Malaysia from Macmillan to Wilson', in Malcolm H. Murfett (ed.), *Cold War Southeast Asia*. Singapore: Marshall Cavendish, 2012.
Murfett, Malcolm H., 'When Trust is Not Enough: Australia and the Singapore Strategy', in Carl Bridge and Bernard Attard (eds), *Between Empire and Nation: Australia's External Relations, 1901–39*. Melbourne: Australian Scholarly Publishing, 2000.
Neilson, Keith, 'Perception and Posture in Anglo-American Relations: The Legacy of the Simon-Stimson Affair, 1932–41', *International History Review*, 29, 2, 2007.
Neilson, Keith, 'The Defence Requirements Sub-Committee, British Strategic Foreign Policy, Neville Chamberlain and the Path to Appeasement', *English Historical Review*, 118, 2003.
Neilson, Keith and Otte, Thomas, *The Permanent Under-Secretary for Foreign Affairs*. Abingdon: Routledge, 2009.
Nicolson, Harold, 'British Public Opinion and Foreign Policy', *Public Opinion Quarterly*, 1, 1937.
Nicolson, Harold, 'The Colonial Problem', *International Affairs*, 17, 1938.
Nicolson, Harold, 'What France Means to England', *Foreign Affairs*, 17, 1939.
Nicolson, Harold, *Why Britain is at War*. Harmondsworth: Penguin, 1939.
Nish, Ian, *Alliance in Decline: A Study in Anglo-Japanese Relations, 1908–23*. London: Athlone Press, 1972.
Nish, Ian, 'Echoes of Alliance, 1920–30', in Ian Nish and Yoichi Kibata (eds), *The History of Anglo-Japanese relations 1600–2000: I: The Political-Diplomatic Dimension, 1600–1930*. Basingstoke: Macmillan, 2000.
Northedge, F.S., *The Troubled Giant: Britain among the Great Powers, 1916–1939*. London: LSE and Bell, 1966.
O'Hara, Glen, 'Attempts to Modernize: Nationalization and the Nationalized Industries in Post-War Britain', in Franco Amatori, Robert Millward and Pier Angelo Toninelli (eds), *Reappraising State-Owned Enterprise: A Comparison of the UK and Italy*. London: Routledge, 2011.
Olson, Lynne, *Troublesome Young Men: The Rebels Who Brought Churchill to Power*. New York: Farrar, Straus & Giroux, 2007.
Orde, Anne, *Great Britain and International Security, 1920–1926*. London: Royal Historical Society, 1978.
Orde, Anne, 'The Origins of the German-Austrian Customs Union Affair of 1931', *Central European History*, 13, 1980.
O'Riordan, Elspeth, *Britain and the Ruhr Crisis*. Basingstoke: Palgrave Macmillan, 2001.
Osada, Sadao, 'From Washington to London: the Imperial Japanese Navy and the Politics of Naval Limitation, 1921–30', in Erik Goldstein and John Maurer (eds), *The Washington Conference, 1921–22: Naval Rivalry, East Asian Stability and the Road to Pearl Harbor*. London: Frank Cass, 1994.

Osterhammel, Jürgen, 'China', in Judith M. Brown and Wm Roger Louis (eds), *The Oxford History of the British Empire, vol. 4: The Twentieth Century*. Oxford: Oxford University Press, 1999.
Otte, Thomas, 'Nicolson', in G.R. Berridge, Maurice Keens-Soper and Thomas Otte (eds), *Diplomatic Theory from Machiavelli to Kissinger*. Basingstoke: Macmillan, 2001.
Overy, Richard, *Air Power, Armies and the War in the West, 1940*. Colorado Springs: US Air Force Academy, 1989.
Parker, R.A.C. *Chamberlain and Appeasement: British Policy and the Coming of the Second World War*. London: Macmillan, 1993.
Pearce, Robert D., *Attlee's Labour Governments 1945–51*. London: Taylor & Francis, 2006.
Pearl, Cyril, *Morrison of Peking*. Sydney: Angus & Robertson, 1967.
Peden, George C., *Arms, Economics and British Strategy*. Cambridge: Cambridge University Press, 2007.
Peden, George C., *British Rearmament and the Treasury, 1932–1939*. Edinburgh: Scottish Academic Press, 1979.
Penders, C.L.M. and Sundhaussen, U., *Abdul Haris Nasution: A Political Biography*. St. Lucia, QD: University of Queensland Press, 1985.
Peters, Anthony R., *Anthony Eden at the Foreign Office 1931–1938*. Aldershot: Gower, 1986.
Pickering, Jeffrey, *Britain's Withdrawal From East of Suez: The Politics of Retrenchment*. London: Macmillan, 1998.
Pham, P.L., *Ending 'East of Suez': The British Decision to Withdraw from Malaysia and Singapore 1964–1968*. Oxford: Oxford University Press, 2010.
Pollitt, Christopher, 'The Central Policy Review Staff 1970–1974', *Public Administration*, 52, 1974.
Prados, John, *Operation Vulture*. New York: IBooks, 2002.
Pratt, Lawrence, *East of Malta, West of Suez: Britain's Mediterranean Crisis, 1936–39*. Cambridge: Cambridge University Press, 1975.
Pratt, Lawrence, 'The Anglo-American Naval Conversations on the Far East of January 1938', *International Affairs*, 48, 1971.
Ransome, Arthur *The Chinese Puzzle*. London: George Allen & Unwin, 1927.
Ratcliff, R.A., *Delusions of Intelligence: Enigma, Ultra, and the End of Secure Ciphers*. Cambridge: Cambridge University Press, 2006.
Reynolds, David, *Britannia Overruled: British Policy and World Power in the Twentieth Century*. London: Longman, 1991.
Reynolds, David, *From World War to Cold War: Churchill, Roosevelt, and the International History of the 1940s*. Oxford: Oxford University Press, 2006.
Reynolds, David. *In Command of History*. New York: Basic Books, 2007.
Ricklefs, Merle C., *A History of Modern Indonesia since c.1200* (4th edn), Basingstoke: Palgrave Macmillan, 2008.
Roberts, Andrew, *'The Holy Fox'. A Biography of Lord Halifax*. London: Weidenfeld & Nicolson, 1991.
Roi, Michael L., *Alternative to Appeasement. Sir Robert Vansittart and Alliance Diplomacy, 1934–1937*. Westport, Praeger, 1997.
Roi, Michael L., 'From the Stresa Front to the Triple Entente. Sir Robert Vansittart, the Abyssinian Crisis and the Containment of Germany', *Diplomacy and Statecraft*, 6, 1995.

Roosa, John, *Pretext for Mass Murder: The September 30th Movement and Suharto's Coup d'état in Indonesia*. Madison: University of Wisconsin Press, 2006.
Rose, Norman, *Harold Nicolson*. London: Jonathan Cape, 2005.
Rowse, A.L., *All Souls and Appeasement*. London: Macmillan, 1961.
Ruggiero, John, *Neville Chamberlain and British Rearmament: Pride, Prejudice and Politics*. Westport, CT: Greenwood Press, 1999.
Sale, Tony, 'The Colossus of Bletchley Park – The German Cipher System', in R.H. Rojas (ed.), *The First Computers: History and Architecture*. Cambridge, MA: The MIT Press, 2000.
Self, Robert, *Neville Chamberlain: A Biography*. Farnham: Ashgate, 2006.
Self, Robert, 'Perception and Posture in Anglo-American Relations: The War Debt Controversy in the "Official Mind", 1919–1940', *International History Review*, 29, 2007.
Shay, Robert P., *British Rearmament in the Thirties*, Princeton, NJ: Princeton University Press, 1977.
Shih, Hu, 'The Renaissance in China', *Journal of the British Institute of International Affairs*, November 1926.
Short, Anthony, *In Pursuit of Mountain Rats: The Communist Insurrection in Malaya*. Singapore: Cultured Lotus, 2001.
Smith, Michael, 'An Undervalued Effort: How the British Broke Japan's Codes', in Michael Smith and Ralph Erskine (eds), *Action This Day*. London: Bantam, 2001.
Smith, Michael, *The Emperor's Codes: Bletchley Park and the Breaking of Japan's Secret Ciphers*. London: Bantam, 2000.
Stambrook, F.G., 'The German-Austrian Customs Union Project of 1931: A Study of German Methods and Motives', *Journal of Central European Affairs*, 21, 1961–62.
Stedman, Andrew David, *Then What Could Chamberlain Do, Other Than What Chamberlain Did? A Synthesis and Analysis of the Alternatives to Chamberlain's Policy of Appeasing Germany*. PhD thesis, University of Kingston, 2007.
Stripp, Alan, *Codebreaker in the Far East*. London: Frank Cass, 1989.
Subritzky, John, *Confronting Sukarno: British, American, Australian and New Zealand Diplomacy in the Malaysian-Indonesian Confrontation, 1961–65*. Basingstoke: Macmillan, 2000.
Sundhaussen, U., *The Road to Power: Indonesian Military Politics 1945–1967*. Oxford: Oxford University Press, 1982.
Suzuki, Shogo, *Civilization and Empire: China and Japan's Encounter with European International Society*. London: Routledge, 2009.
Tan Tai Yong, *Creating 'Greater Malaysia': Decolonization and the Politics of Merger*. Singapore; Institute of Southeast Asian Studies, 2008.
Tan Tai Yong, 'The Cold War and the Making of Singapore', in Malcolm H. Murfett (ed.), *Cold War Southeast Asia*. Singapore: Marshall Cavendish, 2012.
Tarling, Nicholas, *Britain, Southeast Asia, and the Impact of the Korean War*. Singapore: NUS Press, 2005.
Thorpe, D.R., *Eden. The Life and Times of Anthony Eden. First Earl of Avon, 1897–1977*. London: Chatto, 2003.
Tiersky, Ronald, *Francois Mitterand: A Very French President*. Lanham, MD: Rowman & Littlefield, 2003.

Trotter, Ann, *Britain and East Asia 1933–1937*. London: Cambridge University Press, 1975.
Trotter, Ann, 'Tentative Steps for an Anglo-Japanese Rapprochement in 1934', *Modern Asian Studies*, 8, 1 (1974).
Tuck, Christopher, *Confrontation, Strategy and War Termination: Britain's Conflict with Indonesia*. London: Ashgate, 2013.
Turnbull, Constance M., *A History of Modern Singapore 1819–2005*. Singapore: NUS Press, 2009.
Ven, Hans van de, 'Bombing, Japanese Pan-Asianism and Chinese Nationalism', in Antony Best (ed.), *The International History of East Asia, 1900–1968: Trade, Ideology and the Quest for Order*. London: Routledge, 2010.
Waddington, Geoff. T., ' *"Hassgegner"*: German Views of Great Britain in the Later 1930s', *History*, 81, 1996.
Walker, David, *Anxious Nation: Australia and the Rise of Asia 1850–1939*. St. Lucia, QD: University of Queensland Press, 1999.
Wark, Wesley K., *The Ultimate Enemy. British Intelligence and Nazi Germany 1933–1939*. Oxford: Oxford University Press, 1986.
Webster, Sir Charles and Frankland, Noble, *The Strategic Air Offensive against Germany, Vol. I*. London: HMSO, 1961.
Weinberg, Gerhard L., *The Foreign Policy of Hitler's Germany. Starting World War Two, 1937–39*. Chicago: University of Chicago Press, 1980.
Weinstein, F.B., *Indonesia Abandons Confrontation: An Inquiry into the Functions of Indonesian Foreign Policy*. Singapore: Equinox Publishing, 2009.
Weinstein, F.B., *Indonesian Foreign Policy and the Dilemma of Dependence: From Sukarno to Soeharto*. Singapore: Equinox Publishing, 2007.
Westad, Odd Arne, *The Global Cold War: Third World Interventions and the Making of Our Times*. Cambridge: Cambridge University Press, 2007.
Wilby, Peter, *Eden*. London: Haus Publishing, 2006.
Yong, C.F. and McKenna, R.B., *The Kuomintang Movement in British Malaya, 1912–1949*. Singapore: Singapore University Press, 1990.
Yoshimura, Michio, 'Nichi–Ei kyūtei kōryu shi no ichimen: sono seijiteki seikaku to hiseijiteki seikaku', in Yoichi Kibata, Ian Nish, Chihiro Hosoya and Takahiko Tanaka (eds), *Nichi–Ei kōryu shi, vol.1, Seiji–Gaikō*. Tokyo: Tokyo Daigaku Shuppankai, 2000.
Young, John W., 'The Wilson Government's Reform of Intelligence Co-ordination, 1967–68', *Intelligence and National Security*, 16, 2001.
Zheng, Yangwen, *The Social Life of Opium in China*. Cambridge, Cambridge University Press, 2005.

Newspapers and Periodicals

English Review, 'Current Comments', February 1927.
The Daily Telegraph, 'Obituaries: Lt-Cdr Teddy Poulden', 20 November 1992.
The Round Table, 'The Imperial Conference', September 1921.
The Round Table, 'The Problem of Japan', June 1930.
The Spectator, 'News of the Week', 29 August 1925.
The Times, 1 March 1845; 12 August 1936; 3 October 1936; 18 March 1939.

Index

Note: 'n.' after a page reference denotes a note number on that page.

Abyssinia, 5, 98, 113–14, 116, 118, 133n.24, 138, 140–1, 143
Académie française, 18
Acheson, Dean, 193, 231, 232n.1
Acton, Harold, 33
Aden, 171
Addis Ababa, 118
Admiralty, 6, 71, 73, 75–6, 100, 160–2, 167
Afro-Asian bloc (*see* Non-Aligned Movement)
Agincourt, 26
air defence, 76, 86, 88–9, 93, 97, 101–4, 106
Air Ministry, 100
Alexandria, 166
All Souls College (Oxford), 13, 146
Allen of Hurtwood, Lord, 119
A.M. Azahari, 194
Amery, Leo, 143, 147–9
Anderson, HMS, 242
Andrew, Christopher, 20
Anglo-American relations, 3, 8, 29, 34, 41, 50, 65–73, 77–8, 81–2, 131, 165, 193, 241
Anglo-French relations, 41–2, 105, 114
Anglo-German Naval Agreement (1935), 5, 113, 122
Anglo-German relations, 5, 104, 112, 117–18, 120–2, 124, 126–9, 139
Anglo-Japanese Alliance (1902), 6, 26, 29–30, 34, 69–70, 79, 159–60
Anglo-Japanese relations, 27–8, 35, 75, 78
Anglo-Malayan Defence Agreement (AMDA), 175, 184–5
Anschluss, 43, 113, 130
Anson, HMS, 242

anti-aircraft defence, 89, 91, 93, 95, 98, 103
anti-colonialism, 194–5
Anti-Comintern Pact, 5, 120, 122
ANZAM (Australia, New Zealand and Malaya), 172
ANZUS Pact (1951), 172, 181, 200
appeasement, 1, 4–5, 12, 19, 53, 64, 67, 81–2, 128, 136–7, 139–40, 142, 145–6, 148–54, 165, 174
Army (*see* Royal Army)
Army Council, 99, 105
artillery, 89, 93, 102–3, 107, 162
Asia-Pacific, 160
'Atlantic Charter', 167
Atlas Computer Laboratory (AERE Harwell), 247
Attlee, Clement (Earl Attlee), 7, 147, 169–73
Australia (*see also* forward defence), 159
  defence agreements, 172–3, 175, 185, 192n.114, 200
  defence bases for Southeast Asia, 201, 215, 217, 225–8
  Far East 7, 22, 172, 221, 225–6, 230–1
  France, 207
  Japan, 28–30, 161
  Konfrontasi 195–6, 203, 210, 212, 217, 221–3, 226
  Maphilindo, 178
  signals intelligence (Sigint), 242
  Vietnam, 218, 223, 229, 236n.44
  'White Australia' policy, 30
Austria, 3, 43–4, 48, 52, 87, 92, 113, 125, 127, 143, 145, 152, 165
Author's Club (London), 28

Automatic Data Processing,
    243-4
automatic message switching, 243
Axis Powers, 36, 103

Baden Pusat Intelijen (BPI), 194, 209
Baldwin, Stanley, 78, 87, 94, 113, 118,
    124-5, 138, 165
Ball, George, 219, 222
Bangkok Agreement (1966), 228
Bank of England, 47, 56
Bank of France, 47, 51
Bank of International Settlements, 48,
    50, 57
Barlow, Sir Alan, 105
Basle, 51
Basle Committee, 57
BBC (British Broadcasting
    Corporation), 18, 148, 150
Beijing, 23-4, 28, 176, 190n.69, 217
Belgium, 4, 92, 103, 119
    defence of, 59, 87, 90-1, 94, 98, 100,
        107, 120, 141
    independence of, 88, 101, 141
Benn, Anthony Neil Wedgwood
    ('Tony'), 244-5
Bennett, Gill, 107
Berchtesgaden, 130, 147
Berlin, 43-5, 51-5, 57n.8, 58, 113,
    115, 121, 124, 136, 140, 172
    German government, synonym for,
        3, 5, 47-50, 52-3, 72, 112,
        124-6, 129-30, 167
Berliner Tageblatt, 54
Berthelot, Philippe, 47, 56
Bevin, Ernest, 173
Bickers, Robert, 23
Bingham, Robert, 73, 75
Birmingham, 165
Blair, Anthony Charles Lynton
    ('Tony'), 192n.113
Blake, Robert (Lord Blake of
    Braydeston), 10
Bletchley Park, 240-1
Blomberg, General Werner von, 124
Blue Shirts, 36
Blum, Leon, 119, 165, 187n.16
bomber aircraft, 4, 87, 89, 94-5, 103,
    107, 212

Bond, Brian, 107
Bonham Carter, Violet (Baroness
    Asquith of Yarnbury), 145
Boothby, Robert John (Baron
    Boothby), 140, 145, 147, 150
Bonsall, Sir Arthur Wilfred ('Bill'), 242
Borneo, 178, 194-5, 202-3, 209-10,
    217, 220, 223
Borough, John, 242
Boxer Rebellion (1900), 25
Boyd, Alan Lennox- (Viscount Boyd of
    Merton), 15
Boyle, Sir Edward (Baron Boyle of
    Handsworth), 15
Bradford, 120
Briand, Aristide, 42, 46, 50, 52, 55
Bridges, Sir Edward (Baron Bridges),
    97, 101-2
British Army of the Rhine (BAOR), 212
British Columbia, 28
British Council, 150
British Defence Coordination
    Committee Far East
    (BDCCFE), 172
British Empire, 2, 6, 28, 30-1, 80, 141,
    168-70
British Expeditionary Force, 4, 86-92,
    94-8, 100-4, 106-7
British Institute of International
    Affairs, 32
British Leyland, 245
British Military Administration, 169
British North Borneo (*see* Sabah)
British withdrawal from Singapore (*see*
    Singapore)
Brotherton Library (University of
    Leeds), 16
Brown, George (Baron George-Brown),
    181-3
Brown House (Munich), 123
Brunei, 177-9, 193-4
Brüning, Dr Heinrich, 42, 46, 49,
    51-4, 58
Brussels Conference (1937), 81
Budapest, 43
Bulgaria, 148
Bullitt, William C., 72, 124
Bülow, Prince Bernhard von, 54, 57-8
Burma, 171

Butler, Richard Austen (Baron Butler of Saffron Walden), 10
Butterworth, 172

Cabinet, 87, 92, 161
  (1931), 47, 49, 55
  (1933–4), 66, 68–9, 75, 77, 80, 86, 89
  (1935–36), 93, 96–7, 115, 118, 133n.40
  (1937–40), 86, 88, 98–102, 104–5, 121, 123, 128, 130, 143, 147
  (1945–51), 170, 172
  (1957–63), 174, 178
  (1964–70), 180, 183–4, 215, 221, 224, 226
Cabinet Office, 241–2, 246, 248–9
Cadogan, Sir Alexander, 11, 19, 129
Cahill, J.R, 47
Callaghan, James (Baron Callaghan of Cardiff), 180–1, 183
Cambodia, 199, 220
Canada, 20, 28, 78
Canadian Studies Committee (University of Leeds), 13
Canberra, 6, 172, 229
Carey, Sir Peter, 246
Caribbean, 167
Carlton, David, 123, 152
Carrington, Lord, 184–5
Castro, Fidel, 176
Cato, 65
Central Department (Foreign Office), 44, 116, 125
Central Europe, 43, 45, 51, 111, 127, 145
Central Intelligence Agency (CIA), 203
Central Policy Review Staff (CPRS), 245–6
Ceylon, 171, 242
Chamberlain, Sir Austen, 42, 58–9
Chamberlain, Hilda, 91–2, 114, 125
Chamberlain, Neville (*see also* Hilda Chamberlain; Harold Nicolson; Sir Thomas Inskip; Sir John Simon; Sir Robert Vansittart; Sir Warren Fisher), 1–3, 11 114, 124, 144–5, 154, 157n.85
  appeasement policy, 5, 12, 19, 80, 125–6, 129–31, 134n.70, 137, 142, 146–50, 153
  Chancellor of the Exchequer, role of, 3, 90–1, 97–8
  Chiefs of Staff, relations with, 87, 90–1, 97–8
  Eden, relations with, 126, 128, 130, 143, 146
  Prime Minister, 99, 125, 151
  rearmament policy, 4, 68, 77, 86–107
  US, attitude towards, 64–70, 72–5, 78–82
  USSR, attitude towards, 152, 165
Changi, 168
Channon, Sir Henry ('Chips'), 139, 144
Chatfield, Admiral Sir Ernle (later Lord), 71, 73, 75–7, 104–5
Cheltenham, 240–1, 246, 248
Chiefs of Staff (COS), 81, 86–8, 90–2, 97–8, 101, 103–4, 128, 166, 171–3, 229
China, 2, 21–9, 31–6, 68, 70, 72–6, 80–1, 98, 152, 161, 167 (*see also* People's Republic of China)
Chinese Civil War, 171, 196
Chippewa Falls (Minnesota), 241
Chirol, Sir Valentine, 23
Churchhouse, Professor Robert ('Bob'), 247
Churchill, Sir Winston, 5, 151–2, 164, 173
  Anglo-American relations, 64–5, 81, 173, 242
  appeasement policy, 1, 140, 143–4, 147–9, 154
  Attlee, Clement, relations with, 169–70
  Chamberlain, Neville, assessment of, 64–5
  defence policy, 142–3, 145, 150, 152, 198
  Eden, relations with, 1, 130
  rearmament policy, 87–8
  Singapore, 6, 167–9
Ciano, Count Galeazzo, 135n.88
Clifford, Nicholas, 23, 32

Index

Clinton, President William Jefferson ('Bill'), 192n.113
Clunies Ross, Ian, 24
'CoCom' (Coordinating Committee for Multilateral Export Controls), 245
COINS (Community On-line Intelligence System), 243
Cold Store, Operation, 190n.69
Cold War, 1, 7, 20, 171–3, 175–6, 182, 195–6, 198, 201, 203–7, 209, 216, 219, 231
collective security, 7, 33, 114, 118, 164, 194–6, 199, 201, 211, 214–17, 219–21, 224–5, 227–31
colonial administration, 29, 169–71, 194, 196, 200, 204, 208
colonial questions, 116, 120–4, 127–8, 130–1, 134n.53, 146, 173
Colonial Exhibition (Paris), 51
Comert, Pierre, 43–4
Committee of Imperial Defence (CID), 86, 88–9, 102–3, 161
Committee on Higher Education (1963), 15
Commonwealth (*see also* Commonwealth Strategic Reserve; *Konfrontasi*), 2, 6–7, 201, 216
   British withdrawal from Singapore, 183–5
   Five Power Defence Arrangement, 184
   Japan, relations with, 2, 164
   Malaysia, formation of, 194–6
   Southeast Asia, defence of, 6–7, 163, 167–9, 180, 202, 208, 210, 217, 220–1
Commonwealth Strategic Reserve (CSR), 172, 175
Commonwealth Youth Exchange Council, 13
communications, 28, 101, 107
Communications-Electronic Security Group, 240
communications security, 250n.1
communications technologies, 8, 243, 246
communism (*see also* PKI), 84n.25, 196
   dangers posed by, 171, 173, 196, 198
   Germany, possibilities in, 45–6, 119–20
   Southeast Asia, threat to, 8, 171, 176, 195–6, 198–201, 204–5, 208–9, 215–16, 221, 226
   Vietnam, threat posed in, 7, 181, 197, 205, 209, 214, 216, 218, 223
computer industry (UK), 241–9
'Computer Mergers Scheme', 244
Confrontation (*see Konfrontasi*)
Congress (*see also* Senate), 64–5, 75, 79, 81–2, 197, 209
Connaught, Prince Arthur of, 27
Conservative and Unionist Party, 10, 33–5, 87, 144, 149, 152, 169–71, 173, 175, 179, 184
conscription, 105, 113
containment, 64, 114, 197–8, 207–8, 211, 221, 226–7
continental commitment, 3–4, 66, 86, 90, 102–3, 106
continental warfare, 102, 104, 106
Cooper, Alfred Duff (Viscount Norwich), 94–7, 99, 120, 141, 148–9
Cooper, Arthur, 241
Cooper, Josh, 241
Cottrell, Sir Alan Howard, 245
counterinsurgency operations, 198, 209, 212, 226
Craigie, Sir Robert, 71–2, 76, 82
Cray, Seymour, 241
CRAY supercomputers, 241
Creditanstalt, 165
Cripps, Sir Stafford, 172
Crossman, Richard, 182
cryptanalysis, 244, 246
cryptography, 240–1, 244
Cuba, 176
Curtius, Julius, 50, 52–4, 57–8
Curzon, George Nathaniel (Marquess Curzon of Kedleston), 10–11, 26
Customs Union (Austro-German), 43–6, 48–52, 59

Cyprus, 208
Czech army, 103
Czechoslovakia, 4, 105, 127, 141, 146–8, 150–1, 165, 208

Dallas, 206
Danat Bank, 51
Danube, 44
Danzig, 127, 150
Davis, Norman, 70, 79
De Gaulle, President Charles, 207–9, 217
Deakin, Alfred, 28
decolonisation, 170, 194–6, 201, 208
defence estimates, 181, 227, 244
Defence Intelligence Staff, 243–4
Defence Loans Act (1937), 101
Defence, Ministry of, 86, 180, 184, 210, 249
Defence and Overseas Policy Committee (OPD), 215
Defence Plans (Policy) Committee, 99
Defence Policy and Requirements Committee (DPRC), 94
Defence Requirements Sub-Committee (DRC), 65–9, 72–3, 75, 77, 79–80, 88–96, 98, 104, 112, 114, 125
Defence Reviews, 171, 182, 211, 222, 224, 226
Defence Signals Bureau (DSB), 242
Defence White Paper (1957), 175; (1966), 228–9
Democratic Party (US), 196
Democratic Republic of Vietnam (DRV), 196, 204, 208–9, 218
Denmark, 166
Department of Pensions, 249
Department of Trade and Industry, 245, 248
deterrence, 6, 82, 87, 90–1, 94–5, 100, 103, 106–7, 162, 167, 173, 201, 212–13, 247
Deutschland, 48
devaluation crisis, 8, 179–80, 183–5
Deverell, Sir Cyril, 96, 99
Dewar, Captain A.R., 74
Dien Bien Phu, 197, 199
Dilks, David N., 1–2, 9–20, 37, 87, 137, 193, 231

Dilks, Jill, 14
Dilks, Richard, 14
diplomacy, 4, 29, 43, 82, 87, 96, 114, 129, 139, 155n.10, 199, 202
  Chamberlain's diplomacy, 147–8, 151, 165
  China, diplomacy towards, 198
  'direct diplomacy', 127
  'gunboat diplomacy', 34
  Hoare's diplomacy, 138
  Japan, diplomacy towards, 66, 76–7
  Locarno diplomacy, 45, 55, 59–60
  'new diplomacy', 41
disarmament, 44, 46, 58–9, 67, 69, 73, 128, 132n.23, 139, 151, 160, 164
Disarmament Committee (UK), 65, 73, 76–7, 89–90, 92, 94
Disarmament Conference (1932–4), 45–6, 51, 53, 68, 70, 72, 77, 79, 112, 119, 132n.23
Disraeli, Benjamin, 192n.113
Dobbie, Major-General Sir William, 166
Dodd, William E., 72
Dominions Office, 75–6
'domino theory', 7, 171, 197, 199
Draft Treaty of Mutual Guarantee, 41
Drax-Backhouse scheme, 167
Dreyer, Admiral Sir Frederick, 74
Drinkwater, Derek, 150, 153
Drummond, Sir Eric, 43
Dulles, John Foster, 173
Dutch East Indies, 74
Dutton, David, 153

East Asia, 2, 21–40, 69, 74–6, 152, 159, 172
East Indies Fleet, 242
east of Suez (*see* Suez)
Eastern Europe, 41, 43, 45, 48, 119, 122, 124, 128, 131, 141–2, 145, 148, 153, 208
Eastern Fleet, 168
economic crisis, 42–3, 45, 65, 67, 112, 181
economic sanctions, 79, 141

Eden, Sir Anthony [Earl of Avon] (*see also* Eden Group)
   Anglo-American relations, 79, 81, 165
   appeasement, opposition to, 1, 5, 128–9, 131, 135n.88, 142
   Blum, Leon, relations with, 119
   Chamberlain, Neville, relations with, 125–6, 128, 130, 143, 146–50
   Germany, engagement with, 4–5, 111, 113, 115–18, 120–31, 132ns.20, 23, 133n.40, 139–40, 153–4
   Suez crisis, 174, 189n.58
Eden Group, 149, 151, 154
Edge, Walter, 49
Egypt, 101–2, 106, 173–4
Eisenhower, President Dwight D., 171, 173, 177, 184, 189n.58, 197
Elliot, Walter, 80
Elliott Automation, 244
Ellington, Sir Edward, 71
Emmerson, James, T., 140
Emrys-Evans, Paul, 144, 146, 156n.38
English Electric-Leo-Marconi Computers, 244
English Review, 30, 33
Eurasian community, 169
Europe, 3, 5, 41, 129, 240 (*see also* Central Europe; Eastern Europe)
   Anglo-American relations and their effects upon, 65, 72–4, 76–7, 79–80, 82, 172–3, 195, 198, 211, 225, 230
   economic crisis in, 43–5, 47–8, 51
   Hitler's attitude towards, 115, 117–18, 120–8, 133n.40, 141, 145, 148
   political stability in, 44–5, 53, 55, 58–60, 118, 140, 152, 163–5
European affairs, 2, 45, 113, 119, 122–3, 125–8, 142, 153, 224
European colonialism, 22, 29, 208
European decline, 168, 196, 200
European diplomacy, 41, 43, 45
European Economic Community (forerunner of European Union), 174

European nations, 4, 22, 35, 43, 46, 59, 94, 98, 114, 124
European security, 67, 73–4, 119, 244–6
European warfare, 76, 86–7, 94–8, 101–4, 106, 166–7
Europe in Arms, 100
expeditionary force (*see* British Expeditionary Force)
Evening Standard, 136
Eyre, Dean, 225, 227
Eyres-Monsell, Sir Bolton, 71, 76, 78, 84n.25

Falklands War, 174
Far East (*see also* 'Singapore Strategy'),
   Anglo-American relations and their effects upon, 67, 70–2, 74, 76–7, 81–2, 165, 167, 218
   Chamberlain's views on, 68
   Cold War in, 172, 175
   instability within, 65, 67
   'near north', 7, 22, 172
   strategic problems posed by, 72, 91, 160–1, 163, 166–7, 172, 175, 182, 221, 224–7
Far East Appreciations, 167
Far East Command, 178, 182, 184–5, 194, 210–13, 217, 223–4, 226–7, 230, 237n.53
Far Eastern crisis (1931–3), 67, 76, 79, 81–2
Far Eastern Department (FO), 68, 71–2
Far Eastern Fleet (*see also* Eastern Fleet), 161
Far Eastern theatre, 91, 160–1, 166
Farrell, Brian, 168
fascism, 35–6, 120, 136–8, 154
Fascists, British Union of, 136
Federal Reserve System, 47
Feiling, Sir Keith Grahame, 65
field force (*see also* British Expeditionary Force)
Fisher, Sir Warren, 68–71, 73, 75–8, 80, 89, 92, 95–6
Five-Power Defence Arrangements (1971), 185, 192n.114

Five-Power Naval Limitation Agreement (*see* Washington Conference 1921–2)
Fleming, Peter, 32
Flowers, Sir Brian Hilton (Baron Flowers), 246
'flying squadron', (*see* Force Z)
'Force de Frappe', 244, 247
Force G, 167, 188n.29
Force Z, 6, 168, 188n.29
Foreign Affairs, 142
Foreign Affairs Committee (House of Commons), 128, 139–40, 142–4, 146
Foreign Office (*see also* appeasement), Anglo-Soviet relations, impact of, 245
  Chamberlain, Neville, relationship with, 134n.70
  computers, effectiveness of, 247
  de-colonisation, issues of, 208
  France, opinion of, 48, 51, 55
  Germany, attitude towards, 4–5, 51, 111–12, 114–16, 118 120–7, 129–31, 148
  Japan, policy towards, 70–1, 73
  political truce, idea of a, 43–4
  Southeast Asia, problems of, 210, 215
  Treasury, relations with, 49, 51, 56–7, 75–6, 81
  US, attitude towards, 68, 71, 73, 245
Foreign Policy Committee, 124
'forward defence', 200, 208, 227, 229, 231
Foster, Paul, 248
France, 4, 187n.16, 244
  Anglo-French alliance, proposed, 141–2, 149
  colonial issues, 196–7
  defensive preparations, 100
  Germany, issues with (1935–8), 111, 117–20, 130–1, 133n.27, 140, 145–6
  Hoare-Laval Pact, 138
  Locarno diplomacy, a new stage of, 41–52, 55, 59
  SEATO, membership of, 173
  security concerns, 70, 140, 152
  warfare in, 87, 89, 94, 98, 100–4, 107, 166
Franco, General Francisco, 36, 142, 145
Franco-German relations, 42–3, 53, 55–6, 59, 112
Franco-Soviet Pact, 116, 119
Fraser, Admiral of the Fleet, Sir Bruce (Baron Fraser of North Cape), 242
French, David, 107
Fujitsu, 248–9

Gainer, St Clair, 123
Gaitskell, Hugh, 189n.58
Gamelin, General Maurice, 103
Gandhi, Mahatma, 127
GCHQ (Government Communications Headquarters), 9, 240–8
GCHQ, X Division, 248
General Electric, 244
Geneva (*see also* Disarmament Conference), 68, 70, 72, 77, 79, 112, 119, 132n.23, 220
Geneva Agreements (1962), 207, 214
Geneva Conference (1954), 197, 199
Geneva Protocol, 41
George VI, King, 82, 124
Germany (*see also* entries for Brüning; Hitler; League of Nations; Stresemann), 3, 5, 29, 132n.23, 133ns.24, 27, 40, 137, 139–41, 147, 165, 213
  Austro-German relations, 43, 48, 51–2, 59
  colonial appeasement, opportunities for, 116, 120–4, 127–8, 130–1, 134n.53, 146
  Deutschland, construction of, 48–52
  domestic politics, 42–3, 59
  economic crisis in, 47–8, 50–1, 56–8, 61n.32
  France, relations with, 45–6, 48, 51–2, 58–9, 61n.32
  Italy, relations with, 35, 146, 164
  Japan, relations with, 30

Germany – *continued*
  military threat posed by, 65–71, 73, 76–7, 80–1, 86–92, 94, 96, 98, 103–6, 112, 137, 141–3, 145, 151–2
  revival of, 42–3, 70, 111–19, 121–31, 140, 143, 147–8, 153
  US, relations with, 44, 48–50
  Versailles, revisions to Treaty of, 41, 44
  war debts, 44, 48–9
  Young Plan, attitude towards the, 42, 44, 48, 50
Global Strategy paper (1952), 174
Goebbels, Joseph, 115, 130, 132n.20
Goering, Herman, 126, 130
Goh Keng Swee, 182, 185
Goldsmiths Company, 15
Gordon Walker, Patrick (Baron Gordon-Walker), 220
Gort, Lord, 103
'Grand Design', 8, 177, 180, 194, 201, 213
grand strategy, 196, 224, 228, 231
Grandi, Count Dino, 144
Great Depression, 2, 43, 59, 112, 165
'Greater Indonesia', 178
'Greater Malaysia', 8, 177–8
'Green Scheme', 162
Grey, Lord, 28
Guernica, 142
'Guided Democracy', 194, 204
'Guilty Men', 65, 137
'gunboat diplomacy', 34
Guomindang (GMD), 22, 33, 36
Gurkhas, 212

Hague Conference, 42
Hailsham, Viscount, 90–1
Halifax, Lord, 104–5, 123, 126–8, 134n.70, 135n.76
Hamilton, Sir Ian, 25, 27–8
Hammerskjöld, Dag, 189n.58
Hankey, Sir Maurice (Baron Hankey), 68, 71, 73, 76, 95, 97–8, 101
Harding, Sir Edward, 76
Harrison, Austin, 30
Hart, Basil Liddell, 4, 94, 99–100, 107
Harvey, Oliver, 129, 149

Harwood Report (1949), 171
Hasluck, Sir Paul, 226, 228–30
Hawaii, 79, 160
Healey, Denis Winston (Baron Healey), 180–5, 211, 221–2, 225–9
Heath, Sir Edward Richard George, 184–5, 245, 249
Henderson, Arthur, 45, 49–58
Henderson, Sir Neville, 130, 134n.53
Hertford College, Oxford, 11
Hevia, James, 25
Hindenburg, Paul von, 50
History, School of (University of Leeds), 13–14
Hitler, Adolf, 1, 3, 5, 82, 104–5, 112–28, 139–41, 143, 145, 165
  Chamberlain, Neville, relations with, 125, 128, 131, 137, 147–51
  Eden, relations with, 113, 115–18, 130, 132n.23, 133n.40, 153
  Halifax, meeting with, 123, 126–8, 135n.76
  Mussolini, relations with, 118–19
  Rhineland, march into, 117, 139
Ho Chi Minh, 7, 171, 196, 208
Hoare, Sir Samuel (*see also* Templewood, Viscount)
Hoare-Laval Pact (1935), 4, 114–15, 118, 138–9, 154
Hobhouse, Christopher, 137
Hoesch, Leopold von, 54
Hohler, Thomas, 27
Holland (*see* Netherlands)
Holmes, Colin, 26
Holt, Harold, 225
Holyoake, Sir Keith, 213
Hong Kong, 160–1, 192n.117, 212
Hopkins, Sir Richard, 105
Home, Alec Douglas (Baron Home of the Hirsel), 10, 179, 206
Hong Kong, 160–1, 192n.117, 212
Honolulu, 74, 79
Hooper, Sir Leonard James ('Joe'), 243–5
Hoover Herbert, 3, 44, 47–9, 51–2, 56
Hoover Moratorium, 44, 47–8, 56
Hore-Belisha, Leslie (Baron Hore-Belisha), 99–105

Hossbach Conference, 135n.76
House of Commons, 47, 88, 130, 136, 138, 140–3, 146–50, 152–3, 192n.113, 211
Howard, Sir Michael, 86, 90, 102, 106
Hu Shih, 32
Hughes, William Morris, 30–1
Hull, University of, 15–18

IBM, 241, 247–9
ICL (International Computers Limited), 244–9
ICL 2900 series, (*see also* 'New Range'), 249
ICL 4–70, 246–7
Iikura, Akira, 27
Immigration Act (1924), 31
Imperial Conference (1921), 30; (1926), 58
imperial defence (*see also* Committee of Imperial Defence), 4, 66, 71, 98, 106, 160, 165
Imperial Japanese Army (IJA), 29–30, 165–6
Imperial Japanese Navy (IJN), 2, 160–2, 166
imperialism, 21, 23, 30, 36, 164, 194
India, 11, 22, 25–6, 66, 159, 171, 199, 208, 220
Indian Ocean, 167, 225, 227
Indochina, 196–7, 205, 208, 217
Indo-Pacific theatre, 225, 227, 230
Indomitable, HMS, 167
Indonesia (*see also Konfrontasi*, Soeharto; Sukarno), 7, 177–80, 194–6, 201–7, 209–10, 212–13, 217, 219, 221, 223–4, 231, 237n.52
infantry, 88–9, 92, 95–100, 102–4, 107, 162, 212, 218
Information, Ministry of, 136
Ingersoll, Capt. Royal E., 82
Ingersoll-Phillips conversations (1938), 165
Inland Revenue, 249
Inskip, Sir Thomas, 95–104
Inskip Report (1937), 99, 102–3, 106
Institute for International Studies (University of Leeds), 16

Institute of Pacific Relations (IPR), 33
intelligence-gathering, 8, 19–20, 92, 103, 180, 194–5, 240–50
Inter-Allied Military Control Commission, 42
International Committee for the History of the Second World War, 18
International Computers and Tabulators, 244
International History and Politics (Leeds), 11–14, 16
international security, 42
internationalism, 25, 32, 34–6
Ion, Hamish, 26
Iriye, Akira, 24
isolationism, 64–5, 95
Italy, 35, 44, 65–6, 80, 98, 137, 142–4, 165
  Abyssinian invasion, 113–14, 138, 141
  Germany, relations with, 125–6, 129, 131, 146, 164

J Division (GCHQ), 242
Jakarta, 179–80, 194, 205, 222–3, 228
Japan (*see also* IJA & IJN), 2–3, 84n.25, 98, 169, 248
  Anglo-Japanese Alliance, 2, 6, 26 30–1, 34–6, 68–70, 79, 101, 159–60
  Anti-Comintern Pact (1936), 120
  European dictatorships, relations with, 129, 131, 137, 142, 165
  Manchurian crisis (1931–3), 67–8, 81
  military threat posed by, 3, 6, 22, 28–31, 35, 64–6, 71–2, 75–9, 82, 88, 91, 129, 142, 152, 161–8, 185
  Western image of, 22–31, 33–6, 71, 73–6, 80–1, 220
Japanese Occupation (Singapore), 6, 169
Java, 223, 237n.52
Jellicoe, Admiral Sir John Rushworth (Earl Jellicoe), 160–2, 164

Jenkins, Roy (Baron Jenkins of Hillhead), 183
Jiang Jieshi, 36
Johnson, Senator Hiram Warren, 77
Johnson, President Lyndon Baines ('LBJ'), (*see also* Cold War; *Konfrontasi*), 180, 184, 218, 236n.44, 243
Johor, 163, 166, 209
Johor Strait, 176
Joint Intelligence Committee, 243
Joll, James, 246
Jones, Howard, 205

Kalimantan, 178, 193, 202, 209, 211–12, 217
Katō Kanji, Admiral, 159
Keith, Commander Bruce, 242
Kennedy, Aubrey L., 52, 55, 113
Kennedy, President John Fitzgerald ('JFK'), 177, 184, 193, 204–6, 219
Kennedy, Robert Francis, 113, 206, 209
Kenya, 208
Keppel Harbour (Singapore), 162
Keynes, John Maynard, 170
Kim Il Sung, 172
King George VI dry dock, 165
Kirkwood, Kenneth, 23
Konfrontasi, 7–8, 178–81, 190n.82, 194–6, 203–7, 209, 211–17, 221–6, 228–31
Korea, 26, 172–3
Korean War (1950–3), 171–3, 197–8
KOSTRAD, 222
Kowner, Rotem, 23
Kuala Lumpur, 177, 179, 183, 203

Labour Party, 60, 136, 144–8, 152, 160, 164, 169–73, 179, 181, 184, 210, 218, 229, 235n.35
Labour Government (1964–66, 1966–70), (*see also Konfrontasi*; Singapore), 218, 235n.35, 236n.44, 244
Laos, 199, 205, 207–8, 220
Laurier, Sir Wilfrid, 28
Lausanne Conference, 57, 68

Laval, Pierre, 4, 45, 47, 52–3, 56, 114–15, 118, 138–9, 154
Layton, Sir Walter, 47
League of Nations, 33, 115–16, 118, 120, 129, 144, 153, 164
  Abyssinian crisis, 5, 138, 140–1
  Covenant of, 30, 41
  Germany's membership of, 45, 67, 112, 116, 128, 139
  Manchurian crisis, 34–6, 79
  Mandates, 74
  US attitude towards, 34, 65, 67, 79
Leamington Spa, 120, 123
Le Bailly, Vice-Admiral Sir Louis, 244
Lee Kuan Yew, 168, 176–7, 179, 181–6 190n.69, 202–3 222, 230
Leeds, University of, 10–18, 20
Leeper, Rex, 55
Leicester, West, 136, 144, 149
Let Us Face the Future, 170
Leith-Ross, Sir Frederick William, 54–5, 124
Lend-Lease, 170
Levant, 171
Liddell Hart, Basil, 4, 94, 99–100, 107
Lim Yew Hock, 176
Lindley, Sir Francis Oswald, 71
Lindsay, Sir Ronald, 48, 74, 82, 165
Lippmann, Walter, 219
Litvinov, Maxim, 113
Lloyd, Selwyn (Baron Selwyn-Lloyd), 189n.58
Lloyd George, David, 32, 41, 144, 161
Locarno agreement (1925), 2–3, 5, 41–2, 45, 58–60, 112, 116–17, 119, 133n.40, 139–40, 163
London (*see also* London Conference (1931); London Naval Conference (1935); London Study Group), 28, 30, 32–3, 45, 47, 50–1, 58, 60, 68, 82, 90, 94, 119, 123, 125, 130, 166, 180, 182, 184–5, 208, 211, 215, 218–19, 221, 223, 229
  synonym for British government & UK, 2–3, 5, 7–8, 41–2, 44, 49, 51, 64–7, 69, 111, 116, 119, 146, 161, 170, 173, 181, 198
London Conference (1931), 51–7

Index 283

London Naval Conference (1935), 66, 69–71, 73, 75, 77, 80–1, 84n.25
London Study Group, 230
Lothian, Lord (Philip Kerr), 28
Low Countries, 91, 104, 166
LSE (London School of Economics and Political Science), 11, 13–14, 20
Luftwaffe, 89–90, 94, 103, 142
Luther, Hans, 51
Lyons, Joseph, 244

Macapagal, Diosdado, 178
MacDonald, J. Ramsay, 3, 51–5, 57, 67, 78, 164
MacDonald, Malcolm, 145, 172, 177
Machines Bull, 244
Macmillan, Harold (Earl of Stockton), 7–8, 10–11, 147, 149, 174–9, 184, 206, 208, 217
McNamara, Robert, 224
Madras, 160
Maginot Line, 100, 164
Main Fleet (UK), 6, 162–4, 166
Maisky, Ivan, 150, 152
Malaya, 6, 22, 161–3, 166, 168–72, 175–7, 194–5, 198, 202–3, 208–10, 217
Malayan Communist Party (MCP), 8
Malayan Emergency, 7–8, 171, 200
Malaysia (*see also* 'Grand Design'; 'Greater Malaysia'; *Konfrontasi*; *Maphilindo*), 182, 185, 195, 202, 208, 210, 220, 227
Malta, 163
Manchester, 148, 250
Manchester Guardian 32
Manchu monarchy, 28
Manchurian crisis, 35, 112
Manchukuo, 2, 164
Manila, 74
Manila Pact, 7, 199, 202
Mao Zedong, 7, 171
Maphilindo, 178, 202–3
Marco Polo Bridge incident (1937), 164
Marshall, David, 176, 190n.69
Marshall Plan, 172
Masaryk, Jan, 113
Massey, Sir Vincent, 25

Mediterranean, 44, 118, 145, 163, 167
Medlicott, William Norton, 14
Meiji, Emperor, 27
Melaka, Straits of, 209
Mellon, Andrew W., 49
Menzies, Sir Robert, 217–18, 221
MI5, 241
MI6, 241
Middle East, 163, 173, 182
Middlemas, Keith, 126
military withdrawal (UK forces from Singapore), 173–4, 181–5, 192ns.114, 117, 199, 206, 226–7, 231
Ministerial Committee on the Naval Conference, 73, 75–7
Ministry of Defence, 180, 184, 210, 249
Ministry of Information, 136
Ministry of Supply, 105
Ministry of Technology, 244–5
Minorca, 145, 154
mobilisation, 102, 104
modernity, 24–6, 36
Montgomery of Alamein, Field Marshal Viscount, 86, 106
Montgomery-Massingberd, Sir Archibald, 71, 88, 92–4
Moore, Gordon E., 252n.33
Moore's Law, 246
Morrison, G.E., 28
Moscow, 18, 115, 121, 176, 245
Mosley, Oswald, 136–7
Admiral Earl Mountbatten of Burma, 242
Mukden incident (1931), 2–3
Munich, 123
Munich settlement (1938), 12, 103–4, 144, 147–50, 152–3
munitions, 95, 101–2, 106, 112, 115–16, 152
Mussolini, Benito, 118–19, 125, 137–9, 142–3, 165, 174

Nanjing massacres, 35
nanshin-ron, 161
Nasser, Gamal Abdul, 174, 189n.58
National government (UK), 3–4, 6, 60, 66, 87, 143

National Labour Party, 5, 136, 144–6, 148, 152
National Security Agency (US), 241–3, 247
National Socialism (Nazism), 19, 112, 137, 141, 148
nationalism, 8, 22, 32, 34, 59–60, 112, 196, 200–1, 204–5, 208, 216
naval limitation treaties (for 1922 see Washington Conference), 69
Navy League, 87
Nazi (NSDAP) Party, 42, 59, 115, 121, 124, 151
Nazi-Soviet Pact (1939), 166
'near north' (see Far East)
neo-colonialism, 8, 178, 194, 210
Netherlands, 88, 90–1, 103–4, 141, 204
Neurath, Constantin Freiherr von, 49, 52, 129
neutrality, 65, 70, 75, 77, 81–2, 96, 101, 164, 208, 226, 228–30
'new diplomacy', 34
New Life movement, 36
New Party, 136–7
'New Range' (ICL computers), 247–9
new standard of naval strength, 99
New Statesman, The, 113
New York City, 47
New Zealand (see also ANZAM; ANZUS; Konfrontasi; SEATO), 7, 22, 161, 172, 192n.114, 227, 242
Newton, Basil, 49, 52
Ngo Dinh Diem, 206
Nichols, Sir P.B.B., 44, 61n.32
Nicoll, Douglas, 248
Nicolson, Sir Harold George, 5, 121, 132n.23, 136–54, 154n.1
Noel-Baker, Philip, 35, 43, 45–6
Non-Aligned Movement, 195, 204, 208, 216
Non-Intervention Committee, 119, 124
Non-Proliferation Treaty, 244
Norddeustch Wollkämmerei, 51
Norman, Montagu, 56, 70
North Atlantic, 167

North Atlantic Treaty Organization (NATO), 172, 201, 210–13, 224, 232n.1, 237n.53
North Korea, 172–3, 209
North Vietnam (see also DRV & Vietnam), 218, 223, 228
Norway, 166
Nuremberg, 119

'open door', 22, 26, 29
Operation A, 209–10
Operation *Rolling Thunder*, 218
opium, 24
Orde, Sir Charles William, 72
Orientalism, 36

Pacific War, 2, 6, 168
Pacific, Western, 6, 160
Pacific Ocean, 22, 27, 30, 34, 74, 224
Pakistan, 173, 199
Palestine, 101, 171
Panay, USS, 81, 165
Paris, 3, 30, 45, 47–58, 112, 116–17, 124, 130, 138, 141, 244
Partei Rakyat Brunei (PRB), 193–4
Peace Conference (see Versailles)
Pearl Harbor, 74, 79, 82, 160, 168
Peel, Sir Robert, 185, 192n.113
Peking (see Beijing)
Pentagon, 243, 245
People's Action Party (Singapore), 185, 203
People's Army of Vietnam (PAVN), 7
People's Republic of China (PRC), (see also Cold War; Konfrontasi), 7–8, 190n.69, 199, 208, 210, 220
'period before relief', 166
Philippines, 74–5, 80, 160, 173, 177–9, 202–3
Phillips, acting Admiral, Sir Thomas S. V., 168
Phipps, Sir Eric, 72, 114–15, 117, 124
phoney war, 151, 166
PKI (*Partei Komunis Indonesia*), 180, 196, 204–6, 222–3, 237n.52
Placentia Bay (Newfoundland), 242
Plowden, William, 246, 249
Poland, 150–1, 153, 166, 208
Polish Corridor, 44–5

post-colonial states, 21, 194, 196–7, 202
Post Office, 249
Poulden, Commander Teddy, 9, 241–9, 251n.13
Pound, Admiral Sir Dudley, 167
pound sterling, 53, 172, 174, 180–3, 213, 220–3
Pownall, Lt-Gen. Sir Henry, 89, 104
Prague, 150
Pratt, Sir John, 68, 71
Prince of Wales, HMS, 168, 242
'Project 52', 247
public expenditure (UK), 170, 181

Quai d'Orsay, 47, 56, 68

race, 23, 25–7, 30–1, 35, 210
Ransome, Arthur, 32
rearmament, 73, 87, 92–4, 96–100, 104–7, 112–13, 115–16, 118, 120, 125, 128–31, 142–3, 153
'Red Scheme', 162, 164–5
Red Sea, 167
Reichsbank, 51, 61n.32
Reichstag, 42–3, 59
reparations, 44, 46, 48, 56–7, 59, 67–8, 91, 112
Republic of Vietnam (ROV), 205, 209, 218
Repulse, HMS, 168
Rhine, 42, 59, 130
Rhineland, 3, 5, 42, 59, 113, 115–18, 122, 124, 130, 139–41, 152–4
Ribbentrop, Joachim von, 5, 117, 120–4, 129–30
Richards, Sir Brooks, 244
Riefenstahl, Leni, 115
Riley, Basil, 32
Robbins Report on Higher Education (1963), 15
Romania, 148
Rome-Berlin Axis, 120
Roosevelt, Franklin Delano, 3, 64–5, 67, 71–2, 74–5, 79, 81–2, 165, 167, 242
Rose, Norman, 153
Rothschild, Victor (Baron Rothschild), 245–6, 249

Round Table, The, 31
Royal Academy of Arts (London), 33
Royal Air Force (RAF), 4, 66, 86–7, 89–99 106–7, 175, 212
Royal Army, 4, 66, 71, 86–107, 205, 212, 237n.52
Royal Commonwealth Society, 15
Royal Institute of International Affairs, 145
Royal Navy, 4, 6, 66, 87, 91, 97, 99, 145, 166, 168, 175, 212–13, 242
rubber, 177
Ruhr, 2, 42, 92, 101, 112, 114
Rumania (*see* Romania)
Rumbold, Sir Horace, 54, 58, 115
Rusk, Dean, 183, 206, 210, 214, 229
Russell, Bertrand, 33
Russia, 20, 26–8, 66, 80, 98, 142, 146–7, 152, 243, 247
Russian Academy of Sciences, 18
Russo-Japanese War (1904–5), 25, 27
RYAD computer system (USSR), 247

Saar, 5, 43, 113
Sabah (British North Borneo), 8, 194–5, 203
Sackett, Frederic M., 49–50
Sackville-West, Vita, 136–7, 140, 145, 147, 149, 154
Saigon, 206–7
Salter, Professor Arthur, 146
'Salter's Soviet', 146
Sandys, Duncan, 142, 175
Sandys 'Axe', 175
Sankey, Viscount, 80
Sarawak, 178, 194–5, 202–3, 209
Sargent, Sir Orme, 44, 48, 61n.32, 114, 119, 121, 127
Savile, Leopold, 162
Schacht, Hjalmar, 124
Schuschnigg, Kurt, 130
seamen's strike (1966), 181
SEATO (South East Asia Treaty Organization), 7, 172–5, 180, 199–202, 218–19, 225, 228–30
Selat Sinki, 162
Self, Robert, 87, 90–1, 103, 106
Sembawang Naval Base, 162, 164–6
Senate (US), 41

Shanghai, 32, 68
signals intelligence, 240, 242
Simon, Sir John, 3, 67, 70, 73–5, 78–9, 99, 104–5, 113
Singapore (*see also* Far East Command), 6–8, 159, 170, 190n.69, 194, 203
 British withdrawal from, 173, 181–6, 222, 224–7, 230
 Japanese defeat of (1941–2), 167–8, 188n.29,
 Japanese Occupation of (1942–5) 168–9
 Konfrontasi, military base for, 178–9, 210, 221
 Malaysia's attitude towards, 177, 180, 202, 220, 223
 naval base, 66, 74–5, 91, 161–7, 171, 174
 post-war defence policy, 172–86, 200, 209–10, 217
 'Singapore Strategy', 6, 160, 162–6
Sino-Japanese War (1937–45), 35
SIS (Secret Intelligence Service), 243, 251n.13
Sissinghurst Castle, 136
Six-Day War (1967), 182
Smuts, Field Marshal Jan, 6, 163
Snowden, Philip, 56–7
Soeharto, Major-General (later President), 179–81, 222–3, 228, 237n.52
Somerville, John, 242
South Asia, 22
South China Sea, 74
South East Asia Command (SEAC), 169, 242
South Vietnam (*see also* ROV & Vietnam), 205, 214, 218, 220, 226, 230
Southeast Asia (*see also* Cold War; decolonisation; *Konfrontasi*; SEATO; and entries under individual regional states), 8, 22, 159, 161, 163, 167, 177, 183–4, 193, 197, 210
Soviet Union, 119, 171, 176, 245
 Anglo-Soviet relations, 115, 152, 165, 199

Cold War rivalry, 196–7, 208
Germany, relations with, 114, 119–20, 166
munitions, 204, 212
Poland, attack upon, 151
PRC, relations with, 206, 219
Spain, 36, 98, 121, 124, 142, 144–5, 164
Spanish Civil War, 5, 118, 142, 152
Spears, Major General Sir Edward Louis, 145
'Special Relationship', 6–8, 82, 184, 193
St Antony's College, Oxford, 11
Stalin, Joseph, 113, 171–2
Stanhope, Earl, 27–8, 73
State Department (US), 183, 201, 206, 243
Stedman, Andrew, 137
stereotypes, 23, 25, 33, 35
Stewart, Brian, 243
Stewart, Michael (Baron Stewart of Fulham), 219–20, 229
Stimson, Henry, L., 3, 52, 54–5, 57, 67, 70–1, 73, 78
Straits Settlements, 165
Strang, Sir William (Baron Strang), 125
strategic priorities, 101, 212
Stresa Front (1935), 113, 133n.24
Stresemann, Gustav, 3, 59, 112, 140
Subandrio, 178, 194, 205, 207
Subic Bay, 160
Sudetenland, 147–8
Suez, east of, 6, 8, 160, 164, 167, 169, 171–2, 181–4, 214, 225, 228–9
Suez Canal, 7, 144, 173–4
Suharto (*see* Soeharto)
Sultan Omar Ali Saifuddien III (Brunei), 177–8, 194
Sukarno, President, 8, 178–81, 194, 203–10, 217, 222–3, 237n.52
Sumatra, 217
Sussex, HMS, 169
Sydney, 161

Taishō democracy, 2, 164
Taylor, Philip, 8
Tedder, Marshal of the Royal Air Force Arthur William (Baron Tedder), 11

Templewood, Viscount (Sir Samuel Hoare), 138
Ten Year Rule, 161
Tentara Nasional Indonesia (TNI), 195, 205, 209, 212, 217, 222–3
Tentara Nasional Indonesia Angkatan Laut, 212
Tentara Nasional Kalimantan Utara (TNKU), 193–5
Territorial Army (TA), 88–90, 92–9, 102, 104–7
Thailand, 173, 230
The Past Week, 148
The Times, 23, 28, 32, 40n.48, 52, 55, 94, 113
The Times Good University Guide, 18
Thomas, J.H., 78
Thomas, Sir Shenton, 165
Thomson, George (Baron Thomson of Monifieth), 183–4
Tiderace, Operation, 169
tin, 177
Tonkin, 167
Tonkin Gulf Resolution, 209
Toynbee, Sir Arnold, 33
Treasury (UK), (*see also* British Expeditionary Force; Defence Requirements Sub-Committee; Defence Reviews), 78, 81, 99, 105, 180, 245
  Germany, reparation problems of, 49, 51, 54–7, 61n.32
  military expenditure east of Suez, 162, 170, 181–3, 210–11
Trenchard, Viscount, 4, 89, 92, 98, 107
Trend, Burke St John (Baron Trend), 242, 251n.14
Treviranus, Gottfried Reinhold, 43
Tripartite Pact (1940), 167
'Trojan Horse syndrome', 244
Truman, President Harry S, 170, 197
Truman Doctrine, 172
Tunku Abdul Rahman, 8, 175–8, 180, 202
Turing, Alan, 241
'twenty-one demands', 29

U Thant, 203
UKUSA (sigint alliance), 242
unemployment, 43, 45, 47, 87
United Nations, 173, 204, 217
United States (US), (*see also* Anglo-American relations; Cold War; SEATO; Vietnam), 131, 178, 183, 213 243–6
  European security, attitude towards, 64–5, 164
  Japan, attitude towards, 30–1, 34, 74–6, 79–80
  military assistance rendered by, 95, 98, 167
  war debts, issue of, 44, 47, 52
  Washington Conference (1921–2), 159–60
University Grants Committee, 241
Untung coup (1965), 180, 222–3, 237n.52
Upham, Admiral F. B., 74
US Navy, 77–8
USSR (*see* Soviet Union)

Vansittart, Sir Robert (Baron Vansittart), 151, 153
  France, views on, 50, 58, 140
  Germany, formation of policy towards, 44, 69, 77, 81, 92, 118, 121–2, 124–5, 139–41, 145
  Italy, assessment of, 44, 114
  US, attitude towards, 50, 68, 70–3, 75–81, 96
Versailles, Treaty of (1919), 3, 5, 30, 65, 136–7, 139, 161
  repercussions of, 36, 41–3, 58–9, 117, 148, 137, 139
Vienna, 43, 130
Viet Cong, 7, 223
Viet Minh, 171, 197, 199
Vietnam, 7–8, 174, 180–1, 195–201, 204–7, 209–11, 214–20, 222–3, 226–31, 236n.44
VME (Virtual Machine Environment) software, 249

Wall, Sir John, 248
Wall Street Crash (1929), 2
war debts, 56, 67–8
War Office, 95–9, 102–4, 162

Washington Conference (1921–2), 2, 6, 30–1, 34, 69, 160
Washington treaty system, 159, 164
Washington DC, 47–8, 56, 82, 160, 183, 205–6, 213, 224, 242, 251n.13
 synonym for US government, 7–8, 44, 49–50, 57, 64–9, 71–3, 75–81, 173, 181, 245
Webb, Sidney & Beatrice, 26
Webster, Sir Charles, 33
Wehrmacht, 89, 92, 95, 107
Weinstock, Sir Arnold (Baron Weinstock), 248
Weir, Lord, 94
Wellesley, Sir Victor, 68, 72
Wellington, 6, 172
West Point, 232n.1
Western Australia, 227
Western New Guinea, 204
Western Pact, 120, 122, 124, 130, 133n.40
Western Powers, 7, 27, 113–14, 120, 122, 127, 199–201, 204
Whitehall, 3, 7, 42, 120, 129, 159, 171, 175–7, 209–10, 212, 217, 220, 222
'White Australia' policy, 30
'white man's club', 219, 229
White, Sir Dick Goldsmith, 242–3

Why Britain is at War, 151
Wigram, Ralph, 116, 120, 125, 133ns.24, 27
Wiggin-Layton Committee, 57
Williams, Harold, 32
Wilmot, Robb, 249
Wilson, Sir Horace, 105, 148, 150–1
Wilson, James Harold (Baron Wilson of Rievaulx), (*see also Konfrontasi*; Singapore), 8, 218, 245
World Economic Conference, 67–8
World War I, 2, 4, 6, 16, 19, 28–9, 33, 36, 41, 66, 76, 159
World War II, 1, 64, 80, 82, 137, 166, 173, 242

X Division, 242, 248–9
Xenophobia, 34

Yamashita, General Tomoyuki, 168
'yellow peril', 26–7, 35
Yorke, Gerald, 32
'Young China', 32
Young Plan, 42–3, 48, 50–1, 56
'you've never had it so good,' 175, 201
Yugoslavia, 148

Zipper, Operation, 169

Printed and bound by CPI Group (UK) Ltd, Croydon, CR0 4YY